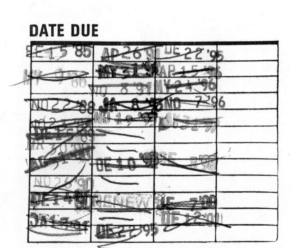

DATE DUE

James Galway's
Music
in
Time

James Galway's
Music
in
Time

written by
William Mann

Harry N. Abrams, Inc., Publishers,
NEW YORK

Credits

Editor
Alexandra Towle

Associate Editor
Clive Unger-Hamilton

Editorial Assistant
Wendy Varley

Designer
Stephen Bull

Design Consultant
Anthony Cobb

Picture Research
Olivia Maxwell and
Vanessa Whinney

Production
Barry Baker

Co-ordination
Sally Fairhead for
RM Productions

Library of Congress Cataloging in Publication Data

Mann, William S.
James Galway's Music in Time

Includes index.
1. Music History and criticism.
I. Galway, James.   II. Title.
III. Title: Music in Time.
ML160.M218 1983 780'.9 82 11351
ISBN 0-8109-1342-9

Published in 1983 by Harry N. Abrams, Incorporated, New York

Typesetting and black and white Reproduction by
Tradespools Limited, Frome, Somerset
Colour Reproduction by Bridge Graphics, Hull
Printed and bound by Koninklijke Smeets
Offset b.v., Holland

Contents

Foreword

This is a book about music and the men and women who wrote it and played it. It sets music against the backdrop of the times in which it was created, tracing its development from the earliest rhythms and songs to the seemingly confused sounds of contemporary music, and it makes a fascinating story. I became involved in the project because I couldn't resist the enormous scope of it, and because I wanted to share with as many people as possible something which I have been privileged to enjoy every day of my life: music.

Everybody in our street played a musical instrument. That's what really started my musical career. I first played the penny whistle, and learned all sorts of tunes like the "Belfast Hornpipe" and lots of Irish reels. Not that I was particularly musical then, for the most important thing seemed to be able to play faster than everybody else.

I took up the violin for a few weeks, but quickly moved on to the flute. Then I knew I had found my true vocation, for in Ireland playing the flute is a way of life. I practised all day long (often when I should have been doing my schoolwork), and went in for competitions—where you were sure to have an audience—and I joined flute bands. Now flute bands (particularly the 39th Old Boys) are very special: they have an enormous repertoire embracing not only traditional folk music but all the symphonies you could possibly imagine. Can you believe that when I was young, I thought that Beethoven's fifth symphony was actually written for fifty flutes? But it sounded great: I'm sure Beethoven would have loved it.

I was lucky to be surrounded by music. There were the other kids with tin whistles, my father played the flute, my mother played the piano, and there was our old wind-up gramophone with a few scratched records of Fritz Kreisler. Despite all my education at music colleges and conservatories and work with the great orchestras, it was our music at home which had the strongest influence on my life and career.

Of course, what I didn't know while I was playing away on my penny whistle was that music, which became my life, had been a potent creative force in the world since the dawn of man, and that reflected in its development was the unfolding story of mankind itself. I later discovered that if you listen to the changing patterns of music over the centuries you can follow the course of history. Haydn and Mozart composed within the balanced confines of eighteenth-century Enlightenment. The structured musical form developed by Haydn was then stretched and broken by Beethoven, whose life was deeply affected by the French Revolution and Napoleonic Wars that shattered the European system of government. In the operas of Verdi you can trace the political upheavals of the unification of Italy. Elgar displays the self-conscious hey-day of the British Empire, and the rousing operas of Glinka reveal the growing sense of national identity in nineteenth-century Russia.

Music is a chronicle of human emotion too. Think of the gentle, romantic traditions of courtly love in the songs of the medieval troubadours and the flowering harmonies of the Renaissance: consider the brilliant confident glitter of Elizabethan keyboard music, the brash optimism in the piano rags of Scott Joplin: the acid wit of the operettas that epitomise *fin-de-siècle* Paris: and the confusion of dissonant voices heard in our own time.

As surely as art or literature, music reflects life. The aim of *Music in Time* is to put the whole fascinating picture in perspective—to place music in the context of its own time—for to understand and therefore appreciate music, it is necessary to know the circumstances under which it was written. For this reason, we decided that the starting point for both the book and the television series had to be the music we can still perform authentically, music that was written down at the time it was composed so that it brings its personality to us across the centuries with as little distortion as possible. (Of course, this means that much folk music and the music of the east which is passed down orally from generation to generation and so changes with each performance, is beyond the scope of this book.)

A hundred years ago, the history of music was thought to be evolutionary. Historians believed that music had steadily improved from the earliest times—so that Wagner was a better composer than Beethoven, Beethoven better than Mozart who, in his time, had made Handel seem old-fashioned. Our own eclectic tastes would have seemed quite eccentric in Beethoven's time. Today, thanks to recording technology, we have a choice such as no previous age has enjoyed—we can learn the musical language of madrigals, appreciate the Classic spirit of Mozart, the Romanticism of Chopin, the vision of Wagner and the restless spirits of every age who have pushed music to its limits to find new forms of expression.

Throughout this ambitious project I have enjoyed a wonderful collaboration with Derek Bailey, director of the television series, and Bill Mann, author of this book and script advisor to the series. We found there was so much we wanted to say, so many perspectives and connections to explore, that we found it impossible to put everything into sixteen hours of television—hence this book.

Working on *Music in Time* has been a marvellous experience for me—apart from meeting a lot of interesting people, it has given me the excuse to revel in favourite pieces, the chance to reacquaint myself with half-remembered melodies and to know the thrill of discovering new ones. I hope that you, too, will be prompted to explore the works of all the composers you will encounter in this engrossing and fascinating book, for together they have created the rich heritage that is our western musical tradition.

James Galway

This book is for
Peter John, Georgina, Bob,
Alexander, and Derek,

with much love to all of them.

Chapter 1
Beginnings

Vibrations and Pagan Rites

The music of nature ♦ Nature teaches man to sing songs of
celebration, magic and bravery in battle ♦ The rhythms of life,
the magic and the mathematics ♦ How the oral tradition
has robbed us of a rich musical past ♦ The first musical
instruments ♦ Reconstructing the sounds
of pre-Christian music ♦

Music, which we rank high among the sophisticated arts of human
communication, is the oldest of them all, the most primitive in intention. It
evolved from the essential rhythms and pulses of the planet on which we
live—from the sounds of wind and water, air and fire.

The Music of Nature
When *Homo sapiens* evolved from the primates, he already had the ability
to make noises through the larynx, as apes have, to warn others of danger,
to frighten an intruder, to attract a potential partner, or just selfishly to
voice strong emotion.

We can observe the beginnings of human speech and song in the
behaviour of young pets, or our own babies. First comes the cry for
attention, varied in pitch and intensity, but uncontrolled—closer to song
than to speech. Eventually the infant learns to vary and define its cry by
copying what it hears and controlling the sounds it makes. The human
infant (like the parrot) copies what it hears in order to make contact with
others—to define a particular feeling or experience. Primitive man, left to
his own devices, had first of all to copy the sounds of his natural experience.
He heard the crackling twigs as he padded circumspectly through the
undergrowth—the soughing of wind in the trees—plashing water in the
brook. Nature herself gave him the first musical instruments.

The First Songs
While man was alone, exposed to merciless elements, clearly he sang partly
to combat danger, partly from fascination with the sounds around him and a
desire to match them. When a partner was found, or a pack formed, song
evolved into speech—verbal symbols for immediate needs. These symbols
resulted in a sing-song poetry whose words and meaning affected the shape

Beginnings
Vibrations and Pagan Rites

The so-called "**Venus of Laussel**" from Périgord, France, is about 28,000 years old. It represents a woman who appears to be playing on an animal horn, probably that of a bison.

and contour of sung melody. Man's first songs were celebratory, paeans to superior divinities, chronicles of past achievement, prayers or exhortations. Music, in early times, was a form of magic, inducing trance-like concentration in the listener. It soon became apparent that music had greater powers, and could be used as active propaganda to inspire a whole tribe, perhaps to bravery in war, and not simply revered as a magical adjunct to sacred rites, like the priests' consumption of intoxicating *ganja*.

The Rising Scale

In the absence of documentation, the origins of music can still be guessed at. In young children, song is suggested before speech. Varied pitch and the articulation of vowels and consonants happen later. The organization of sung music into scales of five or seven notes (or more) must have taken centuries to evolve. The five-note *pentatonic* scale was current in the pre-history of music, and has remained predominant to this day among many Third World peoples. European music, with which this book deals, is predominantly based on the seven-note *heptatonic* scale, which has been traced back to 3000 BC.

Rhythms of Life—Magic and Mathematics

At least as important as pitches and scales is rhythm, the impulsive and varied inner life within the consistent beat, or metre, of the melody. An expert listener can often identify a known tune from its rhythm and metre, rapped out without pitch variation. Primitive man learned rhythm from the elements. He heard the percussion of nature—the tide lapping regularly on the shore, the breeze in the branches.

In the late twentieth century we must distinguish between regular, "straight" rhythms (as in most classical music) and "bent" rhythms, in

The Musical Theories of Pythagoras

The Greek philosopher and mathematician Pythagoras (fl. 540 BC), represented right demonstrating the musical scale upon a set of graduated bells, believed that the theory of numbers could explain much of the universe. Each of the planets, he averred, gave forth a distinct musical note while spinning—the music of the spheres—and these notes together formed a scale.

He ultimately evolved and defined a precise mathematical relationship of the notes of the scale to each other. First came the principle of the octave, discovered by cutting a plucked string in half (and therefore expressed in the ratio 2:1). The interval of the Fifth (C–G on the piano, and expressed as 3:2) gave the scale its "dominant" note; it is a sound that predominates in plainsong, and is much used in music for brass instruments.

A slightly smaller interval, 4:3 (C–F on the piano) was the Fourth—also deemed very important. Musicians know it as the subdominant. Three thousand years later, it is still common to harmonize almost any tune with the "three chord trick", using just the chords of the three most important notes laid down by Pythagoras: tonic (keynote); dominant and subdominant.

which the beats are unequal. "Bent" rhythms are the distinctive feature of rock music, jazz and most traditional black music, as well as much sophisticated white European music in the Baroque eighteenth century.

Rhythm is a basic human activity—sometimes we move our bodies regularly, sometimes in a more diversified, but still phased rhythm, a longer beat followed by a shorter one, more apt to informal dancing. This is my distinction between "straight" and "bent" rhythms, which form the basic difference between classical and popular music, differences which existed centuries ago, perhaps since the dawn of music.

Scales p 129

Beginnings
Vibrations and Pagan Rites

As a general definition, it may be said that all music is an expression of physical movement, every theme and phrase a reflection of some bodily gesture, and that the composer's invention is physically motivated. Music for dancing is an obvious example, but so is lyrical music—whether fast or slow. If it goes at a correct tempo, the listener's body should sense it as physically natural, even in the smoothest, long-phrased operatic *bel canto*, or the most challenging vanguard composition of today. Several attempts have been made to turn this natural pulse into a mathematical formula, but human nature turns away from such tamperings because music inspires the mind through the body. To our ancestors rhythms were religious and magical—for us rhythms are mathematical and physical—and an even more explicit stimulus to the mind and inner senses.

The Oral Tradition

There was plentiful music in the centuries before our *anno Domini*, and enough evidence that it was splendid and highly coloured. Nobody wrote the music down on paper so we cannot perform it now as it was heard then. Music was passed on orally, from teacher to pupil, as a living document, not to be codified. India's high musical culture, several thousand years old, has never been put on paper, nor has the music of Sumeria or Egypt or China (some isolated attempts from 138 BC tantalize the scholar). The resistance to music written down, arrested in its development once and for all, has persisted. No Asian musician would dream of writing down his composition, for unlike argumentative modern western music, the essence is improvisation—the aim is inward contemplation.

*This **Han dynasty relief** shows musicians accompanying an entertainment.*

For the ancient Greeks, the purpose of music was therapeutic, to purify the mind and harmonize the soul through dancing or song. They believed that each of their modes or scales had its own effect on the listener, some harmful, others beneficial—thus one inspired courage, another level-headedness and so on. They discouraged the writing down of music as detrimental to the activity of the memory. So while Classical Greek art can show us the instruments used and representations of music in performance, and the literature can retail for us their theories and systems, we have no inkling how the music sounded. Two hymns and a drinking song dating from the second century BC do exist, but about how these should be performed, scholars cannot wholly agree.

The Invention of Musical Instruments

There is a delightful scene in Wagner's opera *Siegfried* in which the young hero listens to the chirruping of a bird in a tree, and cuts a reed into a pipe to answer the bird-song (his efforts are comically unsuccessful). Primitive man's first musical instrument, apart from the earth as a stamping-ground, may well have been invented in such circumstances.

The earliest extant instruments are a one-note whistle made of reindeer phalanx (dated at 10,000 BC), and bone flutes almost as old, with three or more fingerholes (reed pipes are much easier to make, but quickly perishable). Both whistle and flute were successful attempts to copy nature—the wind whistling down a hollow tree-trunk or through the reeds, the call of an owl. Lithophones, or pitched stones (ancestor of the xylophone) and scrapers made of phallic-shaped bone (associated with courtship in primitive societies even today), date back to the Stone Age—likewise the bullroarer, whirled round the head on a thong and believed to connect man

Siegfried p.237

A dancer and a group of musicians *perform for the entertainment of an Indian prince and his child. Even today, such music is largely improvised around a raga, or sequence of notes. Each raga, and there are hundreds of them, is designed for a specific time of day or night.*

Under the **T'ang dynasty** *in China (AD 618–907), music became increasingly sophisticated. Music for the Chinese was a tool to govern the hearts and minds of the people—this contemporary silken scroll depicts a group of musicians bringing harmony to court.*

17

Beginnings
Vibrations and Pagan Rites

with the souls of dead ancestors. Rattles, like the maracas, mimic the sound of the sea—pottery drums and bells survive from about 2500 BC and suggest a refinement on perishable wooden prototypes, perhaps originally used to counter the thunderclaps in a storm or exorcise baneful influences from this world or beyond.

The first high cultures began around this time—first Sumeria and Ur, followed by Egypt, India and China, then by Judea, Greece and Rome. In Sumeria three-stringed harps are portrayed on writing tablets dated 3000 BC. Lyres, clappers and other simple percussion instruments from a few centuries later have been found in Ur of the Chaldees, as well as drawings of what look like trumpets or megaphones.

Double pipes are portrayed in the art of Ur, such as shepherds in central Europe still play. With them music could be played on two pitches simultaneously, heralding the beginnings of harmony.

Sacred and Secular Music
The Sumerians cultivated music for sacred rites, including funerals, military triumphs and banquets. That remained the pattern until very recently—an art for the élite. Popular music always went its own way, unchronicled but perhaps more mobile and more durable.

It was at Babylon in Sumeria that King Nebuchadnezzar maintained the famous orchestra listed in *Daniel III* (the instruments enumerated in the Authorized Version of the Old Testament are not accurately translated, so modern scholars have found—the Sumerian musical instruments being given Greek names of modern currency). Hebrew music, after the return from Babylon to Jerusalem, had absorbed influences from the courts where the Jews had been captive, notably Egypt and Sumeria. Later domination by Greeks and Romans must have left some mark on the music of Judea, as it did elsewhere. Music in the Temple of Solomon was choral with instrumental accompaniment, though the use of instruments was banned by the time Christianity became an independent religious sect—perhaps to exorcise reminders of the long captivity—just as the Christian liturgy did its best to wipe out all traces of earlier pagan practice.

*A horizontal harp, as well as vertical models and pipes, appears on this bas-relief depicting **a military band** found at Nineveh and dating from the seventh century BC.*

The Sounds of the Pre-Christian Orchestra
The orchestra of these earlier high musical civilizations was reported to be numerous, but even the most enthusiastic descriptions and pictorial representations do not suggest a great variety of instruments, or any music

Ancient Mesopotamia
possessed a considerable musical culture. This stone fragment portrays a piper and a drummer in procession.

that we would call grandly harmonious. The modern concept of harmony is based on the natural phenomenon of resonance or overtones. You can hear them if you depress the sustaining pedal of a modern piano and loudly strike a very low note. It will resonate upper overtones of itself, developing naturally up the scale. These overtones can be heard on quite primitive instruments, like the bell.

One of the principal instruments of the early orchestra was the natural horn—restricted, like every brass instrument without valves, to a low fundamental note and a series of overtones, playable by altering the position of lips and the pressure of air into the instrument.

The harp and its other stringed derivatives (lyre, guitar, viol, etc) were legendarily assumed to be of divine origin. The Greeks believed that the god Hermes bound animal sinews round a tortoise shell, and let the wind blow

A section of the "**Standard of Ur**" shows the king and his court feasting to the sounds of a singer and a lyre player.

Three musicians, a harpist, lutenist and piper, appear on this Egyptian tomb painting from the reign of King Thothmes IV. It was believed that such painted scenes could be brought magically to life, ensuring the dead king pleasure in the next world.

Facing page: **David, King of the Israelites**, is portrayed in this medieval illumination, playing the harp to the accompaniment of his courtiers.

Vibrations and Pagan Rites

through them, exciting sounds of varied pitch—the shorter the sinew, the higher the sound. King David's harp in the Old Testament was similarly, but miraculously, put together. More recently, in the tenth century AD, St Dunstan claimed to have been given such an instrument by God himself—it was what we now call the Aeolian harp, strings fixed to a sounding-board, placed in a draughty spot, and resonated by breezes to enchanting, indeed magical effect. The harp and lyre were current from Sumerian times—at first plucked, then bowed with an archer's bow for greater penetrating power and eventually stopped with the fingers to vary pitch. The brass instruments could only reproduce the harmonic series of upper overtones, but the bowed and stopped harp, or lyre, could vary pitch minutely and so brought about the modern seven-note scale and all its refinements, including tones between notes—or microtones (less than a semi-tone).

Our full orchestra was still far in the future, but there are mentions of a wind instrument with a single reed to blow through, like the clarinet. Brass and percussion were quite sophisticated, and one picture (from perhaps 630 BC) shows a singer squeezing his epiglottis (the cartilage at the root of the tongue), to produce a *vibrato* sound, like a modern operatic singer, or even a male gospel vocalist of today.

When the glory that was Greece yielded to the grandeur that was Rome, music was greatly cultivated: we read of concerts by mixed chorus and large orchestra in AD 284, of the organ as an orchestral instrument, but of Roman musical theory and practice there is nothing. We do know, however, that Nero did not fiddle while Rome burned: he played the lyre. Evidence shows us that Rome seems to have developed an instrument similar to the bagpipes, and there is testimony that music was commonly used during work and in leisure time, as it must have been in earlier times, a spin-off from army, court and religious worship for humbler enjoyment, or incentive to harder work.

A modern listener may well wonder when music began to include dissonance—that clash between adjacent notes which from quite early in the written down literature of music gives such vitality and spice. There is no evidence of such an event in pre-Christian music: the Greeks would have condemned dissonance as barbarous—civilizations farther east outlawed it as hostile to fruitful inward musing—it is, fairly certainly, a phenomenon acceptable only in modern times.

Two muses with a lyre *from ancient Greece—a structured and wealthy society with much leisure to devote to artistic pursuits.*

Scales p 129

Chapter 2
Masses and Motets
The Truth from Above

The spread of Christianity nurtures western
European music ◆ Careers in music ◆ The birth of notation ◆
The Paris school—a burgeoning of talent ◆ Songs for the
people—close harmony and rounds ◆
The ingenuity of *ars nova* ◆ English composers
contribute sweet harmonies ◆

We have seen how mankind first invented music to cheer himself up, to voice his grief, to warn others of danger and to appease superior powers. He still does—the categories might be updated exactly as rock 'n' roll, blues, military bands, and gospel or hymns. We have also seen how little of this early heritage remains. For so long as music consisted only of a simple unharmonized melodic line there was no need to write it down. Musicians were content to pass on by ear their own repertory, whether folk song, ballad or hymn, to their children or disciples. While keeping the traditional songs and dances alive in this way, the music was bound to suffer change as it was passed on, adapting itself subtly to the needs and tastes of each succeeding generation.

A New Religion Demands a New Music
It was the spread of the Christian religion, from a local cult in Judea to become the accepted faith throughout the civilized western world, that brought about the development of European music. Christianity emerged as a branch of Judaism, and accordingly borrowed its music, partly from Jewish chant (cantors got an extra job on Sunday in addition to the Sabbath day), but also from Classical Greece via Imperial Rome.

When the Emperor Constantine proclaimed Christianity as the official religion of the Roman Empire in AD 325, church music borrowed also from local musical dialects wherever the new faith took root, incorporating elements of existing traditional sources both sacred and secular. Before long there were several varieties of music for Christian worship. The Ambrosian Rite (named after the fourth-century St Ambrose), which still flourishes in northern Italy, gave other rites the principle of antiphons, which are plainsong chants responsively sung by two bodies of singers, still called *decani* and *cantoris* in cathedrals and churches. In France there was the

325-1450 The Truth from Above

St Gregory, pope from 590–604, helped to assemble an immense collection of early church music. He is pictured here notating music as dictated by a heavenly dove.

"Music of the Spheres", an illustration from Pratica Musicae *published in 1496 by the Italian musical theorist Franchino Gafori. Here he links the planets of the solar system to the Muses of ancient Greece, via Gregorian modes and the particular emotions each supposedly excites.*

Alleluia! This example of early notation in the form of neumes is preserved at Winchester, England.

Gallic Rite; in Spain church music was dominated from the early eighth century by Christian Moors and in Constantinople there flourished the Byzantine Rite.

Greater Sophistication Brings Greater Complexity

Sacred music had often made use of hymns without meaningful words (the Hebrew *Hallelujah* was a particularly ancient example). While it was easy to learn and remember melodies when each syllable of text had its own appointed note it proved much more tricky when several notes were given to each syllable. So the texts of hymns were expanded with extra words or phrases in order to make a particularly good tune really memorable (the result was called a *sequence*). In time the established hymns acquired whole new intermediary sections of text and melody: they are known as *tropes*, and the more extended they became, the greater the need to write them down for learning by heart.

From Gregorian Modes to Simple Scales

Musical notation was developed as and when it became essential, necessity once again proving its maternal role in invention. In about AD 600 Pope Gregory the Great determined to systematize the varieties of musical scale or mode regularly used in Christian church music. He identified them by letters of the alphabet, as we still do with modern staff notation, and he gave each of them a name, borrowing ancient Greek names already connected with different scales. These became known, naturally enough, as Gregorian modes and they survive most familiarly in Roman Catholic sacred plainsong. The Catholic evening service, Compline, and the High Masses for church festivals, make much of Gregorian plainsong and they are a musical treat to listen to—sacred music at its simplest and purest.

Pope Gregory's modes are also evident in our old folk songs, as well as in some modern pop music. The early songs composed for the Beatles by John Lennon and Paul McCartney, for instance, were often based on modes rather than the established major and minor scales.

As time passed, composers found the simple Gregorian modes too unsophisticated and they were eventually neglected in favour of diatonic scales—scales made up of tones and semitones. The pitches could now be written down with letters, though it was not always obvious whether the leap from one note to another was supposed to be upwards or downwards, let alone whether some notes were to be sung faster than others. Some musicians, attempting to give maximum information about music for words, used accent signs as well as letters, to show which note lasted longer than its neighbours.

Parallel Harmonies

When two people sing a song together nowadays, the second voice will sing "seconds", repeating the tune at a distance of three notes (a third) above or below. In the ninth century AD a book called *Musica Enchiriadis* described music sung and/or played in three distinct simultaneous parts: first the tune, second a doubling of the tune at the octave (*eg* soprano with tenor), and the third, intermediary voice, doubling at the fourth or fifth above or below. This form of harmonic singing was called *organum*, perhaps because the voice was now accompanied by an organ—hitherto banned from

Harmony and Discord brought about by the signs of the Zodiac. Before her collapse upon association with the warlike signs of Mars, the lady is seen placidly strumming a pigsnout psaltery.

325–1450 The Truth from Above

Christian music, like all instruments, as reminiscent of pagan Roman music. However, this strict doubling had its problems and singers often had to cover up ugly juxtapositions with tiny modifications.

Taking Notes

The possibility of a singer making the wrong modification must have hastened the arrival of a more sophisticated musical notation. Sure enough, in about AD 871, a monk living near Tournai in northern France wrote out the Greek and Latin texts of the Gloria in the Catholic Mass, and above the Greek text drew profuse signs to indicate pitch, duration and stress. They are called *neumes* (from a Greek word meaning *nod* or *sign*). They derived from vaguer Byzantine prototypes; and during the tenth century they became commonly used throughout France, Germany and Britain, and developed into staff notation, which was able to give comprehensive and precise directions for musical performance.

In 1054 the Byzantine branch of Christianity severed itself from the Roman persuasion, became the Greek Orthodox Rite, and joined other eastern musics in preserving an unchanging adherence to traditional melody, not to be altered or replaced. It was only the western European Christian Rites, constantly developing their musical identity, which required their increasingly sophisticated music to be written down.

Some time after 900 the monks at Limoges included in their Easter service an interlude called *Quem quaeritis*, in which the three Marys visit Jesus's tomb and converse with the angel, who tells them that Christ "is not here, He is risen". It was sung in Latin by four choristers who also acted out the drama. There is a stage production book for the version acted and sung at Winchester in England, c. 970, as well as the music. Other religious dramas were added to church services at appropriate seasons—forming a link between classic Greek drama and the first Italian operas of the Florentine *Camerata* in 1600.

Those sacred musical playlets must have been matched by secular operas, which may well have preceded them. The Church never espoused the artistic vanguard, even in its most powerful days, but was always ready to borrow a good tune from the Devil, as Martin Luther put it much later. The secular operas, unfortunately, were not set down on paper until the *Play of Robin and Marion*, a French pastoral comedy with songs by Adam de la Halle (c. 1237–1288), who was in the service of Charles of Anjou—that was three hundred years after *Quem quaeritis*.

Troubadour Traditions

Secular music such as for the eleventh-century lengthy epic poems, *chansons de geste*, the crusaders' songs (from 1096) and the songs of troubadours all seem to be monophonic—one line of unaccompanied melody. No music for *chansons de geste* survives, but writings suggest that the verses were all sung to the same tune and that some of the tunes may have been existing church melodies. They must sometimes, somehow, have been accompanied on an instrument.

Romantic literature has instilled in us a picture of the humble troubadour (whose language was Provençal, the *langue d'oc*) and his colleague the *trouvère* (who sang in northern French, *langue d'oeuil*) singing their lays while accompanying themselves on a lute or similar instrument. Historical evidence does nothing to bear out this notion. The

*An exercise from **Guido d'Arezzo's** treatise on the composition of melody, which relates the vowel sounds in a line of Latin text to various notes of the scale (written sideways on the far left of the page). He acknowledges that melody requires more than mechanics: "Like silver," he says, "you must purify and polish the melody according to your own musical taste."*

Camerata p 229
Martin Luther p 78–80

song that Richard the Lionheart, himself a *trouvère*, wrote in captivity in Dürnstein shows it to be an aristocratic calling.

A particularly famous troubadour was Bernard de Ventadorn, whom Eleanor of Aquitaine brought with her to England when she became Henry II's queen and mother to Richard the Lionheart. In Germany, around 1180, troubadours emerged calling themselves *Minnesänger* or minnesingers, meaning singers about love—but love of the courtly kind without expectation of sexual fulfilment. Their songs also survive as unaccompanied words with melody (often borrowed from the troubadours). The best known minnesinger was Walther von der Vogelweide (*c.* 1170–1230), who is portrayed in Wagner's romantic opera *Tannhäuser* (1845), a story of minnesingers and their musical contests.

A Musical Career

Music had given itself a female patron saint, the second-century martyr St Cecilia, who allegedly sang hymns while being roasted alive in a bath over hot coals. In spite of her patronage music remained a man's career, perhaps until Francesca Caccini in 1600, the first famous woman composer. A secular musician was either a nobleman, like the Duke of Aquitaine or King Richard I of England, or else an itinerant *jongleur*, clever but untutored, or

Young men playing an **Aubade**—*early morning music for the entertainment of a fair lady who lies abed. An Aubade (from the French* aube *meaning dawn) is to morning what a serenade is to evening.*

Die Meistersinger p 238
Francesca Caccini p 69

325~1450
The Truth from Above

Richard I, the Lionheart, a charismatic king and a gifted musician, at his coronation in 1189.

simply a workman singing as he toiled, perhaps inventing songs as they came to him.

A musically gifted boy would hope for a career, at first as a chorister, either at court or in the Church, which amounted to much the same thing. If recruited early enough, he would be thoroughly educated in all general subjects but most carefully in music. It was his only opportunity to become an expert musician, whether playing, singing, or composing.

Often he would become a monk to further his career—celibacy is not impossible, some musicians maintain, with so demanding a mistress as St Cecilia. It will come as no surprise, however, to learn that not all monks were strict in the observation of their vows. The monastery of Benediktbeuren in Bavaria owns a thirteenth-century collection of songs, called *Carmina Burana*, much concerned with drinking, dancing and love-making. Many of these roisterous songs are by *goliards*, or wandering scholars who left the monastery and took to the road.

Employment as a church musician did not preclude secular composition: but without appointment to a court chapel, or to an ecclesiastical foundation, no common-born musician could hope to succeed.

First Steps to the Stave

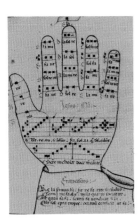

The Guidonian hand, in addition to teaching notation, was also used to teach sight-singing through an ingenious system based on the finger joints.

Such a musician was the monk Guido, choirmaster to the cathedral of Arezzo in Tuscany, and in charge of the choir school around 1030. Evidently well-informed about musical developments elsewhere, and himself an inventive musician, he devised a system for learning music by ear. He found a secular tune, each line of which began a note higher than the previous one. He matched the tune to another Latin text, sacred this time, whose first syllable on each line could give a name to each note of the musical scale.

Then he wrote out each mnemonic on a drawing of the human hand: *Ut*queant laxis, *Re*sonare fibris, *Mi*ra gestorum, *Fa*muli tuorum, *So*lve polluti, *La*bi reatum, *Sa*ncte Ioannes.

Each joint on Guido's hand was allied to an interval of the scale, so that his choirboys in Arezzo knew at once which note to sing: Guido claimed that music could be learned in a few days instead of weeks. *Solfège* or *solfeggio*, as the system became known, caught on fairly rapidly among singing students for the memorization of vocal exercises. During the nineteenth

Scales and Modes

Church music of the Middle Ages was based upon a system of simple octave scales, known as Gregorian modes. These were basically six in number, two of which approximate to the more familiar major and minor scales. These two, the Ionian and Aeolian modes (the white notes on the piano from C–C, and from A–A), were, however, at the time no more important than the others: the Lydian, Mixolydian, Dorian and Phrygian modes.

Throughout the Middle Ages, various theorists propounded refinements and extensions of this system. Certain intervals within the various modes were seen as harsh and ugly and were accordingly sharpened or flattened in performance (musica ficta or "musical faking"). Such complexities led, in time, to the neglect of the modal system in favour of our major and minor scales with their chromatic additions.

A musical scale is a sequence of notes arranged in step-wise order (ascending or descending), from which a piece of music is composed. Though there are countless varieties of scale, three types predominate:

Pentatonic: *As its name implies, this is a five-note scale, equivalent to the black notes on the piano. It is much used in folk music, in the music of the Third World, and also in Rock.*

Diatonic: *The seven-note (heptatonic) scale, preferred in European music, is a variable sequence of tones and semitones. It has two important forms, major and minor, as well as a number of earlier modal types.*

Chromatic: *This scale includes all twelve available semitones: the notes between two adjacent Cs on the piano, for example. Later twentieth-century composers, following Schoenberg and Webern, developed an elaborate technique of composition based on the dodecaphonic (twelve-note) scale.*

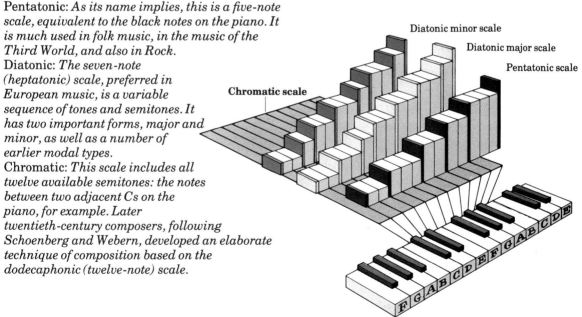

Chromatic scale

Diatonic minor scale

Diatonic major scale

Pentatonic scale

325–1450 The Truth from Above

century Guido's system was adapted to become the tonic sol-fa we know today, and used to teach non-musicians how to sing choral music. It was at this time that some pitches were renamed to make them easier to sing. Ut became Do, Sa became Te (in French, Si).

Guido of Arezzo also wrote much about a new system of notation, using a stave of many lines, F and C particularly marked with coloured ink to denote pitch. Guido's hand and his system of notation quickly flourished and encouraged other composers to make music more elaborate and interesting.

Round about the middle of the thirteenth century, the subtlety of musical organization was such that it demanded a new, more precise method of notation to show the exact length of each note, as well as intervening rests.

Bars and bar-lines were yet to be invented, but musical metres were already divided into *perfect*, triple time (connected with the Holy Trinity and therefore best suited to church music), which was indicated by a circle; and *imperfect*, duple time, marked with a semicircle like a C. The Church disapproved of C and recommended O: in modern terms, Viennese waltzes

Notation

Nearly all tunes, from medieval plainsong through nineteenth-century Lieder *to the current hit parade, have a keynote around which the melody revolves. A simple way to write any tune down was to draw a line to represent the keynote and place marks above, on and below the line as the notes of the melody rose and fell. These marks could also be spaced to give an indication of whether a note was to be held for a long time or only to be of short duration.*

A sign could be placed at the beginning of the line to indicate which note the tune was to start on. This was the origin of the present system of clefs: the treble clef 𝄞 is a refinement of the letter G, the bass clef 𝄢 : of the letter F, and the third sign 𝄡 is the C clef, used by the viola, cello and others.

From having one line to represent a note, it was a fairly obvious step to evolve a whole system of lines and spaces to define accurately the notes of a tune. Sharps ♯ and flats ♭ were added to represent any chromatic notes that didn't belong to the key in (or scale on) which the tune was to be performed.

Rhythmic precision was achieved gradually, through the use of differently shaped note signs to indicate how many beats (counts) each note was to last. The tune could also be divided up into regular groups of beats (bars) for convenience of reading and to show where the stresses fell. (The bar-line is generally placed immediately before each strong beat.)

were in, and marches out. Folk dances have always preferred O, but Anglican hymn-tunes, like Lutheran chorales, are mostly in C; there are, of course, exceptions and mixtures—like the jig, which is two-times-three, $\frac{6}{8}$ time (the tune *Lilliburlero* is a well-known example). Modern staff notation on treble and bass clefs did not become standard until 1600, and has continued ever since to become increasingly explicit—until modern times, that is.

The Paris School—a Burst of Creativity

Artistic change of direction usually affects music last of all, as will constantly be suggested in this book. One exception was the coincidence in Paris, during the latter half of the twelfth century, of an enlarged university with two schools, the building of a new cathedral dedicated to Notre Dame de Paris, and the appearance of a large book of music for divine service there. It embraced every occasion in the church year and contained music of a hitherto unknown sophistication. The original manuscript of this book, the *Magnus Liber Organi*, has long disappeared, but copies of it, each differing slightly, have been found in Spain, England and Italy—indication that music was already circulating internationally. From two musical scholars of rather later date, a Parisian in about 1240 called Jean de Garland and an anonymous writer, probably English, of 1275, we understand that the "Great Book of Organum" was first assembled by "Master

*The tomb of **Francesco Landini**. The outstanding exponent of Italian ars nova, was a brilliant musician also widely acclaimed as a poet and a philosopher. He was blinded by smallpox while still a child.*

A medieval French chanson, *beautifully copied in the form of a heart, probably a love token from the anonymous composer to the object of his affections.*

Léonin" between 1163 and 1182, then revised by his successor "Pérotin the Great" between the late 1190s and perhaps 1225.

All we know of these composers comes from this supposedly English scholar, identified by a nineteenth-century editor as "Anonymous IV". Modern scholars are extremely coy about admitting to the achievements of Léonin and Pérotin, and you may have cause to wonder if they were not figments of Anonymous IV's imagination. But the music is there, and it bears witness to two styles, arguably of two succeeding generations, and two individual musicians sufficiently important to be remembered with respect by a foreigner a century after the book was started.

Léonin's speciality was relatively freestyle harmony for two or three voices. Pérotin's approach was more rigid. His *quadrupla* (music for four

Masses and Motets
The Truth from Above

Singing angels by Jan Van Eyck.

voices) look, on paper, automatic and soulless, but they sound completely human and very expressive. Two of Pérotin's works—*Sederunt Principes* and *Viderunt Omnes*—are available on record, as are other pieces from the *Magnus Liber*.

Expanding Horizons
The new concentration of musicians in one sophisticated cultural centre, Paris, understandably accelerated the development of music. It is not surprising that music for two voices rapidly expanded to music for four voices, each moving along its own horizontal path, yet coinciding vertically with agreeable effect (nobody talked about harmony, though that is what we call the result). It is also expected that named composers should begin to emerge even if only one at a time and at fairly long intervals.

Although it was still the Church that provided the only developing and lucrative career for an ambitious musician, the thirteenth century is largely remembered for the mutual influence of secular and sacred music.

Songs for the People
The musical form of the thirteenth century was the motet (French *mot*, meaning word), whose essence was the introduction of secular texts in the vernacular. In France, Spain, Italy and England we find hymns set to native language, not Latin texts, and secular music written down and sometimes composed with real sophistication.

That popular music was not unsophisticated, we know from Gerald Cambrensis, a Welsh writer of 1175, who mentions that in a gathering of his compatriots, as many vocal parts were to be heard as there were singers among the company. We can be sure that some of them followed their neighbour, as we do, and that they harmonized then in thirds and sixths—those mellifluous intervals which the Church disdained, but which later English composers were to spread around Europe. Did they also copy the melody a little after the singer next to them, and so create a round or canon, as in *Sumer is icumen in*, and later *Three blind mice* and *London's burning*? The concept of canon is at once intellectual and childish. The child is delighted and fascinated to discover that harmony results when one person follows the tune started by the companion; the cerebrally inclined composer delights to create such intricacies and take them much further.

Ars Nova: Brilliant and Inventive
A movement towards the freeing of musical style from its rigid shackles, *ars nova*, started in Italy at the beginning of the fourteenth century and spread rapidly to France, where it coincided with a great surge of intellectual and artistic development. Philippe de Vitry (1291–1361) was the man who wrote the textbook of *ars nova* and composed the examples, which are as beautiful as they are ingenious, with politically inflammatory texts in case a listener might lose interest.

Guillaume de Machaut (*c.* 1300–1377)
The *ars nova* heralded a brilliant period in French music—it encouraged the devices of imitation and canon which were brought to new eloquence by Guillaume de Machaut. Machaut was the flower of the *ars nova* and one of the greatest composers of all time. He delighted in musical conjuring—evident in his rondeau *Ma fin est mon commencement* ("My end is my

The creation of Man and his expulsion from the Garden of Eden—the epitome of **Gothic style**, *from the Duke of Bedford's Book of Days.*

beginning") in which the text instructs the three singers to read a single line of music in three different ways, backwards and forwards, with completely harmonious effect.

Machaut's masterpiece is certainly his *Messe de Notre Dame*, the work which associates him with the Parisian School—though when he was not travelling Europe with war-waging royal employers, he seems to have spent all his time in Rheims. The technical cunning is supreme, the glory of the music best realized in performance when the singers are matched with instruments of the period. The greater part of Machaut's music was not for

325-1450 *The Truth from Above*

the Church; his vocal settings of secular music, ballads, rondeaux, lais and virelais are sophisticated in design, buoyant in expression. Here too the spirit of the music presupposes instruments with voices, perhaps fidel (the ancestor of our fiddle), lute, psaltery (a sort of lyre), and a keyboard instrument such as the chekkers from England, forebear of the harpsichord.

French music of this time flourished by export and import. Italy's leading composer, during the last years of Machaut's life, was the blind Francesco Landini (*c.* 1325–1397), employed as church organist and choirmaster in his native Florence, but remembered now for his choral song-dances or *ballate*, sometimes brilliant and joyous, most impressive when the texts are poignant and the music heart-rending. He left almost no church music, but that is not exceptional: the Church may have been school and employer but it was not sole master of one's creativity, as many composers of that time attest in their music.

The Anglo-French Connection
France and England were closely linked, across the Channel, by the manacles of power. Normandy had conquered England in 1066. England, in return, subsequently spent centuries in strife for dominion in France. Around 1430 the English presence was particularly strong in Burgundy, a cultured as well as powerful court whose Duke Philip was related by marriage to the Duke of Bedford in England. Artists, architects and musicians worked in both countries. Gothic architecture, which displaced the Romanesque in France at about the time when the older Notre Dame was built, flourished on both sides of the Channel; painters matched one another, and English musicians were particularly welcomed in France for the sonorous beauty of their music.

English musicians quickly imbibed influences from France in matters of musical technique and, notwithstanding the Church's disapproval of innovations, English music cultivated pleasing harmonies that became specially favoured on the Continent.

The leading English composer in the French style was John Dunstable (*c.* 1390–1453) employed by the Duke of Bedford, his local liege lord. Dunstable was accordingly exported to Burgundy, where he and his music were greatly welcome. He was singled out as one of the greatest musicians of his time, and as the principal influence on the next important composer working in France, Guillaume Dufay, likewise acknowledged as the leading musician of his day.

Dufay travelled widely in France and Italy, but ended his life in his native Flanders—in the cathedral city of Cambrai, as monk and musician. Dufay is the link between the Parisian school, begun with Léonin, and the Flemish school, which found its supreme master in Roland de Lassus. Music had moved away from Paris, the metropolis of learning, to quieter, less hectic centres where the searching mind could thrive.

Harpsichord p 87
Violin p 65–7

Chapter 3
Patronage

Royal Court and Renaissance

The genius of Dufay ◆
Music on a grand scale at the court of Burgundy ◆
The artful innovators of the Lowland school ◆
Josquin and the musical Renaissance ◆
The Reformation ◆ Three giants of music:
Palestrina, Lassus and Victoria ◆

It is never possible to pinpoint the end of one artistic period and the beginning of another. When a new movement becomes popular it does not annihilate the rest. As far as music was concerned at the close of the fourteenth century, the rigid traditions of earlier church music existed alongside the intellectual intricacies of *ars nova* and the joyous music of the people.

Guillaume Dufay (*c.* 1400–1474)
Dufay is the man generally acknowledged to have bridged the gap between sacred and secular, staid and sensuous, intellectual and purely physical responses to music. He had enormous influence in his lifetime and his disciples in their turn dominated European music for almost two hundred years, influencing other composers wherever they went.

Dufay's music was a personal statement—it grew and changed and developed as he did. His compositions can immediately be slotted into various parts of his career: at home as a choirboy in Cambrai, the enchanting, peaceful and staid centre of music in fifteenth-century Flanders; later in Constance on the border of Germany and Austria; then in Italy, at Pesaro and Rimini as chief musician to the influential Malatesta family, during which time he took holy orders and a degree in law. He moved to Rome, working for Pope Eugene IV, then to Savoy, where his master was the Duke Amadeus. He returned finally to Cambrai, working there until his death.

His are the first complete masses by one composer known to us after the single example by Machaut, and beautiful indeed they are, with their chains of comforting harmonies learned from Dunstable, their delight in alternative duetting, first above, then below their long, tuneful melody lines. The most captivating of them all is, arguably, the mass based on *Se la*

1430–1600 *Royal Court and Renaissance*

Dufay, standing in front of the organ, in conversation with his cheerful-looking colleague **Binchois**, *who holds a harp.*

face est pale, a free-flowing motet of his own composition whose careful adherence to rules may easily be overlooked in its divine euphony.

Dufay's most celebrated mass has, as its theme, or *cantus firmus*, the secular song *L'homme armé* ("The armed man") by an English composer, Robert Morton, who worked at the Burgundian court and visited Dufay at Cambrai. From the frequency with which *L'homme armé* was taken as a theme by other composers, we may assume that it was a widely disseminated popular song.

Earlier composers celebrated a grand occasion as best they might: Dufay was the first to compose music whose component vocal parts create, deliberately, the alternation of harmony and discord according to a now accepted set of rules. His motet *Vasilissa*, composed for a royal wedding, is a monument of ingenuity and splendid composition—the voices blazing forth in celebration. The grander the occasion, sacred or secular, the more ambitious was Dufay's music for it: the Berne–Freiburg treaty between Pope Eugene and King Sigismund inspired the grandiose motet *Supremum est mortalibus*, which interweaves their names in soft chords. When Dufay sensed the approach of death he wrote his last mass, for his own funeral, basing it on the melody of his beautiful and emotional motet *Ave regina coelorum*, and interspersing the text with tropes for his soul's repose.

Renaissance Music

Every great composer spans what went before and what comes after and Dufay has been called the bridge between medieval music and that of the Renaissance. In painting and architecture the Renaissance, which historians reckon to have begun around 1430, brought a preference for the Greek

The Mass

The Roman Catholic Mass, and its medieval plainsong setting, have been a constant inspiration to composers for hundreds of years. In the sixteenth century, to such great composers as Byrd, Palestrina and Victoria, music was essentially for worship. It was only in the Baroque period that orchestration and virtuoso solo singers developed the Mass into more of a devotional showpiece.

The text of the Mass is divided into five basic sections, with numerous variable subdivisions: Kyrie, Gloria, Credo, Sanctus *and* Agnus Dei. *The* Gloria, *for example, may have its* Laudamus te *or* Cum Sancto Spiritu *sections singled out for separate treatment. (There is a magnificent setting of the former, for soprano and orchestra, in Mozart's C minor Mass; and of the latter, in Rossini's* Petite messe solennelle.) *From the* Credo, *Bach's setting of the* Crucifixus *in his immense* Mass in B minor *is one of the most powerful pieces of choral writing in all music. The* Sanctus *section of the Mass contains both the* Hosanna in excelsis *and the* Benedictus, *while the final* Agnus Dei *includes the words* Dona nobis pacem, *which are also often set as a separate movement.*

and Roman Classic virtues of simple, flowing lines as a reaction from the ornate style of the Gothic (which was itself "reborn" in the later emergence of Baroque).

The musical parallel of this Italian-based rebirth was twofold: a progression from polyphony—several voices or instruments moving independently at the same time and creating agreeable harmony while doing so—and a new concern for the audibility and musical matching of the sung words which led to the cult of one harmonized melody, rather than several melodies going on at the same time.

There was a third result; the emergence of a secular music at least as important, sophisticated, advanced and emotionally affecting as church music. That was the musical Renaissance: it happened with the arrival of the madrigal, at first in Italy, then in England and elsewhere. But music had been moving for some time towards the idea of harmony for its own sake, not just because polyphonic voices happened to collide agreeably. There was an awareness that a verbal text was not just a collection of

***The Duke of Burgundy's
hunt**, c. 1419. The revellers
are entertained by a small
group of wind musicians, to
the left of the picture.*

sounds to be accommodated, but an expression of feelings and ideas to be reflected as closely as possible in the music.

The Lowland School—Ingenious Puzzles

The Lowland (or Burgundian) school, of which Dufay was a founding figure, was united chiefly in the pursuit of music distinguished by supremely artful complexity, the more ingenious the better. The text, like the basic melody, was only a foundation for the proliferation of cunning musical design, as intricately woven as possible. Sometimes composers set puzzle canons, to be solved by the singers like difficult crossword-puzzles—given the clue of one vocal line, the singers had to work out the music for at least four voices.

Music of this elaborate nature required exact notation if it was to be sung correctly; and promptly there arrived a new system of mensural notation that could supply all details about the duration and pitch of notes in music. It was not yet the all-informative stave notation of our day, but a clear step towards the sixteenth-century method of giving *all* musical information.

Europe was on the verge of the Renaissance: men came to the Continent from England—some musicians dabbling in espionage, for they travelled most freely from court to court—and the arts began to acquire an extra, intellectual edge.

The Influence of the Burgundian Court

The court of Burgundy was at Dijon. It included a large musical establishment, with a library of music to match. Under Duke Philip the Good (1419–1467) the chapel had twenty-three musicians—more than the French King employed—and by 1506 there were thirty-three musicians. Most of them were singers, some composers as well. There was a separate instrumental establishment, which might join the choir for important religious feast-days, but was chiefly required for secular music, to which the Dukes of Burgundy attached great importance. The most popular instruments there were the noisy ones for outdoor occasions: shawms (a sort of oboe), bagpipes, trumpets and tambourines. There were also flutes, lutes, crumhorns (a gentler sort of oboe with a distinctive buzzing sound), harps and vielles (ancestors of the viol family).

On 17 February 1454 Duke Philip held a Feast of the Pheasant at Lille, during which twenty-eight minstrels played music for the instruments just named, seated in a monstrous pie-dish. Might this event have been the inspiration for the English nursery rhyme *Sing a song of sixpence* with its "four and twenty blackbirds/baked in a pie./When the pie was opened/the birds began to sing"?

The court of Burgundy had strong ties with England, political and musical. Both Dunstable and Morton worked there. The musicians of the Burgundian court were usually recruited from the royal and papal chapels (this was the period of Schism when one pope ruled in Rome and his rival in Avignon), but almost all the music makers came from the Low Countries, in which the Dukes of Burgundy spent most of their time.

Ockeghem *leading a group of singers. An illumination from a Rouen manuscript made about thirty years after the composer's death.*

Binchois (1400–1460)

Gilles Binchois was a Lowlander from Mons, who worked for most of his career as a lay singer and composer. Binchois composed some jolly, quite sophisticated *chansons* and *rondeaux* with French secular texts, such as *Filles à marier*, whose words enjoin marriageable girls not to wed and whose music bounces along deliciously. He had a serious side too, but for all his years of work in chapel, Binchois left little church music and no complete setting of the mass, though what remains to us is of highest quality, favourably influenced by the euphony of Dunstable's harmonies.

Musical historians writing soon after Binchois' death ranked him with Dufay and Dunstable as the composers most influential on new music. His compositions must have been internationally popular, since their tunes turn up all over Europe as themes in other music for decades afterwards. Among medieval composers, Binchois was particularly loved as a person, so literary references suggest; his joyous personality is mentioned more than

1430-1600 Royal Court and Renaissance

The Chansonnier de Tournai, an early collection of love songs and ballads, which includes work by Josquin and Ockeghem.

once, and when he died he was commemorated in musical laments (*déplorations*) by Dufay and the greatest composer of the next generation, Jean Ockeghem.

Jean Ockeghem (*c.* 1410–1497)

Ockeghem's early years are blurred by time—there is a distinct possibility that he spent some time at the Burgundian court, working with Binchois and learning the newest techniques. In 1451 he moved to the royal chapel of the French King Charles VII at Tours, and he served that king's successors, Louis XI and Charles VIII, as musical director, working for part of the time at Notre Dame in Paris. Ockeghem seems to have attained eminence and royal favour without taking holy orders, which in those times was unusual, although in his will he left all his estate to the Abbey of St Martin in Tours, where he had held the office of treasurer.

Ockeghem was admired by succeeding generations chiefly as a virtuoso of musical mathematics, the epitome of the Lowlands *ars nova* in all its ingenious complexity. Historians drew attention to his *Missa cujusvi toni* ("Mass in whatever key"), written without clefs because it made agreeable music wherever the clefs might be fixed: and his *Missa prolationum*, an extraordinary feat of contrapuntal skill for four voices. Those later historians may never have listened to Ockeghem's music, only have read and deciphered it, since musical taste, until the late eighteenth century at least, usually preferred new music to old. Since the modern cult of Ancient Music grew up, we can hear Ockeghem's contrapuntal marvels, and the chief marvel is that those pieces do not sound complicated to the ear, but melodious and harmonious—exquisitely beautiful.

Modern historians are more likely to admire Ockeghem for his musical innovations: when he based music on a theme, he was as likely to place the melody in one of the highest voices as in the conventional bass or tenor lines. Sometimes the melody migrates from one voice to another. Sometimes Ockeghem simply states his chosen theme at the start of each movement, like a motto, then elaborates freely and boldly, without further need of a thematic linchpin. Even in his masses he veered at will between so-called "perfect" triple time, and supposedly ungodly duple time. Where earlier composers carefully marked off a musical piece into sections, separated by cadences, like paragraph ends, Ockeghem did his best to conceal the

Gilles Binchois, *a portrait by Van Eyck.*

cadences, weaving the end of one section into the start of the next without an obvious seam, as sixteenth-century composers were to do almost as a matter of course. Ockeghem anticipated them also in his love of dramatic cumulative effects, working towards a climax, and he made a point of moving outside the middle register of vocal music into unusually high and low sonorities for special purposes connected with the text (eg "He ascended into heaven"). He loved to match words with a musical equivalent, and for "The dead" even set the word *mortuorum* in black notes (crotchets) for mourning. Most important for the evolution of music was his concern with the meaning and clarity of words which led him into passages of

*A page from a beautifully illuminated manuscript, showing the Kyrie of Josquin's Mass **Ave Maris Stella**.*

homophony, one chord to a syllable, the chord often repeated (similar to the chanting of psalms in the modern Anglican liturgy) to draw special attention to some important passage of text.

Ockeghem often used secular songs for his themes such as Morton's *L'homme armé* or his own rondeau *Fors seulement*, which must have enjoyed the popularity of a hit-song, so often was it borrowed and newly worked by other composers. Modern musical ethics might call it plagiarism; the Middle Ages called it *parody* when a composer took an existing composition and improved on it, either by ornamenting it, or by adding extra voices.

Ockeghem was evidently much loved, not only as the most important musician of his day, and a great influence on composers after him, but as a person: in his old age he was singled out as a fine singer, a handsome man and a living example of all the Christian virtues. Among the funeral tributes was a Latin poem by Erasmus and a glorious motet with a double text in two languages, *Nymphes des bois* and/or *Requiescat*, by his most famous pupil and immediate successor, Josquin Desprez, who was working just then as musical director to the Pope in the Sistine Chapel at Rome (its ceilings as yet undecorated by Michelangelo).

The Procession of Composers—Major and Minor

In one sense, the history of music is a procession of great composers. The first two chapters of this book are full of incident, despite the fact they are not about a great composer at all until Guillaume de Machaut came on the scene in about 1325. This is because music goes on at many levels that posterity does not subsequently record. The history of music is shaped, almost entirely, by musicians whose names are unknown, and by composers who are unnamed in history books because the innovatory music that they wrote was surpassed and validated by somebody later and reputedly greater. The big name takes the credit, the inventor is forgotten.

Josquin Desprez, who composed the lamentation for his master Ockeghem, is the next major name in the procession, but there are a couple of important intervening composers who should not be overlooked. Pierre de la Rue (*c.* 1460–1518) was a Lowlander who built on the Burgundian tradition. He was, on available evidence, the most cunning intellectual of the whole crossword-puzzle school. He kept the Lowland tradition alive at the Burgundy court, visited Spain, whose music was shortly to blossom profusely, and developed Ockeghem's investigation into expressive choral sounds, especially for music about death and the grave. Unlike Dufay and other Lowlanders, Pierre de la Rue made a feature of unexpectedly wide vocal jumps, giving his music a jagged quality quite unlike the gentle flow that we associate with the English-influenced Lowlanders. I should also mention another major master of the Lowland music, Jakob Obrecht (*c.* 1450-1505), who wrote songs in Italian, French and Dutch, reflecting the musical styles of the countries where he lived and worked, and who followed Ockeghem in his close attention to the mood and meaning of the text.

Josquin Desprez (*c.* 1440–1521)

The composer who personally brought music out of the Middle Ages into the Renaissance was not so much Dufay as Josquin. He did it not by innovation, but by building on all that he learned from Ockeghem about drama, about ingenuity, about sweet-sounding harmony and word-painting—the essential ingredients of sixteenth-century music. If we compare the music of

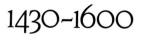

Josquin with that of Palestrina, his most famous Italian successor in the sixteenth century, we can of course find contrapuntal ingenuity in common—the Italian variety much smoother, purged of emotional ardour, the Lowland style far more vivid and searching. Italian music preferred that smooth euphony in church music, and in secular music such firmly rhythmical pieces as the *frottola*, a very popular, flirtatious dance that conquered the rest of Europe. When the Lowlanders got hold of the *frottola* they weighed it down with intellectual counterpoint, but its spirit was to surface again with the madrigal.

Josquin was born in Vermandois, part of Picardy, on the French side of the modern Belgian frontier, near St Quentin, and he died in the same part of France, near Valenciennes. The territory was part of Burgundy, culturally as close to Belgium and Holland as to Dijon, where the ducal court was. He was a chorister at Milan Cathedral in 1459, and by 1474 was in the musical service of the ducal Sforza family in Milan. In 1486 Josquin was working at the papal chapel in Rome, but by 1493 had returned to France in the service of the French royal chapel under Louis XI and Louis XII. History is unsure for which King Louis Josquin wrote the four-part *chanson*, *Guillaume se va chaufer*. The king had asked Josquin for a chanson in which he could take part and since the monarch was a poor singer, Josquin gave him a part consisting of one note only, sustained throughout (Purcell did the

The only known likeness of **Josquin Desprez**, *perhaps taken from a portrait that reputedly hung in a Brussels church.*

Early Music Printing

The printing of words was evolved in Germany by Gutenberg in the mid-fifteenth century, and in England by William Caxton. Soon after that, there appeared books for liturgical use illustrated with plainsong engraved on wood blocks.

In Venice, Giovanni Petrucci used movable type for printing music as early as 1501; over the next twenty-five years he published more than fifty volumes of instrumental and vocal music. This example was printed in 1503.

The technique of printing music had spread to London, Paris and Germany by the middle of the century. The finest are made up from a triple impression, i.e. the staff, the notes and the words printed separately and superimposed.

same in a string fantasia, likewise Rossini in an aria for a singer whose voice he mistrusted). It is a curious, jagged piece with a dogged, droning bass line supposedly to help the king keep in tune.

Josquin twice found his employers slow to pay his salary: when Count Sforza hesitated, Josquin composed a mass on the notes La sol fa re me,

1430–1600 *Royal Court and Renaissance*

Louis XI (*1461–1483*, left), nicknamed *The Spider, and* **Louis XII** (*1498–1515*), *two great patrons of the arts.*

meaning *Lascia fare a me* ("leave it to me")—the Count's promise. When Louis XII failed to pay up, Josquin reminded him in the motet *Memor esto verbi tui* ("Remember your promise"), and he acknowledged payment in a further motet.

In 1501 he was appointed musical director to Duke Hercules of Ferrara, in Italy, and composed a mass on the musical letters of his employer's name. His best music was probably written in Italy, where his style was given full freedom, but he was temperamentally a Netherlander and (unlike the Italians) a contrapuntist. All his finest work makes a feature of close vocal imitation, one voice chasing another, like a canon, then roving more freely. In Italy such pieces were called *caccia*, or "chase". Josquin was among the first composers to have his music printed in Italy by Giovanni Petrucci from 1501 onwards.

The printing of music was as much a triumph of communication as Caxton's printing of words. Chiefly it was important to disseminate culture as widely as possible, not only to encourage composers, but to give pleasure to singers and instrumentalists who might want to perform a favourite piece at home. Home music-making was common in sixteenth-century England, France and Italy, so music publishing developed in all three countries, and soon spread through the civilized world.

Facing page: **A band of Flemish musicians** *assembled on the church steps. Their instruments include crumhorn, pipe & tabor, lutes, triangle and a portative organ* (*foreground*) *being directed by a figure in the centre of the picture.*

Josquin was not an innovator like Ockeghem, but he used all the Lowland techniques for his own expressive purposes. His masses are much admired, but his motets more truly display his genius. The detailed correspondence of text and music made others describe it as *musica reservata* (maybe because it could only be fathomed by musical initiates who had solved the secret of the notation). He was fond of word-painting, as we hear in *Absalon, fili mei*, with its poignant descending motif for David's descent to hell (composed for the death of an employer's son).

Of his many masses, the *Missa pange lingua* is the most famous, though any one of them will stir a newcomer by its beauty of line, occasional passages of chords and thoughtful treatment of words. He was one of the first composers to set the psalms and other passages from the Old Testament as motets. His mature music belongs to the Renaissance rather than the Middle Ages. It is real music, not just old and interesting, but moving, even to those for whom the cult of the Virgin Mary means nothing.

Josquin's last composition was a motet coupling the *Pater noster* ("Our Father") with *Ave Maria* ("Hail Mary") and for his funeral he composed *Absolve, quaesumus*, in which he quotes from his own music as a sort of memorial. When he died, his contribution to art was likened to that of Michelangelo, a comparison that proposes a monumental romanticism uncommon in modern performances of Josquin's music. What we do hear in Josquin's music is a contrapuntal depth, the various voices laid out with a unique clarity. And there is a muscularity also that stands comparison with Michelangelo's art, as may be heard in the lament for Ockeghem; there is also a delightful, frivolous quality, as in *El grillo* ("The cricket").

The German Scene—Heinrich Isaac (*c.* 1450–1517)
As the Burgundian musical establishment grew less important it began to infiltrate the Hapsburg court of the Holy Roman Emperors. In Germany, a country hitherto backward in music, the *Minnesänger* and later *Meistersinger* (still active in the sixteenth century) continued to sing their simple unaccompanied songs, while the rest of western Europe was revelling in rich, intricate, textured sounds.

Our music-making and listening in the twentieth century is so dominated by the German musical tradition, from J.S. Bach to Stockhausen, that it is strange to consider the centuries before Bach when the

finest music was not being composed by Germans at all. There were, of course, great composers in Germany before Bach—Buxtehude, Pachelbel, Schütz are names that turn up at concerts or on records all the time these days. The pre-Bach German tradition was due to Emperor Maximilian I, who visited Italy in 1496 and met the Lowlands composer Heinrich Isaac. Isaac had been employed by the Medici family in Florence as singer and composer at their court, but Medici influence was declining and Isaac accepted a post as court composer to the Holy Roman Emperor. He brought Netherlands compositional technique to Germany, adopted German musical ways—masses based on plainsong rather than secular tunes, special motets for saints' days and songs for many voices with the melody sung by the tenor. His most famous song, *Innsbruck ich muss dich lassen* ("Innsbruck I must leave you"), became a standard hymn-tune through its melodious top part (much used in the Passion settings by J.S. Bach and

*In this engraving from **The Triumph of Maximilian I** (1517), a camel proudly draws the celebrated organist Paul Hofhaimer.*

47

others) not for its leading tenor tune. Isaac brought German music to a level comparable with the rest of Europe, but his life remained, musically and personally, just as closely linked with Italy—he was a dab hand at the *frottola*, and his wife came from Florence. His musical style in Italian and German music was always Lowland-based, intricately worked and rooted in English sweet harmony. His music was widely distributed in Europe and influenced composers everywhere at a period when such sounds were particularly appreciated.

The Effects of the Reformation

The other great influence on German music, and elsewhere, at this time was Martin Luther (1483–1546), who declared an independent rift from the Catholic Church with his list of ninety-five complaints nailed to the church door at Wittenberg on 31 October 1517. It was the Reformation: henceforth music was either Catholic or Protestant. Religious dispute, like war, has never been good for music. Artistic quality, the only real criterion, becomes sullied with contentious issues.

The Reformation at first affected music chiefly in England, where Henry VIII employed Lowland musicians to bring out the innate talent of English composers (c. 1495–1545). The talent was already there in John Taverner and Thomas Tallis, and later William Byrd. All three wrote superb church music in English and in Latin—it was as well to be flexible since changes of monarch sometimes brought reversions to the Roman Rite. Tallis's choral setting in Latin of the *Lamentations of Jeremiah* is a masterpiece of this period. In Catholic countries, the immediate result was the Counter-Reformation (1562). The Pope in Rome determined to veto secular practices such as harmony and folk melody in church music. His ideal was to revert entirely to plainsong—the simple fixed patterns of traditional church music.

Palestrina, Lassus and Victoria

It did not take long to establish exceptions to this austere papal ruling. Giovanni da Palestrina (c. 1525–1594), arguably the greatest Italian composer of music for unaccompanied voices, wrote harmonic masses of such moving beauty that he won a papal dispensation and the papal title "Prince of Music".

Palestrina's music follows the learned, intricate style of the Netherlands, but adjusts it to Italian taste, which was for smoother, melodious invention, more like the old English style of Dunstable. Palestrina's most vivid music lies outside his masses, for example in his *Exultate deo* with its evocations of musical instruments. His was an ecclesiastical counterpart of the buoyant, often risqué Italian secular songs such as those composed by Clément Jannequin (c. 1485–1558). Little is known of Jannequin's life or indeed of his personality, but his songs *The cries of Paris*, *The Battle of Marignan* and *The calling of birds* are vividly onomatopoeic, and great fun to sing or hear, very close to music for dancing.

The vigour of the period is best observed in the music of two non-Italians, the Netherlander Roland de Lassus (c. 1530–1594), who worked chiefly in Bavaria for Albrecht V, and the Spaniard Tomaso de Victoria (c. 1548–1611), who emphasized the pain in religious faith and its actuality in human experience. Victoria (like Palestrina in his motet *Stabat mater* for two choirs) invented a two-choir type of responsive singing that was

Facing page: A portrait of **Martin Luther** *by Lucas Cranach the elder. Luther was an accomplished singer and performer on the lute and flute. As a young man, he sang in the streets for money.*

Dunstable p 34

Luther p 78–80

1430–1600 Royal Court and Renaissance

Left: ***Giovanni da Palestrina***. *He wanted to enter the priesthood, when his wife, brother and two sons died of the plague.*

Far left: ***Roland de Lassus***. *As a boy, he was a chorister in the service of the fabulously wealthy Gonzaga family.*

miraculously what composers at the Cathedral of St Mark in Venice (where two balconies spanned the congregation) found most desirable in church music. The Venetian antiphonal style was chiefly developed by Andrea Gabrieli (1520–1586) and his nephew, a much more self-assertive Venetian, Giovanni (1557–1612). With them the story of music moves from the Lowlands to make its central point in Italy, where the madrigal and the opera arose, bringing with them a new age in music.

Chapter 4
Madrigals and Masques
The Golden Age

Europe turns now to Italy for musical inspiration ♦ The rise of
secular music spawns madrigals, dance and
instrumental music ♦ The English lute-song: a recreation for
gentlefolk ♦ Engish keyboard music ♦ The emergence of the
violin ♦ Opera is born in the musically fertile courts of Italy ♦
The *castrati* ♦ Restoration England: Henry Purcell,
the end of the Golden Age ♦

The action moves away now from the Lowlands to Italy—always an
important country for music, indeed central for the Roman Catholic Church.
The scene is set for the renewed dominance of Italian music and for the
growth in popularity of secular music, which was soon to become as
important as the music that accompanied the church service. The story
takes us to the birth of opera, and the dawn of Baroque music.

Italian Madrigals
During the first half of the sixteenth century Italian poets and other artists,
including musicians, became newly fascinated with the works and style of
the fourteenth-century poet Petrarch, whose *canzoniere* (book of poems to be
sung) was published in Venice in 1501, and much reprinted thereafter. In
Florence and Rome, where the High Renaissance was in full flight,
composers were setting Petrarch's songs and sonnets as *frottole*. However,
connoisseurs of such matters decided that the frottola style, with its plain
texture, regular rhythms and repetitious form, was no worthy match for
Petrarch's sophisticated, deeply felt love poetry.

French and Lowland composers then working in Italy found a more
flexible, expressive and emotional sort of music for the favourite Pet-
rarchian verses and their contemporary imitations by Tasso, Ariosto,
Michelangelo and the like. By the 1520s such pieces were being called
madrigali. Etymologists cannot agree on the derivation of the word, some
say from *mandra* (a sheepfold), others *matrix* (the mother tongue), or
materialis (free-formed). The first of these new Italian madrigals appeared
spasmodically in the 1520s; from 1533 they turned up in great profusion.

The music was intended primarily to be sung by anything from three to
seven voices unaccompanied, the cadence and rhythms of the music closely

Madrigals and Masques
The Golden Age

*A young maid plays the cittern to a **lute** accompaniment. "Any lutenist who attains the age of eighty years," said Dowland, "must surely have spent sixty of them in the tuning of his instrument."*

*Facing page: Andrea Gabrieli was commissioned to write the music in celebration of the **victory of the Venetian Republic over the Turks at Lepanto** in 1571.*

reflecting the sentiments of the poetry, even to individual words such as "grief", "die", "heart" and of course "run", "ascend" and "descend"—a musical device known in English as *word-painting*.

Nowadays these madrigals are commonly sung by choirs, with several voices taking each part; but they were intended for one-voice/one-part performance by a few courtiers, or a family of gentlefolk, since every educated person was expected to sing and play an instrument decently. Madrigals were domestic, informal music: if there were not enough singers the missing voices could be played on an instrument—usually the lute.

By the middle of the century, long narrative passages from Virgil or Dante, or the epics of Ariosto and Tasso about Charlemagne and his crusaders were also being set as sequences of madrigals. To keep the text clearly intelligible, the less emotive bits of narration were often set as declamatory chords, anticipating the sung *recitative* of opera. When the words did become emotionally intense, the music became increasingly juicy in harmony, with outlandish chords that we call chromatic—chords with notes not contained within the prevailing key. The new masters of these innovations in the madrigal were the Lowlander Cyprian de Rore (1516–

Andrea Gabrieli p 54, 78

Ow is the Month of Maying, when mer-ry Lads are play-ing; Fa la la la

la la la la la la la la la la; Each with his bon-ny Laſs up-on the gree-ny

Graſs; Fa la la la la la la la la la la la la la la la la.

*A section of the first printing of Morley's "**Now is the Month of Maying**". The clarity of the printing was of prime importance: one copy had to serve for many singers.*

1565) and the Italian Luca Marenzio (1553–1599), whose emotional style of music particularly influenced English madrigalists towards the end of the century.

Varieties of Madrigal

For lighter entertainment Italian composers wrote *balletti*, songs in several verses with a "fa-la" refrain, set to crisp, dance-like music. Giovanni Gastoldi (*c.* 1555–1622) was best known for his balletts (the spelling has stuck to avoid confusion with *ballet*), though the most famous example is English, Thomas Morley's *Now is the Month of Maying*. The simplest, lightest, most harmony-conscious pieces of the madrigal type were called *villanelle* from *canzone villanesca alla napolitana* (Neapolitan peasant songs) or *canzonette*, a style that became quite popular in England.

The madrigal itself became more complicated and varied. In place of elegant love poems in the manner of Petrarch, Andrea Gabrieli set to music poems for important social or political occasions and popular, even vulgar, comic verse. Palestrina brought this essentially secular form of music back into the Church's domain with his "spiritual madrigals", to be sung at home or at court during Lent. It was Orazio Vecchi (1550–1605), chief musician to the court of Modena, who, with his *L'Amfiparnaso*, pioneered the "madrigal comedy", a series of madrigals following the course of a *commedia dell' arte* play in three acts. The character parts were represented by all the singers together (so for a female character the men sing falsetto, for an old man they all adopt quavery voices). No stage action or costume was envisaged, but the madrigal was moving towards opera. It was to get there in the work of Claudio Monteverdi.

The madrigal began to travel outside Italy. Lassus, having been trained and employed for some years there as Palestrina's predecessor at St John Lateran in Rome, moved to the Bavarian court in Munich, where he inspired other musicians to write madrigals, two volumes of them. Philippe de Monte, another Lowlander, deserves a mention here on two counts: he exported the madrigal to the Imperial court in Prague and Vienna, and he was the most prolific of all madrigal composers, publishing more than a thousand of them, sacred as well as secular. But it was in England that the madrigal, together with its lighter forms, found a second home.

Developments in England—Tye, Tallis and Byrd

England under the Tudors was as keenly devoted to music as to the other arts. The plays of Shakespeare and his contemporaries abound in musical references, presumably understood by the humblest spectator in the commercial theatre. The substantial yet comfortable architecture of Hampton Court Palace is reflected in the portraits of English notabilities by Hans Holbein and in the agreeable sounds of sacred motets by Christopher Tye and Thomas Tallis. Henry VIII's Reformation of the Church had an interesting side effect on English musical talent—the conflict between Protestant and Catholic gave contemporary composers experience in writing for both English and Latin liturgies. Some uncompromising Catholic composers were persecuted, of course, but Elizabeth I sensibly allowed Latin church music to be sung in places of learning, and so masses and motets continued to be composed and sung, alongside anthems and settings of the Protestant service in English.

Commedia dell' arte

The name commedia dell' arte *belonged to the "guild comedies" performed by troupes of itinerant actors in sixteenth-century Italy. Their performances were very stylized, being a mixture of improvised clowning, traditional comic business (*lazzi*), stock characters and predictably romantic plots.*

Best remembered today are the names of some of the characters, which still survive in Christmas pantomime: Harlequin (Arlecchino) with his bright, lozenge-patterned costume and domino mask; Columbine (Colombina), Harlequin's true love and the servant of another, more aggressive and cowardly commedia character, Captain Fracasso. But the best known remains Pulcinella, the hook-nosed scoundrel who evolved into Mr Punch. One more character, Pedrolino, became especially popular in France, where he eventually became the wistful and hapless Pierrot.

Commedia performances took place as a rule out of doors, on a light, collapsible stage that belonged to the troupe of zanni *(as these clowns and tumblers were known). They became famous all over the mainland of Europe and were a popular form of entertainment until late in the eighteenth century. A film by Marcel Carné,* Les Enfants du Paradis, *re-creates with brilliance and sympathy the life of such a troupe.*

The commedia dell' arte *characters, shown here, were a collection of pranksters and buffoons. They have served as models for comic figures throughout the Western world.*

Although much of the music of the fifteenth and sixteenth centuries was religious in content, there was a secular side also, and early public performances frequently accompanied theatrical productions. **The Globe** *in London was Shakespeare's theatre and provided the setting for many presentations of popular music. The playwright himself included many musical metaphors in his plays.*

William Byrd was perhaps the most go-ahead composer of the time. He was co-organist with Tallis of the Chapel Royal in London and wrote four settings of the English service, but being a staunch Catholic, he was persecuted for his faith, and he defiantly continued to write Latin masses and motets for rich Catholic families with private chapels. Byrd's early secular domestic music consisted of solo songs accompanied by a group (*consort*) of viols or recorders, or a mixture of both. His friendship with Philippe de Monte (they exchanged Latin motets) explains Byrd's awareness of new developments in Italy, especially among the Lowland-born composers.

The English Madrigal Tradition

Thomas Morley (1557–1603) was organist of St Paul's Cathedral in the city of London and he too composed Latin and English church music. His chief claim to fame, however, was as the leader of the English Madrigal School, which took root in 1588, the year of the Spanish Armada, and thereafter flourished marvellously and survived for a quarter of a century after his death. Henry VIII is known to have sung and played the lute, and is credited

Facing page: *Lassus, directing the musicians of* **the Bavarian court at Munich**, *where his career began. So wonderful was his voice as a child that he was twice kidnapped from school. Both times his parents retrieved him, though they abandoned matters at the third attempt, when he was abducted to the service of the Viceroy of Sicily.*

less certainly with some compositions (in those days one could claim authorship merely by adding a part to an existing piece). His daughter Elizabeth, Morley's Queen, certainly played the virginals and the lute, she sang and was particularly keen on dancing. Her courtiers were expected to do likewise, although the rules of courtly etiquette, which were formulated in an Italian book—a bestseller during her reign—insisted that well-bred persons never made music in public.

Both Henry VIII and Elizabeth I kept Italian musicians at court. One of them, from 1562 onward, was the madrigalist Alfonso Ferrabosco (1543–1588), greatly admired at the time by English colleagues, though his music now seems much inferior to theirs. Copies of Italian madrigals had been circulating in England since the early years of Henry VIII's reign.

In 1588 a chorister of St Paul's Cathedral, Nicholas Yonge, published an anthology of Italian madrigals chosen from volumes he had been sent by friends there that he had fitted to English verse texts. He called the collection *Musica Transalpina* ("Music from across the Alps"). Luckily, English poets such as Edmund Spenser, Michael Drayton and Sir Philip Sidney had begun to emulate the sophisticated, sentimental imagery of Petrarch. It was this fashion that made the English madrigal possible—music closely linked to poetry in the Italian style. Three more collections of *Italian Madrigals Englished* were published in London and sold in quantity; Byrd wrote his only madrigals (two settings of the same poem in praise of his protectress the Queen) for one of these collections.

The English Madrigalists

The popularity of madrigals in musical homes encouraged other English composers. In 1593 Morley produced his *Canzonets* or *Little Short Songs to Three Voices*—light and tripping Italian-style madrigals in miniature, a musical parallel to the exquisite miniature paintings by Nicholas Hilliard and in complete contrast to Morley's grave, austere sacred music. During the next four years he published further volumes of canzonets, madrigals and balletts, often borrowing freely from Italian originals. He also wrote a teaching book, *A Plaine and Easie Introduction to Practicall Musicke*, much of it in the form of dialogues between a master and two pupils, one industrious, the other lazy; it too included short madrigals as examples.

Other composers followed his example, among them notably Thomas Weelkes (1575–1623), who was organist and choirmaster in Winchester and Chichester. His vivid pictorial imagination finds marvellous scope in the double madrigal *Thule, the Period of Cosmography*, a sequence of wonders reported by recent explorers of the world, musically portrayed in bold, even violent harmony. Weelkes's madrigals and balletts range easily from lovesick melancholy as in *Say, dear, when will your frowning leave*, with its agonized ending "And kill my soul with double smart", to the profound grief of the sacred madrigal *When David heard that Absalom was slain* to the frank, earthy jollity of *Since Robin Hood, Maid Marian, and Little John are gone-a* or *Come, sirrah Jack ho, bring some tobacco* (Sir Walter Raleigh's latest innovation from travel in America). *O Care, though wilt despatch me* is, curiously, a sad ballett, with positively doleful fa-la refrains. He also set the street-cries of London hawkers to music in madrigal style.

Weelkes's virtuosity of style is rivalled only by John Wilbye (1574–1638), a Suffolk man who, unusually, held no church appointment but spent

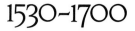

most of his life in the service of a rich family outside Bury St Edmunds as household lutenist and general musician. Wilbye's two books of madrigals display an exceptional poetic sensibility and refined musical invention. His songs are elegantly and sensuously Italianate, serious by temperament even when entertaining, for instance in *Sweet honey-sucking bees*, or in the eccentrically inhibited canzonet *Flora gave me fairest flowers*. Wilbye's genius is heard at its grandest and most affecting in the gently melancholy nocturnal double madrigal *Draw on, sweet night*, with its grave, spacious final section "I then shall have best time for my complaining".

Several other collections of English madrigals appeared during the 1590s. In 1601 Thomas Morley produced *The Triumphs of Oriana* to which twenty-three composers contributed madrigals in honour of Queen Elizabeth, each ending with the couplet "Then sang the shepherds and nymphs of Diana/Long live fair Oriana". Oriana, or more often Gloriana, was a loyal nickname for Elizabeth I, with pastoral associations in the tradition of Petrarch's poetry. Orlando Gibbons (1583–1625) was the outstanding English composer of his day, supreme in Anglican church music, in music for keyboard and the instrumental consort; and his one volume of *Madrigals and Motetts, apt for viols and voices*, published in 1612, is a glorious achievement, though scholars insist that its finest pieces, such as *The Silver Swan* and *What is our Life?* (the poem supposedly written by Raleigh on the night before his execution), are too serious in mood and too obviously solo songs to count as real madrigals. But by 1612 the English madrigal was in decline. The Italian original from which it

Orlando Gibbons *became a choirboy at Cambridge and at twenty-one, the organist to the Chapel Royal of James I of England, a post that he held for the rest of his life.*

From **John Dowland's First Book of Lute Songs**. *The tablature for lute accompaniment is seen on the left-hand page, while the voice parts, nicely placed for a group of singers reading from one volume, are on the right.*

1530-1700 The Golden Age

King Henry VIII was a musician of surpassing skill, who wrote devotional motets and fetching love-songs. Also seen in this illustration is probably William Cornyshe, a musician of the king's court.

sprang had moved on to become something else, more virtuoso, with essential, independent instrumental accompaniment for professional singers expert in rapid vocal decoration.

The English Lute-song

England still held that music was for performance by cultivated amateur gentlefolk, and in England the madrigal gave way to the "English ayr" or lute-song for voice accompanied by lute, sometimes but not necessarily the same performer. The lute had become a popular instrument in well-to-do homes during the time of Henry VIII and instruction manuals began to appear early in Elizabeth's reign. The first lute-songs were published as part of one such book in 1596 with the instrumental accompaniment notated in *tablature*, each dot showing where the fingers should be placed on the strings (popular guitar music today is still generally written out in similar fashion). The poetry of these songs is also remarkable for its fine quality, and meticulous attention was paid to the setting of the words. Some of the composers, incidentally, were their own lyricists.

Elizabeth I, *who enjoyed dancing as much as performing on the lute, also played the virginals; her instrument is shown below. Interested royalty were the chief patrons of composers during this period.*

John Dowland (1563–1626)

Dowland was the greatest English song composer, internationally celebrated in his lifetime as a lutenist, partly through publication of his songs and lute pieces in several European countries, partly because he spent much of his life working in France, Italy, Germany and Denmark (Shakespeare wrote _Hamlet_ during Dowland's period at the court of Elsinore, a tantalizing coincidence). He was a Catholic and unwilling to be harried by Protestant authority—hence the extensive travelling—but he did not flaunt his faith: he dutifully composed sacred songs in English and harmonized psalm tunes for the Anglican Rite.

Dowland's lute solos, mostly in the manner of popular dances, often allude to friends and members of English society as well as himself, most characteristically in the Pavan _Semper Dowland, semper dolens_, a Latin pun on his name, since _dolens_ means grieving.

Dowland's most typical music is of a melancholy character, as we constantly find in his songs: _Weep you no more, sad fountains, Sorrow, stay, If floods of tears could cleanse my follies past, Flow, my tears_, which was famous all over Europe as Dowland's _Lachrimae_ pavan, and from which he elaborated _Seven passionate pavans for lute and five viols_. The most glorious and tragical of them all is the song _In darkness let me dwell_, truly sombre in colour, with an unforgettable refrain, "Down, down I fall, never to rise again".

The Irish have claimed Dowland for their own, Dolan being a common Irish name, but evidence suggests that he was a Londoner and he spent his last years in the City, where he owned a house in Fetter Lane, nowadays part of London's newspaper district.

Dowland was the leader of a flourishing and influential English school of lute-song composers that had begun with Morley: it included respectable lesser figures such as Thomas Campion (1567–1620), a poet in his own right, Robert Jones and Philip Rosseter. Today, all are likely to be heard when a singer and lutenist give a recital together.

An autograph setting of the **Lord's Prayer** by John Dowland, the greatest lutenist of them all.

Instruments and their Music c. 1600

The age of the madrigal was also the age of the rise of the solo keyboard piece and of music for instrumental ensemble, sometimes dance music, which resulted in the _suite_. It also saw the birth of a free-formed abstract music, unconnected with words or with dance-steps, which led to the _sonata_.

When Dowland wrote music for the lute, he composed from special appreciation of what his instrument could do. Other composers who wrote for consorts of viols or recorders or organ simply wrote as if for a choir of voices singing that polyphony which had been the distinctive mark of the Christian Church for several centuries. Sometimes they called their pieces _Fantasia_, to indicate an extemporization written down, _Ricercar_, meaning carefully worked out, or _recherché_ (that signified some sort of fugue). Or else a composer would stipulate _canzon da sonar_ ("a song to be played"), and this led to the alternative _sonata_, which was how Giovanni Gabrieli in Venice described such compositions in 1615: he proudly called one of them _sonata pian e forte_ because he had alternated soft and loud phrases in it for two separately disposed consorts of brass instruments at a time when degrees of dynamics were always left to the discretion of the performers.

An important instrumental form from the late sixteenth century onwards was the set of variations on a well known theme, decorated or

Polyphony p 86
Sonata p 90

Early Keyboard Instruments

The terminology of early keyboard instruments was nowhere more confusing than in England. The most common instrument was the virginals (though this word was also used to refer to the larger harpsichord and, more rarely, the clavichord).

The virginals was generally a small, single-manual instrument whose strings were plucked with quills. Though it has no tonal variety, the sound is most distinctive, with a full, somewhat spongy bass and bright, shrill notes in the treble.

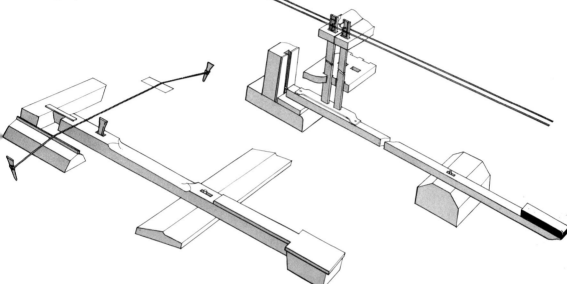

The spinet, in the sixteenth century more in use on the Continent than in England, was in essence a small, inexpensive version of the harpsichord: the equivalent of today's upright piano compared with the concert grand. Its function seems to have been mainly that of an accompanying instrument in the home. While the harpsichord family is one of plucked instruments, it is the simpler and more gentle striking action of the clavichord that spawned the pianoforte in the eighteenth century. The accompanying illustrations show both principles.

altered in mood or rhythm. Spanish lutenists from early in the century had been writing *diferencias*, which are variations in this manner, and variations are common in the English collections of keyboard music.

A favourite variation method, in all countries, was based on the use of a ground bass—a theme several bars long, repeated continuously beneath varied music. It was also called a *chaconne* or a *passacaglia*, the harmonic patterns of which relate to twentieth-century boogie-woogie. The most popular theme used in this way was *La Folía*, a simple, haunting melody based on a Portuguese folk dance which swept through Europe at about this time and is still used today.

Variation treatment in Italy was first used to connect dance pieces, such as the slow *padovano* from Padua which became the *pavane*, and the quick *saltarello* or *galliard* and the energetic Italian *lavolta*. Other favourite types of dance were the *Allemande* or Almans from Germany, the *coranto*, a fast dance, the *bransle* (in English brawl), the jig, the hornpipe and the English dump, which was slow and stately (gloomy people were described as "down in the dumps").

The dance pieces are found in all the virginals books and also in consort music (music for a group of instruments), especially for the "broken consort", which Morley's *Consort Lessons* (1599) names as consisting of treble and bass viol, recorder, cittern (a variant of the lute plucked with a plectrum), lute and pandora (or "bandora", a sort of bass lute). English consort music was much admired and copied on the Continent, though the instruments varied according to availability.

The English Virginalists

"The oftner you shall heare it, the better cause of liking you will discover." Those words of William Byrd, written at the end of the sixteenth century, remain true even three hundred and fifty years later. The world of Elizabethan keyboard music is small in range, form and, particularly, timbre. Yet it is possible to be as emotionally stirred by a galliard played upon the virginals as by listening to Chopin on a big modern grand piano: our ears, however, more accustomed to the latter, must adjust to the small, thin sound within which the composers worked.

The music tends to be short, for while the harmonies were still based on modes, extended works could all too easily sound monotonous. A favourite form was the pavan and galliard, a pair of linked dances, one slow and the second faster, in triple time. The jig and the almans appear in the later Baroque suites.

Elizabethan keyboard music abounds with ingenious and lovely variations on street-cries, popular songs or even simpler note sequences. William Byrd (1543–1623) was a master of the form. His variations *The Bells* involve nearly one hundred and fifty repetitions of a simple, two-note pattern, yet in a continuously developing and exciting arrangement. Other sets by him, such as *O Mistris Myne* or *Have with you to Walsingame*, have a freshness and charm unmatched in the music of his contemporaries. It is bold and brilliant music. A good piece to hear first is his short, merry variations upon *Lavolta* (a favourite dance of Queen Elizabeth, thought at the time to be not quite *comme il faut* since it involved high jumps that exposed the ankles).

A contemporary of Byrd was John Bull (1562–1628), who, like Scarlatti, Chopin or Liszt in later generations, chose to write almost exclusively for keyboard. He too delighted in the variation form, subjecting his themes to ever more florid and fantastic treatment. Bull must have been a virtuoso of the highest order: much of his music has an improvised air about it, and if in addition one considers that keyboard players used predominantly just the three middle fingers of each hand to perform the pieces, Bull's repeated notes, hand crossings and rapid scales give us an idea of how unique his keyboard mastery must have been. Even four hundred years later, keyboard players approach his whirlwind sets of variations with caution. The best known must be *The King's Hunt*, where he uses all his technical command of the instrument to depict the jingling harness, hoofbeats and glittering pageantry in a magnificent display of tone painting and virtuosity.

Much of the music for virginals by Byrd and Bull is to be found in a

John Bull's musical career began innocently enough as a choirboy in the Chapel Royal of Elizabeth I, where he later became organist. But with maturity came other interests which led to his dismissal as professor of music at the newly founded Gresham College, London. His amorous inclinations earned him many accusations of adultery. According to the then Archbishop of Canterbury, George Abbott, Bull had "more music than honesty, and is as famous for marring of virginity, as he is for fingering of organs and virginals".

Liszt p 185–7

D. Scarlatti p 91–2

Chopin p 180–4

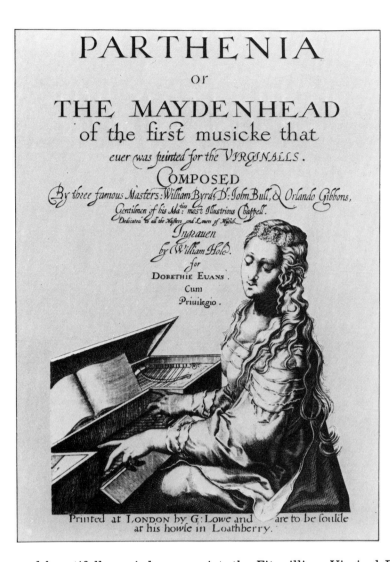

PARTHENIA
or
THE MAYDENHEAD
of the first musicke that
euer was printed for the VIRGINALLS.
COMPOSED
By three famous Masters: William Byrd, D: John Bull, & Orlando Gibbons,
Gentilmen of his Ma:ties most Illustrious Chappell.
Dedicated to all the Masters and Lovers of Musick
Ingrauen
by William Hole.
for
DORETHIE EUANS.
Cum
Priuilegio.

Printed at LONDON by G: Lowe and   are to be soulde
at his howse in Loathberry.

Parthenia (1711) was the first keyboard music to be printed in England. It contained paired dances by the three great masters of the genre: Bull, Byrd and Orlando Gibbons.

large and beautifully copied manuscript, the Fitzwilliam Virginal Book. This is by far the biggest collection of keyboard music of the period, containing just under three hundred pieces by various composers such as Giles Farnaby and Thomas Morley, as well as the two discussed above.

The third great composer in this medium (born just too late for inclusion in the Fitzwilliam collection) was Orlando Gibbons, already mentioned for his church music and his madrigals. His music for virginals places him firmly with the earlier masters. Gibbons liked the free form of the Fantasia and he wrote many rich and sombre examples for the instrument. Perhaps his greatest work for virginals (and, incidentally, a short one) is his pavan *The Lord Salisbury*; its restrained passion and tragedy transcend the tinny sounding instrument for which it was written.

The Rise of the Violin
The violin did not emerge until the middle of the sixteenth century. It differed from the viols in being played on the arm like the *lyra da braccio*,

Morley p 57–8

not between the knees, with the possible advantage that it could be played while walking about—café violinists have gained more than others by this facility—and also by having an unfretted fingerboard. Viols had frets to show the amateur where to find the notes: the violin was for the professional musician who knew without looking where to find every note of the music and how to alter the pitch minutely for expressive effect—like a blues singer's "blue" notes—officially called *microtones*, being less than even a semitone, which is the smallest step possible on conventional keyboard instruments. The violin, viola and the cello (still played between the knees, but unfretted) seem to have developed together. The missing instrument, the double bass, is shown in a painting of 1518, but it did not have its own music until 1690 and it only replaced the bass viol in the orchestra after the 1760s.

By 1556 the family of violins was established and socially discredited as essentially minstrel-proletarian, good for dancing and "easy to carry", not for the aristocracy, who had servants to carry and fetch. But the violin quickly became respectable in France and in Italy, where the finest violins were made in Cremona. Virtuosity on the violin was greatly forwarded by Biagio Marini (1597–1665), who first coaxed double stops and chords from his violin, as well as the *tremolo* sound and the *pizzicato*, or plucking effect.

Centres of Music in Italy

The development of Italian vocal music during the last half of the sixteenth century was closely bound up with life at court. Musical activity had been profuse and important in Rome, the capital of Christendom, and in Venice, a less austere city, rich and flourishing. Venice was musically dominated by the basilica of St Mark, with its two organ galleries, from which choirs of

The violin was at first deemed unfit for cultured performances and was relegated to common musical forms—peasant dances and the like—except in the French court, where the instrument was highly regarded and soon displaced the more cumbersome viol.

Violin

The birthplace of the violin was Italy. At Brescia, Gasparo da Salò (1540–1609) seems to have been the first successful maker of the instrument. In nearby Cremona, the illustrious Amati family refined Salò's design, and later Amati generations passed on their skill to others: most notably Andrea Guarneri (1626–1698) and Antonio Stradivari (1644–1737). Stradivari made more than one thousand instruments; violas, cellos and other instruments as well as violins. The Tyrol became another centre of violin manufacture in the seventeenth century. Master craftsmen such as Matthias Klotz and the eccentric Jacob Stainer produced magnificent instruments to rival those of Cremona.

Violin making is a complex art. There are about seventy components in each instrument, and the wood for each must be fastidiously selected and meticulously crafted by hand. Several different woods are used: the back, sides and neck are of a hard wood, usually maple, while the belly is fashioned from a soft wood such as spruce. When finished, the instrument is "tuned" by coating with varnish: a soft varnish reduces the intensity of the higher notes, while a harder varnish has the effect of adding to their brilliance.

Antonius Stradivarius Cremonenfis
Faciebat Anno 1724

These illustrations are views of the famous "Le Messie" Stradivari violin, now in the Hill Room at the Ashmolean Museum, Oxford. Its history is as unique as the instrument itself, being in "as new" condition; the state in which it entered the collection, in 1775, of Count Salabue from Stradivari's own workshop. In 1827, after Salabue's death, the instrument came into the hands of Luigi Tarisio, a carpenter by trade, who had given up his profession to concentrate his energies on collecting rare and costly violins. A great collector, Tarisio was also a true businessman, and soon began supplying Parisian dealers with valuable instruments. On his visits to Paris he would sing the praises of this one exquisite violin, always promising to bring it with him on his next trip. On one occasion, Tarisio was enthusing in the presence of the great violinist Alard, who exclaimed, perhaps in exasperation, "Ah, ça, votre violon est donc comme le Messie; on l'attend toujours, et il ne parait jamais": "your violin is like the Messiah; we are always waiting, but he never comes."

When Tarisio died, in poverty in spite of his grand collection, the dealer Vuillaume went to Italy and, in 1855, purchased "Le Messie" from Tarisio's heirs, along with a perfect Bergonzi, an immaculate Guarneri and two beautiful Guadagni, paying a reported £3,166 for the collection.

Detail from **The Triumph of Venus** *by the fifteenth-century artists Francesco del Cossa and Cosme Turé in the Palazzo Schifanoia, Ferrara, a city renowned for its love of pastoral musicals, which is reflected in the composition of this fresco.*

voices and instruments could answer one another. Florence, the seat of the Medici family, was the acknowledged source of the purest Italian language, the Italian of Dante and Petrarch. The Medicis were keen, active musicians: many significant composers worked for them, and it was in Florence that what we call *opera* was born.

Ferrara (between Padua and Bologna) was the home until 1598 of the Este family, as rich and powerful as the Medici clan and equally devoted to music. All the great Lowland composers, from Josquin to de Wert, had been there. During the sixteenth century, plays with music, usually on pastoral themes, were presented there on important occasions. Ferrara's pride and joy was its group of professional singers, expert in florid running passages of music. Particularly famous were three ladies, Tarquinia Molza, Laura Peperara and Lucrezia Bendidio, as beautiful and gifted in the arts of love as of music, so we are told. Composers came from far and near to hear and write music for them. Two were sopranos, the third an alto, and it was because their voices blended so well that Italian madrigals grew from four voices to five: two sopranos, alto, tenor and bass. Also through their virtuosity the madrigal became a more brilliant and ornamented form of music, for professionals rather than amateur gentlefolk, with independent instrumental accompaniment and frequent passages for solo and duet, as

Josquin Despréz p 42–6

well as dramatic narrative sections sung to repeated notes, almost like speech—they became known as *recitative.*

Claudio Monteverdi (1567–1643) and the Birth of Opera

The new style of madrigal is chiefly associated with the music of Monteverdi, who was born in Cremona, home of the violin. He worked for many years at the court of the Gonzaga family in Mantua and in 1613 was appointed director of music at St Mark's in Venice, where he spent the rest of his life. Monteverdi called his new tuneful and chromatic style of music his "second practice" (*seconda prattica*), as distinguished from the contrapuntal unaccompanied "first practice" (*prima prattica*) of the Lowland composers in Italy and elsewhere. Other composers of his time took up the "second practice", and it was central to early opera.

In all those great Italian courts, spectacular musical shows called *Intermedii* or "interludes" (they sometimes lasted several hours) were staged to celebrate a wedding or birthday, or to honour an important guest. They were like an opera, except that they did not tell a story. Songs, madrigals, instrumental movements and ballets followed one another in gorgeous stage settings.

In Florence there lived Giovanni de Bardi, the Count of Vernio, who hosted meetings of artists and thoughtful amateurs, a sort of culture club, which they called the *Camerata* or companionship and where they met to discuss artistic topics. Bardi himself improved the content of the *intermedio* by giving it some vague story-line, a connecting link between the various items, and calling the result a *masque*. The Camerata's members included Vincenzo Galilei (father of Galileo the astronomer), a singer and lutenist, and a musical theorist who argued that the ideal art-form in history had been ancient Greek drama in which noble poetry was not just spoken, as it is today, but sung, accompanied by an orchestra of flutes and lyres. He decried both polyphonic music and florid solo song, recommending an accompanied recitative in which the words and their audible expression took precedence, supported by instrumental accompaniment. Galilei died in 1591 without seeing the practical fruit of his theories, achieved by other members of the Camerata, the poet Ottavio Rinuccini, the singer/composer Giulio Caccini (1550–1616), whose daughter Francesca was the first woman composer, Jacopo Peri (1561–1633), Emilio de Cavalieri (1550–1602) and Marenzio, who wrote no opera but was the most experienced composer of them all.

After various experiments, Rinuccini wrote a poetic play for music on the subject of the Greek nymph Daphne, who was loved by Apollo and, frightened by his ardour, persuaded Jupiter to transform her into a laurel-tree (there is a modern opera on this subject by Richard Strauss). Peri set it to music and it was produced during the Carnival season of 1597 (between Christmas and Lent) at the Palazzo Corsi in Florence. Very little of the music survives. The first opera to have survived until now is *Euridice*, text by Rinuccini, music by Peri with some choruses by Caccini, composed to honour the wedding of Maria de Medici and Henry IV of France and first performed in Florence at the Pitti Palace on 6 October 1600. There are recitatives to move the story forward which are not dull at all, there are tuneful solo songs, choruses and instrumental linking bits. The singing voice was usually accompanied by a bass instrument playing the bottom musical line that dictates the harmony, with lutes and keyboard instruments filling in the necessary chords. Earlier in 1600, Cavalieri had

*Of the twenty-one theatre compositions created by **Claudio Monteverdi,** only three survive intact. One year following the performance of his first operatic work,* Orfeo, *Monteverdi's wife died. The compositions after this date reflect the deep sadness he felt at his loss, in particular, the "Lament" from* Arianna, *which reduced the opening night audience to tears.*

Richard Strauss p 300–6, 319–21

produced the first sacred opera, *The Representation of Soul and Body*, for performance in Rome. It is a noble piece, still performed nowadays, but typical of starchy, smooth Roman taste. Rome liked grand spectacle, and even pioneered comic opera (which became a speciality of Naples), but the audiences there did not have the taste for bold, florid operatic music, and so supremacy in matters operatic was held by the courts farther north in Italy.

It is just about possible to perform some of these early operas today, but the first one to hold a respected place in the modern repertory is Monteverdi's *Orfeo* (1607), written for the court of Mantua and based on the same story as Peri's *Euridice*, using much the same resources but with infinitely greater intensity of musical invention. When you have seen it, you remember afterwards the choruses of shepherds; Orpheus's lilting solo, which he sings to the trees, "*Vi ricorda, o boschi ombrosi*"; the Messenger's account of Euridice's death with its refrain, "*Ahi, cosa acerba*" ("Ah, what a bitter thing"); Orpheus's plea to Charon to take him across the river Styx, again with a lovely refrain, "*Rendetemi il mio ben, Tartari numi*" ("Give me back my beloved, O gods of hell"), that sticks in the head and touches the heart. Music of those days does not often indicate the orchestral instruments involved, but Monteverdi's *Orfeo* does: there were thirty-six players, though most of the music is only for keyboard instruments, lutes and harps, not strings, wind or brass, which were kept for special effects.

We are lucky to have the music of *Orfeo* still. Monteverdi went on to write many more operas, but of this later work only the last two have survived, *The Return of Ulysses* and *The Coronation of Poppaea*, both of them masterpieces of music and drama and very striking theatrical experiences. They are not just interesting remnants of musical history, but eloquent, vivid music-dramas, as modern productions everywhere have shown. Serious as his existing operas are, they contain—as good drama should—a leavening of comic or amusing characters: Charon in *Orfeo*, Irus in *Ulysses*, the Servant and his sweetheart, the poet Lucan, and the Nurse Arnalta in *Poppaea*.

If you have never heard a Monteverdi opera, but have heard his sacred *Vespers* of 1610 (which may have been his testimonial exercise for the musical directorship of St Mark's), you can appreciate the brilliant, totally involved, *avant-garde* nature of his "second practice". You can also hear it in *Il ballo delle ingrate* ("The Ballet of Unkind Ladies"), and the *Duel of Tancred and Clorinda*, which is a chamber opera for three characters; they were both included in his *Madrigals of Love and War*, which feature a new, disturbing musical manner which Monteverdi named his "excited style" (*stile concitato*). For his madrigals, his church music and his operas, Monteverdi deserves a top place in anybody's list of the great composers. The time was right, the circumstances were favourable and Monteverdi's genius was ripe.

Francesco Cavalli (1602–1676), Monteverdi's successor at St Mark's and probably his pupil, left many operas, several revived nowadays, which are even more tuneful, often comic, and always highly expert. *Calisto* is the funniest, *Ormindo* attractive, *Giasone* supposedly the best. Cavalli was a clever second-rate worker on what his predecessor Monteverdi achieved. Cavalli concentrated on superior music for vocal virtuosi, and led the way to the castrato-dominated opera of later Italy. Vincenzo Galilei must have turned in his grave to think that his ideal return to the dramatic world of

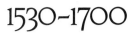
the ancient Greeks had deteriorated into a glorification of the eunuch. At this time, the star of every opera's cast was the *castrato*, a male soprano or contralto who, because of a lovely singing voice in boyhood, had been gelded so that his voice would never break but develop power and tone-quality— artistry as well.

Italian Opera Goes Abroad

The new Italian opera quickly spread across the frontier to Vienna, capital of the Holy Roman Empire: operas by Monteverdi and Cavalli were soon performed there. France was still obsessed with nobility of style and the importance of the dance to form a complete artwork. It took the Italian-born

The Castrato Tradition

In sixteenth-century Italy, women were banned from singing on the stage or even in choirs. St Paul's dictum "Let your women keep silent in churches" was rigidly enforced. The castrato voice was evolved to cope with this problem, and proved to be so powerful and flexible that the unfortunate possessors of such voices were soon in demand over much of Europe.

The cruel practice of castration was known from 1565 in the Sistine Chapel of Rome, and common from 1574 in Munich during Lassus's time there. Castrated men grew magnificently tall, but were often oddly proportioned, as suggested by this contemporary caricature.

A castrated boy singer could become a lucrative source of income for his parents. Many a surprised youth was fobbed off with tales of childhood "accidents" such as a fall from a horse, or a vicious nip from a goose. In the eighteenth-century age of Baroque Italian opera, and until the time of Rossini and Meyerbeer in the nineteenth century, castrati *were the male heroes of most operas, and the subsidiary male roles as well. When Janet Baker sings the part of Julius Caesar in Handel's opera, she replaces an Italian* castrato, *as does a baritone hero in Monteverdi's* Orfeo *or a tenor Nero in his* Coronation of Poppea.

In the nineteenth century, the fashion for the artificial sound of the castrato *waned, though some few roles are to be found in the operas of Meyerbeer and Rossini. The last of the* castrati, *Moreschi, died in 1922, having made several recordings at the beginning of the century that give us some idea of this unnatural, virtuoso warbling.*

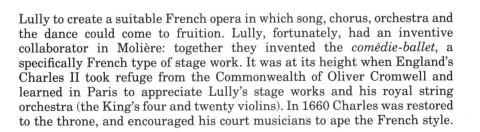

Lully to create a suitable French opera in which song, chorus, orchestra and the dance could come to fruition. Lully, fortunately, had an inventive collaborator in Molière: together they invented the *comédie-ballet*, a specifically French type of stage work. It was at its height when England's Charles II took refuge from the Commonwealth of Oliver Cromwell and learned in Paris to appreciate Lully's stage works and his royal string orchestra (the King's four and twenty violins). In 1660 Charles was restored to the throne, and encouraged his court musicians to ape the French style.

Julius Caesar p 115

An Italian by birth, **Jean Baptiste Lully** arrived in France when he was ten. He was appointed to the Royal Band of the Dauphin (later Louis XIV) and in 1656 trained a group of sixteen chosen violinists, called Les Petits-Violons.

Right: "The British Orpheus" was the nickname given to **Henry Purcell**. He was engaged by Charles II as court composer and at twenty-one he succeeded his teacher, John Blow, as organist at Westminster Abbey. He had the same relationship with Blow that Mozart had with his mentor, Haydn: the student first learning from the master, and the master then learning from, and being influenced by, the pupil.

Henry Purcell (1659–1695)

Purcell was easily able to oblige the king in French-style ceremonial music for birthdays and royal excursions. He was expert in Italian styles too—the Trio Sonata of several movements in different moods and speeds, the Italian song set to English words, the dance suite for keyboard. He could also turn his hand to the English masque, a play with copious, attractive music. Purcell is often referred to as England's greatest composer, and indeed his variety of style and constant poetic eloquence still move the intelligence of a listener. Yet his large works, whether for theatre or concert-room, do represent a backwater in British music which he should not, ideally, have been occupying. His royal odes, his funeral music, his dramatically footling, though musically resplendent, incidental music for plays, all show what he might have achieved in a less parochial, less bigoted artistic climate, just as his compact opera *Dido and Aeneas* (written for schoolgirls to perform) shows how he would have graced the history of opera given more accommodating company. Nevertheless, *Dido* remains a miniature master-piece, not least for the heroine's great lament "When I am laid in earth" towards the close of the piece. Other theatre scores that Purcell produced, such as those for *The Tempest* and *The Indian Queen*, are dramatically satisfying only intermittently. One great exception is the music he wrote for his friend John Dryden's *King Arthur* in 1691.

Chapter 5
High Baroque

"Gentlemen, Old Bach is Here!"

The "unfashionable" music of J.S. Bach ♦ Reformation music enjoys a much-needed boost ♦ Frederick the Great at Sans-Souci ♦ The life and times of a court musician ♦ The Three S's ♦ Germany adopts French music and manners ♦ French keyboard music ♦ The sonata and concerto in Italy ♦ Public subscription concerts ♦ The genius of J.S. Bach—his heritage and his legacy ♦

In the story of *Music in Time*, Johann Sebastian Bach (1685–1750) is the great contradiction. For most of the nineteenth and twentieth centuries he has been revered as the greatest of all composers, the figurehead of that German sound which has dominated the world's music in all but the most Teuton-hating countries from his age up to our own time. During his lifetime he was esteemed only in his native Germany, and not as a composer at all, but as a virtuoso organist and specialist in the mechanics of organ building. When he applied for his last job in 1722, he was at the height of his powers, having completed most of the masterpieces for which he is now renowned throughout the world. But the interviewing board for St Thomas's Church, Leipzig, were not at all certain whether he was sufficiently eminent for such a post as *cantor* (organist and choirmaster) to their great church. Bach was not famous outside his native Saxony, and therefore only grudgingly accepted when his more admired colleague Telemann refused the job. He remained a provincial musician throughout his life.

The "Unfashionable" Music of J.S. Bach
The music of J.S. Bach is now regarded as the climax of the Baroque movement, which had started in Venice with Andrea Gabrieli at the end of the sixteenth century and was already giving way, during Bach's lifetime, to the light, elegant *style galant*, an entertaining and unmonumental style which Bach's composer-sons espoused, as did his contemporary, Handel (whose music Bach much admired). They were all international figures as J.S. Bach, who never travelled abroad, even for study, was not. He knew what was happening to music in Italy and France, and used that knowledge in his keyboard suites and instrumental concertos, but in his own old-fashioned way—founded on Lowland counterpoint. He was not drawn to

Andrea Gabrieli p 78

opera, except as a member of the audience, but his settings of Christ's Passion are vividly dramatic in their music. He could, and did, write tunes with chordal accompaniment: an example is his simple, elegiac setting of *Komm süsser Tod*. There are also all those hymn-tune harmonizations (distinguished, for no sensible reason, in English as "chorales") which recur in his church cantatas and oratorios, so that the congregation would have opportunity to join in the performance. Even in those hymns the lower vocal parts are all independently interesting, each of them tuneful, as everyone who has sung *Jesu, meine Freude* ("Jesu, priceless Treasure"), or the *Christmas Oratorio*, or the *St John* and *St Matthew Passion* settings will readily admit.

Counterpoint was in Sebastian Bach's blood. To prove that, compare any of Bach's Brandenburg Concertos with any of Handel's *concerti grossi*: neither is artistically superior in any way to the other—both are designed as entertainment music, but to get the best out of Bach's concertos you need to listen more attentively to what happens between the top line and the bass; and it isn't just chords, as it often is with Corelli, Vivaldi and Handel.

Bach devoted most of his working life to the Lutheran Church as organist, choirmaster, teacher, and composer of sacred music. Many of his works have been lost because they were not considered important, but more than a thousand remain with us. The pages of manuscript of the six sonatas for unaccompanied violin, for example, were found in a grocer's shop about to be used for wrapping up butter, while the autograph of the cello suites was discovered making excellent protection for some fruit trees against the frost. Music had a much greater ephemeral quality for past generations: it was not normally thought important to preserve such works for posterity, for once they had been performed they had served their purpose and would be superseded by newer (supposedly better) music. The great reverence shown for the music of the past is largely a twentieth-century phenomenon. Some of Bach's finest works may never have been written down at all: his contemporaries reckoned him unsurpassed as an extemporizer at the keyboard, improvising great music on the spot, unpremeditated. It was said that if he walked into a church when the organist was playing the subject for an improvised fugue, Bach could say instantly just which devices of fugal technique could and could not be applied to the theme, and was as maliciously delighted if the player ignored the possible, as when he attempted the impossible and came to grief.

At a time when church music was in the doldrums, through official policies of anti-innovation, or composers' preference for entertaining secular music, Bach's church cantatas and similar works gave sacred music a fillip such as it has never known at any other time. Nowadays, of course, his organ meditations on Lutheran hymn-tunes, known as chorale-preludes (such as *Wachet auf*, where a busy counterpoint accompanies the hymn sung in English as *Zion hears her watchmen's voices*), or his cantatas, including the *St Matthew Passion*, are considered as much a part of everyone's regular listening as Handel's *Messiah*, Beethoven's nine symphonies or Wagner's four-part epic, *The Ring*.

Sebastian Bach married twice and fathered twenty children, several of whom were successful composers: the most famous were Wilhelm Friedemann, Carl Philip Emanuel and Johann Christian. They referred, in private, to their father as "the old periwig", for which an exact modern translation would be "old hat". Towards the end of his life he travelled to

Bach's monogram. *The initial letters JSB are reversed and superimposed, forming a calligraphic design of great elegance.*

Facing page: *J.S. Bach's portrait (1746) by Haussmann shows him as the serious, sober Lutheran churchman that he was. He is holding a copy of his Canon Triplex a 6 Voci.*

Handel p 99–102, 113–20   Vivaldi p 90–1
Corelli p 89–90

1600–1760 "Gentlemen, Old Bach is Here!"

*Adolph von Menzel's finely detailed Das Flötenkonzert (1852) shows **Frederick the Great** playing the flute to the accompaniment of his first harpsichordist C.P.E. Bach at Sans-Souci. Quantz, Frederick's flute teacher, is standing on the extreme right, and he would, according to Dr Burney, cry out "bravo!" to his royal scholar, at the end of the solos. But on hearing wrong notes Quantz would cough, once causing Frederick to remark sharply that something should have to be done about poor Quantz's cold.*

*These fine **ivory flutes** belonged to Frederick the Great. Each modification of the flute necessitated a corresponding change in fingering: this **chart** was drawn up by Quantz for his employer.*

Potsdam to visit his son Emanuel at Sans-Souci, the court of Frederick the Great, a keen practical musician when not waging war. On hearing of Bach's arrival, Frederick called out, "Gentlemen, Old Bach is here!" It is always supposed that, by "old", the King meant not young Emanuel. But Frederick's taste was French and modern, and his remark may well have had deprecatory connotations about his own composer's fuddy-duddy father.

As well as C.P.E. Bach, Frederick had two other outstanding musicians working at his court: Johann Quantz (1697–1773) and Carl Heinrich Graun

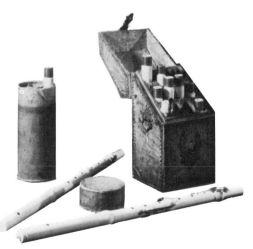

A Musical Career

When his training was over, and if he were not taking holy orders, there were few options open to a young musician. Until the end of the eighteenth century, any work he found was almost certain to be involved with a wealthy or noble household, such as playing in a private band, or in a tutorial capacity. Very often such work would be accompanied by duties of a domestic nature. Giuseppe Sammartini, for example, a fine oboist and competent composer of the first half of the eighteenth century, worked for the Prince of Wales not only as a musician but also as major-domo of his household.

Some, like Haydn, were fortunate indeed with their masters. Though the lot of the court musician was menial, Haydn's music won such fame for himself and for his master that he became a most favoured member of the household, a highly prized possession—but still a possession. His work would be divided between composing occasional music for domestic use, ceremonial pieces for important occasions such as birthdays or royal visits, operas for the court theatre (even, in Haydn's case, for the court puppet theatre), finding the necessary singers and players, rehearsing them, being responsible for the instruments, arranging and copying the music, conducting, teaching and looking after all the problems of the many musicians in his care.

But all these duties did give the composer an opportunity to have his music performed, with an orchestra and an opera-house at his disposal. Bach, for example, who worked for most of his life as organist and choirmaster of a provincial church (eventually a large one), was expected to devote valuable time to teaching Latin to the boys of the choir-school. For any secular music he needed to hear, he had to find musicians among his friends and colleagues to form any kind of orchestra.

It was not, therefore, upon merit but upon public exposure that success depended. Handel (who had all but completely taken over the London musical scene) and Haydn could publish all their music: indeed they could scarcely produce it fast enough for a greedy public. Less fortunate musicians such as Bach or Schubert, who achieved little more than local fame, died with the bulk of their masterpieces unknown and in manuscript, left for posterity to discover.

Haydn p 136–46
Schubert p 163–8

(1701–1759). Quantz was the leading German flautist of his generation, and was appointed Frederick's chief court musician. It was he who invented the adjustable sliding endpiece of the flute that facilitated accurate tuning. The King paid Quantz a handsome salary, and in return he composed some hundreds of concertos and chamber compositions for his master to play. Graun too wrote flute compositions for Frederick, though his main work lay in organizing the Berlin Opera: going to Italy to bring back the best singers, and writing Italian operas for them. He also composed a quantity of choral music, including a splendid *Te Deum* in celebration of one of Frederick's victories.

Bach's contemporaries may have thought of him as "old hat"—time gives a different perspective. With J.S. Bach, the Baroque more or less ends (apart from some welcome hangovers), but Bach's inspiration remains as potent as that of any composer in musical history. The Roman god Janus had two faces, one looking backwards, the other forwards. Johann Sebastian Bach is the Janus of western music. This chapter traces his roots and the fruit of his tremendous creative industry, which blossomed through his sons, and whose influence extends to the present time.

The Music of Luther's Reformation

When Martin Luther nailed his ninety-five objections to Roman Catholicism on the door of the Castle Church at Wittenberg on 31 October 1517 and set the Reformation of the established Church in motion, one of his major plans was that church services should be understood by those who attended them. He had nothing against Catholic Latin music (his favourite composer was Josquin), but he wanted a liturgy in the language of the congregation, and he wanted them to join in, rather than let the choir sing their prayers in recondite Latin which few in the pews could understand. Luther was a keen musician, playing the recorder and lute, and singing also. Many celebrated hymns are associated with him, most of all *Ein feste Burg* ("A stronghold sure"), of which he wrote the words, and perhaps the melody also.

Luther retained the Latin mass in his liturgy, shortened to the first two sections, *Kyrie* and *Gloria*. Few German Lutheran composers were interested in it, though J.S. Bach set this short mass four times and eventually put together a whole mass in Latin, partly for his own satisfaction; the so-called *B minor Mass*. The work appears to have received one performance during its composer's lifetime—in Dresden, where his son Wilhelm Friedemann was working as organist.

The Lutheran composer of the early seventeenth century in Germany could either set a hymn-tune simply, in four-part harmony with the tune at the top, for ordinary congregational use; or he could treat it line by line contrapuntally, in the manner of a Lowland motet. Roland de Lassus worked for the Catholic court in Munich, but his influence spread throughout Germany (and elsewhere), into Lutheran centres as well, where his motets were sung in German. Hans Leo Hassler (1564–1612), a Lutheran himself from Nuremberg, studied in Venice with Andrea Gabrieli, learning to write madrigals in Italian and German, then worked for a Catholic banking family, but finally won a post at the Protestant Dresden court, and published books of Lutheran hymns treated in both styles, "simple" and "fugue-wise" as he put it. His best known composition was, nonetheless, a secular song, *Mein G'mut ist mir verwirret* ("My mind is confused by a pretty girl"), which soon became a Lutheran hymn-tune, and was particularly used

Facing page: *A title page from Michael Praetorius'* three-part **Syntagma Musicum**. *The first part of this encylopedic treatise deals with sacred music; the second part discusses the instruments, especially the organ; and the final part considers prevailing musical forms.*

A. Gabrieli p 54

1600-1760 "Gentlemen, Old Bach is Here!"

Schütz was thirteen when his talent as a singer was spotted by the Landgrave Moritz. His musical career, which he was to follow much against his parents' wishes, started at Moritz's court in the electorate of Hesse-Cassel.

Schütz's Christmas Story is based on the combined texts of the gospels according to Matthew and Luke. Schütz's commitment to Luther's cause—the use of the vernacular—explains his use of German texts.

by J.S. Bach in his Passion settings and the *Christmas Oratorio*: it is sung in Protestant churches everywhere as *O Haupt voll Blut* ("O Sacred Head") at Passiontide. That is a good example of Luther's precept that the Devil must not have all the best tunes.

The same hymn-tunes were often made the basis of variations, suites or chorale-preludes for solo organ. Michael Praetorius (1571–1621) published copious volumes of Lutheran church music in all these forms, short masses as well, for choirs small and large, in all styles known to him, Italian, German and Lowland. He wrote theoretical works too about musical instruments and performance practices. His complete works run to twenty-one volumes, but he too is mainly known for one hymn tune, *Es ist ein Ros entsprungen* (sung in English as "The noble stem of Jesse").

The Three S's

Monteverdi's liberating, eminently Baroque influence touched Praetorius at the end of his life, but only began seriously to affect German music in the work of three Lutheran composers born one hundred years before Bach and known to students of musical history as the Three S's; Schütz, Schein and Scheidt (in contrast to the venerated Three B's; Bach, Beethoven and Brahms).

The oldest of them, the longest lived and the greatest, was Heinrich Schütz (1585–1672). Schütz studied composition with Giovanni Gabrieli in Venice and learned there to compose music for multiple groups of voices and instruments separated spatially (*cori spezzati* was the Italian term). After publishing a book of his Italian madrigals in Venice, he returned to Germany and brought out the first German opera, *Dafne* (1627, the music is lost). He then concentrated entirely on sacred music, mostly in German but including a volume of Latin motets for a Catholic patron. He left no music for instruments alone. Schütz set the *Psalms of David* (1619) for *cori spezzati* in the Gabrieli manner. His *Geistliche Konzerte* ("Sacred Concertos", 1636–1639) are Lutheran hymns dramatically treated, *à la* Monteverdi,

G. Gabrieli p 62

Continuo

The principle of continuo (short for basso continuo*), figured bass or thorough bass came into use early in the Baroque era. It refers to a type of accompaniment that was written down as a form of musical shorthand. The instruments used for this were, most commonly, harpsichord and cello; though organ, viola da gamba or bassoon are not unknown. It existed to support, reinforce and keep together the melodies that were being woven above it, whether in an operatic aria, orchestral concerto or simple trio sonata.*

The music consisted of a single bass line, generally with numbers sketched intermittently beneath it to imply which chords the keyboard player should extemporize with his right hand to keep in harmony with the music, since his left hand was providing the bass line of the work being performed. In chamber music a bass melody instrument would reinforce this line: in paintings of the period, it is common to see a cellist looking over the harpsichordist's shoulder and sharing his or her music. Hence a trio sonata, perhaps for two violins and continuo, would not be a trio at all, needing four players to perform three lines of music.

The system stayed in use, particularly in large-scale music such as opera or symphonic works, up until the first decades of the nineteenth century. The keyboard player was in fact the conductor: he gave the tempo, cued in various instruments and filled out the music where necessary. When Haydn conducted his "London" symphonies at public concerts given during his tours of England in the 1790s, he directed them from the pianoforte.

Haydn p 136–46

1600–1760 "Gentlemen, Old Bach is Here!"

with startling harmonies and dramatic effects. His *Sacred Symphonies*—one of which actually quotes from famous Monteverdi madrigals—become progressively more bold; *Saul, Saul, why persecutest thou me?*, about the conversion of St Paul, is a startling piece. Schütz's *Musikalische Exequien*, funeral motets in German, may be the first German Lutheran Requiem Mass, and he assembled four such motets and called them a "German Mass" (*Deutsche Messe*, 1657).

Schütz also cultivated the oratorio, a sacred vocal work in the vernacular that had begun in Rome and was to develop, particularly in Protestant countries, as a religious opera to be performed in Lent when theatres were shut, or at other times when theatrical performance was impossible. One soloist sang the narrative, other characters were taken by other voices—in Schütz's time, not always the same voices, sometimes two or three together—and a choir acted the crowd, or the believer. An orchestra might be employed, and in Hamburg regularly was: at Dresden, where Schütz wrote his four Passion settings (one for each gospel), the orchestra was forbidden in Lent, and the works had to be unaccompanied. For his *Resurrection Story* (1623), he could have a quartet of viols and a

Modes and Modulations

For Scheidt's generation, diatonic scales were new and exciting; they made mode-based music sound old-fashioned, because music could now audibly shift from one key climate to another, farther away, and then eventually back, an emotionally satisfying journey. Modal music could not switch from one tone-centre to another without going off the monorail travel system of modes. Changing of keys, called modulation, is like being able to travel via an elaborate motorway junction system, whereas modal composers were restricted to one, good quality, narrow byway. The motorway system of key changes caught on and persisted until shortly after 1900; it is still quite alive in popular music today, as indeed is modal music—and even the most advanced composers of modern music may admit that the principles of the key system lie behind their musical thought.

keyboard continuo (Lent being over), though the narrative is intoned rather than declaimed, so that the effect is slightly archaic—apt for an old story. Schütz also set *The Seven Last Words of Christ on the Cross* (c. 1645) and the *Christmas Story* (1660), both in a more Monteverdian, modern manner, though in performance the music will sound more sturdy and muscular than Monteverdi's; closer to Germany, whose national dance the *Almain*, or *Allemande*, was essentially weighted and rather grave.

Whenever I am tempted to lament that the music of Schütz's *Dafne* is lost, I reflect that Schütz is not known to have attempted opera again: perhaps he realized that his own dramatic imagination would be more beneficially applied to Luther's Bible (in any case a new and outstandingly dramatic volume) and so he spent the rest of his long, industrious life doing for church music what Monteverdi did for opera. If you spend two hours or so listening to Schütz's polychoral music in a large, acoustically favourable building, the experience will be enough to convince you that Schütz

Monteverdi p 69–70

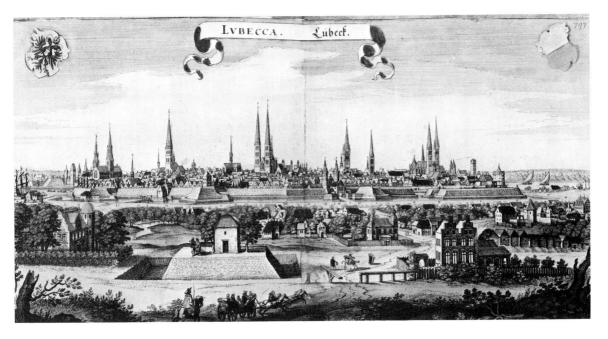

LVBECCA. Lubeck.

contributed as much incomparable music to his time as any composer in this book—some would place him firmly among the world's top ten composers.

The other two S's, Schein and Scheidt, are important for what they did rather than for posterity's urgent concern to perform their works. Johann Hermann Schein (1586–1630) preceded J.S. Bach as cantor at St Thomas's in Leipzig and was writing Monteverdi-inspired sacred cantatas in the tuneful and excited manner as early as 1618. He then brought out a volume of secular songs to be performed in various ways, with voices and instruments, or most easily of all by one singer accompanied on the keyboard. Thus he invented *Lieder*, songs with piano accompaniment, such as Schubert, Wolf and Brahms were to write later, not to mention French *mélodies* and songs of other nationalities with keyboard as partner.

Samuel Scheidt (1587–1654), the organist at Halle where Handel was born, brought the Venetian idea of double choir with separated orchestras firmly into the German Lutheran Church. The ancestors of Bach's double choral music, in the *St Matthew Passion* and *B minor Mass*, were Scheidt's *Cantiones sacrae*. They sound much more German and solid than Schütz's similar works, which do not disguise their Venetian origins, even given German texts. Scheidt, as a professional organist, composed plenty of keyboard music, variations and dance suites particularly, and in his compositions, perhaps for the first time in musical history, there is no doubt that the language is based on scales, not old modes.

All these three German S's, thrilled by the possibilities of massed separated choirs and orchestras, were hit by the religious Thirty Years War, which took men off to fight and discouraged public luxury such as there was, as well as causing famine and every other disaster. Big polychoral works had to be performable by a few musicians, and alternatives suggested for reduced circumstances. The Baroque had to be slimmed down, and that may well have led to the leaner, even more elegant *style galant* and its successor, the highly formalized Rococo, though in music they did not occur until many

A view of Lübeck where *Buxtehude became organist in 1667, probably on the condition that he would marry (which he did) his predecessor Franz Tunder's unprepossessing younger daughter; other unsuccessful applicants for the job had refused. In pursuance of this tradition, Handel and J.S. Bach both turned down Buxtehude's job, for neither wished to marry Buxtehude's daughter.*

Lieder p 166

1600–1760 "Gentlemen, Old Bach is Here!"

Venus and her assistants watch over young lovers about to set off for the Island of Love in Watteau's **L'Embarquement pour L'Ile de Cythère.** *"If God made the world for me he put France there for my entertainment" Frederick the Great had written as a young man, and during his reign the French style emerged strongly in music, painting and language. Frederick is reported to have spoken French to his friends, English to his servants and German to his animals.*

years after the Thirty Years War ended with the Treaty of Breda in 1648, thirty-seven years before Johann Sebastian Bach, archpriest of the high Baroque, was born in what is now East Germany.

J.S. Bach and his Contemporaries

One of Bach's immediate predecessors in Germany was Diderich Buxtehude (c. 1637–1707), the organist at Lübeck whom Bach made a long walk from home to hear. Buxtehude's organ music developed the manner which became Bach's: the pedal-board for feet was used as much to produce the principal melody as for the usual bass line. Buxtehude established the Lutheran church cantata based on hymnal or sacred texts. Bach's generation added commentary by local poets on the chosen text, bringing much greater variety of music and verbal content to the piece. The German fascination for completeness (we find it today in boxed sets of records comprising all one composer's music) led Bach to complete five annual cycles of music for every event in the church year, but he was preceded by Telemann, who had made a complete cycle in 1711, and rivalled in his time by J.P. Krieger (1649–1725), who left no fewer than two thousand cantatas. It is no good concluding that Krieger must be a hopeless composer because his cantatas aren't performed nowadays as often as those by Telemann, let alone Bach. At their time, all their cantatas filled a need, and were not expected to enter posterity. Nowadays we perform Bach and Telemann more often then Krieger, because Krieger's name is unfamiliar, but some day an enthusiast will certainly press the cause of Krieger and make his music

The Couperin family
*produced five generations of
fine musicians. Charles
Couperin, pictured here,
was the father of François,
called Le Grand.*

familiar, as Mendelssohn made Bach's and modern scholars have made those of so many other Baroque composers.

A composer who may have contributed to the appreciation of modern Italian music in Bach's home province was Johann Pachelbel (1653–1706). He came from Nuremberg, where he also spent his last years. But in between he worked as organist at Vienna and Stuttgart: the years in the former city were particularly important, for its Catholic and multinational music (as the centre of the Holy Roman Empire) had made it a home of modern Italian musical development. Himself a staunch Lutheran who wrote quantities of church music in German, his style is therefore more cosmopolitan than that of Buxtehude. Though the music seems relaxed, in his day Pachelbel was held in high esteem as a writer of strict fugue. But for

1600–1760 "Gentlemen, Old Bach is Here!"

later generations, his organ and instrumental music are the most familiar to audiences (particularly a canon and a gigue, both in orchestral arrangements by Karl Münchinger). In recent years too, his Lutheran church music in German has been much admired—if seldom heard—as a guideline to the future, slenderer *galant* manner, a pointer away from German to French and Italian tastes.

A Taste for All Things French

It was just those tastes that Germany preferred in the early eighteenth century. The Prussian court at Potsdam led the fashion for French language and French taste, even when the monarch had abandoned Roman Catholicism for Luther's reformed Rite in German. Germany was not one country, but a network of provinces governed by kings or princes or dukes, each with its own court and musical staff, who all copied the Potsdam style and fancied French courtly manners. They even preferred not to speak German, which they found a coarse language.

Their Frenchified music meant static bass-lines, a firm support for melody above; not natural singing melody, but a mere outline to be decorated, rendered more seemly and graceful. The tyranny of melody pushed the accompaniment away from the ideal contrapuntal pursuit of melody present everywhere, which is what polyphony had meant, and could still mean. In visual terms the French ideal can be seen in the paintings of Watteau (1684–1721), his *L'Embarquement pour Cythère*, an idyllic adventure by water, or his *Gilles*, a portrait of a sad clown, a real man in the clothes of a fool; or in Fragonard's painting of a lady on a swing, the object idealized and set in a swirl of pastel colour, airy and not quite believable, magically hazed.

French Keyboard Music

The harpsichord music of France at the time was brilliant and expressive, tender and exquisitely decorated on a musical line of effortless poise, as in the suites of Jacques Chambonnières (1602–1672), Louis XIV's official harpsichordist, and the man who brought to Paris both Louis and François Couperin, uncle and nephew in a dynasty of musicians destined to develop, sophisticate and enrich French harpsichord music. François Couperin le Grand (1668–1733) composed the most masterly and fascinating keyboard music of his time, published in twenty-seven suites entitled *Ordres*, abounding not only in dances but also in descriptive genre pieces, which are perfect examples of *Music in Time*. Just as the painter was looking with new eyes at the French countryside, François Couperin was ready to respond with his vignettes of particular characters, noble or working-class: *La Majestueuse* and *Les Matelotes provençales*, *L'Enfantine* and *L'Adolescent*. A favourite piece has the enigmatic title *Les Baricades mistérieuses* ("The Mysterious Barriers"), perhaps referring to the melody's persistence in straddling across the bar-lines, with the effect called "syncopation", an essence of jazz and all "bent" music today.

Couperin had been appointed organist as well as harpsichordist to Louis XIV: his house, attached to the church of St Gervais in Paris, can still be seen. As well as his twenty-seven *Ordres* (from which, incidentally, the composer specifies that movements may be isolated and performed separately at will), he wrote an important treatise on harpsichord playing, *L'Art de toucher le clavecin*, which includes delightful advice on performing before an audience, where the player is exhorted to keep a slight smile on his features while at the keyboard. In his capacity as organist, Couperin composed a quantity of sacred vocal music; his three *Leçons de Tenèbres* (1713–1717), settings in Latin of the *Lamentations of Jeremiah* to be sung on Maundy Thursday, are especially fine, in the modern Italian manner, with daring harmonies and fierce, yet controlled, passion.

Couperin's love of Italian music, learned from his revered colleague Lully, can also be heard in his chamber music, the first trio sonatas (two violins and bass, with keyboard continuo) to come out of Italy into France, and a set of magnificent Royal Concerti (*Concerts royaux*) for various instruments with continuo; they declare their intention to combine French with Italian taste in the title of some, *Les Goûts réunis*, and triumphantly succeed because Couperin, for all his delight in Italian innovations, remained completely French in the precision and hard-headed logic of his musical individuality.

Ornaments

Many listeners to Baroque music are confused, if not deterred, by the profuse decoration with which it is so generously endowed. But this apparent overabundance has two vital structural functions that originate in two deficiencies of the harpsichord: its lack of sustaining power and of accent.

As long as a note is blown or bowed, it will continue to sound. On a harpsichord (as on a modern piano if you do not use the sustaining pedal), as soon as a note is struck it begins to die. Performers, who were also largely the music's composers, evolved an elaborate system of prolonging notes that they wished to continue sounding, with trills, arpeggios and other devices. The very last chord in a slow piece is an obvious place for embellishment, for example. Such a convention spread easily into other branches of music.

Similarly, the principle of accenting a note by hitting it harder is impossible upon the harpsichord (or upon the organ, for that matter). Strong beats could be given a shake, turn or appoggiatura to bring them out from their neighbours: there are literally hundreds of variations of these devices that have to be studied by the performer of early music. The interpretation of the various signs used was by no means a matter of agreement between composers: those of Couperin are different from Bach's, those of Bach differ from the signs used in England, and no two contemporary treatises on the matter are in detailed agreement. The example right *is from a book of ornamentation exercises for singers and instrumentalists published in 1593 by the Italian virtuoso singer Giovanni Conforti.*

Before examining the instrumental music of Italy, however, two other French *clavecinistes* should be mentioned. Elisabeth Jacquet de La Guerre (1659–1729) was a protégée of Mme de Montespan and, like Couperin, worked for much of her life at court. She wrote a quantity of keyboard music, as well as choral works and a successful opera, *Céphale et Procris*.

Jean-Philippe Rameau, *an intellectual of no mean standing, wrote harpsichord suites of great originality.*

Most appealing is a set of violin sonatas, owing much to the influence of Corelli's compositions, which show a rare refinement and melodic gift. More important as a harpsichord composer was Jean-Philippe Rameau (1683–1764). Even as a child, his ability to sight-read and perform upon the instrument was outstanding. As a teenager, he was sent to study in Italy, then worked in numerous provincial French towns as an organist for some years before settling in Paris. His four books of harpsichord pieces show a highly individual approach to keyboard writing, with a bold use of chromaticism and of keyboard figuration. The massive suite in E minor contains splendid examples of Rameau's imposing keyboard genius, and is often featured in harpsichord recitals today. A rondeau with two *doubles* (variations), *Les Niais de Sologne*, and a magnificent Gavotte with six variations (from the suite in A minor) are two more frequently heard examples of Rameau's brilliant musical imagination. Though the composer possessed a strongly intellectual personality—he corresponded on a wide variety of subjects with his friend, Voltaire—in his harpsichord pieces he seems to show us the happy and tender aspects of his complex personality. His music heralded the simple elegance of the eighteenth century.

Sonata and Concerto in Eighteenth-century Italy

These instrumental forms, sonata and concerto, have, with the later symphony, remained the principal ones in instrumental music until our own time. Both came from Italy at the beginning of the sixteenth century, and quite soon discovered their ideal dimensions. Both quickly became popular throughout Europe around the lifetime of J.S. Bach.

During the seventeenth century composers used the terms *sonata, concerto* and *sinfonia* to describe any sort of instrumental, even vocal, music. The idea of expanding a trio sonata to include musical dialogue with a larger body of strings, referred to as the *concerto grosso* (literally "big concert"), was practised by Alessandro Stradella (*c.* 1645–1682) in 1675, and seriously taken up by Corelli around 1700 in his so-named *concerti grossi* written to impress the guests of his employer, Cardinal Ottoboni.

Arcangelo Corelli was born near Bologna in 1653, and early acquired a reputation as a formidable virtuoso on the violin. He tried his luck as a musician in Paris, but may have fallen foul there of the all-powerful Lully, who resented his enviable skill. Another impediment to his success as a performer was said to be his habit of grimacing eccentrically while playing,

*Vivaldi was employed in 1703 to teach the violin at the Pio Ospedale della Pietà, an orphanage for girls in Venice. The occasional concert there attracted the favourable attention of foreign visitors as well as the local aristocracy. **This painting by Gabriele Bella** commemorates the concert given by children from different Venetian orphanages at the **Casino Filarmonico** for the visiting Russian Grand Duke Paul and Grand Duchess Maria Feodorovna.*

and "rolling his eyes as if in agony". But he was held in high esteem as a teacher and loved by his many friends for his gentle nature and for his qualities as a conversationalist. His *concerti grossi*, while simpler than those of Vivaldi, show above all the qualities of harmonic structure and affecting melody.

In the last of his *concerti grossi*, Corelli gave a particularly brilliant part to himself as principal violinist, and so paved the way for Giuseppe Torelli (1658–1709) and Antonio Vivaldi (1678–1741) who developed the solo concerto as well as the *concerto grosso* for two violins and violoncello alternating with a larger string band. Torelli worked in Germany for the Margrave of Brandenburg (whose successor was to receive those famous concertos from J.S. Bach)—Vivaldi worked at a charitable institution for girls, the Ospedale della Pietà in Venice. Both adopted a new scheme of three movements, quick-slow-quick, for their concertos, derived from the Italian operatic overture (or *sinfonia*), and it has remained the standard pattern for the concerto until now. Torelli's solo concertos are full of brilliant violin music for himself, though we know that the Margrave of Brandenburg's musical establishment was only of modest size. Vivaldi's schoolgirls in Venice were very numerous and included virtuoso performers on the mandolin, flute, recorder, piccolo, oboe, clarinet, bassoon, trumpet, horn and trombone as well as all stringed instruments—he wrote concertos involving all these instruments. Vivaldi, who was nicknamed the "Red Priest" on account of his shock of red hair, liked to give his concertos

The First Sonatas

A sonata *is essentially music "sounded"—ie played, rather than sung* (cantata). *How long does a sonata last? Domenico Scarlatti's hundreds of harpsichord sonatas are in one short movement lasting about three minutes, generally written in contrasted pairs. Beethoven's* Hammerklavier *sonata for piano lasts over half an hour, some modern examples even longer. In Italy the sonata settled, during the seventeenth century, into a free-formed piece of several contrasted sections, usually for violin, or two violins, and continuo. A distinction was at first made between the* sonata da chiesa *(for performance in church) and the* sonata da camera *(to be played at court, perhaps in a cultured home): the former had four standard sections, slow-quick-slow-quick, the latter might include dance sections, as in a suite. By the early 1700s the distinction began to fade and the domestic sonata had acquired the same characteristics as the church variety.*

It was Corelli (shown here), working in Rome, who, from 1681 standardized the number and length of the movements, which he kept separate. The keyboard solo sonata originated in Germany with Bach's predecessor at Leipzig, Johann Kuhnau (1660–1722), as an instrumental work in several movements. The sonata travelled from Italy into Germany and other European countries (Purcell in England, Couperin in France). It was not until later that the movement design "sonata form" was evolved.

Beethoven piano sonata p 161–2

*A caricature of **Vivaldi** drawn in 1723 by Pier Leone Ghezzi.*

fanciful titles such as *The Trial of Harmony and Invention* (a set of twelve concertos which includes the popular *Four Seasons*), *Proteus or the World Back to Front*, *Harmonic Inspiration* and *The Lyre*. He also wrote significant vocal music, including forty-six operas, many now lost. It was Vivaldi who established the design of the concerto, to be followed by his successors including Bach and Handel: two quick outer movements based on a vigorous theme, for all the players, which returned (whence its name *Ritornello*) in whole or part after solo episodes: in between came a slow, melodious and highly decorated movement, largely dominated by the soloist or soloists.

One more Italian composer of instrumental music, Domenico Scarlatti (1685–1757), absorbed entirely new influences. Born in Naples, the son of the great opera composer Alessandro Scarlatti, Domenico devoted his early years to the composition of opera and church music, and even some *concerti grossi*. The results, while competent and attractive enough, are not sufficiently distinguished to place him in the front rank of his contemporaries. But at about the age of thirty-five, he accepted a job as music master to Princess Maria Barbara of Braganza, in Lisbon. Soon afterwards, when she married the heir to the throne of Spain, Scarlatti followed her there, and remained in Madrid for the rest of his life. During this time, he devoted himself almost exclusively to the composition of hundreds of one-movement keyboard *sonatas*: just under six hundred survive today. Within the confines of such a constricting form—nearly every piece is in binary form and of about three minutes' duration—there is a variety of effects, sentiment and virtuosity that is not met with in the keyboard music

***Domenico Scarlatti**, son of Alessandro, and perhaps the greatest keyboard virtuoso of all time.*

*In the courts of Europe music was provided by servant-musicians round the clock. This sketch depicts a **scene at court** in Florence.*

of any other composer of the eighteenth century. Guitar sounds, street-cries, hoofbeats and all the pageantry of the court jostle for attention in these eccentric and wonderful miniatures. Scarlatti must have been the greatest virtuoso of his day (closely followed, perhaps, by the Queen of Spain, if she could play these difficult works): his powers as a performer were vividly described by his friend Roseingrave, who first encountered Scarlatti at a noble gathering where both men had performed. Though pleased with his own performance, Roseingrave relates that when Scarlatti began to play, he thought ten hundred devils had been at the instrument; he had never heard such passages of execution and effect before. The performance so far surpassed his own that, if he had been in sight of any instrument with which to have done the deed, he would have cut off his own fingers. As it was, Roseingrave could not bring himself to touch a harpsichord again for a whole month.

There is a last echo of this wayward genius in the music of a Spanish monk, Antonio Soler (1729–1783). He worked for most of his life at the gloomy Escorial in Madrid, and was a pupil there of Scarlatti. He wrote many one-movement sonatas after the style of his master, as well as concertos for one and two keyboards. Much of Soler's delightful music is possessed of a gaiety and vigour that seems quite at odds with his austere and cloistered life.

The Inventive Genius of J.S. Bach
Although Sebastian Bach never travelled outside Germany, and hardly ever outside his native province, he was informed of all the developments. Travel was awkward, but new music circulated quite quickly to other parts

The Clavier

Bach's Well-tempered Clavier, *a collection of forty-eight preludes and fugues, has a title requiring some explanation. Much of his keyboard music is designated merely as being for "clavier" (keyboard), which could mean either organ, the brilliant glitter of the harpsichord, or the tiny voice of the clavichord—whose sweet and intimate sound made the instrument an especial favourite of Bach. Often, the choice of instrument is a matter of common sense: a brilliant work such as the* Italian Concerto *is quite obviously for harpsichord; while many of the gentler and more lyrical works, the French suites, for example, seem conceived with the clavichord's unique expressiveness in mind. As far as the* Well-tempered Clavier *is concerned, it was never intended to be performed as a single work, and contains pieces that are most suited to each of the three keyboard families, as well as ones that sound well whether plucked (harpsichord), struck (clavichord) or blown on the organ.*

"Well-tempered" refers to the manner in which the keyboard has been tuned. Equal temperament was a system advocated (though not invented) by Bach in this work. Theoretically, the note F sharp is not at the same pitch as G flat, for example, though on the keyboard there is only one note for both of them. G sharp is not the same as A flat, and so on. Bach proposed that all intervals on the keyboard should be made equal (and consequently fractionally out of tune) to facilitate moving into and out of remote keys, avoiding ugly "out of tune" gaps. Equal temperament is the system that remains in use on all our keyboard instruments today.

1600–1760 "Gentlemen, Old Bach is Here!"

of Europe, even to the small towns where Bach grew up and lived before he settled in the great city of Leipzig. He is said to have corresponded with François Couperin in Paris, and he copied one of Couperin's pieces into a musical notebook for his second wife, Anna Magdalena. As a young church organist at the court of Weimar, he had transcribed concertos by Vivaldi and other contemporary Italians for solo keyboard. An early influence too was the Italian Tommaso Albinoni (1671–1750). Bach wrote some fugues on themes by Albinoni, whose music is rarely heard today. (Albinoni's famous *Adagio* is not by the composer at all, but rather a twentieth-century pastiche by Giazotto based upon an Albinoni fragment.)

A youthful keyboard composition of Bach's that should be mentioned here is the *Capriccio on the departure of a Beloved Brother*. It is the only example in Bach of "programme music": its movements depict the bewailing of friends that gather to see the traveller off, a description of all the terrible dangers that may befall him on his journey, the arrival of the coach in which he is to travel and a fugue based upon the call of the post-horn.

Bach contributed significantly to the literature of the Italian sonata and concerto, the French overture and suite, but for most of his working life, music for the Lutheran Church took up the best part of his time—the church cantata, the short mass, the oratorio and Passion, the German motet, organ music—and educational music for his many children took up the rest. In all of these he applied comprehensive musical knowledge, virtuoso technique and a quest for perfection, so that the result surpassed what had been done with them before.

Bach came, like Couperin, from a family dynasty of professional musicians, extending from the fiddler and Stuttgart court jester Hans Bach (born *c.* 1555) to the Elberfeld music teacher Johann Georg Bach, who died in 1874. His forebears included singers, every variety of instrumentalist known in his day, choirmasters, music teachers, instrument-makers and composers. Like Martin Luther, Bach was born in Eisenach, where his father was organist. In his youth he sang as a choirboy and learned to play the keyboard and the violin; later he preferred the viola, as Mozart did, because it is in the middle—at the heart, so to speak—of the musical texture. He taught himself composition by copying out the music of earlier masters, just as he taught himself to improvise elaborate fugues: he studied the playing of every notable organist in his part of the world, sometimes enduring hardship to do so. A famous anecdote relates how, as a boy, Bach had wanted access to a volume of keyboard music belonging to his elder brother. Permission to study it was refused, however, so Bach carefully removed it each night through the latticework of his brother's bookcase and copied out the entire book—it took him six months, working by moonlight and probably damaging his eyesight in the process.

Having had, as an orphan, to fend much for himself (fortunately he was sent to good schools in those years and given a superior academic education), he became both independent-minded and stubborn when he did not get his way. Because of that, he fell foul of many employers during his working life: the Grand Duke of Weimar had Bach imprisoned before letting him take up a post elsewhere. At Arnstadt they complained that he accompanied the hymns too elaborately. At Mühlhausen he had time to take pupils in keyboard and composition, and to compose the first of his church cantatas. At Weimar he composed the greater part of his solo organ music, began his first cycle of cantatas, discovered Vivaldi, who influenced

F. Couperin p 86–7

Vivaldi p 90–1

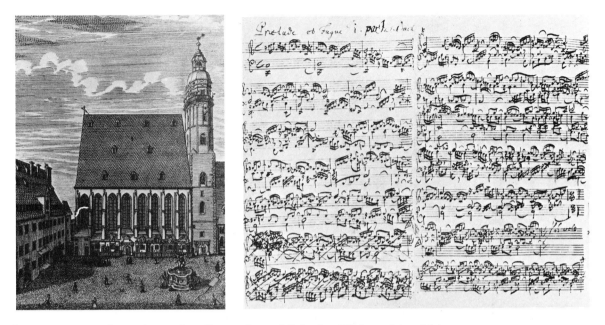

his instrumental music profoundly, and established a lifelong friendship with Telemann. Family squabbles among his Weimar employers made Bach take another post as music director at Cöthen, where the Prince treated him as a friend and fellow-musician, and where Bach wrote much of his instrumental music—church music was not required of him there, the court being Calvinist. The sheer volume of music that he composed during these six years is astonishing, and all of a consistently high quality. The keyboard music includes the first book of the *Well-tempered Clavier* (twenty-four preludes and fugues in each of the major and minor keys); the six French Suites, small-scale pieces of great sweetness and charm, probably intended for the clavichord; and the sets of two- and three-part Inventions, as well as many teaching pieces for his son, Wilhelm Friedemann. Beyond this, at Cöthen Bach wrote the six Brandenburg Concertos, the six unaccompanied violin sonatas (and another six with accompaniment), the cello suites, the flute sonatas and the suites for orchestra. Even when he had a job where his duties were relatively light, Bach was constantly involved in the process of composition.

But eventually the Prince took a new wife who resented her husband's friendship with a servant (a court musician was no more than that), so he applied for, and was eventually offered, the post of cantor (church and town musical director) in Leipzig. There he completed his church cantatas, his concertos and orchestral suites, his five Passion settings (only the St John and St Matthew survive), his forty-eight preludes and fugues for solo keyboard in all the major and minor keys (*The Well-tempered Clavier*), and other instructional works. He developed his encyclopaedic longings that also resulted in the thirty *Goldberg Variations* for harpsichord, each variation in a different style, and *The Musical Offering* for Frederick the Great, a collection of canons and fugues plus a trio sonata, all based on an intriguing, teasing theme given to him by the King. His final work was *The Art of Fugue*, a collection of fugues of every variety, all on the same musical theme or subject: it exists unfinished, but he had probably completed it

A page from J.S. Bach's **Well-tempered Clavier** *manuscript, and an engraving of* **St Thomas's Church in Leipzig** *where J.S. Bach held the post of cantor for much of his life. Leipzig's reputation as one of the leading musical cities of Europe was already established by the time Bach took up this prestigious post.*

Bach & Frederick the Great p 76

before he went blind and died of a stroke after unsuccessful operations on his eyes (there were no anaesthetics in those days).

Those last contrapuntal collections were the result of Bach's renewed study of older composers, particularly Palestrina and Frescobaldi, by then unfashionable and almost forgotten, but still fascinating and instructive to such an avid student of music as J.S. Bach. He still retained his interest in new music and new playing techniques. When the newly invented *fortepiano* (or *pianoforte* as we call it) arrived, Bach tried it out and advised the maker, Silbermann, on various desirable improvements, which were quickly adopted. Bach is generally credited with the invention of the sonata for solo instrument with fully written-out harpsichord accompaniment, a proper solo part, not just chords to be filled in by continuo player (sonatas for violin, viola da gamba, and flute). And whereas the Italian *concerti grossi* had accompanied their soloists with continuo keyboard, Bach in the fifth Brandenburg Concerto again made the harpsichord part fully solo, with a written-out cadenza. He developed the notion in several solo harpsichord concertos, thereby establishing the framework for what turned into the ever popular piano concerto.

The Public Eye

In Leipzig Bach was, for several years, director of the Collegium Musicum series of weekly subscription concerts, founded by Telemann and given in a coffee-house—Banister's London invention had travelled.

Such concerts had been in existence in Paris since 1725 with the celebrated *Concerts spirituels*, and in Hamburg since 1722. Vivaldi gave

The Suite

In modal music, individual pieces tended to be short, for the range of modulation available was extremely limited. Instrumental dances were often written in pairs, the first slow and the second fast, to enable a composer to extend his music for a longer period of time. The Baroque suite (predominantly for keyboard) was evolved in the early seventeenth century, and was in essence two such pairs of dances linked together: allemande *(slow),* courante *(fast),* sarabande *(slow) and* gigue *(fast).*

Frequently other contrasting movements were inserted into this formal structure, such as a pair of minuets, a short air, or an improvisatory prelude at the beginning. The great composer François Couperin constructed some of his suites (ordres) out of so many movements that he gave permission in a preface for the performer to omit some of the movements if he so chose.

The greatest keyboard suites are those of J.S. Bach, who composed his French suites, English suites and partitas in groups of six. Many of these are mighty works, lasting almost half an hour in performance, with several interpolated movements, and usually (as was conventional) having the movements thematically linked. The Partita in C minor *(no. 2 of the set) is a magnificent example of how a series of short, related dance movements can be welded into a sublimely satisfying whole.*

Sometimes a suite began with a French-style overture (slow, quick and fugal, slow again), and so the whole piece was called an overture; in Italian these suites might be called partita, or sinfonia (fast, slow, fast again), which more usually meant the overture to an opera, and eventually became our symphony.

Palestrina p 49

Couperin *ordres* p 86

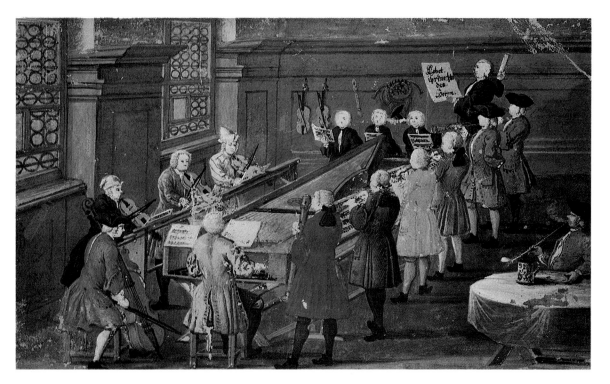

semi-public concerts with his pupils of the Ospedale in Venice, and public opera-houses were becoming successful too. In Hamburg the Goosemarket Theatre opened in 1678 as a public opera-house, with operas by German composers much indebted to good French and Italian models, often sung in two languages more or less simultaneously. A leading light there was J.S. Bach's friend Georg Philipp Telemann (1681–1767), who worked copiously in all the same spheres of music, and also in opera, which J.S. Bach never cultivated.

Telemann was largely self-taught, and became a competent performer on many instruments, including the zither. He had studied science and languages at Leipzig University, and acquired his immense musical knowledge in his spare time, practising instruments and studying such scores as were available. Much of his subsequent life was spent as civic music director at Hamburg. His speed of composition was enviable: Telemann must rank as one of the most prolific composers of all time. "He could", said Handel, "write a motet in eight parts as easily as another could write a letter." Telemann could and did write contrapuntal German music in the Baroque style of Bach; but he had travelled, and he surrendered completely, as Bach never entirely did, to the new French *galant* manner, simpler and frankly entertaining. It was Telemann who was preferred to Bach when they were being considered for the same post, and Telemann whose music was being performed outside Germany. Telemann left many more compositions than Bach—they cost less effort to write—and he lived longer. But few of Telemann's numerous operas have come down to us complete: the best known is *Pimpinone*, a comedy in mixed Italian and German (1725); there is also a *Don Quixote* (1761) and *The Patience of Socrates* (1721); all three all occasionally performed.

Collegia musica were a musical feature in Germany from the sixteenth century. They were essentially gatherings of musically minded people who met to play together, often in coffee-houses as depicted here.

1600–1760 "Gentlemen, Old Bach is Here!"

Inspiration and Influence

Neither Telemann, nor even J.S. Bach, would have suspected that Bach's music would inspire the greatest composers of the next generation. But in the 1780s, the Viennese musical amateur Baron van Swieten, unfashionably convinced that new music was not automatically superior to old, acquired all Bach's music that he could find and showed it to Mozart and Haydn, thereby inspiring both to inject Bach's sublime mastery of counterpoint into their late Viennese classical music. The young Beethoven, too, grew up with Bach's forty-eight preludes and fugues which his teacher, Neefe, had long admired. There was a Bach cult in England headed by Samuel Wesley (1766–1837), a Roman Catholic who named his illegitimate son Sebastian and preached the supremacy of the organ and J.S. Bach's works for it in particular. When Felix Mendelssohn Bartholdy, a Protestant Jew, found and performed the *St Matthew Passion*, he finally established the cult of J.S. Bach in Germany which Schumann, Brahms and virtually all composers after them gladly espoused, especially Reger, Busoni, Hindemith, Stravinsky and Villa-Lobos—and in the present century, even jazz and pop musicians.

Mendelssohn p 173–5

Chapter 6
The Age of Handel

Opera: the Play's the Thing

Italian Opera inspires Europe ◆
Alessandro Scarlatti ◆ Opera seria and
Opera buffa ◆ Handel brings his elegant operas to
England ◆ The birth of Oratorio ◆ The Sons of Bach ◆ The
French opera tradition ◆

In 1703 a young German musician from Halle came to Hamburg's Goosemarket Theatre as violinist and harpsichordist. He was Georg Friedrich Händel (1685–1759); he composed two operas in Italian for Hamburg, then went to Italy for further study. He returned to become the dominant figure in eighteenth-century English music, changing his name to George Frideric Handel.

Handel went off to study in Italy because he realized that the coming musical vogue was going to be Italian opera. He had heard some of the real thing in Germany and his fellow Germans' attempts at copying it. German composers wrote heavier, plodding music, full of accompanying counterpoint, born, as it were, of the keyboard rather than the singing voice. He knew that the two Italianate operas he had composed while in Hamburg were lacking in the clarity, elegance and the suave femininity which made Italian opera so attractive. Handel's music of that period was declared by the best critic of the age, the composer Johann Mattheson (1681–1764)—who gave opera its first *Boris Godunov* in 1710—to be weak in melody, though strong in harmony and counterpoint. So it was to Italy that Handel went to repair that failing.

The Italian/German Fusion
During his two years in Italy Handel wrote one opera for Florence and one for Venice. He met all the best composers. From Corelli and Vivaldi Handel learned about concerto and sonata. From Alessandro Scarlatti he learned the standard Italian opera and solo cantata of the day. With Scarlatti's son Domenico, Handel took part in a keyboard contest, won by Handel in the organ event and ceded to Scarlatti at the harpsichord—a basis for mutual admiration and friendship ever after. Handel learned how to write naturally and brilliantly for the voice and how to control harmonic accompaniment so as not to perplex amateur listeners. He wrote a good number of

Handel *like J.S. Bach, suffered from blindness in later years, and both suffered unsuccessful surgery at the hands of the same English quack surgeon.*

cantatas, which had become mini-operas lacking only a stage—especially popular in Rome, where opera was now officially forbidden. *Lucrezia* is one still performed today (the solo protagonist is not Countess Borgia, but the classic heroine of Shakespeare's *Rape of Lucrece*); another, *Acis, Galatea and Polyphemus*, was later revised into an English serenade-cantata with chorus. It is often performed today and is famous chiefly for Polyphemus's air *O ruddier than the cherry*, much sung by ambitious basses. It was first written for Giuseppe Boschi, a great virtuoso singer of his day, whose huge vocal range and agility in scales and runs brought that low voice, thanks to Handel, out of the gloom imposed by the glamour of the unnatural male soprano.

Facing page: ***Alessandro Scarlatti*** *came from a musical family. His two brothers and two of his sisters were also musicians.*

Handel went back home, into service with the Elector of Hanover. He was now a complete Italian musician, versed not only in opera and chamber-cantata but in Roman oratorio and Latin motet, in the Venetian *concerto grosso* and solo concerto, as well as the domestic instrumental sonata and

1680–1780 Opera: the Play's the Thing

A caricature by Hogarth
of a group of singers
performing Handel's
oratorio Judith.

the art of solo harpsichord-playing in the glittering anti-intellectual manner. He never forgot his German contrapuntal inheritance, fortunately, but he learned when to put it out of mind for immediately practical purpose.

From Hanover Handel might have created a valid German opera, such as I believe nobody did until Wagner. Instead he chose England, perhaps a greater fame, certainly a more international, enduring glory that was not confined to opera, and was influential long after his death and that of Baroque music, which was his birthright. In the field of opera he gave England thirty-six works between 1712 and 1741, very few duds among them, so modern revivals suggest. Their style is his own particular idiosyncrasy—Italianized German, breaking always out of the strait-jacket called Italian *opera seria* ("serious" opera) as formalized by his mentor, the Neapolitan Alessandro Scarlatti.

The Dramas and Comedies of Alessandro Scarlatti
Alessandro Scarlatti (1660–1725) was born in Palermo, Sicily, part of the kingdom of Naples. He was one of eight children, five of whom became musicians (there were two musicians among Alessandro's ten offspring).

Wagner p 229–40, 233–8

Alessandro was sent as a boy to study music in Rome, where he became music director to Queen Christina of Sweden, self-exiled there after she became a Catholic and abdicated. In Rome theatrical shows, like female singers, were banned by the Pope from public performance, though both were cultivated in private, sponsored by wealthy patrons.

Scarlatti composed six operas for Rome, only one of them a grand heroic drama or *opera seria* (*Pompeo*), the others mild pastorals, all with a great many short arias separated by simple recitative. (Two plum arias extracted from *Pompeo*, *O cessate di piagarmi* and *Gia il sole dal Gange*, are among the "old Italian airs" with which singers often begin recitals today.) Scarlatti's first operas were immediately successful, much performed in Italy and abroad. In 1684 he was appointed musical director to the viceroy of Naples, and there settled into his life-work of one hundred and fifteen operas, six hundred cantatas and getting on for forty oratorios, besides masses, motets, *concerti grossi* and numerous sonatas, including the first string quartets ever composed. One of his specialities was the *Siciliano* from his birthplace, a sad, lilting song like a very slow jig, which was eagerly adopted by others. He spent some time in Florence and Venice and was often in Rome, but he had made his home in Naples and spent his last years there. Naples, during Scarlatti's lifetime, succeeded Venice as the headquarters of Italian opera, from which it conquered Europe completely, including Russia, but excluding France.

Senesino (right), the most celebrated alto castrato *of his day, and Francesca Cuzzoni in* **Handel's Flavio**. *Cuzzoni, recalled Horace Walpole, was "short and squat, with a doughy cross face".*

Opera Seria—Dramatic Recitals

Opera has always been the prey of amateur theoreticians. Count Bardi brought it into existence. After a hundred years, his spiritual descendants of the Arcadian Academy in Rome complained that the guidelines were too muddled and the aim of music-theatre uncertain. The principal mouthpiece of reform was Pietro Metastasio (1698–1782), a great poet, and sufficiently a musician to compose and sing music for every aria whose text he wrote, before handing it on to the chosen composer.

As a boy, Metastasio had shown a precocious talent; his gifts for singing, poetry and improvisation had won him a substantial inheritance from a wealthy patron in Rome. In later life, he worked for many years at the Viennese court: most of the librettos by which he is remembered were written there. The most famous of these was probably *La clemenza di Tito* (1734), which was later to form the basis of Mozart's last opera in 1791. Metastasio's success as a librettist rests on the smooth, flowing quality of his verse and imaginative ingenuity of his poetic conceits, rather than on any great depth or passion in his lyrics.

The earliest operas had relieved their seriousness and dignity with comic, even farcical, scenes (such as the Page and Lady's Maid scene in Monteverdi's *The Coronation of Poppaea*, or the fawning glutton Irus in his *The Return of Ulysses*), and they were still there in Scarlatti's operas. Metastasio and his fellow librettist-reformer Apostolo Zeno (1668–1750), who did write librettos for Scarlatti, were determined to separate comedy from serious opera. They did their best to rid serious opera of comics, just as they banished choruses, orchestral interludes, ballet and, for preference, magic. They preferred the plot to echo history or romantic fiction rather than mythology, in order to do away with incredible magical intervention in the love affairs of credible principal characters. They chose to write about rulers (usually benevolent, to flatter royal patrons), their lovers, confidants or advisors, and (only on best behaviour) servants. Spectacle was extremely grand and architectural, a sequence of Palladian back-drops that changed some three times in each act, and might include a spectacular transformation (much more quickly managed then than now!). The subject-matter was always frustrated love, with conflicting loyalties and vaunting ambition as side-issues: the ending always had to be happy.

The purpose of every opera was to show the principal characters, *i.e.* singers, in a great variety of strong emotional situations one after another. Each situation was summarized in a solo aria, set to perhaps four lines of jewelled poetry, two lines expressing the mood of the moment, the next two qualifying it (contrasted music). After that the music returned to the beginning (*da capo* in Italian), with the same music now varied by florid vocal decoration and ending with a long, brilliant, unaccompanied flourish or cadenza before the short orchestral close. This was called a *da capo* aria. As the eighteenth century progressed, the beginning which was also the ending grew larger to accommodate further contrasting themes, until it was as long as a solo concerto movement. In Scarlatti's operas (and Handel's too), the arias are still quite concise, accompanied either by continuo alone, or strings, perhaps with a prominent instrument duetting with the voice—oboe, horn, or trumpet (much favoured with a powerful male soprano).

The poet's job was to give each main character the appropriate number of arias, never two of the same kind, nor too close together. It was a jigsaw-puzzle task. A scene could start with two characters conversing in

*An **opera seria** performance. Typically, the audience pays scant attention, save at the entrance of a favoured performer or during a favourite aria.*

***Maria Barbara, Queen of Spain**, with the playwright Metastasio on her right and the great* castrato *Farinelli to her left. It was Maria Barbara for whom Domenico Scarlatti wrote most of his harpsichord sonatas.*

1680–1780 Opera: the Play's the Thing

A set design for an opera in 1675 by Legrenzi, showing the descent of a god upon his cloud, and the mechanics by which the spectacle is effected.

recitative, then at the appropriate moment one sang an aria and left the stage, after which another entered and the dialogue was resumed. There could be numerous characters on stage, singing arias in turn and departing. When the last one had sung and made the necessary exit, the stage was empty, so the scenery changed—very quickly at the pull of a lever—and the process began again. While all this went on through three acts, with perhaps one duet at the end of an act, but without trios or other ensembles or choruses, the poet had to be advancing the plot towards maximum complication and eventual (rational) resolution.

The composer, for his part, had to make sure that every aria was neatly contrasted with others in the same act—in key, speed, mood and orchestration—another jigsaw puzzle. He also had to compose each aria expressly for the singer contracted; his or her vocal range, best notes, special virtuoso capabilities and whole vocal personality. When an opera was revived later with other singers, they would require other music, which is why some composers set the same text more than once, or imported into an existing opera an item from an earlier opera composed for the same singer. Handel became the great master of re-using old material, not always originally his own, but always improved by his re-working. This was not plagiarism in the modern sense of the word, but legitimate "borrowing", an accepted and acceptable convention of an age in which music had to be turned out at a great rate, to satisfy public appetite.

Often an opera, when produced somewhere else, only needed a few changed arias to fit the new cast: it was thought perfectly respectable to get some other composer to supply them, because musical language throughout Europe was more or less the same, as was understood by the Latin phrase *lingua franca*—the invented common language which hoped to regularize the international communication that music has always achieved of its own accord. Music can never be an international language, because every creative musical voice (*i.e.* composer) has a unique vocabulary and style: the rest of us try to acquire enough common vocabulary to follow the gist of a composer's work.

When Italian *opera seria* died in the early nineteenth century, posterity forgot it. Only in the middle twentieth century and since have we learned to appreciate *opera seria* as a theatrical art-form; not just quaint and artificial history, but music-theatre of an extraordinary but still thrilling nature. It perfectly suited the tastes and customs of the aristocratic society of those days; but even before the French Revolution of 1789 it was aggressively challenged, because it was not as natural and sensible as Metastasio and Zeno had hoped.

The Aria

By the time of the late Baroque era, operatic arias had acquired particular stylized conventions. As a long solo for virtuoso voice and orchestra, it was generally the function of an aria to supply the emotional interest of an opera, holding up the narrative to allow the character to express his (or her) reaction to the story so far.

Eighteenth-century arias are most commonly in A-B-A form: that is to say, with a contrasting middle section interposing an identical first and last section, the latter embellished. Towards the end of an aria there is frequently a cadenza, a florid, unaccompanied passage for the singer to display the range and agility of his or her voice, and which was, as a rule, improvised by the performer.

There were many classes of aria within this form, such as the Aria cantabile, *slow and pathetic in style; the* Aria di bravura, *much faster and filled with brilliant leaps and scales; the* Aria d'imitazione, *which attempted to copy other sounds such as birdsong or martial trumpets: and the little* Arietta *or* Cavatina, *too short and simple to be dignified with the title of aria, and generally without the contrasting middle section.*

It is no good likening the Italian *opera seria*, whether by Scarlatti or Handel, or the Mozart of *Idomeneo* (the greatest, if not latest, of them), with the great tragedies or histories of Shakespeare or Schiller or any other great playwright. They are plays about people. *Opera seria* might be described as a multi-celebrity recital masquerading as a play about people. Writers and critics who had not seen these operas used to describe them as "concerts in costume". Nowadays they are often to be seen in one theatre or another, especially the operas of Handel. When properly staged they come across as

Mozart's *Idomeneo* p 152–3, 158

theatre of a quite idiosyncratic sort, its rules unique, its language greatly eloquent, but only when we have learned its conventions in the same way as we learn a foreign tongue.

Opera Seria Comes of Age

The musical mouthpiece of Metastasio's reformed *opera seria* was chiefly Johann Adolf Hasse (1699–1783). You may be surprised to learn that he was the most popular composer of Italian opera in his lifetime, active in Venice, Dresden, Vienna, Warsaw and Paris, admired too in London, which he never visited, though Handel produced his operas there (and borrowed happily from his melodies). Hasse was on friendly terms with Handel and with Bach in Leipzig.

Hasse came from a dynasty of musicians in north Germany. After vocal studies he joined the Hamburg opera as a tenor singer. His first opera was produced there and in 1721 he left Hamburg, as Handel had done, to study composition in Italy; his teacher in Naples was Alessandro Scarlatti, and there Hasse was soon a busy composer of comic opera and comic intermezzos spatchcocked (as was the fashion) between the acts of heroic operas. His *Artaxerxes* (1730, Venice) has gone down in history for two arias which the great castrato Farinelli, for whom they were written, sang every night for ten years to his employer Philip V of Spain. Hasse's wife was the soprano Faustina Bordoni, who was often engaged in London by Handel—on one disastrous occasion with her great rival Francesca Cuzzoni: the performance ended when the two of them, each envious of the other's success, attacked one another physically on stage and the curtain had to be rung down. Nevertheless they continued to sing together thereafter. Faustina's strength was agility, Cuzzoni's, tender expressiveness: many years later, Mozart parodied their rivalry in his little operetta *The Impresario* (1786).

From Naples Hasse returned to Germany for a post in Dresden with the Elector of Saxony, where he composed quantities of sacred music in Latin, as well as instrumental music. He spent some time in Vienna, giving music lessons to the Empress Maria Theresa and writing operas for her children to perform in the little opera-house at the palace of Schönbrunn. During the early 1770s in Vienna there was heated rivalry between Hasse, as representative of the old *opera seria* guard, and Gluck as the great reformer. Hasse, like Bach, had become "old hat", not least because he declared that the popular comic opera harmed singers' voices. Hasse retained close links with Venice as an opera composer and as music director of an institution for incurables. He retired to Venice with his Faustina; they were a much-loved, friendly, still handsome couple, and he spent his last years composing church music, which he preferred to the rat-race of the theatre. When Italians referred to "the dear Saxon" (*il caro Sassone*), it was not Handel they meant, but Hasse.

Hasse devoted his creative life to the singer's art, to *bel canto*—flowing melody matched perfectly to eloquent poetry, simply but appropriately accompanied. He followed Metastasio, whose libretti he set one after another, in giving as much musical importance to recitatives as to arias, letting the Italian words be savoured like fine wine, restricting orchestral accompaniment to dramatic moments. If the historical museum we call musical repertory were fair, his music would be heard occasionally and represented in record catalogues, though nowadays we require music to be not only perfect but interesting as well, which for us Hasse's is evidently

Facing page: **The Emperor Franz I** and Maria Theresa with their children on the terrace at Schönbrunn. Haydn's symphony no 48 is known as the "Maria Theresa" because she took particular delight in the work when she heard a performance at Esterhaza.

Gluck p 125–6

*So popular was **Arne's opera Artaxerxes** that the management refused to admit the audience at the customary half price. A riot was the result.*

not. Handel and Mozart both admired it greatly and learned from it. In Dresden, where he worked for so many years, his church music was regularly performed until the present century, though elsewhere it fell into a total neglect that has not yet been reversed. Hasse must still be claimed as important a composer in the history of opera as Monteverdi or Mozart, which is why I have written about him at length. We can never afford to neglect great inventors of melody.

Opera Buffa: Comedy for Naples

High art might be better served by Metastasio's recipe, but the fun was missed. Italy had already a grand comic tradition in the *commedia dell' arte*; plays about Pierrot and Harlequin, Columbine, Truffaldino and other stock clowns, the text improvised but never written down. Opera needed them and had used them in the early specimens, including those by Scarlatti. Exiled from *opera seria*, the Italian comic style was destined to show its face in operas entirely devoted to comedy. Alessandro Scarlatti duly produced *Il trionfo dell' onore* ("The Triumph of Virtue", 1718), a real comic opera, just as Handel brought out *Xerxes* (1738), though they were exceptions, like Hasse's few comic operas. (*Xerxes* begins with the Persian King addressing an aria to a favourite plane-tree—the music so beautiful that the words were removed and the piece became popular as Handel's *Largo*.) Comic opera came out of Naples, desperately poor, and therefore ripe for robust amusement. Naples was called the Two Kingdoms because it included Sicily—it better deserved the title, and still does, because opulence and abject poverty have long existed there side by side.

Out of Sicily came Alessandro Scarlatti, bringing with him the *Siciliano*, a song of woe, more or less desperate. Out of Naples came the first comic operas, *opere buffe* in Italian, using dialect texts and cheerful music. A pioneer was Giovanni Battista Pergolesi (1710–1736), whose comic opera *Lo frate 'nnammorato* ("The Monk in Love") set a fashion, and whose *La serva padrona* ("Maid turned Mistress", 1733), originally an intermezzo to a serious opera, almost at once conquered Europe with its inter-sex war and delightful music allied with an amusing story. It is often performed by itself nowadays. Pergolesi's life is surrounded with a confusing tissue of myth and legend. He was educated in Naples, and appears to have been something of a child prodigy, astonishing those who heard him with his capacity for improvising on the violin.

He died while still a young man, before he could reap the rewards that *La serva padrona* would have brought him, and was interred anonymously in a communal burial-pit at Naples. But Pergolesi did live long enough to compose a *Stabat Mater* for two sopranos and orchestra; a typical Italian cantata of its day whose lovable melody and intense feeling have kept it firmly in the concert repertory (though today it is often sung by a female chorus, which blunts the fine Italian edge of the music). J.S. Bach thought sufficiently highly of the work to arrange it in German for use in the Lutheran Church.

La serva padrona has a bass part for an old fellow so plagued by his soprano maid that he cannot refrain from marrying her. The bass voice had fallen out of fashion in heroic opera, which gave its choicest roles to male or female sopranos. Italian comic opera brought back the agile *basso*, especially in the lively roles of foolish old men. In due course, the voice

*An eighteenth-century view across the Elbe to the city of **Dresden**.*

1680-1780 Opera: the Play's the Thing

A typical Italian theatre scene of the eighteenth century (school of Longhi). The audience strolls around and chats, while on the stage a shepherd boy with his maid get on with performing an **intermezzo** *between acts of the opera.*

returned to the heroic stage in Handel's works through the brilliant artistry of a generation of basses from northern Italy. They cut their teeth on strong comic roles, became the kings and fathers of Romantic Opera and, since Verdi, have become as starry and important as any *castrato* of earlier days.

The comic opera brought back duets and trios, other concerted ensembles and thereby the making of music-drama—which as *dramma per musica* was the whole intention of early opera. *Opera seria* was devoted to one character with one emotion at a time, but drama is always about two or more people and needs duets at least.

Comic opera quickly proliferated in Italy and sped abroad. At first the humour was very broad and the characters coarse—the clowns of the *commedia*. Carlo Goldoni (1707–1793), a contemporary of Metastasio, created a brilliant new style of comedy, largely derived from close observation of the manners and morals of Venetian society. As a child he had run away for a spell with some travelling players. Later, after qualifying as a lawyer, he continued writing for players he encountered. In 1749 he began to publish his comic opera texts: they were very funny indeed, but also carefully and cleverly put together—fairground-show turned into high art. The characters were modern types even when derived from the *commedia*, the drama scrupulously turned. The speciality was the

Verdi p 215–24

finale, which gradually brought more and more characters on stage as the musical pace increased. There are countless examples in operas never performed today; the perfect example, by any standard, came later—the second act finale of Mozart's *The Marriage of Figaro*, a comic, amazing piece of spirited musical invention, never surpassed and inexhaustible. But Goldoni's innovations are sometimes difficult to appreciate in the light of all that has passed since his time. Often the subject of bitter attack in his own day, he turned to writing plays in French, as director of the Comédie-Italienne in Paris. On his retirement, in poor health and with failing eyesight, Goldoni received a small pension from the French king. But even that was stopped with the coming of the Revolution in 1789, and Goldoni died in neglect.

Cimarosa and Paisiello

But there were, before *Figaro*, many popular comic operas nowadays forgotten. Two of them are still popular. *Il matrimonio segreto* ("The Secret Marriage") by Domenico Cimarosa (1749–1801) is based on a play by the English actor David Garrick. It suffers by comparison with Mozart's great comic operas, but in its own right, and well performed, it grips hold of a listener and brings its period to life. It was written for the Emperor Leopold II, while Cimarosa was music director to the Viennese court. The Emperor was so delighted with the work that, as soon as the performance was finished, he commanded it to be repeated after supper.

Carlo Goldoni organized the improvised tradition of the commedia dell' arte *into a system of written comedy.*

Cimarosa was indeed a gifted and fortunate man. While still in his twenties, he had been appointed chamber composer to Catherine the Great in St Petersburg, before moving to Vienna. After the Emperor's death, he accepted a post as director of music at the Neapolitan court, though he was imprisoned for a spell there because of his Republican sympathies. He eventually died on a journey back to Russia. A famous story connected with Cimarosa tells how a painter friend declared him a greater composer than Mozart. "What nonsense," he replied, "What would you take me for if I said that *you* were greater than Raphael?"

An Italian contemporary of Cimarosa, Giovanni Paisiello (1740–1816), also enjoyed success with a comic opera, *The Barber of Seville* (1782), anticipating Rossini by thirty-four years. He had studied at the Conservatory in Naples for many years and, like Cimarosa, worked for Catherine the Great in St Petersburg. His *Barber* was written for the court there, and became so popular throughout Europe that the Italian public would at first have nothing to do with Rossini's later version when it appeared. Paisiello's bold orchestration was particularly admired. In later life he worked for a period for Napoleon, though not without arousing resentment among his colleagues in Paris. In all he wrote about a hundred operas (most of which are now forgotten) before dying in Naples in reduced circumstances.

Handel in England

While Handel was in Venice, he was invited by Prince Ernest of Hanover to visit that court, and by the Duke of Manchester (English Ambassador to Italy) to visit London. Having obtained the post of musical director to the Elector of Hanover, he soon set out to visit London, where he produced his next opera, *Rinaldo*—now famous for the moving aria *Lascia ch'io pianga*, in triple time with a *chaconne* stress on the second beat of the bar. Other solos, greatly praised, had been taken over from his earlier operas or

cantatas, and this was to be his economical practice for the rest of his life. London, never until now a capital that properly appreciated opera (indeed made fun of it), paid far less attention to the splendid music of *Rinaldo* than to the release of a flock of birds from a cage—an artful device employed in one scene.

Handel returned to Hanover, but almost at once applied to the Elector for leave of absence and came back to London. He over-stayed his leave being plentifully occupied with work—in fact he stayed until his patroness, Queen Anne, died and was succeeded by Handel's ex-employer, the Elector of Hanover, now King George I of England. The King was not a little upset to find his reluctant employee flourishing in his newly acquired realm. But the King forgave him, perhaps after hearing a Handel *Te Deum* in the Chapel Royal, perhaps by the intervention of a friend and prominent courtier, Baron Kilmansegg, whose wife was the King's mistress. A pleasant legend has it that in order to curry forgiveness, Handel followed the court on a royal progress by barge down the Thames from Westminster to Chelsea, serenading the King with seductive airs—one suite on the way up, suite two during supper, and suite three for the return journey. Many such musical anecdotes of old provenance have been discounted by modern scholarship, but whatever circumstances surrounded its creation, Handel's *Water Music* remains a concert favourite. A report from the *London Daily Courant* of 19 July 1717 told the story as follows:

"On Wednesday evening about eight, the King took water at Whitehall in an open barge, wherein were also the Duchess of Bolton, the Duchess of Newcastle, the Countess of Godolphin, Madam Kilmanseck and the Earl of Orkney, and went up the river toward Chelsea. Many other barges with persons of quality attended, and so great was the number of boats, that the whole river in a manner was covered. A city company's barge was employed for the musick, where were fifty instruments of all sorts, who played all the way from Lambeth (while the barges drove the tide, without rowing, as far as Chelsea), the finest symphonies, composed express for the occasion, by Mr Handel: which His Majesty liked so well that he caused it to be played over three times in going and returning. At eleven, His Majesty went ashore at Chelsea where a supper was prepared, and then there was another very fine consort of musick which lasted until two: after which His Majesty came again into his barge and returned the same way, the musick continuing to play until he landed."

In London Handel produced thirty-six new Italian operas of the serious variety, without comic interludes. They include some great pieces, such as *Radamisto, Alcina, Rodelinda* and *Julius Caesar*, all nowadays likely to be seen on stage, and virtually all exciting experiences for a musical theatre-goer, though they are pre-eminently Baroque *opera seria* in style. However perverse the conventions of *opera seria* must seem to be for those who look for drama in a theatre piece, Handel's operas still hold an audience, even without the singers he and his audiences took for granted. He had learned in Italy how to write real, beautiful melody; fluent, emotional and adjusted precisely to suit the voice of one particular singer with particular vocal strengths and weaknesses—we try today to recapture the original impact of the piece, inevitably in vain.

Facing page: ***Cimarosa*** *in 1785. At his death, on the way to St Petersburg, there were rumours that he had been poisoned.*

1680-1780 Opera: the Play's the Thing

As further witness of the strict conventions that composers were expected to follow in *opera seria*, Goldoni recounts in his delightful memoirs the instructions given to him in all seriousness by the director of an Italian opera company:

"The three principal personages of the drama should sing five airs each; two in the first act, two in the second, and one in the third. The second actress and the second soprano can only have three, and the inferior characters must be satisfied with a single air each, or two at the most. The author of the words must furnish the musician with the different shades which form the *chiaroscuro* of the music, and take care that two pathetic airs do not succeed one another ... He must, above all things, avoid giving impassioned airs, bravura airs, or rondeaus, to inferior characters; these poor devils must be satisfied with what they can get, and every opportunity of distinguishing themselves is denied them."

Macheath and Lucy, from a 1786 production of Gay's **The Beggar's Opera**, *"performed at The Little Theatre with great applause".*

While Handel lived and worked in England he was, to some extent, deliberately independent of opera in Italy, rather like Sebastian Bach was in Leipzig. Handel knew about the greater simplicity of Italian music, the triumph of Rococo over Baroque, but he geared his work to his London audience, and hardly concerned himself with musical fashion across the Channel. His operas are a particular blend of Baroque and *galant*. He wrote French overtures, slow-quick-slow, not the new Italian operatic overture, fast-slow-fast, that Alessandro Scarlatti espoused and made standard. Handel's blend is entirely his own.

A Change of Taste

Eventually fashion overturned him. Handel's operas were thought old-fashioned and staid compared with the modern Italian comic product. He was given the warning light by *The Beggar's Opera* (1728), the text by John Gay (1685–1732), the music anthologized by Gay's music director, Pepusch (1667–1752), from well-known tunes by Handel and others. Gay, a genial poet and playwright with a talent for satire, got the idea for *The Beggar's Opera* from his friend Jonathan Swift, who had mentioned to him that "A Newgate pastoral might make an odd pretty sort of thing". It was staged by the actor-manager John Rich (who introduced pantomime to England) and succeeded beyond their wildest dreams, making, it was said, "Gay rich, and Rich gay". A sequel, entitled *Polly*, immediately became a best-seller, though its scurrilous allusions banned it from the London stage. In general, ballad-opera, set among London's criminal classes and full of satirical jibes about corruption in high places, suited English taste better than Handel's heroic operas. The actor, composer and playwright Charles Dibdin (1745–1814) enjoyed particular success with the medium. Though now he is remembered solely for his song *Tom Bowling*, written when his brother was drowned while serving at sea, operas he wrote such as *The Waterman* (1774) enjoyed an immense vogue in the late eighteenth century.

The Birth of Oratorio

Handel persevered with Italian opera in London until 1741. His last two operas were unsuccessful: London taste remained as frivolous as in Purcell's time. But Handel had already found a more popular substitute—sacred opera in English. The Church would not allow Bible stories to be acted in

Purcell p 72

Julius Cæsar:
AN
OPERA.
Compos'd by
G. Frederick Handel,
of London, Gent.

LONDON,
Printed at Cluer's Printing-Office in Bow-Church-Yard,
and sold there, and by B. Creake at ye Bible in Jermyn street, St.
James's.

*The title-page of **Handel's Julius Caesar**. Dainty continuo players perform for some listening angels in the clouds above.*

Handel's autograph *of the bass part for the chorus "And the Glory of the Lord" from* Messiah.

the theatre, so Handel produced his *Esther* (1732) "after the manner of an oratorio", in concert performance. During the next decade he alternated between Italian opera and English oratorio, which was performed sometimes in the theatre, sometimes in concert halls (only exceptionally in a church, since orchestras were thought too worldly for a sacred building).

Handel's most famous oratorio is *Messiah* (1741), a grand and inspiring anthology of passages from the Old and New Testaments relating to Christ before, during and after His life on earth. When King George II attended a performance in London, the power of the chorus "Hallelujah!" forced him to rise to his feet: the rest of the audience followed his lead, and the practice has continued until now. Haydn, on a visit to London, was similarly overwhelmed: "Methought the heavens did open" was his comment, and he was, from that moment on, inspired to compose oratorios of his own along Handelian lines—*The Creation* and *The Seasons*.

But *Messiah* is untypical of Handel's oratorios. Like *Israel in Egypt* (1739) it is non-dramatic by intention, though the music is marvellously vivid. Like *Theodora* (1750), it is about Christianity. Handel's other oratorios are on Old Testament stories, such as *Saul* (also 1739), *Samson* (1743) or *Jephtha* (1752). Their English texts are laid out as for a play, with

Haydn's oratorios p 141, 143

stage directions, and characters each portrayed by a different singer: the chorus represents crowds, or sometimes posterity, and Handel's music is perfectly operatic in manner. In modern times they have been performed in the theatre as operas, in costume and with stage production and have proved at least as effective as any of Handel's true operas. Indeed, for those who cannot accept the conventions of *opera seria*, his oratorios are the more effective because their dramatic style is a natural one. The judgment of Solomon between two women claiming the same child, or the scene where David tries to cure Saul's madness by playing to him on the harp, or the double chorus of Israelites and Babylonians deriding one another in *Belshazzar*, all cry out for stage presentation. Handel's genius certainly flowered in a drama that permitted duets and trios and choruses, and in which human character was realistically portrayed. His Biblical heroes were sung by tenors and basses, not *castrati*; his choral sopranos and altos were choirboys and lay clerks—female choristers did not appear until after his death.

Keyboard Music and Music for State Occasions

In between the acts of his oratorios, Handel was accustomed to play an organ concerto: he left sixteen of them, works as original as Sebastian Bach's harpsichord concertos of much the same time, though unfortunately only sketched out in many places. Handel, we know, possessed an especial genius for improvisation: the solo part of these brilliant works, designed for the composer himself in performance, necessitated only a rough idea on paper of what he would play on these occasions. Handel also published oboe concertos and two sets of grand concertos (English *concerti grossi*), one with the conventional *concertino* of two violins and cello, the other with mixed woodwind and string soloists, rather as in Bach's Brandenburgs but less adventurous in their instrumentation.

*Handel wrote the music for the **Fireworks in Green Park**, on 27 April 1749, in celebration of the Peace of Aix la Chapelle.*

J.S. Bach's Brandenburg Concertos p 95–6

Handel's prowess as a keyboard player is also shown in his suites for harpsichord solo, particularly in the first set of eight suites, published by the composer in London in 1720: "because Surrepticious and incorrect copies of them had got abroad. I have added several new ones to make the Work more usefull which if it meets with a favourable reception: I will Still proceed to publish more reckoning it my duty with my Small talent to Serve a Nation from which I have received so Generous a protection." The Seventh Suite (in G minor) begins with a magnificent French Overture and concludes with a Passacaglia of mighty proportions, while the Fifth Suite of the collection contains the well-known variations which are called *The*

Concerto Grosso

*The concerto grosso form was the creation of the Baroque period. It was a composition for string orchestra, where a small body of instrumentalists was set in alternation and in combination with a larger group. The smaller section (*concertino*) usually consisted of two violins and cello; while the larger,* ripieno, *section stated the themes in an opening* ritornello, *which functioned as a point of departure (and return) for the soloists.*

Exceptions to this set of rules are innumerable. Wind instruments such as oboes make not infrequent appearances in concerti grossi, while perhaps the most famous set, Bach's six Brandenburg concertos, explore the possibilities offered by a different line-up of instruments for each concerto. The most constant rule for the concerto grosso form is its pattern of three movements, fast-slow-fast, which was predominantly adhered to and became the preferred structure as well for the later Classical solo concerto.

*From being a provincial church organist, **Charles Burney** went on to become one of the most eminent men of letters of his day. His biography was written by his novelist daughter, Fanny.*

Harmonious Blacksmith, because Handel was said to have heard the tune whistled from inside a forge he was passing.

Although he did not hold the official post of Master of the King's Music, Handel was well-favoured by the English monarchs, salaried by them, and asked to compose music for state occasions such as the coronation of George II (1727), to which he contributed the anthem *Zadok the Priest* (performed ever since at coronation services). For the Treaty of Aix-la-Chapelle (1749), which ended the War of the Austrian Succession, he provided music specially for a grand and jubilant fireworks display given in London's Green Park which is still often played at concerts as *Music for the Royal Fireworks*. Handel was the first composer in history whose music remained popular and much performed after his death. His memory dominated British musical life throughout the fiercely patriotic, empire-building period of the nineteenth century.

Handel never married. Beyond the fact that he made a wealthy living from his music, enabling him to live in the heart of Mayfair, disappointingly little is known about his private life. Portraits show him as a large man, and he was reputed to be extremely fond of food and drink as well as being physically very strong. He seems to have lived a quiet and devout life, deriving much enjoyment from his collection of pictures, among which he numbered works by Rembrandt.

Handel's Successors

Handel left two major apostles in London. Thomas Arne (1710–1778) wrote an Italian opera, another *Artaxerxes* (1762), with an English text that he himself translated from Metastasio's original; and two ballad-operas (which the English preferred to opera), *Thomas and Sally* (c. 1760) and *Love in a Village* (1760), which are still sometimes performed. His masque *Alfred the Great* (1738) gave England her unofficial second national anthem, *Rule, Britannia*. His settings of songs in Shakespeare's plays, such as *Where the bee sucks* or *Come away, Death*, remain the standard ones. His finest masque is based on Milton's *Comus*. The Master of the King's Music during Handel's last years was William Boyce (1710–1779), whose eight tuneful and attractive symphonies of 1750 (really theatre overtures) and concertos closely reflect Handel's manner.

Another interesting composer of the period, Maurice Greene (1695–1755), was a friend of Handel—until the latter discovered Greene's friendship with an operatic rival of his in London, Bononcini. Greene worked for some years as organist of St Paul's Cathedral. Above all, he was a church musician, and published a famous collection of choral music, *Forty Select Anthems* (1743), which includes the lovely setting of *Lord, let me know mine end*. A more important musical figure was Charles Burney (1726–1814), whose *General History of Music* is an important source book for the eighteenth century in particular. Burney travelled all over Europe collecting material and interviewing musicians (and wrote in addition delightful and perceptive accounts of his journeys). Among his friends were numbered Dr Johnson, King George III, Gluck and Haydn. Musical scholarship continues to owe an immense debt of gratitude to the tireless researches of Dr Burney.

The Sons of Bach

In 1762 another German composer trained in Italy, settled in London—J.S. Bach's son Johann Christian (1735–1782): his place is in the next chapter, which deals with the rise of orchestral music, though he tried, as unsuccessfully as Handel, to interest London in his Italian operas.

Wilhelm Friedemann (1710–1784), Sebastian's eldest son, was considered by his siblings to be the most talented of the composer's many children. He must have been a precocious performer while still a child, to judge by the difficulty of a book of pieces written for his instruction by his father. But much of his life was wasted. He became disappointed at the lack of success that he and his compositions found throughout Germany, though his powers of improvisation won him respect. He was eventually reduced to selling pieces he wrote, claiming they had been composed by his father. What remains of his music—a few symphonies, keyboard pieces and sacred vocal works—has failed to enjoy an enduring popularity with audiences, and failed in his lifetime too, despite the admiration of his successful brother, Philipp Emanuel.

The most interesting composer among Bach's sons was surely Carl Philipp Emanuel (1714–1788), the leading keyboard-player and teacher of his time, who spent nearly thirty years as harpsichordist to Frederick the Great. He produced a great quantity of keyboard music for that instrument, as well as for the clavichord (which he loved best, as his father did, for the expression of quiet inward emotions). Eventually he composed for the emerging pianoforte and wrote the authoritative *Essay on the True Art of*

Thomas Arne *seems to have had a truculent disposition. While working at Drury Lane Theatre with the affable William Boyce, it was reported that the two were seen to be "much in each other's way".*

J.C. Bach p 129–131

Keyboard-playing (1753), a treatise that goes beyond keyboard technique to discuss ornamentation and extemporization.

Eventually C.P.E. Bach left the Prussian court to become music director to the city of Hamburg, in succession to his godfather, Telemann, a post similar to his father's in Leipzig. It involved him in composing Lutheran church music in German including a thrilling *Resurrection* oratorio, though his Latin *Magnificat* is as fine as his father's. Emanuel Bach's keyboard music had a vital effect on the development of sonata-form. It includes twelve brilliant harpsichord concertos and many more sonatas, often "with varied repeats", so that the theme never reappears twice in the same guise. Both Haydn and Beethoven profited from study of C.P.E. Bach's keyboard music and his espousal of the Frenchified "sentimental style" (*Empfindsamer Stil*), which involved very bold harmony and lightning changes of mood. "A musician cannot move others unless he too is moved," he said. Charles Burney visited him at home, and gave a compelling description of Philipp Emanuel's playing:

"After dinner, which was elegantly served and cheerfully eaten, I prevailed upon him to sit down to a clavichord and he played with little intermission till near eleven o'clock at night. During that time he grew so animated and possessed that he not only played but looked like one inspired. His eyes were fixed, his underlip fell, and drops of effervescence distilled from his countenance."

*An engraving after a portrait of **Carl Philipp Emanuel Bach**.*

Emanuel Bach took his responsibility as warden of his father's library and posthumous reputation seriously. The nineteenth-century Bach revival could not have taken place without Emanuel's constant propagation of Sebastian's music.

Emanuel was a keen student of literature: his friends were more often writers than musicians—Lessing, Klopstock, Claudius, major German authors of their day, were among them, and they often discussed the relationship of poetry and music. It was the topic of the day, nowhere more so than in France, where yet another national solution to the thorny problem of music-drama had been found. When Christian Bach arrived in Paris to produce his last opera, *Amadis des Gaules* (1779), an Italian opera of his own style with a French text, it flopped. It was not to the French taste, which had become accustomed to a much closer alliance between text and music, spectacle and sound.

French Opera from Lully to Gluck

Lully's invention of the *comédie-ballet*, in collaboration with Molière as author, has been previously mentioned—it was a way to introduce the new form of opera into France—a country which always loved the theatre and music, and which has always regarded common-sense and logic above every other virtue. The aim in opera for France, as for Italy in Count Bardi's day, was to resurrect the classical Greek drama of the fifth century BC. Monteverdi had proposed one solution. Lully saw that the dance and choral elements, so important to French taste, were vanishing in Italian opera in favour of star vocalists and their arias, and that Greek dialogue, viz. Italian recitative, was being continually reduced to accommodate longer arias. In 1673 Lully produced his first *tragédie en musique*, *Cadmus et Hermione*. The text was most scrupulously set at length, the recitative all orchestrally

The Opera Audience

It was not until the present century that auditorium lights were extinguished in the opera-house during performances. Until shortly before the First World War, audiences could follow the foreign text from a printed libretto with translation into the vernacular. Before that, the attraction was to sit in a box, gamble at cards, eat, gossip and ogle the rest of the audience while the recitatives were going on. Attention was only drawn when a favourite aria began or a favourite singer entered. This painting by Panini depicts the sociable goings-on during a concert given in honour of the birth of the Dauphin.

Opera seria *was not audience-involving: it set a scene and an atmosphere in which an audience might be attracted to attend for a while and leave their other diversions. The superstars in the cast behaved just as nonchalantly: the composer Benedetto Marcello satirized the situation in* The Fashionable Theatre *(1720):*

"All the while the ritornello of his air is being played the singer should walk about the stage, take snuff, complain to his friends that he is in bad voice, that he has a cold, etc, and while singing his aria he shall take care to remember that at the cadence he may pause as long as he pleases, and make runs, decorations, and ornaments according to his fancy; during which time the leader of the orchestra shall leave his place at the harpsichord, take a pinch of snuff, and wait until it shall please the singer to finish. The latter shall take breath several times before finally coming to a close on a trill, which he will be sure to sing as rapidly as possible from the beginning, without preparing it by placing his voice properly, and all the time using the highest notes of which he is capable."

The fourteen-year-old **Louis XIV** *as "Le Roi Soleil" in Lully's* Ballet de la nuit.

accompanied and there was plenty of mechanical spectacle. The airs were short and free-formed, without vocal virtuosity: clarity and intellect were demanded of the singers, qualities not high on the Italian list of operatic priorities. And yet Lully's serious operas spend much time on entertainment inessential to the dramatic action—there is plenty of pomp and spectacle and homage to the King in chorus and dance. The orchestra, Lully's pride, was as large as eighty players.

Lully died in 1687 of blood poisoning, having pierced his foot with the stick he used to bang on the floor to mark the beat for his players, while he filled in missing harmony on the harpsichord with his left hand. French taste had become less solemn and formal, more *galant*, by the time his great sucessor, Jean-Philippe Rameau, produced his first opera in 1733. *Hippolyte et Aricie* deliberately followed Lully's model—"beautiful, simple nature". Recitative was now fused with aria, more than before, and the orchestral music was richer and more varied. Of his later operas, *Castor et Pollux* (1737), *Dardanus* (1739) and *Platée* (1745) are most likely to be heard today; even more admired is the opera-ballet *Les Indes galantes* (1735), revived by the Paris Opéra during the 1950s. The noble, sensitive and thoughtful art of Rameau in the opera-house well repays study.

As in Italy, the development of opera in France worked to the detriment of comedy which, in music, fended for itself in the cheap, plebeian *opéra comique*, which was essentially satirical and musically notable for its *vaudeville*, a song in several verses sung by different characters to the same simple tune. It was raised to respectability by Rameau and by the author-actor Charles-Simon Favart, who found a home for the French comic opera in Paris's Italian Theatre, later to be Rossini's last stamping-ground. Among the first great successes of *opéra comique* was *Le Dévin du village* ("The Village Soothsayer", 1752) by the musician-philosopher Jean-Jacques

Rameau p 88

Rousseau (1712–1778), who determined to compose an opera about people with dirty hands—the working class. Rousseau was the prophet of the Enlightenment which so altered European social thinking in the eighteenth century; the philosophy of common-sense and sociability; the herald, perhaps remotely, of the French Revolution.

French opera, idealistic but still dramatically affected in style, unnatural, was ripe for reform. As so often in music, it came from abroad. The instigator was Christoph Willibald Gluck (1714–1787), a Bohemian (now part of Czechoslovakia, but then part of the Holy Roman Empire based on Vienna).

As a youth he studied violin and cello, and became a pupil for four years with Giovanni Sammartini, Giuseppe's younger brother. In England he wrote two operas, though at that time London audiences still preferred the Handelian style. (Gluck, incidentally, conceived a great reverence in London for Handel, of whom he always kept a portrait in his bedroom.) Then he worked for a while in Germany, where he worked as an operatic conductor and married the daughter of a wealthy banker before his move to Paris. He returned to Vienna in 1780, and set about making Italian opera more simple, noble and natural: in Paris he had learned the right lessons from Rameau, including the one about *opéra comique*, which he applied in his own comic opera *La Rencontre imprévue* (elsewhere usually known as *The Pilgrims of Mecca*).

Like Vincenzo Galilei, Metastasio and Lully, Gluck regarded opera as an attempt to revivify ancient Greek drama and, like them, he found his own solution in collaboration with his Italian librettist, Raineri Calzabigi. Gluck first outlined his proposals for operatic reform in the preface to his opera *Alceste* (1769), though he had already worked with Calzabigi in *Orfeo* (1762), their most popular work. Their aim, like that of Lully and Rameau, was to get rid of Italian *opera seria* conventions, to restore dramatic characterization and, by careful setting, to make the linking dialogue more exciting than the dry recitative of the Italian product. *Orfeo* is still very

Madame de Pompadour in a court performance of Lully's Acis et Galatée *at Versailles in 1749.*

1680-1780 Opera: the Play's the Thing

Right: **Gluck** *was fortunate to achieve financial independence early in life, through marriage to a banker's daughter.*

Far Right: **Rousseau's** *opera* Le Dévin du village *(1752) was parodied by Mozart in his* Bastien & Bastienne, *though the former remained popular in Paris for more than fifty years after its composer's death.*

formal, but nowadays is the most famous Gluck opera, often performed (I suspect) because it includes the celebrated, extremely touching plaint of Orpheus for his dead wife: *Che faro senza Euridice* ("What shall I do without Euridice"). *Alceste* (1767) is grander—even more so when the Italian version was revised for Paris in 1777, with its drastically improved central air *Divinités du Styx* (the two versions can be fascinatingly compared on records). Still finer and more dramatic is *Iphigenia in Tauris* (1779), wholly French and wholly Classical in style, with dance, choruses, ensembles, solos, orchestra, great feeling and marvellous vocal music, all merged together without clear-cut breaks for detachable "highlights" as was then usual. Starry egotism and fireworks were banished, but not superb singing. At last Hamlet's words, "The play's the thing", could be applied to opera, though only to this noble, rather reverential sort of opera. The comic variety was quite soon to rival, and perhaps even to surmount it, in the last works of Mozart.

Chapter 7
The First Symphonies

Enter the Orchestra

The Symphony evolves at Mannheim ♦ J.C. Bach and the first
public concerts ♦ The amazing orchestra of Johann Stamitz ♦
Orchestras in Vienna, Dresden, Leipzig and Stuttgart ♦
Chamber music ♦ Esterhaza ♦ "Papa" Haydn:
the father of the symphony ♦

Orchestras had been playing since the masques and intermezzos which were
opera's predecessors. Bach had orchestras to accompany his major sacred
choral works, no more than two players to a part. Vivaldi had his
schoolgirls' orchestra in Venice, and Handel the strings and wind orchestra
for the *Water Music* and *Fireworks Music*.

The balanced band of woodwind, brass and strings that we call the
symphony orchestra grew out of such beginnings and was more or less
standardized by 1750 with local variations. It developed with the orchestral
symphony—a new musical form with which eighteenth-century Europe was
much preoccupied. Symphonies developed side by side with music for the
string quartet—which was not only the basis of the symphony orchestra,
but also the provider of intimate drawing-room music composed for just four
string players. The key figure will be Joseph Haydn, who excelled in the
symphony and the string quartet. But he had important predecessors and
contemporaries, their music less famous, but likely nowadays to be played
in concerts or on records. People often use the terms *galant* and *Rococo* to
typify much of this music. But when Baroque musical style faded out, the
style that replaced it can more simply be described as Classical—the term
we use for the great masters of symphony and string quartet, Haydn,
Mozart and Beethoven a label which equally applies to their immediate
forerunners.

Sinfonia: Overture to an Opera

Symphony comes from a Greek word that means "consonance"—sounding
together, whether done by players or singers (Schütz's sacred symphonies
were for choirs and groups of instruments). For J.S. Bach and Handel it
meant the introduction to a larger piece of music, as small as an air or as
large as an opera. The first orchestral symphonies were just that: operatic
overtures, either French (slow-quick-slow), or Italian (quick-slow-quick). In

Schütz p 80–3

due course, Vivaldi and his contemporaries extracted their opera overtures for use in orchestral concerts. Some of Vivaldi's overtures, or symphonies, exist which are not identified with any of his operas—they may have been composed purely for a concert, though many of his operas are lost. His younger colleague from Milan, Giovanni Battista Sammartini (c. 1700–1775), who began life as an oboist, composed seventy-seven symphonies, very few derived from operatic overtures; the earliest are like trio sonatas, only three parts written out. From 1732 he sometimes included a minuet as finale, and throughout he recognizably worked to contrast themes and invent the sort that could be set off against one another and provoke musical argument—the essence of a symphony. Simple as these pieces are, they sound like real symphonies rather than sonatas, concertos or any other form. Sammartini's symphonies were often played around Europe, including Salzburg, where they made an impression on young Mozart. Gluck was Sammartini's pupil. He was also much admired and studied by J.C. Bach, Boccherini and Haydn, all important to this episode of *Music in Time*.

Keys and Forms made the Symphony

All Classical music of the eighteenth century is inspired and balanced by the diatonic system of key relationships which had only recently become recognized as the natural ambit of music. For J.S. Bach and Corelli, Handel and Vivaldi, a piece of music was grounded in one key: it may move elsewhere, but must eventually return to the key which is its home.

Early in the eighteenth century, composers of sonatas and concertos recognized that an extended piece of music needed a stronger polarity. The science of acoustic resonance, backed up by human experience, showed that the natural antithesis of the home-key, the "tonic", was five steps up or four steps down—called the "dominant". For best satisfaction, a longish piece of music should move from tonic to dominant, bring out a new, contrasted tune, and a further clinching group; then explore other keys, perhaps other aspects of the given ideas, before returning to the home-key, there to restate the original ideas, which had won new significance from being argued in the "development" section. That was sonata form: variety of character and variety of key, imbroglio, then new perception. It was also the essence of the orchestral symphony. Early sonata movements clung to the binary form accepted by Domenico Scarlatti and his disciples. The music there moved from tonic to dominant, then after a full-stop reversed the process with some rethinking so that the home-key remained stable by the end. The variety possible within sonata form kept composers busy on the symphony until the Romantic nineteenth century gave them new possibilities of content for the recently settled form.

The story of the arrival of the symphony is also the story of orchestras in musical centres: how big and expert an orchestra, where, and directed by whom. In Berlin in 1754, Frederick the Great had quite a large orchestra with twelve violins, four flutes, three oboes, and four bassoons, two horns, lute, viola da gamba and two harpsichords—an orchestra made for Baroque music, not for modern symphonies. And Frederick, with all his *galant* French taste, was a musical reactionary who hated modern music—even the new ideas of Carl Philipp Emanuel Bach, who did not show his worth as a symphonist until after 1768, when he moved from Berlin to Hamburg and could publish his *Symphonies with twelve obbligato voices*, meaning twelve different instrumental lines. They are scored for two flutes, two

Sonata p 90
D. Scarlatti p 91–2

oboes, bassoon, two horns and the normal strings: two violins, viola, cello and double bass. The music is fiery—a mixture of French, Italian and German styles, thus rather slow-moving but tender in sentiment and still given to old-fashioned counterpoint, his father's bequest.

In London his brother Johann Christian's symphonies could call on clarinets and trumpets and drums too. Some are for two orchestras alternately. They are much less German in tone of voice; more Italian with some French grace, their influence on Mozart quite apparent. When J.C. Bach died, Mozart borrowed a melody from one of his symphonies in a piano concerto, K414 in A—a touching quotation, though Christian had borrowed the tune from his brother Emanuel in the first place. In London J.C. Bach gave the first ever solo public performance on a fortepiano, the hammer-action keyboard instrument which displaced the harpsichord and became our pianoforte. J.C. Bach also presented subscription concerts in partnership with his compatriot C.F. Abel. Abel (1723–1787) may have been a pupil in Leipzig of J.S. Bach. He settled in London around 1760, as a gamba player, and lived together with his friend and co-promoter, J.C. Bach. Their concerts, first in Soho Square, and later moved to the Hanover Square Rooms, were immensely successful and saw the first London performances of several of Haydn's symphonies. Mozart heard their symphonies on his first visit to London, aged eight, and imitated them in his own first symphonies, written for a smaller orchestra of oboes, horns and strings. (One of these, attributed to Mozart, is not his but Abel's, copied out by young

Tonality

The major scale is a sequence of seven notes. The scale of C major is easiest to think of, for it uses no black notes. Of the twelve possible notes that make up the chromatic scale, five are therefore omitted (in the case of C major, the "sharps and flats" are left out to produce the melody that the ear recognizes as the major scale). All the other scales need various black notes to produce a similar-sounding sequence containing the same five gaps in corresponding places.

The first note of the scale (known as the "keynote" or "tonic") is harmonically closely related to the fifth note ("dominant") and fourth note ("subdominant"). In the key of C, these would respectively be G and F. If a composer wishes to write a piece of any length, he will at some point have to change key (modulate) to avoid monotony, and it is to the dominant that his first departure usually takes him. Beyond that, there are many other keys available for visiting before he returns home (depending on the length of the piece of music), some of which may be in the minor.

The minor scale is merely a different pattern of seven notes and, like the major, can exist in any of the twelve possible keys. The scheme of modulations has a different order of priorities, however; the main alternative to the home key being the major key of the third note of the scale. This is not nearly as complicated as it sounds: in the case of A minor, for example, which has no black notes, the third degree of the scale is the note C. C major is, of course, a close relative of A minor for it also has no sharps or flats. Hence the third note of the minor scale is the keynote of its "relative major".

Such a scheme of modulations was the backbone of all music of the Baroque and Classical periods: it is only in the mid-nineteenth century that such a reliable, flexible and satisfying construction began to be supplanted by key relationships of a less predictable and more impressionistic character.

Mozart in London p 149

Mozart so as to learn from it.) J.C. Bach's skilful interweaving of orchestra and solo in his concertos came as a revelation to the young Mozart, who also imitated his fondness for the trotting, broken chord bass in keyboard figurations. He even arranged three of J.C. Bach's sonatas as piano concertos. Sebastian Bach was dead, his music virtually forgotten: but his influence was carried over to his successors—to Haydn through Emanuel Bach, to Mozart through Christian (and eventually in Vienna they were both able to study Sebastian's own music).

The best known English symphonies of this period are those of William Boyce. They are theatrical overtures of the old Baroque kind with courtly dance movements—unoriginal but perfectly irresistible. In France, the spectre of old Lully haunted composers, and the symphony only inspired François Joseph Gossec (1734–1829).

The son of a Belgian peasant, Gossec had taught himself to play on a home-made violin while tending cattle. As soon as he was old enough to leave home he made his way to Paris and, after studies with Rameau, found work as a conductor and principal violinist in a rich taxman's private orchestra. His thirty symphonies are serious and skilled and in three movements only, as French taste preferred. Gossec includes clarinets among his woodwind as Mozart would do in his *Paris Symphony*.

Stamitz and the Mannheim Orchestra
During the third quarter of the eighteenth century, the court of the Elector Palatine in Mannheim was considered supreme for orchestral performance

*A view across the Rhine to the beautiful city of **Mannheim**, painted in 1812.*

Facing page: ***Johann Christian Bach***. *His keyboard works were such "as ladies can execute with little trouble", wrote Dr Burney. Bach was the great master of the galant style, and himself a keyboard virtuoso, though he wrote music for others more often than for himself.*

Rameau p 88, 124

and for its cultivation of the symphony. It owed this reputation partly to the number of musicians from Bohemia (part of modern Czechoslovakia) who had been on the court's musical strength since 1718 or so; partly to the Bohemian violin virtuoso Johann Stamitz (1717–1757). Stamitz's family seems to have been composed almost entirely of musicians, and Johann spent years practising the violin until his amazing skill performing at the coronation of the Hapsburg Emperor Charles VII was noticed by the new Elector of Mannheim, Carl Theodor. At the age of only twenty-four, Stamitz was brought back to direct the orchestra of the Mannheim court. He soon transformed it. As the ubiquitous Dr Burney noted on a visit there:

"I found the Mannheim Orchestra to be indeed all that its fame had made me expect: power will naturally arise from a great number of hands; but the judicious use of this power, on all occasions, must be the consequence of good discipline, indeed there are more solo players and composers in this than perhaps in any other orchestra in Europe; it is an army of generals, equally fit to plan a battle as to fight it."

Stamitz's employer, Carl Theodor, was an eager patron of the arts, a proficient, versatile musician himself, who liked nothing better than to take his orchestra to his country palace at Schwetzingen and play chamber music with them.

Under Carl Theodor, Stamitz built up the Mannheim orchestra to a strength of four flutes, two oboes, two bassoons, ten first and ten second violins, four violas, four cellos and two double basses. He could count on four horns from the Elector's huntsmen, twelve trumpeters and two drummers from his military force (the Elector, like every self-respecting ruler, could not sit down to dinner without a fanfare of trumpets, and of course some "table-music" while he ate). Stamitz made his orchestra famous for its perfect unanimity in rapid rising scales, for its controlled slow *crescendo* from soft to loud, and *decrescendo* from a thunderclap to a whisper, and again for sudden alternations of *piano* and *forte*, or the "Mannheim Sigh", a poignantly modulated lean from one note to its neighbour. Since many members of the orchestra were virtuoso instrumentalists and composers too, they wrote music to display the orchestra's special accomplishments; other composers visiting Mannheim went home and used those effects in their own music. Johann Stamitz wrote almost seventy such symphonies, as well as "orchestral trios" which could be played as trio sonatas or by full orchestra. In 1754 the Elector sent him to Paris for a year and there Stamitz discovered clarinets: he composed the first clarinet concerto as well as concertos for harpsichord, violin and other instruments. His late symphonies include clarinets, which joined the Mannheim orchestra soon afterwards. Stamitz's contemporaries at Mannheim included the older, less go-ahead, Franz-Xavier Richter (1709–1789), Christian Cannabich (1731–1798), who succeeded Stamitz and even improved the orchestra's finesse, and Stamitz's son Carl (1745–1801), a prolific composer of symphonies, concertos and the favourite Parisian hybrid the *concertante symphony*, an enlarged *concerto grosso* with two or more soloists (the best known examples today are two by Mozart and one by Haydn). Carl Stamitz left Mannheim quite young to travel Europe as a violin and viola virtuoso. Mozart visited Mannheim when Cannabich was in charge, and though he pronounced the orchestra "excellent and very strong", what impressed him most there was

Carl Ditters von Dittersdorf. *In addition to his copious musical output, Dittersdorf was the author of a lively autobiography.*

the clarinet playing, which was to prove the start of a long relationship between the composer and the melancholy sound of the clarinet. (Another relationship from Mozart's stay at Mannheim was with Aloysia Weber, with whom Mozart had fallen in love, and whose younger sister Constanze he was eventually to marry.)

The Mannheim symphonists experimented boldly in all directions—though their sonata structures sound unsophisticated beside those of Haydn and late Mozart. Their real importance in musical history is the influence of Carl Theodor's orchestra on performance standards elsewhere, at first from Mannheim, later from Munich, where he removed his musical establishment when he became Elector of Bavaria. Mannheim has nevertheless remained an important musical centre in Germany, if no longer at such an international level of importance.

There were important orchestras at Dresden and Leipzig and Stuttgart, and of course in Vienna, seat of the Holy Roman Empire. At Dresden, Hasse was in charge; at Leipzig, J.A. Hiller; in Stuttgart it was Niccolo Jommelli (claimed as the inventor of the Mannheim crescendo). Jommelli (1714–1774) was a close friend of the poet Metastasio and an opera composer of

Sonata form p 141

1730–1800 Enter the Orchestra

distinction. He worked in Germany for many years, writing church music as well as operas. But when he returned to his native Naples, it was to find his work considered lacklustre and out of date. Jommelli never recovered from this disappointment, though posterity has been kinder to his undoubted gifts as a melodist.

In Vienna Florian Gassmann was the least insignificant of several musical directors. The Viennese composers of symphonies included Karl Ditters von Dittersdorf (1739–1799), who also composed operas and string quartets. As a young man, Ditters travelled in Italy together with Gluck. His skill on the violin later brought him to the attention of the Bishop of Breslau, who appointed him music director and eventually ennobled him:

*A silhouette of a **string quartet** circa 1750. Note only the cellist is seated.*

*"Morning Employments".
An English engraving in the style of Sir Joshua Reynolds.*

henceforth Ditters became Ditters von Dittersdorf. He wrote more than one hundred and thirty symphonies, including a set contrasting the taste of five nations, and one reflecting the *Metamorphoses* of Ovid. Johann Vanhall (1739–1813), another Bohemian composer who settled in Vienna, composed some one hundred symphonies and a like number of string quartets. When Haydn visited Vienna during the 1780s he dearly loved playing string quartets as first violin, with Dittersdorf as second violin, Mozart on viola and Vanhall as cellist. They must have made the most distinguished string quartet in musical history.

String Quartets

Music in the home might be for keyboard, or keyboard with another solo instrument such as the violin (the duo sonata), or, now less frequently, the trio sonata. The keyboard filling-out of the continuo became increasingly redundant as composers learned to write out harmony complete. While orchestral music developed, the dedicated string players clung to their domestic, one-to-a-part music, without the support of a keyboard instrument—the musical equivalent of bareback horse-riding or nude swimming.

VIEW OF MADRID FROM THE TOLEDO ROAD.

Published by Nuttall Fisher & Cᵒ Novᵣ 1.1814.

Alessandro Scarlatti (*c*. 1720) was the first to write music for these four players without the usual extra keyboard player. Galuppi wrote some in 1740, Sammartini some more, Baroque in form but melodious. Real string quartets, though simple in structure, came out of Mannheim with its superlative string players. The first violin was the leader, with the most elaborate music; especially in the cantabile slow movement. Somewhere a fugue would give prominence to other instruments as well, but the violin-orientated Mannheim quartets belonged to the species later designated as "brilliant quartets", meaning violin concertos for just four players. The essence of a good string quartet is that no one player should appear more prominent than any other, but it took time for virtuoso violinists to learn that. In some centres where a flautist (like Frederick the Great) was in charge, the violin had to share the limelight with a flute; London also cultivated this propensity, if only because the instrument was generally popular there.

The first composer to play string quartets in public was Luigi Boccherini (1743–1805), who was born in Lucca, a most musical city, where he learned his instrument, the cello. He then travelled to Spain, where he

*A view of **Madrid** from the road to Toledo, dated 1814.*

A. Scarlatti p 102–3

spent the rest of his life, writing quintets with two prominent cellos (he played one of them), as well as string quartets and concertos, largely for his own instrument. The sheer number of his compositions is astonishing. Though there are more than twenty-five symphonies, there exist one hundred and two string quartets, sixty trios and one hundred and fifty-five quintets for various groups: Boccherini's heart was in chamber music, as witness his *Aviary Quintet*, which mimics birdsong, or the quintet *Street Music at Night in Madrid*, a work so particular in appeal that Boccherini did not want it published outside Spain. His music is extraordinarily forward-looking: there are a few Spanish effects such as we enjoy in Domenico Scarlatti; but in Boccherini's music the harmony brings constant surprises, jarring discords or tonal dislocations, emotionally stirring and very un-Classical. This is something more disturbing than Emanuel Bach's *Empfindsamer Stil*, not a gentle stroke but a blow. Boccherini was trying to break away from his Classical style, and surprises of that kind, very frequent in his music, make one think of Schubert or even Mendelssohn. Boccherini composed a quantity of the best Italian eighteenth-century music. He was the heir to a great style; that of Corelli and Vivaldi. Through the interest of Prince Friedrich Wilhelm of Prussia, a keen cellist, he was in touch with musical developments elsewhere. His musical vision, nevertheless, must have been extraordinary: only Haydn and Mozart, apart from him, could write music in the eighteenth century that belongs, by its sound, to the nineteenth century. The strength of his music is its mixture of Italian ease with the complexity which we associate with German composers. The critic who dubbed Boccherini "Haydn's wife" probably meant that Boccherini had the qualities of invention and the questing, exploring spirit which also typify Haydn's music. It is charming as well, but entirely masculine. The real Haydn's wife was a shrew, a quality that Boccherini's beautiful music never suggests.

Viennese Classicism—Haydn

Vienna, the seat of the Holy Roman Empire, had all the power but not much music to speak of. The age of the classical orchestral symphony had its climax in the work of composers who are usually represented as the Viennese Classics: Haydn, Mozart and Beethoven—Schubert perhaps appended. Only Schubert was actually Viennese.

Franz Joseph Haydn came from a part of lower Austria, Rohrau, where Hungary, Moravia, Slovakia and Croatia all met, each with its own national variations of popular culture, including music. Haydn retained an interest in folksong and used tunes in his own music from the countries amid which he was born. They give a piquancy to his music whenever he uses one. At the age of eight he was packed off to Vienna as a choirboy, from which he acquired a fine, complete education. He is known to have remained after his voice broke—so the story of his expulsion for snipping off another boy's pigtail during church can be discounted. Another story that Haydn liked to tell in later years was how, as a boy, when it was explained to him by his teacher that he could have his lovely soprano voice preserved for ever, Haydn was keen to have the "small operation" that would effect this miracle. He was only prevented on the very day it was to take place, when his father came to hear of it. He continued to sing as a lay clerk in St Stephen's Cathedral, Vienna, earning extra as an assistant organist and as principal violin in orchestras. His parents wanted him to become a priest,

Luigi Boccherini. *Note the manner in which the composer supports the cello, the spike being not yet in general use.*

financially a secure job, but Joseph was intent on a musical career. He took lodgings in a house where one of his neighbours was Metastasio, who found Haydn work as keyboard accompanist to singers—notably for the composer and singing teacher Niccolo Porpora (1686–1768), who had been Handel's rival in operatic London. Porpora used Haydn as his manservant and taught him composition: he also brought Haydn out into Viennese musical society as harpsichordist. Another neighbour was the Hungarian dowager Princess Esterhazy, whose son, Prince Paul Anton Esterhazy, was so taken by a hearing of an early symphony by Haydn that he promptly engaged him in 1761 as *Vice-Kapellmeister* (assistant musical director) under an aged and ailing musician whom the Prince did not want to pension off. In practice Haydn had full musical responsibility at the Esterhazy court, which was situated first at Eisenstadt, outside Vienna, and later at Esterhaza in Hungarian Galanta, a new, grand palace built by Prince Nicholas Esterhazy, who succeeded his brother in 1762 and was even more devoted to music.

Haydn remained in the service of Prince Nicholas until his master's death in 1790. His life was quite lonely. His relationship with the Prince was strictly formal; his contract required him to keep at a distance from his musicians so as to maintain their professional respect. His wife was no comfort to him (he had, self-admittedly, romances of a clandestine nature with other ladies, being a warm-blooded central European). And in Ester-haza he was far removed from contact with musicians elsewhere. As he

Haydn's orchestra at Esterhaza during an opera performance there. The continuo group, with the composer at the keyboard, is on the left.

Facing page: Portrait of *Joseph Haydn by the English artist Thomas Hardy, painted during his first visit to London in 1791–1792.*

*The Esterhazy family was the richest in all Hungary. Their palace of **Esterhaza**, where Haydn worked, boasted a theatre with a capacity of 400.*

Eysenstatt.

***Prince Paul Anton Esterhazy** (1786–1866). The family kept its connections with music beyond the age of Haydn: Hummel spent some years in their employ, and Liszt was brought up on the estate.*

***Prince Nicholas Esterhazy** (1714–1790), with whom Haydn enjoyed a happy and privileged relationship for thirty years.*

himself later recalled: "I could, as orchestral director, experiment, remark what made an impression, and what weakened it, so improving, adding, cutting and taking risks. I was set apart from the world. There was nobody near me to confuse or frustrate me in my work and so I had to be original."

In 1766 Haydn's nominal superior died shortly after complaining, surely from motives of jealousy, about Haydn's indolence. Haydn promptly wrote out, and subsequently maintained, a catalogue of every work he had completed as proof of his industry. The categories were symphony, of which he composed more than one hundred and four; party music; works for his Prince's instrument, the baryton or lyre-organ (a sort of viol); concertos, operas and cantatas; and church music. The list omits his masterly string quartets and increasingly superb keyboard sonatas. He had to provide music for concerts twice weekly, for accompaniment to meals, for operatic evenings (he produced, edited and rearranged operas by other composers, as well as writing many new ones of his own) and, after the death of his old boss, regular church music.

When the Esterhaza musical establishment was disbanded in 1790 after Prince Nicholas's death, Haydn retired to Vienna and more convivial contact with friends and fellow-musicians. He had been able to spend some time there in previous years, making friends with his mutually admiring colleague Wolfgang Mozart, and playing string quartets with him and others. Haydn's contribution to string quartet writing was seminal. Others before him, like Alessandro Scarlatti, had written music for two violins, viola, and cello, as a consort, and it took Haydn a while to recognize the serious and adventurous possibilities of what first seemed a form of intimate party music for home performance. Eventually he came to understand perfectly the separate and combined sonorities of violin, viola and cello, and his eighty-three quartets show a marvellous ripening of his approach to the form. The early works are divertimento- or serenade-like in quality: later come quartets that resemble miniature violin concertos, with a florid first violin part, the other three lines supplying the accompaniment. The twelve quartets that make up opus numbers 54, 55 and 64 were probably written for the virtuoso violinist Johann Tost, which may explain the predominance of the first violin role in them: the *Lark*, opus 64 number five, is a well-known case in point.

The late quartets show Haydn continuing to explore all the possibilities of the medium. Unusual harmonic relationships occur to miraculous effect: a marvellous example is in the D major work, opus 76 number five, which has a *largo* slow movement in the remote key of F sharp major. Goethe summed up Haydn's achievement in the quartet field when he remarked, "One listens to four intelligent people conversing with each other, one expects to gain from their discourse and to learn to know the peculiarities of the instruments."

Like Mozart, Haydn made the acquaintance in Vienna of Baron Gottfried van Swieten, who had met Emanuel Bach in Berlin and been fired to collect copies of Sebastian Bach's major works, which he had performed every Sunday morning in his house. Haydn's study of these works resulted in his late choral works, *The Creation* (1798) and *The Seasons* (1801), striking improvements on his earlier Viennese academic oratorio *The Return of Tobias* (1775).

Sonata Form

Classical sonata form was essential to the music of the Classical age: about four-fifths of all the music Beethoven wrote is in sonata form. The term is as applicable to symphonies and string quartets as to sonatas—a symphony is a sonata for orchestra. There are also solo sonatas for melody instruments, such as the violin unaccompanied.

There are four movements, the first being the most extended, with possibly a slow introduction. If it is in a major key, after the first theme the music will soon modulate to the dominant for a contrasting, usually more feminine, second theme. There will be a substantial development section discussing these and any other ideas before a return to the tonic for a restatement of the opening themes and a concluding coda.

The second movement is generally the slow one, and set in a contrasting key. It is often inclined to operatic, decorated cantabile *(a legacy of Corelli's violin concertos, so good that composers were unwilling to propose anything else). Very occasionally, in some of Haydn's string quartets for example, the second movement may change places with the third—a minuet. This merry dance in triple time was found to be ideal for leavening an experience that could all too easily become overpowering. Within the minuet there is a trio: a bucolic little dance-within-a-dance.*

The symphony (or sonata, quartet, etc) closed with a fast, dancing finale, marked Molto allegro *or* Presto. *Often it was in rondo form (with an intermittently recurring theme), or it might even be a theme and variations. The latter is more common in chamber and instrumental music than in a symphony. Sometimes it again approached sonata form.*

Most of Haydn's, Mozart's and Beethoven's music conforms approximately to this pattern. Yet it was not a restricting form, as their immense and marvellous output testifies: rather it had gradually evolved as the most useful and well-balanced mould that could contain the expression of their genius.

*The impresario **Salomon** painted in 1791 when he introduced the composer Haydn to English audiences.*

In 1791–1792 and 1794–1795, Haydn visited London at the invitation of the violinist and impresario Johann Peter Salomon, to compose and direct new symphonies. His music was especially popular there. Before leaving, he took a tender farewell of his dear friend Mozart, and hoped that he too would soon go to London. But before Haydn returned to Vienna, Mozart was dead. In between his visits to England, he gave composition lessons to Beethoven, newly arrived in Vienna, but their opposing temperaments ensured that these were not a success. He used his time in England to travel, take an honorary doctorate in music at Oxford University (his *Oxford Symphony*, which he performed on that occasion, was one of a set commissioned for a concert series in Paris), and make good new friends. A romantic attachment with a widowed lady in London inspired him to compose his *English Canzonets*, which include settings of Shakespeare (*She never told her*

Beethoven's lessons with Haydn p 160

love) as well as the excellent *Sailor's Song* and other poems from her own pen. The English national anthem fired Haydn to compose an Austrian hymn, *Gott erhalte Franz den Kaiser* ("God preserve the Emperor Francis"), still current. Haydn used it as a theme for variations in his C major *Emperor* quartet. He was a great favourite of the English royal family. King George III invited him to spend the summer of 1795 with them at Windsor and, though Haydn declined, he performed at Buckingham Palace and elsewhere more than thirty times. When he left to return to Vienna, he was overburdened with gifts that ranged from a talking parrot to manuscripts by Handel.

Haydn last appeared in public at a performance of *The Creation* in 1808, conducted by Salieri. But it was too much for him, and he had to be taken out. Before his death, Haydn asked to be carried to his piano, where he played his Austrian hymn. His body lies buried at Eisenstadt.

Haydn became known as the "father of the symphony" and "father of the string quartet"; indeed his younger colleagues, Beethoven for example, called him "Papa" to his face. We know now that the symphony and the string quartet were going concerns before Haydn became involved with them. More or less exiled in Esterhaza, committed to produce a new symphony very often for concerts twice a week, so imaginative and creative a musician could not help pushing the orchestral symphony in more directions than any other composer of the eighteenth century. His orchestra was quite small: eleven violins, led by him—probably six first and five second—two each of violas, cellos and basses, two oboes, two bassoons, two

Haydn (seated, foreground) at a performance of The Creation in Vienna, 1808. This painting is a copy of a lost original that was executed on a box-lid.

horns, sometimes a flute, and trumpets with drums. A harpsichordist was still necessary to hold the rhythm together. It was not a famous orchestra as the one in Mannheim was. His operatic establishment was famous and put on all the best new operas from other places as well as Haydn's own (low be it spoken, he was a dogged, uninspired opera composer; many of his operas are recorded and may help you to think more highly of them, though I recommend starting with *Orlando Paladino* (1782), which is good fun and splendid music). The Empress Maria Theresa, who lived in Vienna, said, "When I want to see good opera, I have to go to Esterhaza," a strong testimonial for Haydn's work.

Drama came more naturally to Haydn in his church masses, especially the so-called *Nelson* mass (1798), composed to celebrate the British admiral's recent victory at Aboukir Bay (Nelson and Emma Hamilton visited Haydn at Eisenstadt on their way home: Haydn presented Lord Nelson with his pen, and received the gold watch that Nelson had worn at

Sturm und Drang

The cradle of the Sturm und Drang *("storm and stress") movement was Germany, a country that in the eighteenth century had lacked the peace and prosperity of England and France. It was primarily a literary movement, though many composers of the late Classical and Romantic periods reflected its spirit in their works. Such dramatists as Goethe, Schiller and Lessing wrote of epic conflicts between good and evil. Schiller's* Maria Stuart *exemplifies well the feelings of the* Sturm und Drang *writers. At the first performance of another of Schiller's plays,* Die Räuber *(1781), the audience was deeply affected: "Complete strangers fell sobbing into one another's arms, and fainting women tottered towards the exits. The effect was of universal release, as when a new creation bursts forth from out of the mists of Chaos."*

the battle of Aboukir Bay. Lady Hamilton also sang several of Haydn's songs). The drama of his symphonies is sufficiently attested by some of their nicknames: the *Surprise*, no. 94 (a loud chord to awake sleepy listeners), the *Miracle*, no. 96 (a glass chandelier fell and broke in the concert-room, but hurt nobody because the audience, carried away by the power of the music, had crowded to the edge of the platform—actually this event took place in Symphony 102, whose Adagio is the greatest Haydn ever wrote), the *Philosopher*, no. 22, with its grave solos for the old *cors anglais*, so-called English horns; *La Passione*, no. 49, one of Haydn's minor-key, high-mettled dramatic works, later called his *Sturm und Drang* ("Storm and Stress") period. The *Farewell* symphony, no. 45 in F sharp minor, was composed as a reminder to the Prince that his musicians were impatient to return home to Vienna: in the finale, the players stop playing one by one, snuff out the candles on their music-desks and leave the platform, until finally only two solo violins are left playing in the extravagant key of F sharp major. The Prince is reported to have understood the message. The *Military* symphony, no. 100 in G (1794), is said to have been inspired by a royal review of troops, something like the annual Trooping the Colour on Horseguards Parade in

London's St James's Park. Haydn's Symphony no. 104, his last, is simply called the *London* symphony. But Haydn's un-nicknamed symphonies are treasure-trove as well: no. 88 in G, 95 in C minor and 98 in B flat (Haydn directed from the piano and wrote out a brief flourish for himself in the finale) are at least as marvellous as *The Bear, The Hen, The Schoolmaster* and others.

Haydn wrote more than fifty piano sonatas, most of which were for a long time treated as lightweight, didactic music. While it is true that many of the earlier works were probably written for teaching purposes at a period when the composer was earning his living by giving piano lessons, the sonatas provide constant delight for listener and player alike. They span a period of more than thirty years in the composer's life, culminating in three magnificent works he composed for a pianist in London, Teresa Jansen (later Mrs Bartolozzi). These sonatas, in C major, D major and E flat major, are the masterpieces of them all—in particular the E flat work, with a finale

The Pianoforte

The suddenness with which the harpsichord became obsolete when the piano appeared on the musical scene around 1780 is astonishing. Within fifty years, it had altogether vanished. There were two main reasons for this: a harpsichord of sufficient size for full-scale solo work was an expensive and unwieldy

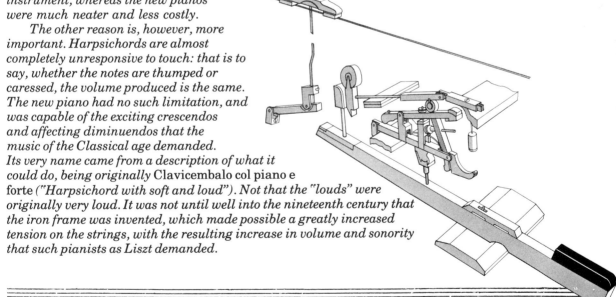

instrument, whereas the new pianos were much neater and less costly.

The other reason is, however, more important. Harpsichords are almost completely unresponsive to touch: that is to say, whether the notes are thumped or caressed, the volume produced is the same. The new piano had no such limitation, and was capable of the exciting crescendos and affecting diminuendos that the music of the Classical age demanded. Its very name came from a description of what it could do, being originally Clavicembalo col piano e forte *("Harpsichord with soft and loud"). Not that the "louds" were originally very loud. It was not until well into the nineteenth century that the iron frame was invented, which made possible a greatly increased tension on the strings, with the resulting increase in volume and sonority that such pianists as Liszt demanded.*

reminiscent of the ending of Schubert's last sonata. One other keyboard work should be mentioned: an exquisite set of double variations in F minor, composed between his two stays in London. Its air of tender sadness and affecting simplicity conceals an artistry of the highest order.

In the 1930s Donald Tovey, a great musical scholar and performer, wrote a challenging essay called "Haydn the Inaccessible": very few of

Schubert's sonatas p 164–5

1730-1800 Enter the Orchestra

The opening bars of a
Haydn Symphony *taken
from a hand-copied
catalogue published in the
1850s.*

Haydn's works were then available, even in print, for study. Nowadays we can listen to all his symphonies, piano trios, masses, string quartets, piano sonatas and operas on commercial gramophone records and decide which are our favourites. Inevitably some are less thrilling than others, but every one of them testifies to a lively, fine, musically masterly mind completely in tune with his time. Many of them suggest that, in all history, his was the time when to be alive and a musician was, despite war, filth, penury and disease, not to mention class distinction, infinitely preferable to life at any other time. If Haydn had lived in another age, he might have written music just as idealistic, though no other composer did. The Viennese Classical style, which Haydn so signally represented, was made by the age and by individual musical geniuses. Haydn was not alone, however unique, as the next chapter will show.

Chapter 8
The Classical Era

Vienna

The Classic spirit ◆ Vienna—a gathering place for musical
genius ◆ Mozart; a prodigious talent ◆ Beethoven, the
revolutionary ◆ Franz Schubert heralds
the Romantic age ◆

The capital city of European music has shifted from one country to another
in the course of history. We have followed it from Paris to Dijon, to Rome, to
Venice. Between about 1780 and 1828, it was located in Vienna, where, at
one time or another, four of the world's greatest composers were living and
working—Haydn, Mozart, Beethoven and Schubert. The previous chapter
ended with Joseph Haydn: now it is time to consider the three other
composers generally lumped together in the pigeon-hole called Viennese
Classicism.

Viennese Classicism
"Classic" means, essentially, "top class", or unsurpassable, and implies that
what followed after in musical history, which was the age of Romanticism,
must in some way be deemed inferior—which is nonsense. Chopin,
Schumann, Berlioz, Verdi and Wagner, to go no further, are also, each in his
own way, unsurpassable, and later on I will suggest that each of them
inherited the Classic spirit—which is the instinct and the ability to seek
perfection of form and content, a great idea flawlessly presented, such as we
admire and can study endlessly in the music of the Viennese Classical
masters.

In their lives they had to endure hardship and personal wretchedness,
but they never allowed momentary melancholy to colour the music they
were creating just then. While Mozart was in despair about lack of money,
he wrote his symphony no. 39, which is full of high spirits: likewise young
Beethoven composed his joyous second symphony in full realization that he
was going deaf; or Schubert, pessimistically undergoing hospital treatment
for syphilis, then an incurable disease, during which he wrote that gentle,
contented song *Der Einsame*. I am reminded of the actor who, cast as a
clergyman and asked whether he was a pious Christian, answered, "Do I
need to kill somebody before I can play the part of a murderer?", or Jacques-
Louis David, French painter and master of the Classic style: "What does the
truth matter so long as the pose is noble?" The English musical scholar

The sumptuous interior of **the Schlosstheater at Schönbrunn**, *during a performance there in the presence of the Emperor Joseph II and his family.*

E.J. Dent, a great teacher, discussing the Viennese Classical style, echoed David's words, saying: "Sincerity is a virtue with which art is not concerned." Finally Beethoven, appalled at the prospect of his imminent deafness: "Artists are fiery, and do not weep." *That* is the Classicism with which this chapter deals.

Mozart (1756–1791)

If ever a composer could be considered unsurpassable it must be Johannes Chrysostomus Wolfgangus Theophilus Mozart—so he was baptized, the first two names after the saint on whose day (27 January) he was born, the fourth, meaning lover of God, after his godfather. Wolfgang (his personal name) usually signed himself Amadé—the French version of Theophilus, or Gottlieb in German, though posterity uses the Latin form, Amadeus.

Vienna claims Mozart, since he worked there for the last ten years of his short life, during which time he was shabbily treated by his fellow-Viennese, it must be said, considering his ability and fame elsewhere. While he lived in Vienna, Mozart poured out great music, operas, symphonies, piano concertos and an immense quantity of chamber and incidental music. The enlightened Emperor Joseph II, though amiably disposed towards him, had only a minor court post for Mozart. Subscription concerts given by Mozart attracted few customers. He had to borrow money and write begging letters. Vienna did not praise him until he was dead and buried—but that has always been the way of the superficial, reactionary Viennese.

As a complete musician, Mozart owed little to Vienna, but much to Salzburg, where he was born, grew up and worked at court as violinist, organist and composer. Chiefly he acquired mastery in every form of music from the extensive travels he undertook in his boyhood, and for a while later, at the instigation of his father—an expert professional musician who recognized his son's precocious genius and felt duty-bound to reveal it to the rest of Europe. Leopold Mozart was in service, as violinist and composer, at the court of the Archbishop of Salzburg, a small but not unimportant musical establishment.

In the year of Wolfgang's birth, Leopold Mozart brought out his book on violin-playing, a classic of its kind, still valued along with C.P.E. Bach's on keyboard-playing; Quantz's (Frederick the Great's flute teacher) on the flute; and the Viennese J.J. Fux's *Gradus ad Parnassum* on composition (the only equivalent volume on how to sing, by P.F. Tosi, is much less thorough, though still invaluable). From these books, we today can learn how music was performed in the eighteenth century, not a bit as the printed notes suggest, but subject to accepted conventions, sounding on instruments of those days quite unlike their modern equivalents—hence the new interest in performance on old instruments.

Early Travels

Leopold Mozart taught his son the violin and clavier, musical theory, Latin and other academic subjects. Father Mozart was a highly knowledgeable and intellectually cultivated person, a composer of merit (he wrote the *Toy Symphony*, often attributed to Haydn), though he gave up his own career as soon as Wolfgang's genius manifested itself, for the sake of his prodigious son. Wolfgang's elder sister Nannerl (Annie) was also a decent harpsichordist, so Leopold took them on tour, first to Munich and Vienna, then to France, England, the Netherlands and Italy. The strain of so much travel on a young boy, with all the public display involved, must have adversely affected Wolfgang's physical constitution, and contributed to later bouts of illness and a premature death. Nevertheless it was through all those travels in so many countries and musical centres that Wolfgang Mozart mastered the Italian, French and German styles of music, elements of which he was to combine in his mature work, filtered through his personal creative genius.

As a little boy in London, he astonished royalty, nobility and the general public with his keyboard improvisations, not to mention playing with a cloth to cover the keys (very easy really, but apparently magical to the untutored), and reading difficult music at sight. More important was his

contact with J.C. Bach, the composer who most influenced him then, and whom he revered like another father, or his singing lessons with the great *castrato* Manzuoli. In London, while his father was ill, he wrote his first orchestral symphonies (some now lost). In Rome he heard Allegri's *Miserere*, a piece forbidden performance elsewhere, and wrote it out after one hearing. He was also given the papal order of Knight of the Golden Spur and commissioned to compose his first operas.

Return to Salzburg

Returned from instructive travels, Mozart was able to enliven Salzburg's old-fashioned music. He was given a job as violinist, in which capacity he wrote five splendid violin concertos in 1775 for himself as soloist, though he wrote better solos still in the *Sinfonia concertante* of 1779 for violin and viola solo, K 364. (K refers to Baron Köchel's chronological catalogue of all Mozart's works, everybody's way of referring to them.) He composed copious orchestral serenades for festive occasions, such as Salzburg University passing-out parties—these are symphonic at a light level, with extra dances, a march to start and finish, often a violin concerto in the middle (K 320, called *Posthorn*, and K 250, called *Haffner*, for example). There were symphonies, more and more striking (25, 29 and 34, despite the numbers, belong together as a brilliant, varied trio). He began to compose concertos for himself, at first as harpsichordist (K 271 in E flat is the finest of them), though he soon preferred the fortepiano, and for the newer instrument he composed, during his Vienna years, his most marvellous and original instrumental works.

The Salzburg court had no facilities for opera, Mozart's self-acknowledged strong suit by now (he had written old-fashioned serious operas for Italy with resounding success—the best is *Lucio Silla*), though his talent had been acknowledged by semi-concert performances of several stage works. The new Salzburg Archbishop Colloredo—it was an aristocratic rather than clerical post—gave Mozart small scope to develop church music, no chance in opera, and grudging permission to travel. In 1777 Mozart journeyed to Paris, via Mannheim, where he fell in love with the soprano Aloysia Weber. She was the second of four daughters in the family of a professional musician (the uncle of the composer Weber, incidentally). The family was extremely kind to Mozart: no doubt they hoped he would be able to advance their fortunes. Aloysia and her elder sister were singers and the third daughter, Constanze, was studying singing—Mozart eventually married her. He planned to travel to Italy in the company of the sixteen-year-old Aloysia and write operas there, but was dissuaded in no uncertain terms by his father in a stormy correspondence.

In Paris he wrote his *Paris* Symphony, also a *Sinfonia concertante* for four wind instruments, now extant only in a dubious transcription. One soloist was the Bohemian horn-player Punto, whose own horn concertos borrow from Mozart's four (written for a Salzburg friend and colleague), and make highly enjoyable listening. Other works from Paris include a delightful set of piano variations on a theme we know as *Twinkle, twinkle, little star*, and an impassioned, almost hysterical, piano sonata in A minor, K 310. He also had an introduction to the Duc de Guines, a gifted amateur flautist whose daughter played the harp. The Duke commissioned the Flute and Harp Concerto for himself and his daughter to play—though he kept forgetting to pay the composer for it.

Weber p 170–3   J.C. Bach p 129–31

Castrati p 71

Vienna

The extraordinary hold exercised by the city of Vienna over European musical life is first of all the story of the Hapsburg Emperors. As far back as the seventeenth century, these cultured and musical rulers were importing Italian operas, composers and performers to their court, and were sometimes (as in the case of Leopold I, 1640–1705) gifted composers themselves.

Early in the succeeding century, court opera was given an immense boost in Vienna by the genius of Giuseppe Galli-Bibiena, an Italian theatre architect and stage designer. His gorgeous and dramatic perspective sets were a legend in the operatic world, as was his invention of transparent scenery.

Later in the century, the court monopoly of musical life diminished, and there arose numerous wealthy patrons who attracted such giants as Haydn and Beethoven to Vienna. The Viennese public enjoy a reputation for their musical connoisseurship, though in truth they have always seemed just as susceptible to the latest musical novelties as audiences everywhere. Mozart certainly had little to thank them for. By far and away the majority of the great "Viennese" composers came from outside the city: Schubert and Johann Strauss were the only two significant musical natives of Vienna.

The city is probably best known today for the excellence of its Philharmonic Orchestra. Founded in 1842 by the composer Nicolai, the Vienna Philharmonic has numbered such luminaries as Richard Strauss and Mahler among its resident conductors (though neither of them was Viennese).

In the present century, three native-born Viennese composers brought a rather different reputation than that for melody to the city. Arnold Schoenberg, with his disciples Berg and Webern, evolved the twelve-note system of composition, setting out to remove all sense of tonality and of the traditional melodic gift that had made Vienna famous. Schoenberg hoped that one day his music "would be whistled in the street by errand boys".

1760–1828 *Vienna*

*A portrait of **Mozart** as a child prodigy by Hans Hansen.*

During that Paris visit, Mozart grew up. His mother died; his fame brought him little work; he hated the French and their proud, superficial taste. He was offered a prestigious post as church organist and turned it down, but accepted a less glorious one in Salzburg. A commission from Munich prompted the heroic opera *Idomeneo* (1781). The form was out of date, but Mozart was now under the spell of Gluck's reforms: choruses, few recitatives, noble melodious airs, ballet, ensembles, orchestral set-pieces and high gripping drama. They are all in *Idomeneo*, which is as great as any later, more famous Mozart opera.

The old heroic opera of Scarlatti, Hasse and Handel was quite dead, except among the staunchest conservatives who included the opera's most

regular customers. *Idomeneo* did not suit them: it had too much emotional recitative with excitable orchestral accompaniment, too much counterpoint in the orchestral music altogether. The arias were quite divine, but the whole had so absorbed Gluck's teaching in Paris that opera's old heroic image was hardly perceptible—this was a new sort of musical drama. Mozart knew how to follow it up, but he had to go elsewhere to fulfil his operatic ambitions. After the first three performances of *Idomeneo* in Munich, he was recalled to the service of the Salzburg Archbishop, just then staying in Vienna for the funeral of Maria Theresa, and the accession of her son Joseph II. The success of *Idomeneo* irked the Archbishop: he was not willing to congratulate one of his servants on a success elsewhere. In June 1781 Mozart asked for a better post; the Archbishop refused. His life there was ignominious, the accepted lot of many less talented servant-musicians, as he well knew. Writing to his father about a trip to Vienna with the Archbishop, Mozart said:

The Mozart family, painted in 1780/1781 by J.N. della Croce. Wolfgang and his sister, seated at the keyboard, are overlooked by a portrait of their dead mother and by their father, the violinist Leopold.

"We lunch about twelve o'clock, unfortunately somewhat too early for me. Our party consists of two valets . . . the confectioner, the two cooks and—my insignificant self. By the way, the two valets sit at the top of the table, but at least I have the honour of being placed above the cooks. Well, I almost believe myself back in Salzburg! A good deal of silly, coarse joking goes on at table, but no one cracks jokes with me, for I never say a word, or, if I have to speak, I always do so with the utmost gravity; and as soon as I have finished my lunch, I get up and go off."

Mozart soon resigned and was physically booted out of the Archbishop's service. He became a freelance musician in Vienna and, with great difficulty, survived in that way of life until his death, just ten years later.

The Vienna Years

In Vienna Mozart became acquainted with Joseph Haydn (whose brother Michael had long been a leading musician at the Salzburg court) and in 1785 dedicated six string quartets to his older friend, from whose opus 33 quartets he had learned much about form, and about how to write four independently interesting string parts so that together they sounded coherent, and even more beautiful. The series was published as Mozart's opus 10, but the quartets are known nowadays by their Köchel numbers, between K 387 in G, which Mozart composed in 1782 after the experience of Haydn's latest, and K 465 (called the Dissonance Quartet, because the slow introduction makes a feature of harsh discords miraculously resolved into harmonious consonances). Haydn, accepting the dedication, told Leopold Mozart, who was staying in Vienna with his son: "Before God I tell you, and as an honest man, that your son is the greatest composer known to me in person or by name. He has taste and, what is more, the greatest knowledge of composition." That must be the noblest compliment ever paid by one great composer to another.

Mozart's wife, Constanze. He wrote the great C minor Mass, K 427, in celebration of their marriage.

The Patronage of Emperor Joseph II

When he settled in Vienna in the summer of 1781, Mozart hoped to make a living, if possible, from a post at court. But the Imperial musical establishment, formerly large and distinguished, had become run down during the reign of the Empress Maria Theresa (1740–1780), whose prime interest was political and military ambition, although she was musical herself. Her son Joseph II found more time for good works, including patronage of the arts. He formed the short-lived German-language opera company for which Mozart composed *Die Entführung aus dem Serail* ("The Abduction from the Harem", 1782), a comic opera with spoken dialogue (the German term is *Singspiel*, meaning "sing-and-play"), in an oriental setting, popular at the time of the Turkish wars. It is partly knockabout nursery farce, partly romantic rescue-opera, a type due for popularity rather later—after the French Revolution of 1789 and its repressive aftermath. *The Seraglio* (its commonest English title) was quickly taken up by other opera companies. Until Mozart's death it was his most successful opera; his later, greater comic operas were not widely performed until afterwards. Coincidentally the heroine has the same name, Constanze, as the wife whom Mozart married while writing the opera.

Haydn's string quartets p 140–1

It was at this time that Mozart had his celebrated duel at the piano with Clementi. Muzio Clementi (1752–1832) was a gifted pianist and composer who had been brought up in England by a wealthy cousin of the eccentric William Beckford (whom Mozart had known as a child in London). At the contest, organized for the amusement of the Emperor, both had to show off their sight-reading ability with some sonatas by Paisiello, and improvise together on a given theme as well as perform their own music. Clementi was greatly impressed by his rival, though Mozart had little to say concerning Clementi's prowess: "He is an excellent keyboard player, but that is all. He has great facility with his right hand. His star passages are thirds. Apart from this, he has not a farthing's worth of taste or feeling; he is a mere *mechanicus*."

The Austrian Emperor did not have a job to offer Mozart until his court composer Gluck died (in 1787). He did commission the little comic German opera *Der Schauspieldirektor* ("The Impresario", 1786) for a court party at the palace of Schönbrunn outside Vienna. He approved the production of *Le nozze di Figaro* ("Figaro's Wedding", 1786), and saw it through the usual Viennese jealous antagonism to a première so successful that he had to forbid the repetition of favourite numbers, so many were there of them. Joseph II is credited with suggesting the plot of *Così fan tutte* (1789)—the Italian title means "All women behave alike". When it was produced, the Emperor was at the wars, and sent home a barbed message that he assumed the piece would be too erudite for a Viennese audience.

The Piano Concertos

Mozart had to make a living by giving public subscription concerts, for which he composed new works, notably his latest piano concertos (twenty-seven in all, the first four not original works). Since J.S. Bach's day, the keyboard concerto had become the public's favourite instrumental music. Mozart, with the new improved fortepiano, alone raised it to a perfection that later composers could only try to copy, without hoping to surpass the ideal model.

In the Romantic nineteenth century, audiences preferred K 466 in D minor and K 491 in C minor, because these are stormy, dramatic musical tragedies. Modern audiences have learned, through a Swedish film, *Elvira Madigan*, to love K 467 in C, which has the most magical slow movement of all. The most magnificent of the set is K 503 in C major, which as much deserves the nickname "Emperor" as Beethoven's fifth piano concerto. But K 482 in E flat is almost as grand and brilliant. K 488 in A major has a sparkle and tenderness of its own. The last of the set, K 595 in B flat, is the most mellow, often looking forward, for a moment at a time, to nineteenth-

The opening bars of Mozart's Rondo in A minor, K 511, for piano, one of the noblest works he wrote for the instrument.

Gluck p 125–6

1760–1828 Vienna

*The entrance to the Queen of the Night's palace: a set from Act I of Mozart's **The Magic Flute**, designed by the architect Schinkel for a Berlin production in 1816.*

Anton Mesmer. *The inventor of mesmerism was a friend of the Mozart family. The composer's early opera* Bastien & Bastienne *was first performed in his house.*

century music: the Rondo theme of the finale used a nursery song about a child in winter looking forward to warm weather, which Mozart set to music at the same time. I could dwell on these piano concertos for pages and pages and only scratch the surface of their splendour and allure. I can only suggest purchase of the whole lot in a box of records (there are several sets available to choose from), and constant listening until your own selection of favourites emerges.

Later composers mostly took other models for their piano concertos, or explored different territory. Those who tried to emulate Mozart's often misconstrued his methods. Beethoven, who played them often in concerts, did not understand the form until his fourth and fifth piano concertos, which are in the same top class as Mozart's. So is Brahms's no. 2 in B flat major, which adopts the Mozart ideal model. All three begin by introducing the soloist very soon, which Mozart only did in K 271 in E flat, an early work for harpsichord—the important lessons of Mozart's late piano concertos are heard in what Beethoven and Brahms did after the opening.

Mozart's Pupils

To keep his new family in funds, Mozart gave lessons copiously: in 1787 one of his pupils was J.N. Hummel (1778–1837), best known today for a splendid trumpet concerto. So impressed was Mozart with Hummel's playing that he took him into his own house for two years when the boy was only seven years old and grew very fond of him. In later years Hummel toured all over Europe as a virtuoso: some said his playing rivalled that of Beethoven. Hummel became a fine composer—his A minor piano concerto

Brahms's piano concertos p 187

(1820) was Chopin's model, his Piano Quintet, op 87 (1820), the model for Schubert's *Trout* Quintet, his Septet a splendid and unique piece.

At a party in a Viennese palace, Mozart heard Beethoven improvise at the piano and told the company: "Mark my words, that young fellow is going to cause a stir in the world." Mozart had many noble piano pupils, and wrote music for some of them, especially young ladies. He had all the characteristics of the star sign Aquarius—genius, impatience with authority, devotion to the other sex, laziness coupled with immense industry. The story that he could work out a composition in his head, while playing billiards, before writing it out in complete full score, is most attractive but untrue.

It is important to remember that Mozart's piano music was written for a much lighter and sweeter-toned instrument than those we hear today, and with a much more delicate action. Mozart was always exhorting his pupils that musical passages should "flow like oil", and his works for piano solo demand this *legato* approach. Many of the eighteen sonatas are used as teaching pieces, though their composer's original intention was not necessarily didactic. Two of the greatest must be the sonata in A minor, referred to above, that Mozart wrote in Paris when his mother died, and another stormy work in C minor, K 457 (to which is attached a magnificent Fantasia in the same key, that gives us some notion, with its effortless developing of ideas, of Mozart's powers as an improviser). Beyond the sonatas, there are also many sets of variations, dances, rondos and isolated movements. A sublime Rondo in A minor, K 511, is one of the most profound pieces he ever wrote for the piano. There is also a splendid body of work for piano duet, from which there is only room to single out a magnificent sonata in F, a set of variations in G, and a C minor fugue for 2 pianos.

The title page of Mozart's **Così fan tutte** *depicts Dorabella and Fiordiligi ministering to their lovers, who pretend to have taken poison. They are finally restored to life by mesmerism.*

More Concert Music

Mozart's piano concertos were not, of course, enough of an achievement for the finest pianist in Europe. For his public concerts, and those in the palaces of Viennese noblemen, who had to replace the Imperial court as leading lights of music when the emperor forsook the throne for the warhorse, Mozart composed piano trios, a piano quintet with woodwind, all fine, but surpassed by his piano quartets in G minor and E flat major (both 1785), which are marvellous drawing-room-scaled piano concertos. There is too a marvellous quantity of music for wind band, outstanding among which are two serenades: in E flat, K 375, and C minor, K 388. For the drawing-room he also composed his string quintets (with two violas, one being himself)—late works with a special radiance and opulence of sound. The last three of Mozart's Viennese symphonies (numbers 39–41) are magnificent, the *Prague*, number 38 in D, at least as fine, the *Haffner*, in D major, number 35, a work of glittering bravura. They do not surpass the string trio (violin, viola, cello) called Divertimento in E flat, K 563: the title denotes party music, as do Serenade and Cassation in Mozart's works, but K 563 is a big, serious work, captivating at every level. The best known of all must be Mozart's string serenade *Eine kleine Nachtmusik* ("A Little Night Music"), cheerful, exquisitely refined party music, evidently the sequel to *A Musical Joke*, a burlesque of feeble compositions, terrible and hilarious in effect.

The Operas

Figaro was only moderately successful in Vienna (too new, too complicated for musical ignoramuses who thought themselves the cream of audiences),

1760–1828 *Vienna*

but in Prague, capital of Bohemia, the most musical country in Europe, it hit the jackpot: no ball, no concert, was complete without tunes from *Figaro*. As a result, Mozart was commissioned by the Italian opera company in Prague to write a new opera. He chose the old Spanish tale of Don Juan—a popular favourite.

While composing the opera in the summer of 1787 in Prague, Mozart stayed with Franz Xaver Dussek and his wife Josepha. Dussek (1731–1799) was an old family friend of the Mozarts and a fine pianist, not be confused with J.L. Dussek (1760–1812), who worked in England and France and composed many piano sonatas greatly in advance of the time. The Prague Dussek's wife was a fine soprano, and for her Mozart wrote the concert aria *Bella mia fiamma*, K 528. Apparently she had to lock Mozart up in his room to get him to finish the piece; he responded by making it excessively difficult and insisting that she sing it at sight. While in Prague, working on *Don Giovanni*, Mozart's librettist was called back to Vienna on business. Mozart, in need of help with the text, was fortunate to be able to call upon the services of another visitor to the city, Casanova (whose own experiences as a Don Juan were already legendary).

Don Giovanni, supposedly a grand spiritual thriller, though cheerfulness keeps breaking in, surpassed the intrigue and social realism of *Figaro*. *Don Giovanni* proposed a dynamic, super-heroic drama of destiny and heroism, far more intense than any comic or serious opera had ever known (except in Mozart's own *Idomeneo*, and perhaps vestigially in Gluck's *Iphigenia in Tauris*). For the romantic nineteenth-century, *Don Giovanni* was, in the words of E.T.A. Hoffmann, "the opera of all operas". Mozart's librettist in *Figaro* and *Giovanni* was one of the Viennese court poets, and an amateur Don Juan, called Lorenzo da Ponte, whose memoirs are worth reading. He wrote a third opera libretto for Mozart, *Così fan tutte*, the story of a gamble about the fidelity of girls to their sweethearts; the drama is ironic and painful, the music Mozart's most subtle and magical.

Da Ponte is a fascinating character. He was an unfrocked priest and soldier of fortune, who worked for a time as poet to the Imperial Theatre in Vienna and finished up teaching Italian in New York. His description of writing the libretto for *Don Giovanni* in Prague exposes him as the right man for the job:

***Lorenzo da Ponte**, Mozart's raffish collaborator of genius, who wrote the librettos for* The Marriage of Figaro, Don Giovanni *and* Così fan tutte.

> "I sat down at my table and did not leave it for twelve hours continuous—a bottle of Tokay to my right, a box of Seville [snuff] to my left, in the middle an inkwell. A beautiful girl of sixteen—I should have preferred to love her only as a daughter, but alas...!—was living in the house with her mother, who took care of the family, and came to my room at the sound of the bell. To tell the truth the bell rang rather frequently, especially at moments when I felt my inspiration waning ...I worked twelve hours a day every day, with a few interruptions, for two months on end."

Finally Mozart wrote the German opera for which he had been pining, not a grand, serious story, but a knockabout comedy, *Die Zauberflöte* ("The Magic Flute"), which Mozart managed to turn into something of the serious sort he wanted, partly amusing, partly thrilling, also partly idealistic and religious, along the lines of Freemasonry to which he had become strongly allied. It is partly rescue-opera, partly sacred, partly the farcical

To all Lovers of Sciences.

THE greateſt Prodigy that Europe, or that even Human Nature has to boaſt of, is, without Contradiction, the little German Boy WOLFGANG MOZART; a Boy, Eight Years old, who has, and indeed very juſtly, raiſed the Admiration not only of the greateſt Men, but alſo of the greateſt Muſicians in Europe. It is hard to ſay, whether his Execution upon the Harpſichord and his playing and ſinging at Sight, or his own Caprice, Fancy, and Compoſitions for all Inſtruments, are moſt aſtoniſhing. The Father of this Miracle, being obliged by Deſire of ſeveral Ladies and Gentlemen to poſtpone, for a very ſhort Time, his Departure from England, will give an Opportunity to hear this little Compoſer and his Siſter, whoſe muſical Knowledge wants not Apology. Performs every Day in the Week, from Twelve to Three o'Clock in the Great Room, at the Swan and Hoop, Cornhill. Admittance 2s. 6d. each Perſon.

The two Children will play alſo together with four Hands upon the ſame Harpſichord, and put upon it a Handkerchief, without ſeeing the Keys.

Mozart knew international fame only as a young boy, when he toured Europe often billed as a scientific phenomenon, like a performing monkey.

adventures of the comedian bird-catcher Papageno. Mozart put into this motley pudding, concocted by his friend Emanuel Schikaneder (who played Papageno), the grandest of all his musical invention. Schikaneder (1751–1812) was a playwright, actor and director who had started his career as a travelling player and violinist before he made Mozart's acquaintance in Salzburg. He eventually became manager of the Theater auf der Wieden in Vienna, for which he commissioned *Die Zauberflöte*. Essentially he was looking for a "magic opera", complete with transformation scenes. But, like Mozart, Schikaneder had been admitted as a Freemason, and included elements of this ritual in his tale

Bernard Shaw claimed "The Magic Flute" as the music of his own private church, and most of us would agree with him, however much we may love Mozart's formal sacred music in his incomplete *C minor Mass*, a thank-offering for his marriage to Constanze Weber, or the *Requiem*, which he also left incomplete on his deathbed. Picaresque stories of his death by poisoning have been disproved. Mozart died very young, exhausted by long, hard work. In nearly thirty-six years of life, he achieved more than gifted composers who survived into their eighties. The game of "who is the greatest composer" is pointless, because every composer is himself, in his own time. If we must play it, my own candidates would be J.S. Bach and Wolfgang Mozart, as I have attempted to demonstrate.

Beethoven (1770–1827)

Another candidate was already working in Vienna when Mozart died. Ludwig van Beethoven had been born into a musical family in Bonn, a cultured city in northern Germany. His father, Johann, was a court musician there and had every intention of turning Ludwig (who was small

*A silhouette of the boy **Beethoven**, in his sixteenth year.*

*A miniature portrait of the
young **Beethoven**, now in
the Beethovenhaus at Bonn.*

for his age) into a child prodigy. The child was by turns beaten, overworked
and neglected. He was removed from school at the age of eleven in order to
concentrate exclusively on a musical career, but was fortunate to be put in
the care of C.G. Neefe, a reputable composer and a J.S. Bach adherent, in
the Baroque tradition of counterpoint and keyboard improvisation. In 1787
Beethoven visited Vienna and may have studied with Mozart. After a brief
return home to sort out family affairs, he returned to Vienna to study with
Haydn. He had some money from the elector in Bonn, and rapidly made his
name by his formidable skill at the piano, especially as an improviser. He
had lessons as well from Salieri and from a learned contrapuntist, Johann
Albrechtsberger. A friend and pupil of Beethoven's, Ferdinand Ries, recalls
that "All three valued Beethoven highly, but were also of one mind touching
his habits of study. All of them said Beethoven was so impetuous and self-
willed that he had to learn much through harsh experience, which he had
refused to accept when it was presented to him as a subject for study." But
Beethoven certainly loved his teachers enough to dedicate his set of opus 2
piano sonatas to Haydn, and, in his fortieth year (that of the *Emperor*
concerto) to refer to himself as "pupil of Salieri".

The big pond of Vienna suited Beethoven perfectly. He did not seek a
court appointment as Mozart had wished. Beethoven was able to live
comfortably on commissions, sales of music (hand-copied, as well as

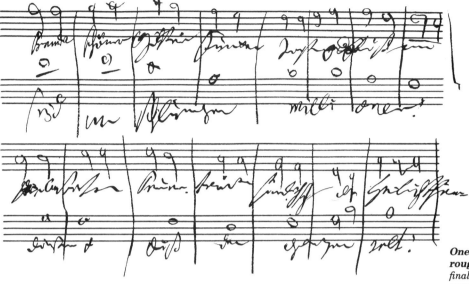

One of Beethoven's rough sketches for the finale of his ninth symphony.

printed), public concerts and grants of money from noblemen who did not want him to seek employment elsewhere. Beethoven's lifestyle appeared poorer than it actually was. He was forever moving from one apartment to another after rows with his landlords, and the state in which he generally kept his rooms gave them good cause for grievance. But though he was niggardly with himself, Beethoven remained always generous towards his friends. In 1815, when his brother died, the composer became guardian of his nine-year-old nephew, Karl, though not without protracted litigation involving the boy's mother. Karl grew up to be unstable and graceless, rejecting the love (though not the money) that his uncle gave him.

With the arrival of the nineteenth century, Beethoven saw himself as the spokesman of a new age; he had already shown himself a pioneer in his first symphony and his first two piano concertos (no. 2 was started before no. 1). In 1801 he discovered that he was losing his hearing—for a musician an appalling occurrence. Beethoven obliged himself to continue a musician's career, notwithstanding. He was not a theatrical musician, though his one opera, *Fidelio* (1805–1814, several times revised), is a thrilling and moving work, with spoken German dialogue, full of superb music, as witness Leonora's aria *Abscheulicher* and the canonic quartet *Mir ist so wunderbar*—indeed every number surpasses expectation.

Beethoven's music is usually divided into three periods: the pieces orientated to the eighteenth century; the middle period, when he cultivated the Heroic Style appropriate to post-French Revolution ideals (his epoch-making *Eroica* symphony and *Kreutzer* sonata were intended to secure him a post in Paris, a city and culture he preferred to Vienna); and the late, near-mystical period of the last string quartets.

The Revolutionary

Beethoven's piano sonatas, more than Mozart's or Haydn's, drive music into new spheres of drama and philosophy. As early as the opus 2 sonatas, there is a breadth of thought and structural command that breaks away from the

A sketch of Beethoven by J.P. Lyser, whose signature appears beneath that of the composer.

Mozart's piano sonatas p 157
Haydn's piano sonatas p 145

eighteenth-century elegance of Haydn and Mozart. After 1800 indeed, in his piano sonatas Beethoven started to expand sonata form on a Romantic scale. The A flat work, opus 26 (the first to be composed after that date) opens with a slow theme and variations, follows with a headlong, rushing scherzo, a funeral march *on the death of a hero* and a whirlwind finale. This was followed by the two sonatas *quasi una Fantasia* (the second of which is the "Moonlight") that are anything but conventional in form. The next milestones in Beethoven's writing for the piano came around the same time as the great crisis in his life over his rapidly encroaching deafness. The brilliant *Waldstein* (named after a princely protector) and the mighty *Appassionata* sonatas were again so revolutionary in their thinking that even Beethoven forebore to write any more for piano solo for the next few years. But the peak of his pianistic achievement must be the last four of the thirty-two sonatas from the *Hammerklavier*, which proposes an absolutely unprecedented pianistic technique, through to opus 111 in C minor—the key that Beethoven used for his *Sturm und Drang* music, such as the fifth symphony in C minor.

Beethoven had first made his name as a pianist, playing Bach's *Well-tempered Clavier* and his own early works, but above all as an improviser of exceptional powers. He managed to survive in Vienna as Mozart never did. Audiences there enjoyed Beethoven's fiery, genial piano extemporization and, more cautiously, his works for orchestra. He felt least unhappy there.

For the Archduke Rudolf he composed a series of cadenzas to his piano concertos, as well as the glorious trio for piano, violin and cello, called the *Archduke*, and the tremendous Mass in D major (*Missa solemnis*) for soloists, chorus and orchestra, intended for the Archduke's enthronement. It is a work full of music about mankind's tiny relationship to the immensity of God, and the terrible suffering of Christ on humanity's behalf. Even an atheist can appreciate Beethoven's interpretation of the Catholic Mass (he was no conventional Christian himself).

It was in orchestral music that Beethoven chiefly showed his greatness. With his third symphony, the *Eroica*, he honoured Napoleon Bonaparte. The first movement is longer than whole symphonies by his predecessors, crammed with incident of the most dramatic order; the slow movement is a funeral march (Napoleon was very much alive), really a funeral oration, when one considers the glorious melody of its second subject and its grand, purposeful fugue. The scherzo, amazingly vivid and dynamic, with a fizzing trio for horns, and the finale, a set of variations (on a theme which Beethoven had already composed for a ballet about Prometheus, who gave culture to mankind), lift this symphony above every sort of music hitherto known. Beethoven wanted his audience to regard music not as the entertainment accepted by earlier audiences, but as some sort of sermon about the godlike nature of man. He was surely thinking of Goethe's play about Prometheus, where the hero is portrayed defying the gods in a thunderstorm.

Beethoven went on to further deeds of musical heroism in his fifth symphony: "Fate knocks at the door," he said, but the music triumphs over Nemesis and the finale is a doubly effective achievement in the face of that fate which the deaf Beethoven had experienced. His sixth symphony, the Pastoral, celebrated man's glad acceptance of nature, however inclement: it proposes man's affinity with our surroundings, humanity as part of a larger environment, uncertain, dramatic and imperious, the real controller of our

Sturm und Drang p 144
The Well-tempered Clavier p 93

lives. The seventh symphony is more secular, a celebration of man's delight in his own physical energy, a glimpse of divinity. Beethoven's ninth symphony opened new doors, windows, everything, to reveal the whole universe as man's realm. It is called the Choral Symphony, but the choral finale, set to Schiller's poem about spiritual joy, relates to the previous movements in which man passes through uncertainty, elation and serenity before encountering an infinitely greater expanse—a vision of perfection and eternal human bliss.

Uncharted Territory

Beethoven, perhaps because he was deaf, could perceive more than ordinary mortals. So, at least, we may hear in his last piano sonatas and string quartets, works which explore territory uncharted by other musicians, mysterious, humorous, sacred. Unaccepted by the public for many years, much of his late music still sounds ugly and was not meant to woo the ear, because Beethoven was then chiefly concerned with truth, not beauty. In his

Piano Duet

Pianistic homes specially love music for four hands at one keyboard. It has a history that reaches back to the Elizabethan era. It is essentially a social medium, though as a small child Mozart appeared frequently in public at the keyboard together with his elder sister. Schubert, who above all other composers enjoyed the social side of music-making, wrote a large output of music for piano duet which he played with young ladies of his acquaintance. It has even been suggested that many instances of the players' hands crossing over each other in these works were designed to create effects more erotic than musical.

But there was, in addition, a more serious and didactic value in the piano duet. The symphonic and operatic repertoire of the nineteenth century was seldom available to music lovers, unless they happened to live within reach of a big city. Music publishers hastened to bring out versions of popular orchestral works arranged for piano duet (four hands being much more able than two to cope with the intricacies of, say, Beethoven's symphonies). Even today, though orchestral colour of course is lost in such an arrangement, struggling through such reductions at the piano teaches more about the inner workings of an orchestral piece than listening to any number of recordings can ever hope to do.

last string quartet, opus 135 in F major, he descended to the level of banality—his housekeeper asked if a bill must be paid and Beethoven admitted that it must. Then he turned that question and answer ("Must it be?" "It must be") into music infinitely greater: a satisfying conclusion to his life's work.

Schubert (1797–1828)

Franz Schubert, unlike the other Viennese Classics, was actually born in Vienna, lived there for almost the whole of his life (his holidays were always spent within Austria), and died there at the age of only thirty-one.

He knew no glory in his working life, though his gifts were as dazzling as those of Mozart or Beethoven. They were keyboard virtuosos admittedly,

Schubert accompanies his friends during a charade. His evenings were often spent playing games and making music in convivial company: such gatherings were called Schubertiads.

as Schubert was not, though he was a decent pianist, useful at a party when dance music was required. He longed always to compose a successful opera and wrote operas throughout his life, though none were popular and few even staged. He wrote symphonies all the time: his eighth, the *Unfinished*, and ninth, the *Great C major*, are two of the world's greatest symphonies, nowadays as much loved as any by his contemporary, Beethoven. But neither was performed during his lifetime. Schubert's first six symphonies were composed for an amateur orchestra. Nowadays they are quite popular because their music is charming, though number four is called *Tragic*.

Schubert wrote copious music for solo piano, the instrument he loved most. It is extraordinary that so much of it, apart from the Impromptus and a certain *Moment musical*, is unfamiliar. Fifty years ago, the great pianist Rakhmaninov confessed to ignorance of the existence of any piano sonatas by Schubert. Including incomplete works, there are twenty-two sonatas, among them some of the loveliest in the entire literature. Perhaps one reason for their neglect is what Schumann called "heavenly length". Perhaps another reason is more traditional: that they never had a chance to become well known. For Schubert himself was no public performer—he was not a good enough pianist. But the listener who fails to discover the B flat

Rakhmaninov p 278–80

*A pencil caricature of **Schubert** (who was only just over 5 feet tall) and his friend, the singer Vogl, "setting out to fight and conquer".*

sonata, the last and greatest, the penultimate sonata in A major, or the one in G (which is especially abundant in beautiful ideas) is missing a great deal. Schubert also wrote an enormous quantity of music for piano duet— four hands at one piano. Outstanding among many masterpieces he composed in this medium are a Fantasy in F minor, one of Schubert's last compositions and replete with the sadness of his final years; the Grand Duo, symphonic in scale, and considered by some to be a symphony arranged for performance at the piano; and an early sonata in B flat that contains some of the composer's most eloquent and persuasive melodies.

Perhaps because, unlike Beethoven, he was no more than a competent pianist, Schubert never made a public success in the Vienna of his day. Not even his string quintet in C major, perhaps the most eloquent piece of chamber music ever composed, conquered the world in his lifetime. His popular *Trout* quintet took time to be appreciated, as did his Octet, a lovely, highly original piece, full of new ideas. There are about fifteen string quartets, some of them works of his early youth. Those in A minor, G and D minor (known as *Death and the Maiden* from the variations on the song of that name) are the greatest, together with an isolated first movement, the *Quartettsatz* in C minor. A great champion of Schubert's chamber music during his lifetime was the violinist Ignaz Schuppanzigh (1776–1830).

1760–1828 Vienna

Schuppanzigh, who had taught Beethoven the viola and given the first performance of many of his quartets, took the first violin part at the première of Schubert's Octet, and soon after received the dedication of the great A minor quartet just mentioned.

Schubertiads

Schubert had a large circle of friends in Vienna: he was popular and gregarious, always in love though never durably attached—he was not

The Lied

Literally the German word for "song", Lied refers specifically to German song of the nineteenth-century Romantic movement. But there are particular features that distinguish Lieder from ordinary song settings. In the first place, the text chosen is meticulously matched in the piano accompaniment, as, for example, the turning of the mill-wheel in Schubert's Das Wandern or the ringing of the blacksmith's hammer in Brahms's Der Schmied. Though the texts chosen are predominantly German, this is not always the case: in the works of the great Lieder composers, Schubert, Schumann and Hugo Wolf, there are settings of Shakespeare, Byron, Walter Scott and even Michelangelo and Cervantes.

As implied above, the piano part has much more than a mere supporting role to play, rising above the role of accompaniment to that of an equal partnership with the singer. Instead of creating specific images, the piano may set the mood for the entire piece, such as in the opening song of Schumann's Dichterliebe cycle, or in the bleak accompaniment of Gute Nacht at the beginning of Schubert's Winterreise.

physically handsome, and was nicknamed *Schwammerl*, which means "mushroom" but is better translated as "Fatty" or "Fatso". He and his friends often met at a café or tavern for an evening's entertainment, which they called a *Schubertiad* because it always involved dancing to music extemporized at the piano by Schubert, and sometimes written down afterwards. When the dancing stopped, Schubert would play his latest compositions, perhaps an *Impromptu* or a *Moment musical*, but especially his songs, particularly with the well-known operatic baritone Michael Vogl as his singer.

Vogl introduced Schubert's two great song-cycles *Die schöne Müllerin* ("The Miller's lovely Daughter") and *Winterreise* ("Winter Journey"). Both were set to verses by Wilhelm Müller, not a famous poet but one with a vivid imagination for nature and the rustic scene, so stirring for a romantic composer living in urban Vienna and longing for the countryside a short coach-ride away.

Die schöne Müllerin is about a travelling miller's labourer who falls for his employer's daughter but is jilted for a local forester. The poems are full of inspiring references to the minutiae of country life, any one of which Schubert enhances in his music. As a tunesmith he has few rivals in the history of song, and among his six hundred or so songs there are melodious gems: for example Goethe's *Heidenröslein* ("Hedgerose"), or Hölty's *Seligkeit* ("Bliss"). Song for Schubert meant more than that. When he set the

*Tischbein's famous portrait of **Goethe** in Italy.*

*Another **Schubertiad**. The composer accompanies the singer Vogl at the house of their friend Josef von Spaun (turning the pages beside Schubert).*

finest poetry, Goethe's *Gretchen am Spinnrade* ("Gretchen at the Spinning Wheel") or *Erlkönig*, he followed the poetic images in the music launched by the particular atmosphere (spinning in the former, galloping hoofbeats in the latter). Both those Goethe songs were composed when Schubert was a boy. Later he learned even greater variety and subtlety. Some songs may sound as if they were strophic (one tune for all verses of a poem): *Das Lied im Grünen* ("The Song amid the Greenery") does so, but actually the music varies slightly from verse to verse. So does that of the poet Rellstab's *Ständchen* ("Serenade"—often billed as "Schubert's Serenade"), and particularly imaginative adjustments follow the verses of *Gute Nacht* ("Goodnight"), the first song in *Winterreise*, and later in *Der Lindenbaum* ("The Lime Tree"), which is virtually accepted in Germany as a folk song. Each song in *Winterreise* paints the scene which determines the musical form, and melody is always at its centre, not only for voice but often for piano, as in *Frühlingstraum* ("Dream of Spring").

To explore Schubert's songs takes a long time, and is an artistic education well worth the trouble. One must understand throughout how the music responds to the German words. Translations do not always convey every shade of meaning, but records usually include literal translations which help one capture the allusion of music to text.

At Beethoven's funeral Schubert was one of the coffin bearers, and followed him all too quickly to the grave. He left behind, in the Great C major symphony, a living legacy of Beethoven's example, and boundless inspiration to the Romantic composers who succeeded him. That he was poor and his genius largely unrecognized did not shake Schubert's faith in his own abilities. He was generally a happy and bohemian personality and, still young, looked forward to the recognition which would have so soon been his. He died of typhoid fever, heavily in debt, and his death was mourned by the many friends who loved him. He was buried, at his own wish, near the grave of Beethoven, with an inscription on his tomb by the Romantic poet Grillparzer: "The art of music has here interred a rich possession, but still far fairer hopes."

Chapter 9
Music and Poetry

Romanticism

Romantic self-expression—music tells a story ◆ Weber and his "Gothick" tales ◆ The elegance of Mendelssohn ◆ Schumann and the Lied ◆ Chopin the virtuoso pianist ◆ The Abbé Liszt ◆ The lyric melodies of Brahms ◆ The waltzing Strausses ◆ Anton Bruckner and the grand symphonic manner ◆

Everybody knows what Romanticism in music means: this chapter is about Weber, Mendelssohn, Chopin, Schumann and Liszt. The great musical Romantics also include Berlioz, though for the purpose of this story I prefer to discuss him with Napoleon's composers elsewhere. The greatest of all Romantic composers was surely Wagner and I have postponed him until we come to the subject of music-drama.

Romantic Inspiration
In 1813 E.T.A. Hoffmann (hero of Offenbach's last opera *Tales of Hoffmann*, and the composer of *Undine*, a typical Romantic opera about a knight who marries a water-nymph), wrote an essay on the Romantic qualities of Beethoven's music. We may agree with him: take for example the hero-worshipping element in the *Eroica* and the countryfied inspiration of the *Pastoral*; take the human idealism of *Fidelio* and the Choral Symphony. C.P.E. Bach's *Empfindsamer Stil* (music of sensibility) was also essentially Romantic.

Romantic elements were always in music, and still are. It does not have to be "wild and fanciful" as Dr Johnson suggested in his Dictionary, though an element of piquancy, the bizarre, often enhanced the appeal of Romantic art. It does not have to be nationalistic, though that too was a feature of Romanticism. It does not even have to voice the longing to be somewhere else, another country or another period in history more sympathetic than the irksome present—much though Romantic artists stressed that. The Romantics were keen on self-expression and subjective emotion, but they did not abandon responsibility for the overall design of the piece—professional composers never do.

We can say that nineteenth-century Romantic music was closely influenced by themes from literature and art, or natural scenery—the countryside and its attendant attractions becoming so desirable as an idea

Berlioz p 205–11   C.P.E. Bach p 121–2

Wagner p 229–40

Music and Poetry
Romanticism

Carl Maria von Weber.
His opera Euryanthe, *while much admired by Beethoven (and later by Hugo Wolf, who considered it a model for aspiring operatic composers), was condemned by Schubert as "anti-musical".*

and a reality as cities expanded with the Industrial Revolution. Music, more than before, sought to paint a picture or tell a story.

Carl Maria von Weber (1786–1826)

There are good examples in the music of this early Romantic German composer. His *Invitation to the Dance*, a concert-waltz for piano solo (1819), begins with a slow section in which a young man at a ball is imagined approaching a girl and requesting the pleasure of the next dance. She is heard replying demurely, they converse briefly, then take the floor together and dance a sequence of waltzes, at the end of which the boy escorts his partner back to her seat and politely takes leave of her. The waltz had, since 1792, been all the rage of Berlin dance-halls, the new, daring, even scandalous dance. Weber's *Invitation* was the first composition to give it respectability and to outline the chain-form it would develop in the work of the Viennese Lanner and the Johann Strauss family.

Another work by Weber, the Concert Piece (*Konzertstück*) in F minor for

Lanner p 191

piano and orchestra (1821), is in four movements rolled into one. Weber described it in terms of a medieval lady in the tower of a castle. Her knight has been abroad at the Crusades for many years; she trembles to imagine him lifeless on some foreign battlefield. As she mourns for him, she sees an army approaching; he is returning and they are blissfully united. The contents are very close to those of Beethoven's *Les Adieux* piano sonata (1809). But whereas in that classical work the three movements are each in a prescribed musical form, in Weber's Concert Piece the four movements are free-formed, like consecutive numbers in an operatic scene (though without recitatives). This is, in effect, Weber's third piano concerto, but he did not want to use the conventional structures: sonata form, an aria in three sections, and sonata-rondo. So he invented his literary programme and set it to music apt for each situation. This departure from classic instrumental forms was to be typical of Romantic nineteenth-century music: Weber's one-movement fusion of several old movements particularly affected Liszt in his B minor piano sonata and the two piano concertos. Schubert worked

*Max, the hero of Weber's **Der Freischütz**, is lured to the Wolf's Glen by his wicked friend Caspar, to mould some magic bullets. Ghastly spectres flutter by them while the woodsmen cast their spell.*

Liszt p 185–7

similarly in his *Wanderer* fantasy for piano solo (1822), in which the four movements also have common themes, a feature adopted by Liszt.

Weber, it may be guessed, was himself a virtuoso solo pianist of wonderful smoothness and agility. He had been well trained. As his parents were members of a travelling opera company, the young Weber came into contact with music in many different cities—and with a variety of musical pedagogues, among them Michael Haydn (working as court musician to the Archbishop of Salzburg), and with Hummel and Joseph Haydn in Vienna. At the age of fourteen his first opera, *Das Waldmädchen*, was produced with some success in the Austrian capital. So precocious were the youth's musical talents that he was appointed *Kapellmeister* to the Breslau theatre before he was eighteen years old (though Weber's career nearly came to a precipitous end there when he accidentally drank a glass of nitric acid). But he soon moved on, and secured a non-musical post as private secretary to Duke Ludwig at Stuttgart. There he wrote another opera, *Silvana*, spent a short time in prison for having incurred royal displeasure, and continued to write for the piano.

His two piano concertos and four piano sonatas are extremely brilliant, sometimes eloquent, elsewhere less inspired. The finale of the first sonata is a *tour de force* of perpetual motion in music. He composed a bassoon concerto and numerous concerto-like works for the clarinettist Bärmann. But he chiefly cultivated the opera, writing it all his adult life and working in opera houses. Weber was among the first conductors to relinquish keyboard or violin and beat time with his arms, a scroll of paper in his hand, standing up in front of the orchestra.

His great operatic success was his seventh opera, *Der Freischütz* (1821): the title is hard to translate without outlining the plot: the hero, a crack shot with a rifle, buys seven magic bullets from the Devil so as to win a contest: six of them will hit the bullseye, the seventh will go where the Devil directs it—a "free shot"—the title's literal translation. The elements of magic and the supernatural appealed to Romantic taste; the scene in the Wolf's Glen, where the magic bullets are cast, revels in stage magic and spooky music. The rustic setting also appealed, with its contests of marksmanship, dancing by peasantfolk (another waltz!), a chorus of huntsmen and another of bridesmaids. It has contrasted solos for the solemn, pious heroine and her jolly younger cousin, as well as for the sinister Kaspar, the Romantic hero Max, and the pious hermit in the finale. Modern audiences have been known to scoff at such nursery stuff; but if *Der Freischütz* is strongly staged, warmly and well sung, and the dialogue convincingly spoken, it can still make a worthy impression.

Weber attempted to repeat its success with *Euryanthe* (Vienna 1823), a preposterous tale of chivalry and calumny, with sung recitatives and marvellous music—drama in need of rescue. His final opera was *Oberon* (1826), an English *Singspiel*, again saddled with an absurd plot, composed for Covent Garden in London. The heroine's big solo, "Ocean, thou mighty monster", is still sometimes heard at concerts as, frequently, are the excellent overtures to all these three operas.

Weber was a weakly child and constantly suffered poor health. His zeal for work and financial worries left him worn out when he reached London to conduct *Oberon*, and he died there. His piano music influenced many subsequent virtuosos and his operas also had a wide effect on his successors, notably Richard Wagner. The shivery, supernatural element (evident in

Lucia Elizabeth Vestris
as Fatima in Weber's
Oberon, *handmaiden to the lovely Reiza and rescued from slavery by the fairy king.*

Felix Mendelssohn was especially revered in England, where his oratorios were adored by respectable Victorian society.

Wagner's *Lohengrin*, 1851), was much favoured in English "Gothick" novels of the nineteenth century (*i.e.* Mary Shelley's *Frankenstein*, 1818), and taken up by opera composers (notably *The Vampyre*, 1827, by Heinrich Marschner, one of Weber's assistants at Dresden Opera).

Felix Mendelssohn Bartholdy (1809–1847)
Another superfine virtuoso pianist from a generation later, a Romantic of a less pioneering order, Felix Mendelssohn Bartholdy, showed astounding musical talent as a boy, composing a brilliantly polished Octet for strings at the age of sixteen and in the following year a concert overture for orchestra, inspired by reading Shakespeare's *A Midsummer Night's Dream*. *The Dream* is a masterpiece by any standards, technical, imaginative or whichever way you look at it. Four orchestral chords, soft and mysterious, raise the curtain; the fairies are seen in airy flight, then the lovers in the forest, then the "rude mechanicals" and Bottom with the Ass's head.

One of the strongest images that Mendelssohn retained from his tour of Scotland was of **Fingal's Cave,** *on the Isle of Staffa.*

Drawings by Mendelssohn—Below: a sketch of **Edinburgh**, *made during his tour of Scotland in 1829. Right: a watercolour of the* **Leipzig Gewandhaus**—*Mendelssohn was the conductor of the orchestra there.*

Mendelssohn's other incidental music for the play, including the Wedding March, the Nocturne (with evocative horn solo, so dear to the Romantic soul) and the Scherzo, with its thistledown whirlwind solo for flute, were composed sixteen years later and still seem to inhabit the same territory of a brilliant boyhood.

Mendelssohn grew up in a wealthy banker's home. His musical talent was encouraged, he was given a liberal but thorough education and was a decent amateur painter. His father sent him away to travel when school-days were done. In Scotland Felix visited the Isle of Staffa and turned the

experience into his concert overture *Fingal's Cave* (or *The Hebrides* 1832—both titles are current), a brilliant seascape in sunshine and storm, noted with a painter's eye. Other visits to Scotland prompted Mendelssohn's *Scottish Symphony* (1842), which evokes the ruined chapel of Holyrood, the hills above the Firth of Forth and the Braemar Gathering. Likewise a tour of Italy provoked the *Italian Symphony* (1833), a work of outstanding spirit and luminosity.

His education over, Mendelssohn proved himself a hard worker, chiefly as conductor in Leipzig, though popularity in England took him there often, prompting the very fine oratorio *Elijah*, and two less persuasive companions, *St Paul* and *Christus*. Although Jewish by birth, he was raised as a Lutheran and acknowledged it in his *Reformation Symphony* (1840), which quotes *A Stronghold Sure*, written by Luther himself, and the Dresden *Amen*, another Lutheran favourite. Mendelssohn's keyboard works sometimes borrow Lutheran chorale-prelude technique, best known in Bach's examples. Mendelssohn was responsible for the revival of Bach's *St Matthew Passion*, after a century's neglect, thus restoring to circulation one of posterity's best-loved choral masterpieces. Mendelssohn's teacher, Carl Zelter (1758–1832), presented to his pupil the autograph of the work, which he had acquired years before. Mendelssohn also prevailed upon his teacher to allow the performance of the work, which took place on 11 March 1829—and its first publication. Very active in this project was the composer's friend, the actor and singer Eduard Devrient (brother of the more famous Emil), who sang the part of Christ at the first performance.

For the Victorian English, Mendelssohn was as great an idol as Handel or Beethoven. He was cheered in the streets wherever he went, fêted by society and a great favourite with Queen Victoria, who graciously consented to receive the dedication of the *Scottish Symphony*. Prince Albert, her husband, was a keen amateur composer (of less than overwhelming music); the royal couple loved to pass musical afternoons in Mendelssohn's company, playing the composer's *Songs without Words* and singing selections from his oratorios.

But eventually taste swung against him. His music was reckoned too demure and comfortable, though his Violin Concerto in E minor (1844), a work of wondrous lyrical beauty and vividness, always remained popular. Our own late twentieth-century age can appreciate Mendelssohn's music more objectively, for example in the piano concertos (much in Weber's vein) and the volumes of *Songs without Words* for piano solo. These short pieces instantly establish a particular mood, a new and typically Romantic idea, and are most attractive piano music for the drawing-room pianist. Though not now as popular as in our grandparents' day, copies of Mendelssohn's *Spinning Song*, *Spring Song* and *The Bee's Wedding* are still to be found in piano stools everywhere. Time is nowadays also found for Mendelssohn's piano trios and string quartets, which are full of interest, much less sedate than was supposed by the early twentieth century.

Robert Schumann (1810–1856)

We have to thank Mendelssohn for convincing his friend Schumann that admirable poetry need not suffer by being set to music. Young Schumann, drawn to both arts, believed that poetry and music should be kept apart. He was in any case chiefly devoted to the piano, was prepared for a virtuoso's career and wrote all his music for his own instrument. His teacher was

Bach's *St Matthew Passion* p 75

Music and Poetry

Romanticism

The young virtuoso pianist **Clara Wieck**, *before her marriage to Robert Schumann.*

Friedrich Wieck, whose daughter Clara, nine years younger than Schumann, was likewise being trained by her father for the career of a virtuoso. By the time she was nine years old, her musicianship was such that she was making concert appearances all over Germany, playing concertos. All this, however, was at the expense of her personality and her general education: her father, a bully by temperament (as well as a great teacher), neglected all other studies and recreation. Schumann soon fell in love with her, to her father's horror, and the young man rapidly became anathema to Friedrich Wieck. Schumann was forced to abandon ideas of becoming a concert pianist when the fourth finger of his left hand became paralysed: it was long thought that this was due to a device he had evolved to try and strengthen it, though recently it has been suggested that the disease was venereal in origin. After some years of despair and adversity, including protracted litigation with Clara's father, the pair were eventually married in 1840, and the years that followed were the happiest in the composer's life.

Schumann began to compose songs with encouragement from Mendelssohn, chiefly to poems by Heinrich Heine and Joseph von Eichendorff, though many less eminent poets, as well as the great Goethe, were involved. Schumann was a magnificent composer for piano, as his greatly endearing Piano Concerto (1845) leaves no doubt: it is youthful, attractive, garrulous, eloquent, very feminine music. Of his three sonatas for piano solo, the second in G minor (1838) is the finest, the invention radiantly alive throughout the piece.

His grandest piano solo composition is surely the Fantasy in C major (1836). It was his contribution to a Beethoven memorial with quotations from Beethoven's songs *To the Distant Beloved*. His large piano output includes music for young people (his own children); also several suites of short mood pieces and the suite *Carnaval* (1836), which describes personages and events at a party. In it Chopin and Paganini are evoked, as are Schumann's literary alter egos, the ardent Florestan and the quieter Eusebius (he was a respected and progressive writer on music), and a final anti-Philistine demonstration by the acolytes of Romanticism. Many other fine solo piano pieces by Schumann are built along this principle of musical sketch-portraiture, notably sets called *Kreisleriana* and *Davidsbündlertänze*. Florestan and Eusebius recur in the *Faschingsschwank aus Wien* ("Carnival Jest from Vienna", 1830), which quotes from the *Marseillaise* at a time when its performance was forbidden because of the current democratic revolution in France. *Papillons* and *Kinderszenen* ("Scenes from Childhood") are two more lovely sets of short, linked pieces, the latter containing the very popular *Träumerei*. A brilliant *Toccata*, composed around the same time as the *Davidsbündlertänze* when Schumann was still playing the piano, shows his obsession with the study of technique. Two of Schumann's four symphonies bear descriptive titles: No. 1, *The Spring*, a hymn to nature, and No. 3, *The Rhenish*, which dwells on the majesty and importance of the Rhineland district where Schumann now lived, including the grand cathedral at Cologne, where he observed the coronation of a new Archbishop—the whole symphony is Romantically vivid.

Facing page: **The Chalk Cliffs of Rügen** by Caspar David Friedrich, epitomizes the yearning that was the Romantic movement. Composers abandoned carefully wrought structures such as the aria and sonata in favour of a freer and more self-indulgent approach to musical expression.

As a good Romantic, Schumann essayed Byron, most Romantic of poets at that time, with his *Manfred* (1849), seldom heard nowadays apart from its overture, but a rare treat when it occurs. His chamber music is worth exploring, even beyond the popular Quintet for piano and strings (1842).

1820-1897 Romanticism

Robert & Clara Schumann.

Fine as are the piano works of Schumann (the *Humoreske*, 1839, for example, a suite that ought to have a literary background but doesn't acknowledge one, deserves greater popularity), his greatest achievement is in song. Schumann was highly literate; his music criticism is a pleasure to read, even about composers long forgotten, though he did hail Chopin and Brahms when both were still virtually unknown.

He had a fine taste in poetry, and a poet's imagination. His first settings of Heine, a so-called *Liederkreis*, though no song-cycle at all, generously prepares one for the *Dichterliebe* ("Poet's Love"), another tale of love won then lost (like Schubert's cycles), but one totally idiosyncratic, the piano and voice even more closely linked than in Schubert, so that some songs are like duets for voice and piano. A Schumann speciality is the song ended with a piano commentary (at the end of *Dichterliebe* and of *Frauenliebe und leben*,

Clara Schumann
accompanying the great violinist Joachim.

"Woman's life and love" for example) that recalls an earlier mood, now even more poignant. Schumann wrote songs after 1840: an especially fine set brings together five poems supposedly written by Mary Queen of Scots. Schumann set them to music in 1852 and they have a maturity and impressiveness even beyond his 1840 songs.

The last years of the composer's life were miserable. He was beset by depression and melancholy that seems to have had its roots in the troubled period of his young manhood. He suffered hallucinations and early in 1854 threw himself into the Rhine from a bridge in Düsseldorf. The remaining two years of his life were spent in a private asylum at Bonn where, in spite of treatment and visits from Clara, Brahms and Joachim, he gradually lost hold upon reality.

After her husband's death, Clara continued to play and teach for another forty years, touring all over Europe and finally settling in Frankfurt, where she taught at the Conservatory. She was an ardent champion of Robert's music and, as a widow, played every concert dressed in black. Her playing was the opposite of Liszt's, eschewing all unnecessary display. Bernard Shaw, when as a young music critic he first heard her perform, called her "the Grail of the critic's quest".

Loewe's Songs

In the context of song, mention must be made of the brilliant, jolly and sensitive work of Carl Loewe (1796–1869). Loewe came from Saxony, had taught himself the piano by playing Bach's *Well-tempered Clavier* and, unusually for a composer, was himself a singer of outstanding ability. He worked as *Kapellmeister* at Stettin for much of his life and died, it is recorded, "in a state of trance". (Five years before his death, he had gone into a trance that lasted for six weeks.) Loewe specialized particularly in the ballad, a long, usually dramatic narrative poem, set to music that varies

Brahms & Schumann p 189   *The Well-tempered Clavier* p 93
Liszt p 185–7

A Romantic portrait of **Chopin** *by his friend Delacroix.*

with the poetic situation. His *Eduard* and *Erlkönig* (the same Goethe poem that Schubert set) are often sung, likewise *Kleiner Haushalt*, the brilliant bejewelled description of the miniature domestic set-up for a miniature lady—comic and endearing in its music, and in Rückert's verses. A ready wit is typical of Loewe's songs; so too, is an agile vocal technique: they are not songs for drawing-room amateurs.

Frédéric Chopin (1810–1849)

It was Schumann, in his capacity as music critic, who drew the German public's attention in 1830 to the arrival of an important new composer, when he greeted the publication of Chopin's Variations on *La ci darem la mano* from Mozart's *Don Giovanni* with the words, "Hats off, gentlemen, a genius!" It was a timely remark: in that year, the twenty-year-old Fryderik Franciszek Chopin left his native Poland to find fame and fortune in western Europe. The next year he settled in Paris, and called himself

Frédéric François: in a sense it was a sort of homecoming, since his father was a Frenchman who had moved to Poland to escape conscription into the French Revolutionary Army. But father Chopin was proud of his new country and brought up his son as an enthusiastic Polish patriot.

As a boy, Chopin heard peasants singing folk songs in the fields, and grew up with Poland's national dances, the *mazurka*, *krakowiak* and *polonaise*. When he began to compose music himself as a boy prodigy, he adopted instinctively these national dance-forms: his first *polonaise* was published when he was seven. He made his concert début as a pianist a year later.

Piano-playing came naturally to Chopin: he largely taught himself to become a leading virtuoso in an age of great pianists—though visits to Warsaw by Hummel and the violinist Paganini prevented Chopin from becoming smug about his prowess. His musical studies were chiefly concentrated on theory and composition, and as late as 1841 he gave himself a refresher course in academic counterpoint. One might hardly guess that from Chopin's music, which is all for the piano (there are songs to Polish verses and works for cello and flute, with piano accompaniment, as well as a piano trio): it all seems directly inspired by the physical activity of piano-playing. Indeed Chopin did always compose at the piano and his written compositions largely derived from extemporizations. It was said that he never played any of his pieces twice in the same manner and hated the

Liszt at the piano. The distinguished audience comprises (left to right): Alexandre Dumas, Berlioz, Paganini, Rossini and, in a scarlet cloak, Chopin's lover, Georges Sand.

Hummel p 156–7
Paganini p 184

finality of setting down on paper a composition that for him could never be finished.

For his first tour of Europe he composed two concertos for piano and orchestra (in E minor and in F minor), closely modelled on those of his current idol Hummel, as can be proved by comparing the Chopin in E minor, phrase by phrase, with Hummel's opus 85 in A minor. Both of Chopin's concertos are attractive and often performed, the orchestral music quite subservient to the piano's flights of fancy. They are audibly less advanced, less personal, than the big piano solo works of later years: the sonatas in B flat minor (1839—the Funeral March third movement was written two years previously) and B minor (1844), both extremely powerful and original; the four Ballades (1831–1843), each matured for several years before being written down, and vaguely suggested by Polish ballad-poems, and the four Scherzos (1831–1842), more quickly completed—but oddly named, since they tend to the heroic rather than the jocular.

There are big pieces among Chopin's sixteen polonaises, notably the last two, both in A flat major (1842 and 1846, the latter called *Polonaise-Fantasy*). But length does not influence merit in Chopin's music. The *Barcarolle* (1846) and *Berceuse* (1844) are not greater than some of his mazurkas, preludes (1836–1839), nocturnes (a type of music that he borrowed from the Irish pianist-composer John Field, 1782–1837, from whose playing Chopin learned much), or particularly his *Etudes*, a formidable and fascinating collection of teaching studies that are little tone-poems in themselves.

His waltzes are miracles of lightness, grace and variety of mood. In these shorter pieces we find much of the cream of Chopin's originality and inventive daring which influenced music, and not only piano music, ever after. He did not give his pieces descriptive titles and except perhaps in the Ballades, did not acknowledge literary inspiration—we may refer to the *Raindrop Prelude* and the *Minute Waltz* and the *Winter Wind* study, but they are not Chopin's names any more than *Moonlight Sonata* is Beethoven's. But each piece seems vividly to paint a picture or set a scene, and nicknames are inevitable—though all of us are entitled to reject what somebody else has foisted on Chopin. The C minor study which ends the first book (opus 10, no. 12) is called *Revolutionary* because Chopin is supposed to have written it in anger after hearing that Poland had capitulated to Russia; but the only evidence is gossip. The superimposing of "programmes" upon Chopin's piano pieces can become ludicrous. The most famous example, perpetrated by the great pianist Hans von Bülow, sets out to describe the ninth (E major) prelude:

> "Here Chopin has the conviction that he has lost his power of expression. With the determination to discover whether his brain can still originate ideas, he strikes his head with a hammer ... In the third and fourth bars one can hear the blood trickle (trills in the left hand). He is desperate at finding no inspiration (fifth bar); he strikes again with the hammer and with greater force ... In the key of A flat he finds his powers again. Appeased, he seeks his former key and closes contentedly."

Chopin must have been a formidable pianist and some of his music can survive the worst attentions of keyboard thumpers and speed-merchants.

Reports of his playing always emphasize its delicacy and refinement and physically he was never robust. Schumann, who loved Chopin and his music, wrote of his playing:

> "Imagine that an Aeolian harp had all the scales and that an artist's hand had mingled them together in all kinds of fantastic decorations, but in such a way that you could always hear a deeper fundamental tone and a softly singing melody—there you have something of a picture of his playing."

Soon after settling in Paris, where he was greatly admired by high society, he found that he could live comfortably by giving piano lessons and selling compositions. Thereafter he gave up public concerts, almost for good, and played only in private. His many love affairs are well documented; the longest and most celebrated was his liaison with Aurore Dudevant, the French writer who called herself Georges Sand.

*Far and away the greatest virtuoso of his age, **Liszt** was the inventor of the solo piano recital, as well as the first conductor of* Lohengrin *by Wagner (who became his son-in-law), and the leading composer in the Music of the Future avant-garde movement.*

Lions of the Keyboard

Romantic music did not need *castrati* for musical heroes: nature was its inspiration and the cruel operation had been internationally banned—not before time. The musical heroes of the age became daredevil superstar instrumental virtuosi. Most were pianists, like Sigismond Thalberg (1812–1871), a Hummel pupil who could play so many notes that he seemed to have three hands; yet he sat erect and motionless at the piano, apparently uninvolved in the furore his playing roused.

The Irish virtuoso John Field cared not at all for Chopin's music, which he contemptuously referred to as "the talent of the sick-room". His opinion was tinged with jealousy—Chopin's nocturnes being more popular than his own. Field was trained by Clementi, in the old "classical" style, and was apprenticed as a demonstrator in the latter's piano showroom in Soho. He became a renowned and poetic pianist, though socially he was graceless and dissipated. Liszt commented on his lack of display in performance which he thought could easily be confused with apathy, but then Liszt's playing was the opposite extreme. There was Alexander Dreyschock (1818–1869), who could play faster and louder than anybody else and whom J.B.Cramer, a great pianist of Beethoven's time, reckoned to have no left hand, but two right hands instead. Dreyschock thrilled his audiences by playing Chopin's

Revolutionary Study, taking the rapid left-hand runs in octaves. Liszt answered by taking another rapid Chopin study that had one note to each hand and playing both parts in octaves at top speed. His histrionics lent an air of mystery to the piano, removing the comfortable aura of domesticity that was associated with the instrument in everyone's mind. Audiences had hysterics and swooned when Liszt played the piano: his personal charisma had a lot to do with it—such reactions were unlikely to be generated merely by a first-class performance of, say, a paraphrase on operatic airs arranged with difficult runs and embellishments.

Later imitators were on the whole less successful. Liszt's flair for showmanship had amounted to genius: some, such as Louis Moreau Gottschalk (1829–1869) from New Orleans, thrilled the public for a short spell with flashy pianistic novelties and were soon forgotten; while others lived by reputation alone. Having developed a phobia for playing in public, Adolf Henselt (1814–1889), a lion of the keyboard, was terrified of audiences. Wearing a red fez, he would play Bach at home, with a Bible on the music stand for him to read while he practised on a piano stuffed with feathers to lessen the noise.

Niccolo Paganini

The greatest circus-musician of all was no pianist but the Italian violinist Niccolo Paganini (1782–1840), whose playing so defied credibility by its agility, accuracy and emotional power, that gossips declared him in league with the Devil. He was only technically much in advance of his time; nowadays music students can throw off his twenty-four caprices for unaccompanied violin before breakfast, though only a few virtuosi trouble to play them complete at concerts. They were exciting enough for Schumann and Liszt to transcribe them as piano studies and the variation-theme of Caprice 24 was re-used for variations by Brahms, Rakhmaninov, Lutoslawski and others. He commissioned but never played Berlioz's *Harold in Italy*. His six violin concertos make lively listening.

Paganini. *His Guarneri violin was a gift from an admirer. He had been forced to sell his own instrument to pay his gambling debts.*

The young Liszt, *looking suitably Byronic, as the great Bohemian virtuoso.*

Ferenc Liszt (1811–1886)

The greatest instrumental virtuoso of them all was the Hungarian, Liszt, who was born at the Esterhazy court (where his father was a servant), long served by Haydn. Liszt studied in Vienna and divided the rest of his long and illustrious life between Paris, his centre as a virtuoso pianist, Weimar, where he was court musical director, conductor, composer and champion of modern music, and Rome, where he took minor holy orders, entitling him to be called Abbé. Like Chopin, he abandoned concert tours as soon as he could, not because any other pianist was his superior, but because other sorts of music and other occupations interested him more urgently (first love, then the Catholic Church). Liszt used his power over his listeners to introduce them to new, often very advanced, music. In Weimar he could produce and perform new operas (Wagner's *Lohengrin* was one). Elsewhere,

Esterhaza p 139–40

Lohengrin p 230

there being no radio or gramophone, Liszt had to transcribe the new music for piano solo and play it in the recitals which he was the first pianist to give regularly in public. When anybody objects to his *Rigoletto-Paraphrase* (1859) or *Réminiscences de Norma* (1841), one must ask how else audiences could then have become familiar with the original music from these operas.

As the ideal piano virtuoso, his finest works are the twelve "Transcendental Studies", of which the published and performed version (1851) is the third and least difficult (but still fearsomely hard). Liszt, unlike Chopin, gave titles to them all: *Mazeppa* (also adapted for orchestra), *Feux-Follets* ("Will-o'-the-Wisp"—as gossamer as the title suggests) and *Harmonies du Soir* ("Evening Harmonies") are highlights in a superb volume of music. Like Chopin and Schumann, Liszt was strongly influenced by the style and virtuosity of Paganini, and in six Paganini Studies tried to transpose for keyboard some impression of the problems involved in playing that composer's music on its original instrument. Schumann said of the result that they were "the most difficult ever written for the pianoforte, as the original is the most difficult ever written for the violin". His two piano concertos both follow Weber's *Konzertstück* in telescoping the movements, and the various themes are transformed between movements; the same happens, even more brilliantly and sensitively, in his B minor sonata for solo piano, the greatest of its kind after Schubert (or even perhaps after Beethoven—I would call it the most marvellous piano sonata ever composed by anybody).

In orchestral music his *Faust* symphony stands out for its dramatic power, bold musical vocabulary and technique of thematic transformation: after movements depicting Faust and his sweetheart Gretchen, the portrait of Mephistopheles skilfully distorts the heroic themes of Faust to diabolic effect.

*A silhouette of **Liszt** in the garb of a Catholic priest.*

Like Chopin, Liszt wrote many short mood-pieces for solo piano. His *Années de Pèlerinage* ("Years of Pilgrimage"—subjects from Switzerland and Italy, composed over a long period) paint scenes in the manner of Chopin. The *Vallée d'Obermann*, the *Villa d'Este Fountains*, the *Sonata after reading Dante* and the *Petrarch Sonnets* (also set verbally as songs) stand at the crown of Liszt's output. As an example of music inspired by painting, a common Romantic practice with few reputable specimens on display, Liszt's daemonic *Totentanz* ("Dance of Death") for piano and orchestra (1859) must be mentioned—it is based on a painting by Orcagna, nowadays in grave disrepair.

For their literary inspiration, so typical of Romanticism, and for highly original, bold music, Liszt's thirteen orchestral symphonic poems deserve anybody's attention. They range from Shakespeare's *Hamlet* and the romances of *Tasso*, to Liszt's homeland, *Hungaria*, and the legendary *Prometheus* and *Orpheus*. Liszt returned to Hungary in later life and hymned his country also in his many Hungarian Rhapsodies for solo piano, some later orchestrated, delightful potpourris of gypsy music, still to be heard whenever a Hungarian gypsy band assembles (Budapest restaurants still employ some of the best), though he wrote them for piano solo. The true Hungarian traditional music was not here, but was later revealed by Kodály and Bartók. Liszt's last piano compositions (eg *Nuages gris* and *Unstern*) range harmonically far into the future, beyond his time to Debussy, and even to Bartók. His harmonic daring much influenced the mature music of Wagner, who married Liszt's daughter, Cosima, and was on

Kodály p 253

Weber's *Konzertstück* p 170–1

Bartók p 253–6

close terms with her father. Liszt was reputedly a noisy pianist. E. Cleary Hugh (Clerihew) Bentley wrote:

> *The Abbé Liszt*
> *Hit the piano with his fiszt.*
> *That was the way*
> *He used to play.*

My own great-aunt heard him play in London on his last visit and recalled his soft, delicate playing—no thunderstorms—a verdict accordant with his late music.

German-speaking Europe, in the late nineteenth century, was split between the supporters of the New Music, represented by Berlioz, Liszt and Wagner, and the supposed product of true tradition, represented by Brahms, a north German, Classicist by persuasion, who moved to Vienna.

Concert Hall

Public concerts, as opposed to music given in great houses under the patronage of nobility, were an English invention of the late seventeenth century. The Hanover Square Rooms and Hickford's in the Haymarket were two of the most renowned, continuing the tradition of concerts started in a City Tavern by a London violinist, John Banister. Above his store in Clerkenwell, a coal merchant named Thomas Britton had established a famous series of concerts even before then, where sometimes his friend Handel would play for the small audience, who each paid a subscription. (Britton, incidentally, was frightened to death by a ventriloquist in 1714.)

The famous Concert Spirituel *series had been inaugurated in Paris in 1725, though at first the concerts were limited to performances of sacred music. The concerts of the Leipzig Gewandhaus came later in the century (1781). But until the post-Napoleonic period, public concert halls were few and far between, and resulted from the decline of private patronage as well as the immense growth of large-scale symphonic music at this time. Big concert halls were essential—not merely to accommodate the dramatic increase in orchestral forces but to hold the large audiences necessary to make such music economically viable.*

The design of such buildings poses numerous problems. The interior must not be too resonant, which produces a confusing echo; nor too sound-absorbent, which muffles much of the music's clarity. The steep raking of the auditorium floor is not primarily so that the audience can see the performers, but to allow the listener to hear the music unimpeded acoustically by members of the audience sitting in front.

Johannes Brahms (1833–1897)

Like every other self-respecting composer of those days, and at least since Sebastian Bach, Brahms was highly regarded as a keyboard player. Born in north-German Hamburg, an elegant, lively and cultured town, as close to France in culture as to Germany, Brahms might be thought well situated. As a very young pianist he formed a duo with a Hungarian gypsy violinist, Eduard Remenyi, and their travels gave Brahms a hankering for the south. Italy enchanted him and at length he made his home in Vienna.

As a pianist of outstanding ability, he wrote virtuoso music for his own instrument: the Variations on Paganini's 24th Caprice, the Variations on a theme of Handel, the two piano concertos, all were considered *ne plus ultra*

in terms of technique for many years. He was as devoted to the female voice as to the ample female singer. Like Schubert, he was always in love, but never married—not even the great love of his life, Schumann's widow, Clara. Brahms had first met the Schumann family when he was twenty years old, some months before Schumann's attempt at suicide. He had an introduction through their mutual friend, the great violinist Joachim, and received valuable help from Schumann in securing publication of his first piano works. For the next two years of the older man's confinement and eventual death, Brahms stayed very close to the Schumanns, helping in whatever ways he could. Such an environment provided an obvious breeding-ground for the germs of romantic attachment.

The Romantic Brahms is well observed in his many *Lieder*, typically Romantic in their fluent melody and rippling accompaniment, not always concerned with niceties of poetic emphasis, but ready always when musical emphasis was needed. They only miss the mark when Brahms refuses to yield his creative all for a climax. It always happens in his music and is a sign of his creative temperament.

Brahms cultivated all instrumental forms with enthusiasm, tempered by his Classic upbringing: he remained always aware that he was the heir of an old, serious, musical tradition. Brahms disliked being played up by the public against Wagner, Liszt and the so-called music of the future; but he was strongly aware of music's past and took an active part in new scholarly editions of old music.

Most people come to Brahms through his symphonies, consciously

Johannes Brahms taking tea with Adèle, the wife of Johann Strauss.

Facing page: *Liszt in his old age. He died in Bayreuth, shortly after attending a performance of Tristan und Isolde.*

Clara Schumann p 176, 179

Lieder p 166

Music and Poetry
Romanticism

A caricature of Viennese society enjoying a brisk Galop *under the baton of* **Johann Strauss the younger**.

conceived as successors to Beethoven, though the relaxation is heard from the second symphony onwards, as the second piano concerto yields a little in expression, after the unrelenting first. The Violin Concerto, written for his great friend, the violinist Joachim, cultivates long melody in typically Romantic vein. Some of Brahms's most beautiful lyrical music is heard in his late piano pieces, given such Romantic titles as *Intermezzo*, *Capriccio* and *Rhapsody*—short, succinct and exquisitely worked music. An early work, very popular, is the *Requiem*, a choral piece set to Luther's German Bible—sombre but often luminously beautiful. Brahms's prolific chamber music includes three very Romantic string quartets, a piano quintet of high quality and a clarinet quintet, one of chamber music's loveliest pieces—the rhapsodic central section of the slow movement links up with Liszt's Hungary. And indeed Brahms did write a number of Hungarian dances for piano duet, several of them still most popular.

Brahms was friendly with, and a leading admirer of, Johann Strauss the Younger—the acknowledged king of the Viennese Waltz, creator of the *Blue Danube*, *Emperor*, *Artist's Life*, *Tales from the Vienna Woods* and other symphonic waltzes. They belong among the treasures of nineteenth-century Viennese music, and generally begin with a free prelude, as in *Wine, Women and Song*, for example, or *Tales from the Vienna Woods*. This is

Liszt p 185–7

The Conductor

In the early days of symphonic music, relatively small forces of musicians were used in performance (and probably less at rehearsal). These would be coordinated by a keyboard player—as often as not the composer himself—who cued in instruments as necessary, set the tempo, helped those who had gone astray to find the place again, and provided a reassuring harmonic support to the ensemble, above all by stressing the rhythmic pulse.

Orchestration, in the age of Haydn and Mozart, was a relatively straightforward matter. With the ever-increasing orchestral resources that came in with the nineteenth century, came the realization that these were impossible to balance from a seat among the players. And there was no way that the entire orchestra could follow a tempo given by someone seated among them directing from a violin or keyboard. It was a simple step from there to the podium, giving out the beat with a baton or roll of music paper (though many preferred, after the fashion of some modern dance-band maestros, to face the audience while conducting the orchestra).

With immense orchestral forces at his disposal by the middle of the nineteenth century, the conductor needed an ever more sophisticated "ear" to judge balance and locate faulty intonation among the players, in addition to a definite headmasterly quality, to keep control over a hundred or more frustrated soloists. Since the recording age, the job of the conductor has become even more complex, with an ever-increasing repertoire to be learned and with a public ever less tolerant of mistakes. Right, Carlo Maria Giulini conducts the Los Angeles Philharmonic during filming for the "Music in Time" television series.

succeeded by a string of perhaps five short waltzes, often with recapitulation, whose rhythm is characterized by a slight anticipation of the second beat of every bar, and by a slowing down of the tempo as each new refrain is introduced. As well as the Strauss family (Johann the Elder and his two sons Johann and Josef), the other great waltz composer of the period was Josef Lanner (1801–1843), who had started as a musician in the orchestra of Johann Strauss the Elder. Many of the Viennese public considered Lanner's waltzes the best: Strauss's music, they said, invited you to dance, but Lanner's music compelled you to dance.

Anton Bruckner (1824–1896)

Brahms's four orchestral symphonies are a marvellous quartet. As they emerged in Vienna, they were regularly and partisan-fashion contrasted with those of Bruckner, a master of musical theory and a greatly imaginative musician, who offended Viennese taste by admiring Wagner's music. The son of an Austrian village schoolmaster, he was orphaned while very young and was sent away to be educated in an Augustine monastery, where he acquired a thorough musical education. When he left, it was to attend teachers' training college, and he returned as a master at the monastery where he had been brought up. Though he composed while there, and became the incumbent organist, the pressures of teaching eventually became irreconcilable with his urge to compose, and he left to pursue studies in counterpoint, orchestration and composition in Linz and Vienna.

A visit to Munich in 1865, where he met Wagner and attended the première of *Tristan und Isolde*, was a turning point in Bruckner's life: Wagner became his idol.

Bruckner's eleven symphonies and three church masses (he was a cathedral organist) seldom show interest in any music since Beethoven and Schubert, but were supposed too modern and harmonically experimental for the pleasure of late nineteenth-century Viennese audiences. Their language is, nevertheless, quite simple. The themes are slowly unfolded, often with spectacular climaxes. Faster and slower melodies are contrasted. The finales are always grandiose, with returns of earlier important themes. The ideals, as in the masses, are simple, the means most elaborate. Once the language is comprehended, Bruckner's symphonies become significant as well as comprehensible, a truly Romantic celebration of man amid nature, as Weber had postulated it so many years before. In the horn-call of the fourth symphony, Bruckner joins hands with the Weber of *Freischütz* and *Oberon*. But in the fanfares of his ninth symphony's *adagio* he is looking forward to a new world, perhaps even beyond ours, and for some of us his symphonies are even more cogent than those of Beethoven and Brahms.

Wagner p 229–40
Weber p 170–3

Chapter 10
Music for the People
Revolution and Grand Opera

Napoleon demands formal Italian music for France's new republic ♦ The Paris Conservatoire ♦ French grand opera gains heart and strength from Italy—Rossini, Donizetti and Bellini ♦ Superstars of the operatic stage ♦ The original genius of Berlioz ♦ A native French opera—Gounod, Bizet and Saint-Säens ♦

During the first half of the nineteenth century, Paris was the capital city of opera, even if, as so often in earlier musical history, the best composers in town were imported from abroad. Considering how much the Lowland French had contributed to Italian music in the sixteenth century, it seems only fair that the Italians should return the favour in the establishment of French *grand opéra*.

The French Revolution
The events of 14 July 1789 and the subsequent Reign of Terror put an end to courtly musical entertainment. Instead of the elegant salon solo cantata there were rousing unison choruses about liberty. Opera was replaced by open-air festivals with massed choirs and orchestras singing about heroic feats of the new France.

Religion was not at first discouraged. The storming of the Bastille was commemorated with a *Te Deum*, it being argued that God, having created the working class, and Jesus having been born to it, must be socially acceptable. Before long the churches were shut, the priests imprisoned and crowds invited to hear Gossec's *Hymn to Liberty*, Rouget de l'Isle's *Marseillaise* and Méhul's *National Song* for three choirs and three orchestras, with soloists and a third small ensemble of instruments separately disposed in the dome of Les Invalides. Already there were doubts about God's classless image, and in 1794 Robespierre instructed the French to praise, instead, the Supreme Being. A major gain to music was the establishment in 1795 of the Paris Conservatoire, musical education for all gifted young musicians: its famous concerts were inaugurated in 1828 with a cycle of Beethoven's symphonies.

When Napoleon became First Consul in 1801 he brought back the Church and its priests, and encouraged Catholic music of a suitably

Gossec p 131   Méhul p 208
Beethoven's symphonies p 162–3

Luigi Cherubini. A *portrait by Ingres, that hangs in the Louvre.*

monumental Classical variety. To lead this musical establishment he brought Giovanni Paisiello (1740–1816) from Naples, already the renowned composer of an opera about *The Barber of Seville* (1782, first performed in St Petersburg), to be musical director of his private chapel. When Napoleon was crowned Emperor in 1804 in Notre Dame, the music had been composed by Paisiello; a *Te Deum* and Coronation mass, with other items by Jean-François Le Sueur (1760–1837), who replaced Paisiello and was Berlioz's chief composition professor.

Napoleon wanted formal, highly melodious, very pompous music for his France. This meant Italian music, which was why he imported Paisiello. He already had Luigi Cherubini (1760–1842), who had been in Paris since 1788, and who produced his greatest opera, *Medea*, in 1797, a typical horror piece of its time but perfectly and eloquently Classical in style. Cherubini specialized in a new, formal Italian Classicism which was French orientated, as can be heard in his C minor *Requiem* (1816), and his monumental *Mass in D minor* (1811). His French rescue-opera *Les Deux journées* (in English its title is *The Watercarrier*, but the French specifies "The Two Days") is rather Beethovenish in style. Beethoven was distinctly affected by the French heroic style and admired Cherubini greatly.

In 1803, a year before Napoleon's coronation, another Italian composer

Facing page: *Liberty at the Barricades by Delacroix captures the spirit of revolution.*

settled in Paris; Gasparo Spontini (1774–1851). Though he came from a poor peasant family, his talent earned him enough attention to warrant music lessons, and his early training qualified him for a place at a conservatory in Naples. While there, his sacred choral music pleased a director of one of the Roman opera houses, who offered him a commission. He soon moved south to Sicily, however, and in 1803 set sail for France. In Paris he saw Gluck's last French operas and determined to emulate their noble style. A new French comic opera by Spontini prompted the writer Etienne de Jouy to offer Spontini his libretto *La Vestale* ("The Vestal Virgin"), which had been rejected by Cherubini and others. Spontini composed it, and thanks to the personal intervention of the Empress Josephine, who appointed him her private composer, *La Vestale* was produced at the Paris Opera in December 1807, and at once recognized as a masterpiece throughout Europe. Its scenes of military pomp and ceremony with heroic music appealed to the men; its human drama of forbidden passion, voiced in noble classic style with fervent singing and rich orchestral accompaniment, attracted the women. French *grand opéra* had arrived. Spontini's later heroic operas, *Fernando Cortez* (1809), politically motivated by Napoleon's military ambition, and *Olympia* (1819), were less successful; and he made himself personally disliked in both Paris and Berlin, where he also worked. *La Vestale* still makes an effect on stage, though it cannot survive comparison with Bellini's *Norma*, a later work (1831) on a very similar story.

Rossini (1792–1868)

The next durably successful *grand opéra* was also by an Italian, who had proved himself in comic opera. But it was an Italian work, *Semiramide* (1823), written for Venice, though to a text based on a French play by Voltaire. Rossini had come from a musical family: his mother sang and his father was a municipal trumpeter (though he doubled as a slaughterhouse inspector, and was imprisoned for republican sympathies). By the time he was thirteen, Rossini could sing and play well enough to join the company in which his parents worked: there can be no better background for an aspiring opera composer than this, and after furthering his studies in Bologna, he was invited by the manager of a Venice theatre to write an opera there.

Eventually Rossini moved to Paris and gave France a truly great example of *grand opéra* in *Guillaume Tell* (1829). Gioacchino Rossini, sometimes called the "Swan of Pesaro", because he was born in that town on the Adriatic Sea, conquered first Italy, then the whole of Europe and the operatic world, starting in 1813 when he produced the serious opera *Tancredi* and the comedy *The Italian Girl in Algiers*. Three years later came his most popular opera *The Barber of Seville*, on the same subject as Paisiello's, which was soon relegated in Rossini's favour. *The Barber of Seville* was the first in a trilogy of plays about the servant, Figaro, by an extraordinary French writer. Pierre-Augustin Caron de Beaumarchais had risen from a humble background to become a royal favourite through his invention of a watch mechanism, from which he soon branched out into arms dealing, and working as a secret agent for the French government. The second of the trilogy, *The Marriage of Figaro*, landed its author in gaol, for King Louis XVI considered it seditious (though Queen Marie-Antoinette herself took the part of Suzanne in a subsequent production at court).

Another sparkling favourite, *La Cenerentola* ("Cinderella"), came out in

Gluck p 125–6

Norma p 204–5

*A photograph of **Rossini** at the age of seventy. Strictly speaking, however, he was then only seventeen years old, for his birthday fell on 29 February.*

1817; also a nearly serious piece, *La gazza ladra* ("The Thieving Magpie"), which deserves popularity though only the orchestral overture is often heard. The same is true of *Semiramide*, except that two arias, the heroine's *Bel raggio* and the hero's *Ah quel giorno* (his is one of the last *castrato* roles in opera), are sometimes heard at concerts.

Rossini confessed to congenital laziness, but he was most prolific, writing thirty-seven operas between 1809 and 1829, after which he lived in Paris until his death, gave musical evenings, entertained lavishly and was greatly loved—but composed hardly at all, save for a few drawing-room pieces (some orchestrated by Respighi for the ballet *La Boutique fantasque*), a *Stabat Mater* and a *Petite Messe solennelle* (Rossini's joke; it lasts almost two hours), but no more opera. Rossini had amply justified his musical existence, with a quantity of exquisite vocal music (think of *Cinderella's* final rondo); delicious comic scenes and ensembles (superb examples in *The Italian Girl*); brilliant finales (the act one *Barber* finale); and grand serious music too—the Prayer from *Moses in Egypt*, the duets in *Semiramide*. He understood the singing voice perfectly, being himself an able singer.

For Paris he composed a delicious comedy of sexual frustration during

Respighi p 318

Rossini. *A portrait that hangs in the Bologna museum devoted to his life and works.*

Isabella Colbran, *Rossini's wife, for whom he wrote "arias and ornamentations designed specifically to expose her virtues and disguise her very considerable deficiencies".*

the crusades, *Count Ory* (1828), in which the trio *A la faveur de cette nuit obscure* ("Thanks to dark night"—two men are simultaneously trying to seduce the same woman, neither aware of the other's presence) has a lyrical and harmonious richness quite new to Rossini's style, French and Italian music perfectly blended. *William Tell*, overlong for modern taste, was heavily abridged in Rossini's lifetime, though in a complete performance the five hours fly past, for the music is supremely grand and touching. Rossini had put heart and charm into the austere classicism of earlier French *grand opéras* by Cherubini and Spontini.

He had given an injection of strength and pace to composers all over Europe—clearly to Schubert, perhaps Beethoven as well (they were mutual admirers in any case) and to many French composers. Auber (1782–1871) was among them—his *Masaniello* (or *The Dumb Girl of Portici*), produced at the Paris Opéra in 1828, used its own blend of French and Italian for serious purposes—in Belgium the revolutionary fervour of the opera is supposed to have started a revolt against Dutch rule. Auber's comic opera *Fra Diavolo* (1830) reflects Rossini's comic style, and remains a repertory piece in some countries.

Meyerbeer (1791–1864)

The challenge of Rossini's *William Tell* was soon taken up by another foreign import, this time not from Italy but from Berlin. Jakob Meyer Beer, like Mendelssohn, was the son of a wealthy German Jewish banker. He learned the piano from Clementi and, as a student, befriended the young Weber. To finish his musical training before he embarked on a career as a concert pianist, he went to Italy, and it was hearing there a performance of Rossini's *Tancredi* that turned him to opera and made him alter his name to Giacomo Meyerbeer. Eventually one of his Italian serious operas, *Il crociato in Egitto* ("The Crusade in Egypt", 1824), gave him an international success, which brought him to Paris. There in 1831 he produced his first

Clementi p 155

French opera, *Robert the Devil*, to a libretto by Eugène Scribe, France's most admired operatic poet at the time. Scribe (1791–1861) was author of more than four hundred works, though he frequently worked with collaborators. Scribe was a master of the "well-made play", his plots were always constructed with scrupulous precision and peopled with characters that the boulevard audiences could fully comprehend. Probably his best known work is the only tragedy he wrote (in collaboration with Ernest Legouvé), *Adrienne Lecouvreur*. *Robert the Devil* is something of an exception in Scribe's enormous output, being a horror-opera that tells of love, wickedness and the supernatural, all three combined in a ballet for half-naked, resurrected, lascivious nuns (hard to stage without provoking laughter nowadays).

Meyerbeer was not a melodist of Rossini's calibre, but he understood the singing voice, and florid music, and theatrical atmosphere in orchestral terms, as well as the French *penchant* for rich, interesting orchestration. He knew when French opera required big, inspiring ensembles with chorus (Verdi, as well as Wagner, learned from him in this), and how to handle the Scribe special dramatic *coup*—something essential to the story and quite unexpected. Meyerbeer quickly became the operatic dictator of Paris. In 1836 he produced *Les Huguenots*, dealing with the conflict of Catholic and

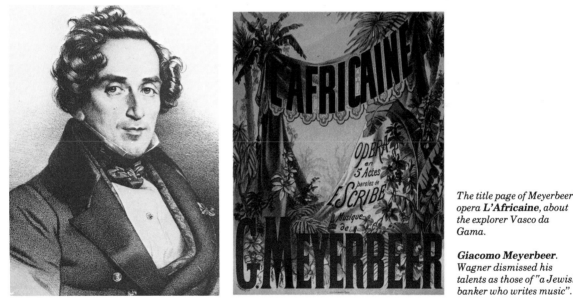

The title page of Meyerbeer's opera **L'Africaine**, about the explorer Vasco da Gama.

Giacomo Meyerbeer. Wagner dismissed his talents as those of "a Jewish banker who writes music".

Protestant in France, centred on the St Bartholomew's Eve Massacre. There are sumptuous crowd scenes, like the Blessing of the Daggers, a ballet of bathing beauties and a glorious love-duet for soprano and tenor. The recipe was absolutely right, until one realized that Meyerbeer's grand opera was as stilted as the Baroque opera it superseded—the opera of Handel and his contemporaries. The spectacle and music failed to heighten one another and disguise the unreality.

The characters are more interesting in *La Juive* ("The Jewess", 1835), by his contemporary Fromental Halévy; even that ends typically with the heroine being deep fried in boiling oil, executed by the judgment of her true

Jenny Lind stars as Alice in this scene from a London production of Meyerbeer's Robert le Diable.

father. Halévy (1799–1862) had studied at the Paris Conservatoire with Cherubini. He began to write opera during his stay there as winner of the Prix de Rome, and composed more than thirty, while doing an arduous teaching job at the Conservatoire, where Gounod and Bizet were among his pupils. (Bizet married Halévy's daughter, and completed his teacher's last opera, *Noah*.)

Meyerbeer's later operas for Paris (and staged everywhere else, for years to come) include *The Prophet*, which is about a false Messiah in Holland—the stage gimmick in this one being ballet on roller-skates, source of a more modern ballet, *Les Patineurs*. After Meyerbeer's death his last opera, *L'Africaine* ("The African Woman"), was performed: it is about the explorations of Vasco da Gama, is highly spectacular, contains much very splendid and lovely music, and concludes with the heroine's suicide by sniffing a poisonous flower.

Donizetti (1797–1848)

Rossini had two major apostles in Italy: Bellini and Donizetti. Gaetano Donizetti came from a poor but musical family in Bergamo, where his precocious gifts were developed by Simon Mayr, a then celebrated opera composer who was working in that city. Donizetti worked as conductor and coach at the San Carlo Opera in Naples, and composed twenty-three operas as well as much other music (hardly ever heard since, but well received at the time) before he became internationally celebrated in 1830 with his tragic opera *Anna Bolena*; the cast also includes Henry VIII and his next wife, Jane Seymour, and its music is quite compelling, especially the

Gounod p 211–13

Bizet p 211–13

The Diva

Opera composers have always tended to write, where possible, for the specific voices that are going to sing their music. During the eighteenth century, it was the castrato *whose artistry most inspired them. Early in the nineteenth century the soprano rose to fame. The first was probably Giuditta Pasta (1798–1865), for whom Bellini wrote the roles of Norma and La Sonnambula. Her star quality lay in the combination of a flexible and thrilling soprano voice with immense stage presence and controlled histrionics: Pasta, shown here as Medea, only sang in opera.*

An extraordinary talent was that of a younger colleague of Pasta, Maria Malibran (1808–1836), daughter of the famous tenor Manuel Garcia. In her tragically short life—she died after a fall from a horse—Malibran packed more singing and touring than most professionals twice her age. Her voice, impetuous acting and, above all, her musicianship had audiences at her feet the world over for the decade's length of her career.

Probably the most famous of them all was Jenny Lind (1820–1887), like Malibran a pupil of Garcia. She first came to fame in her native Stockholm, and acquired an international reputation after a brilliant season at Her Majesty's Theatre in London. Her simple, homely image was in no small part responsible for her attractiveness to the public, and she soon took an offer from Phineas T. Barnum to tour the United States. Jenny Lind excelled in recitals: such songs as "The Last Rose of Summer" were the bastions of her art. Her voice was not especially dramatic but, like her personality, also carefully cultivated, it had an innocence and freshness that men found quite heavenly.

Perhaps the archetypal diva was Adelina Patti (1843– 1919), whose career spanned half a century. Her most famous role was Rosina in The Barber of Seville: *Rossini himself adored Patti's singing in the part. Well past the age of seventy, all work in the opera-house long behind her, she could reduce an audience to tears with "Comin thro' the Rye" or "Home, Sweet Home". (Indeed, she had interrupted a performance of* The Barber *in New York to treat her public to "Home, Sweet Home" and a couple of other favourites.)*

The public itself, of course, creates the legend it adores. It is impossible to judge at this remove the quality of these great voices; but the inspiration and example they left to succeeding generations has preserved the disciplines, devotion and personality that keep alive the idea of a golden age of singing.

famous closing scene where Anna sings *Home, Sweet Home*, so decorated as to be quite unrecognizable to most ears. His *Elisir d'amore* ("The Elixir of Love")—no more mysterious a liquor than red wine, but the bringer together of two lovers—is as much tender and charming as jolly and amusing.

After Mozart, comic and serious operas musically grew together in style even more than he had envisaged. Donizetti's biggest success was *Lucia di*

Mozart's operas p 154–5, 157–9

*"**Donizetti**", said Giuseppe Verdi, "safeguarded the seal of Italian melody" after Rossini ceased writing operas in 1829.*

Lammermoor, based on Sir Walter Scott's novel *The Bride of Lammermuir* (1835), with a marvellous Mad Scene for the heroine and a famous sextet for the principal characters. For Paris he wrote *La Favorite* (1840), a new sort of sentimental semi-tragedy, touching in effect and more in need of rescue than much of his enormous output. In the same year Donizetti gave Paris the sparkling comedy *La Fille du régiment* ("The Daughter of the Regiment"), and three years later another superb comedy, *Don Pasquale* (1843), in which much of the text is also his work. He was an accomplished literary man, who wrote three of his other librettos, all comedies. But the achievement of *Don Pasquale* was the more remarkable because, by 1843, his health had begun to deteriorate seriously (he died miserably of tertiary syphilis), and the death of his beloved wife in a cholera epidemic of 1837 left him bereft of the high spirits and wit that had endeared him to so many people. Trouble with Italian censorship over his opera *Poliuto*, which ended with a martyrdom, and failure to get a post that he wanted, encouraged him to leave Italy for Paris. In *Don Pasquale* he wrote for the celebrated quartet of star-singers, the soprano Giulia Grisi, her husband the tenor Mario, the baritone Antonio Tamburini, and the hugely overweight bass Luigi Lablache. (Lablache, incidentally, worked frequently in England and was held in great affection by Queen Victoria, whose singing teacher he was at the time of her accession.) Donizetti was the first composer to exploit the baritone voice as such, through working in Naples with the greatly admired Giorgio Ronconi—earlier male singers were called either tenors or basses.

Bellini (1801–1835)

Donizetti was still an up-and-coming young operatic aspirant when his junior colleague Vincenzo Bellini scored his first triumph with *Il Pirata* ("The Pirate") at La Scala, Milan. Bellini's career was brief but glorious; it also took him to Paris, where he chose to remain (and died all too soon:

The famous operatic bass **Lablache** *had great stage presence. He is seen here as the charlatan Dulcamara, promoting his elixir of love in Donizetti's opera.*

Henriette Sontag, indisputedly the prettiest soprano of her day, as Rosina in Rossini's **Barber of Seville**.

Cherubini and Rossini were among the pall-bearers at his funeral). Bellini came from a family of musicians in Sicily. At the age of five he was praised for his piano playing. He composed church music from the age of six (his father and grandfather were church organists), and as a boy already showed the unusual sensibility for poetry that marks all his later operas. "Give me good verse, and I will give you good music," he is supposed to have declared. He was lucky, in his first commission for La Scala, to have been given Felice Romani as his librettist, the finest operatic poet of his age. They worked together until Bellini's death, and Bellini's music always faithfully reflects Romani's poetry. Bellini believed that melody was the centre of all music, and practised composing melodies every day, as executant musicians practise scales after breakfast. In that way he built up a stock of tunes that

*Lithograph of **Vincenzo Bellini**. After his premature death, his operas were almost totally neglected until the middle of the present century.*

could be called on later, when he had a libretto to set and a particular dramatic mood to reflect. Like Rossini, whom he admired greatly and befriended in Paris (Bellini could be unnecessarily scathing about other composers, but his life's ambition was no more than to rank as the greatest opera composer after Rossini), he wrote out in detail all the brilliant vocal decorating needed for his operas, in an age when singers still expected to add their own embellishments to existing music, as they had done for centuries. From *Il Pirata* onwards, he worked closely with his preferred tenor, Giovanni Rubini (who tried out every solo with the composer as soon as it was written), and later similarly with his chosen soprano, the delectable Giuditta Pasta.

After *Il Pirata* Bellini's next major success was with *I Capuletti ed i Montecchi* ("The Capulets and Montagues", or *Romeo and Juliet*, 1830, for the Fenice Theatre in Venice). A year later, despite serious illness, he brought out *La sonnambula* ("The Sleepwalker"), a rustic drama which ends happily, unusual in Bellini's output of tragedies, and with a joyous, strongly rhythmical final soprano aria, *Ah, non giunge*, which contradicts (as do many others) the prejudiced gossip that Bellini could only write flaccid, dreamy, slow melodies. Also in 1831, at La Scala, Bellini produced his greatest opera, *Norma*, famous for the heroine's prayer *Casta diva*, for the female duet *Mira, O Norma*, and for the finale, as Norma and her lover go

Pasta p 201

204

to their sacrificial death, with its passionate melody several times screwed up, as if for a climax, only to be relaxed and unfolded again—Verdi reworked the effect later in his operatic finales (as at the end of *Simon Boccanegra*). *Norma* took some time to be appreciated; it was strong meat for conservative opera-goers.

By 1823 Bellini was called to London to direct performances there of *Norma*, *Il Pirata* and *Romeo and Juliet*, all with Pasta, also *Sonnambula* with the great, short-lived Maria Malibran, daughter of Manuel Garcia, who had been Rossini's first Almaviva and who survived to invent the laryngoscope and celebrate his own centenary in London. (Garcia had another famous mezzo-soprano daughter, Pauline Viardot Garcia, who figures in the lives of several nineteenth-century composers as well as that of the Russian author Turgenev.)

Later in 1833 Bellini moved to Paris, again to supervise new productions of his operas, and eventually to compose *I Puritani* ("The Puritans") for the Italian Opera there, another triumph and his last, since he died near Paris soon afterwards. Bellini found himself completely at home in Parisian society: as well as Rossini, he made friends with Chopin (whose brand of melody owes much to Bellini) and the German poet Heinrich Heine, who wrote a vivid memoir of him. *I Puritani* typifies the best and the less admirable qualities of Bellini's music: superb melody, rich orchestration (a French speciality), dramatic passion, also stiff dramatic procedure and cardboard characterization. In some of his earlier operas he seems to be prolonging the artificial method of eighteenth-century *opera seria*, where momentary emotion, not individuality of character, chiefly occupied the composer's attention.

Hector Berlioz (1803–1869)

From all these genial Italian composers working in France, a French native composer of comparable stature was due to emerge. When he did, he proved to be one of music's greatest, most original, figures. His father was a doctor near Grenoble who encouraged a breadth of learning in the boy that included music and the classics. At the age of seventeen he was sent to Paris to study medicine, but such was the lure of music there—particularly the operas of Gluck—that Berlioz soon abandoned these studies and entered the Conservatoire, much to his parents' dismay.

Like many Romantic composers of the nineteenth century, Berlioz was an excellent writer on music: his autobiography, and polemical articles called *Soirées dans l'orchestre* ("Evenings in the Orchestra"), make vivid reading—full of prejudice, enthusiasm and ambition. He also wrote a famous treatise on orchestration, the first comprehensive one of its kind. Berlioz detested his teachers for their musical myopia; they were too blinkered to appreciate music they could not themselves compose. Berlioz was something new in music, an obviously outstanding composer who was not a ranking performing pianist. Others could not believe that any musician, whose instruments were the flageolet (a species of recorder) and guitar, could conceivably write music for a symphony orchestra.

In 1830 Berlioz nevertheless produced his *Fantastic Symphony*. It was a completely new sort of symphony in five movements, held together by a motto-theme (like French early Romantic operas, such as Cherubini's), with a detailed literary programme about the lover who pursues his beloved through bouts of opium-smoking, the hallucinations ever more curious,

*The soprano Adelaide Kemble in a London production of **Norma** in 1841.*

Right: *Jenny Lind sings the role of the orphan Amina in Bellini's **La Sonnambula**.*

until she becomes a malign witch on Walpurgis Night, dancing on the grave of his love. It consists of a fantasy about the beloved, an evocation of a ball (yes, another waltz), a rustic scene, a Napoleonic march to the scaffold, and that nightmare of the witches' orgy. Berlioz's *Fantastic Symphony*, long regarded as virtuoso nonsense, can now be appreciated as a brilliant psychological fantasy in music, its texture finely adjusted to the acceptable music of its period—the Bourbon kings having now emerged from the defeat of Napoleon's Empire. Yet even now, when heard for the first time, it has the effect of a blow to the solar plexus; not even Beethoven's *Eroica* had given such a kick to the cosmic system. Some two years before the appearance of the *Fantastic Symphony*, Berlioz had attended an English Shakespeare season at the Théâtre de l'Odéon and fallen violently in love with the leading lady, Harriet Smithson. But she rejected all his advances, and he began to sketch out this extraordinary work, subtitled *Episodes in the life of an artist*. Its creation helped the composer over this unfortunate infatuation, and he was soon able to condemn the actress as unworthy of his attentions—though he married her first.

Berlioz composed a sequel to the *Fantastic*, entitled *Lélio*, a curious, almost distracted medley of musical ideas that never quite comes off in concert performance. His next symphony, *Harold in Italy* (1834), was commissioned by Paganini as a concerto for viola and orchestra (like most good violinists in history, from J.S. Bach to Pinchas Zukerman and beyond, Paganini had discovered a special affinity with the viola, though he did nothing about it afterwards). When Paganini read the completed work, he found it not exciting enough for the soloist, and never played it. *Harold in Italy* derives tenuously from Byron's poem *Childe Harold* (Byron, like Scott and Shakespeare, was a major inspiration to nineteenth-century Romantic composers). It depicts the hero as bystander in four contrasted situations. It is a weak concerto because the viola solo—representing Harold—is never actually involved, so his music never dominates the orchestral action. Otherwise it is perfectly vivid, rich in thematic material, a highly coloured, strongly felt, admirably formed post-Beethoven literary symphony—impressive in performance nowadays when sympathetic Berlioz interpreters are becoming less thin on the ground.

Berlioz's third symphony, *Romeo and Juliet* (1839), still perplexes those who expect from it a unified musical linking such as a symphony is expected to be. It begins with something like a synopsis: chorus, soloists and orchestra outline the story in several short sections. When the story is completed and you think the piece must be over, Berlioz starts again and re-interprets the bare facts in terms of his own poetry, and at proper length (in four symphonic movements, the finale with bass solo and choir). Everything after the prologue makes symphonic sense: the prologue can perhaps be appreciated in terms of a concert-programme note, or a television trailer. You are primed in advance for the real thing.

Berlioz's last symphony was the *Funèbre et triomphale* ("Funeral and Triumph", 1840), a commemoration of the dead in the 1830 revolution which restored the Bourbons. It dutifully revives the old post-revolutionary Classic style, the Napoleonic heroism, and then adds a personal passion that

Napoleon crowns himself Emperor of the French, in this detail from David's grandiose painting.

Music for the People

Revolution and Grand Opera

Napoleon's composers, Gossec, Cherubini, Méhul, Paisiello, never exhibited because that would have been out of order. Berlioz had no such scruples, and his symphony is as much denunciation as gratitude. Already he had composed his Requiem for the dead in France's catastrophic wars, with his *Grande Messe des morts* (1837), perhaps the most musically eloquent of all his works in melody, harmony and texture. Imagine sitting in a reverberant church—choral and orchestral music resounding everywhere. At the words *Tuba mirum*, about the Last Trump, four brass bands erupt to left and right in front of you, and behind, all at once. It was the greatest surprise imaginable for its first audience, and has not lost its effect. Gabrieli's St Mark's Cathedral music had turned up again, as thrilling as ever, in the harmonic world of a new century.

Berlioz could excel at national music, in the Napoleonic tradition to which he was born. He could not maintain its severe style, nor did he wish to. French literature, with Victor Hugo and Lamartine as inspirational

Orchestration

The skill of combining instruments effectively in a score became much more subtle and problematical in the nineteenth century. Improvements in technology, such as the valve mechanism on brass instruments and improved "plumbing" in the woodwind section, increased the possibilities for larger orchestral forces and exotic instrumental colouring.

The most influential and important work on orchestration at the time was written by the most skilful and imaginative orchestrator of them all: Berlioz. His Traité d'instrumentation et d'orchestration moderne *(1844) was written with the experience of composing the* Fantastic Symphony *and the* Grande Messe des morts *behind him. In addition to a massive body of strings, the latter score called for four flutes and clarinets, two each of oboes and cors anglais, twelve horns, eight bassoons, eight pairs of timpani, four large gongs, bass drum and ten pairs of cymbals—all this in addition to four separate brass bands stationed round the auditorium, and a choir of nearly three hundred singers.*

Richard Strauss, in his symphonic poems, took such ideas to their practicable limit. In the later twentieth century, except for performances of inescapably large-scale works, economy and taste have been to a degree responsible for reducing orchestral forces to Classical or Baroque proportions.

writers, was dominating the arts. Delacroix's paintings, exotic and richly flavoured, typified the age and found a musical echo in Berlioz. His literary idols were Virgil, Goethe and Shakespeare. He used all of them as a basis for great dramatic works: the opera *Les Troyens* ("The Trojans", 1863), the concert cantata *The damnation of Faust* (1846), not a stage work, though regularly and painfully pillaged by theatre producers; and his last opera, *Beatrice and Benedict* (1862), a brilliant comedy on Shakespeare's *Much Ado about Nothing*. His first opera, sumptuously Romantic, was based on the memoirs of the Italian sculptor Benvenuto Cellini (1838). It includes the *Roman Carnival* scene from which comes the popular overture of that title.

When Berlioz died, his new music seemed to have failed. Other countries were not much interested in operas so remote in ideals, so firmly

G. Gabrieli p 50, 62, 80, 352   *Eroica* symphony p 162

Paganini p 184

ROMÉO
ET
JULIETT

L'ENFAN

DU CHRIST.

LES SOIRÉES
DE L'ORCHESTRE

LA DAMNATION

DE FAUST.

GROTESQUES
DE LA MUSIQUE

HAROLD
EN
ITALIE

LES
RANCS-JUGES

TRAITÉ

CHESTRATION

BÉATRIX
ET
BÉNÉDICT

LES TOYENS

Er. CARJAT.

Hector Berlioz. *His last years were made lonely and wretched by the deaths of his second wife and his only son, Louis.*

1789–1890 *Revolution and Grand Opera*

*Mephistopheles flaps across the night sky in one of Delacroix's illustrations for Berlioz's **The Damnation of Faust**.*

set in other ways. His revival happened in the twentieth century, when his music now seems not a bit wildly Romantic but, on the contrary, very restrained in line and texture. Berlioz's music, built on Gluck and Rossini, creates a new French style, missing since the death of Rameau. The remarkable French pianist-composer Alkan (1813–1888)—his real name Charles-Valentin Morhange—won the admiration of Liszt and Busoni, was a close friend of Chopin, and must have been a magnificent pianist, though too correct and classical, not fiery enough for his audiences. Like Stravinsky, he was totally opposed to interpretative licence. Eighteenth-century music was his passion, though his own works link him firmly with Berlioz and Liszt. As a pianist he was a child prodigy and his first compositions were published when he was fourteen.

Almost all his work, highly original in style as well as in pianistic invention, is for piano. There are preludes, studies and sonatas. A symphony and a concerto, both for piano solo (the pianist has to duplicate the roles of orchestra and piano, their music being well differentiated), must be strongly recommended for the understanding of French piano music in this period before Debussy.

Alkan's was a romantic imagination: big, exotic, searching, and aimed at complete keyboard mastery. His piano works, often extensive in size, always individual in style, even eccentric, sometimes have curious titles, such as *The Railway*, *Omnibuses* and *Aesop's Banquet*. There is also a *Funeral March for a Parrot* and a cantata about Eddystone Lighthouse.

The Flourishing of French Opera

The most famous French operas of the later nineteenth century were *Faust* (1859), *Carmen* (1875) and *Samson and Delilah* (1877). Gounod's *Faust* replaces Goethe's aspiration with bourgeois charm, and reflects its composer's own background in the process. Charles Gounod (1818–1893) was the son of cultured parents: his mother was a pianist and his father a successful painter. At the Paris Conservatoire, Gounod won the Prix de Rome: in Italy he immersed himself in the study of church music. Rejecting the priesthood as a way of life, he decided to become a composer and completed three unsuccessful operas before *Faust* won him international acclaim. Indeed, there were those who said that Gounod could not have composed the opera at all, for it was far beyond his musical capabilities. Apart from the operatic field, Gounod's choral music won him many admirers in England, and a delightful *Petite Symphonie* he composed for wind ensemble is quite frequently performed today.

Charles Gounod. *He challenged one critic to a duel, who said that* Faust *must have been written by someone else, so fine were its qualities.*

Bizet's *Carmen* seems the perfect French opera: fiery Spain observed through logical French eyes. Though described as a comic opera (it has spoken dialogue), it is a tragedy in the end, and until then always human, a slice of life. The tender love of the country pair, José and Micaela, interrupted by the amorous gypsy and the incursion of the lusty toreador, create powerful atmosphere which is matched by brilliant music. But it failed at its first production, and its composer never lived to see its gradual acceptance and great popularity: he died three months after the première. Georges Bizet (1838–1875) was an accomplished pianist, whose playing had

The original set for act III of Gounod's **Faust**, *which takes place in the garden of the lovely Marguérite.*

1789-1890 *Revolution and Grand Opera*

Paris Conservatoire

The Conservatoire de Musique was founded under the Revolutionary government in 1795. As early as the turn of the century, it had many important names on its professorial staff, among them Cherubini, Gossec, Adam and Boieldieu.

In 1822 Cherubini became the Conservatoire's director and worked hard in this capacity for twenty years, enlarging the scope of the institution, tightening the rules, and even having a law passed entitling the library to a copy of every piece of music published. Berlioz loathed him.

Cherubini's successor was Daniel Auber, composer of the comic opera Fra Diavolo. *He did much to expand the dramatic aspects of musical training, and revived a custom of holding public rehearsals that were excellent publicity for the school and provided invaluable experience for the students.*

An outstanding period in the Conservatoire's history was under the directorship of Gabriel Fauré, from 1905–1920. On his staff were Dukas and d'Indy holding orchestral classes, Cortot teaching the piano, and the organist Widor giving instruction in composition.

A particular feature of the Paris Conservatoire is the annual award of the Prix de Rome. This coveted prize, the result of competition, enables the winner to spend four years in Rome, living in the Villa Medici (the French Academy). Among the winners since the competition was instituted in 1803 have been Berlioz, Gounod, Bizet, Massenet and Debussy.

*Emma Calvé as **Carmen** in Bizet's opera finds death for all in the cards.*

been praised by Liszt, and who had won a qualified success with an opera, *The Pearl Fishers*, in his mid-twenties. Much of what he wrote, besides *Carmen*, was destined for only posthumous popularity, notably the incidental music he composed for Daudet's play *L'Arlésienne* (1872) and a brilliantly precocious symphony dating from his eighteenth year.

Camille Saint-Saëns (1835–1921), the composer of *Samson and Delilah*, turned to operatic composition in search of excitement. His background was academic: he was organist at the Madeleine in Paris and taught piano at the École Niedermayer (where Fauré was one of his pupils). He had help in his operatic ventures from his friend Auber, an immensely popular composer of *opéra comique*; but even so, the tuneful, spectacular *Samson et Dalila* had to wait nine years for a performance after its completion in 1868. In later years Saint-Saëns turned much more to instrumental composition and was especially successful in his third symphony, with solo organ (1886), his concertos for violin and for piano, and symphonic poems such as *Danse Macabre* (1874). His much-loved *Carnival of the Animals* (1886) was forbidden public performance by him during his lifetime. Saint-Saëns's works and life proclaim him one of France's most endearing, as well as virtuoso, composers.

French opera continued to flourish in the work of Jules Massenet

Georges Bizet *did not live to enjoy his success. Keeping body and soul together with long, gruelling hours of private teaching and routine work for music publishers had undermined his health.*

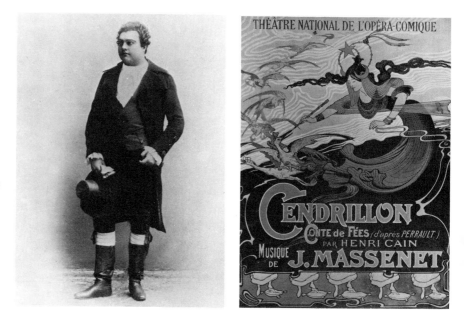

*The young poet **Werther**, in Massenet's opera, played by the tenor Ernst van Dyck (who created the role).*

*Massenet's **Cinderella** was written to try and capture the same success in France that Humperdinck's fairy-tale* Hansel & Gretel *was enjoying in Germany.*

(1842–1912), a gifted young professor of composition at the Paris Conservatoire. *Manon* (1884) was his most successful work. Based on Prévost's sentimental novel *Manon Lescaut*, its unashamed tenderness quickly made it an international success, though there were those who thought his work sensual to the point of indelicacy. He enjoyed subsequent successes with *Le Cid* (1885), *Werther* (1892, adapted from Goethe's novel, *The Sorrows of Young Werther*), *Herodias*, and *Thaïs* (1894). But by then Claude Debussy was already at work on his masterpiece, *Pelléas et Mélisande*, though it did not reach the stage until the twentieth century.

Chapter 11
Verdi and Wagner

Music Drama

Political upheaval in Germany and Italy ◆ Verdi—a popular hero ◆ Puccini and his damsels in distress ◆ La Scala Theatre ◆ Bayreuth festivals ◆ Wagner—a mighty artistic fusion of music, drama and politics ◆

The second half of the nineteenth century was operatically dominated by two composers born in the same year, 1813; one in Italy, one in Germany. They should have met to become mutual influences in the tradition of Haydn and Mozart. But the meeting did not occur, alas, and we are the poorer. The composers in question are Giuseppe Verdi (1813–1901) and Richard Wagner (1813–1883).

The Politics of Change
Both were the heirs of Rossini and Meyerbeer, though they followed different trails. Wagner and Verdi were at one in their philosophy of political liberalism. Wagner's Germany was discontent with petty king-doms and electorates, ill-staffed and oppressive. Germans wanted a whole democratic Germany. Wagner was one of them, and militant, though even he might have regretted what happened after 1933, when Hitler claimed Wagner as prophet of the crazed Nazi policies.

Verdi was strictly Red, as intelligent Italians often are. The country was then divided between France and Austria, much oppressed and harried. The popular longing was for a unified Italy. Verdi responded, well aware that so favoured a medium as opera, visited by people of every class, in every town, must be the most effective weapon of political propaganda.

Giuseppe Verdi
"My youth was hard," Verdi recalled. His father was the tavern-keeper in a hamlet, Le Roncole, near Busseto in the Duchy of Parma, sometimes under French, sometimes Austrian domination—both oppressive to the local peasantry. So violent were the pressures of politics that, soon after his birth, his mother had to hide with him in a nearby bell-tower to avoid the attentions of insurgents. At the age of three his fondness for music impressed the tavern fiddler, who suggested that the boy should be taught an instrument. A spinet was bought for him, and the local church organist taught him so well that when he was nine, young Giuseppe was able to take

Mozart & Haydn p 134, 140, 142   Meyerbeer p 198–200
Rossini p 196–8

1840-1893 *Music Drama*

Verdi, *at about the time of the composition of* Aïda. *The opera was first performed in Cairo a year later than planned: scenery and costumes were unable to leave Paris, under siege from the Prussian armies.*

over his teacher's church duties: in due course an adult replacement was proposed, but the villagers insisted on retaining their "little maestro". He was sent to school in Busseto, where his musical education was rigorously thorough: when he applied for a post there, the examining body declared him ready to be a maestro in Paris or London. Verdi was content to remain in Busseto, teaching music, conducting the town orchestra, and composing an opera. It was turned down by the Parma opera house, so Verdi, now married with two children, moved to Milan where *Oberto* was produced at La Scala, and Verdi was commissioned to write three more operas—one every eight months.

The first of them, a comedy, *Un giorno di regno* ("King for a day") failed. While composing it, his adored wife and only surviving child both died; he lost heart in music, and asked to be released from his contract. One day the impresario of La Scala showed him a new libretto about Nebucchadnezzar. Verdi opened it idly and was captivated by the words of a chorus of lamentation sung by the Israelites captive in Babylon. The impresario persuaded Verdi to compose the opera, and *Nabucco* (to give its standard short title) was the success of the season, soon taken up in Paris and London (the examining body in Busseto must have been proud of its foresight). It had a marvellous title-role for the baritone Giorgio Ronconi and an equally fine villainess part for the admired soprano Giuseppina Strepponi, who soon became Verdi's mistress and eventually his second wife. What chiefly fired the Milanese audience was the eloquent portrayal of the oppressed Israelite people, an easily grasped symbol of Italians under foreign domination.

Verdi made sure that his next opera for La Scala, *I Lombardi* ("The Lombards at the first Crusade"), would also include such a chorus; "O Signore, dal tetto natio" was as much applauded, and sung in the streets, as was "Va, pensiero" from *Nabucco*. Verdi was on his way to becoming a national hero, and became one when nationalists reduced their slogan "Vittorio Emmanuele, Re d'Italia" ("Victor Emanuel, King of Italy") to its initials, VERDI. It was a graffito scrawled on walls and a motto chanted at performances of his operas, which came thick and fast during what Verdi called "my galley-slave period": nineteen operas in fifteen years, for Milan, Venice, Rome, Naples, Florence, Rimini, Trieste, Paris and London—where Jenny Lind, the "Swedish nightingale", was the prima donna in *I Masnadieri* ("The Robbers"). After *Joan of Arc* (1845), Verdi refused to work at La Scala in protest at inadequate working conditions, and throughout his "galley-slave" period he would never agree to compose a new opera until he had been satisfied that the text was approved by the local censor, that it would gratify local taste, and that all the principal roles could be cast from available singers, for whose voices he would then write the music (as Mozart did in the days of *opera seria*).

Most opera librettists of the time looked for thrilling dramatic situations and paid little regard to character or diction; for Verdi the characters came first and he was always complaining about uninspired poetry. He was an absolutely practical musician of the theatre, as well as a progressive composer and a patriotic Italian.

Popular books and plays were the regular stuff of new operas in those days. Verdi's operas draw on Victor Hugo (*Ernani*, *Rigoletto*), Schiller (*Joan of Arc*, *Masnadieri*, *Luisa Miller*, *Don Carlos*), Byron (*The Two Foscari*, *The Corsair*) and his favourite author, Shakespeare (*Macbeth*, and, much later, *Otello* and *Falstaff*). *Il Trovatore* ("The Troubadour"), *Simon Boccanegra* and *La forza del destino* ("The Force of Destiny") are all based on Spanish plays of the spacious, epic sort that Verdi found particularly congenial. *La Traviata* ("The Stray") is a story of thwarted love and may reflect some of Verdi's bitterness at the scandal caused by his long liaison with Strepponi.

Despite his cautious concern for the censor, Verdi had regular trouble with approval of his texts. It reached a peak with *Un ballo in maschera* ("A Masked Ball"), based on Eugène Scribe's libretto about the murder of King Gustav III of Sweden. It had been set by several composers and produced in Italy. But Verdi's version was firmly turned down by the Naples censors, and so many changes were required that Verdi and his librettist could not have an acceptable version ready in time, and eventually it was given a year later in Rome, where, surprisingly, authority was more lenient.

After this débâcle (1858), Verdi moved to his country estate and declared that he would compose no more operas (he was certainly rich enough to retire). It was during this fallow period that the *Risorgimento*

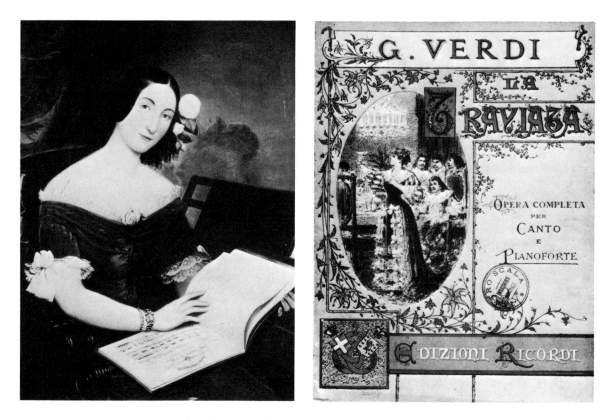

Verdi's second wife,
Giuseppina Strepponi.
*The couple outraged society
by living openly together for
twelve years before their
marriage.*

The vocal score of Verdi's
La Traviata, *composed at a
time when his beloved
Giuseppina was
dangerously ill.*

caught fire—Garibaldi chased the French out of southern Italy, the Austrians were evicted from Lombardy, and Vittorio Emmanuele at last became King of all Italy. Verdi was appointed a member of the first central parliament in Turin, though he did not attend regularly, and in 1865 he resigned.

By then he had been tempted back into opera: he accepted commissions from St Petersburg ("The Force of Destiny", 1862), Paris (first the revised *Macbeth*, 1865, then *Don Carlos*, 1867) and Cairo (*Aïda*, 1871), and with them returned to the grand manner, now at a new level of masterly sophistication. The breach with La Scala was healed with a revised *Forza* (1869), and Verdi was slowly, tactfully persuaded by his publisher, Ricordi, to collaborate with the musician-poet Arrigo Boito (1842–1918), first on a revision of *Simon Boccanegra*, for a cast led by the tenor Francesco Tamagno and the French baritone Victor Maurel; then on two last new Shakespeare operas, *Otello* (1887) and *Falstaff* (1893). Tamagno was his Otello, Maurel both Iago and Falstaff: Verdi worked closely with them during composition.

In 1874, moved by the death of the Italian author and patriot Alessandro Manzoni, Verdi composed a *Requiem Mass* as superb and typical as any of his operas. Verdi was no Christian, and he took delight in showing the clergy unfavourably in such operas as *La forza del destino* (the ridiculous Melitone), *Don Carlos* (the implacable, heartless Grand Inquisitor), and *Aïda* (not Christian priests, but symbols all the same of Verdi's *bête noire*). Yet in the *Requiem* and the even later *Four Sacred Pieces* for choir with and without orchestra (1898, written when he was

Boito p 224

La Scala

The Teatro alla Scala in Milan was built in the late eighteenth century by the Empress Maria Theresa. Apart from its enormous size—it seats more than two thousand—it closely resembles in style many court theatres of the period, with its splendid array of sumptuous boxes wrapped around the rear of the auditorium.

The second decade of the nineteenth century was a period of great success and activity at La Scala, including the premières of Rossini's Il Turco in Italia *(1814)* and La gazza ladra *(1817)*. Later, both Donizetti and Bellini had important first performances there, and by the time Verdi appeared on the scene, La Scala was long and firmly established as one of the world's leading opera houses.

After early failures there, Verdi was disenchanted with La Scala, and worked from 1855 to 1870 writing operas for the Paris Opera and elsewhere. Later operas, such as La forza del destino, Un ballo in maschera *and* Aïda, *were received with less than rapturous enthusiasm when performed at Milan, exacerbating Verdi's mistrust of the opera-house there.

Verdi premièred his greatest work to date, Otello, at La Scala in 1887. Six years later, his last opera and comic masterpiece Falstaff, *based on Shakespeare's* Merry Wives of Windsor, *was given a magnificent first performance at La Scala, setting the seal upon the reconciliation between opera's greatest Italian composer and Italy's finest opera house.

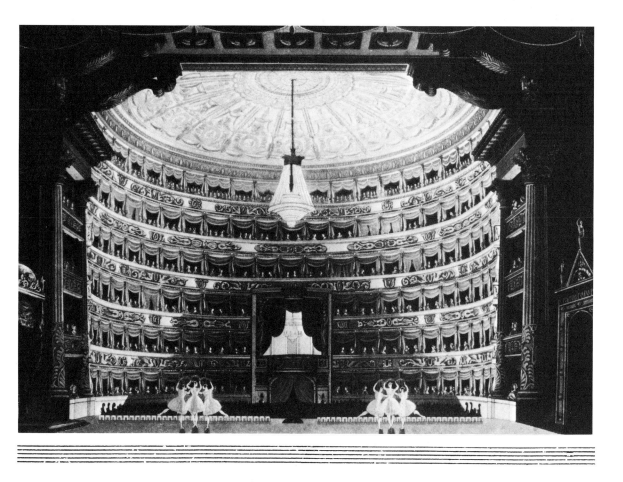

Verdi and Wagner

A cartoon of **Verdi** *in rehearsal.*

eighty-five years old), he could set Christian texts with every impression of devotion and with lofty musical invention, just as his music for scenes of true piety, in his operas, is perfectly convincing.

In the early twentieth century the world had accepted a trio of operas from Verdi's middle period; *Rigoletto* (1851), *Il Trovatore* (1853) and *La Traviata* (also 1853), which were in every company's repertory and hugely popular everywhere (as they still are). Much of their music is familiar to people who never set foot in an opera house: in *Rigoletto* alone there are Gilda's *Caro nome*, Rigoletto's diatribe against his effete fellow-courtiers, *Corteggiani, vil razza dannata* ("Courtiers, vile, damned bunch"—Verdi must have enjoyed composing those words), the solos of the Duke of Mantua, *Questa o quella* and *La donna é mobile*, and the quartet in the final act, *Bella figlia dell' amore*. If I add that the roles of the hunchbacked jester, Rigoletto, and the Duke are both fundamentally unsympathetic and that a musical theme, associated with a father's curse on them both, recurs constantly in the three acts, I have cited two common features of Verdi's operas. He was drawn to tales of unlucky parent-child relationships, and he portrayed his characters in full, subtle colours, not black and white. Another characteristic of Verdi's operas, much less common in those of his predecessors, is the ending, almost invariable, with the death of at least one principal character.

Il Trovatore includes the Anvil Chorus, Manrico's *Di quella pira*, famous for the tenor's loud top C's (not originally asked for by Verdi), Count

Verdi in Paris *in 1894 for a performance of* Otello, *reluctantly photographed with the baritone Victor Maurel in the role of Iago.*

di Luna's *Il balen*, the duet *Ai nostri monti* ("Home to our Mountains") and many another: it used to be said that *Il Trovatore* offers a great new tune a minute, *Falstaff* a new tune every fifteen seconds—a pardonable exaggeration.

If *Il Trovatore* is the rawest of the three, *La Traviata* is the most intimate and the least grand, with Frenchified qualities of charm and tenderness that we may associate with Gounod and Massenet later (though Verdi surely found them in Donizetti). Based on Alexandre Dumas' *The Lady of the Camellias* (still sometimes acted in the playhouse), it is about Violetta, a courtesan who finds happiness with a young man of good family. She is obliged to abandon the relationship for the sake of family reputation, and falls prey to tuberculosis; her lover's father repents, but she is already dying. The orchestral preludes to the first and last acts, portraying the doomed heroine, are sometimes performed separately, likewise the *Brindisi*, or drinking song in the opening scene, *Libiamo ne lieti calici*, the baritone father's solo *Di Provenza* ("From fair Provence") and the heroine's two-part solo at the end of act one, *Ah, fors è lui* followed by *Sempre libera*.

Verdi and Wagner

Music Drama

Aria Conventions

This last is not only a standard favourite, but a good example of aria form in Romantic opera. Violetta's party guests have departed and she is left alone, considering the handsome admirer, Alfredo, whom she has just met for the first time. "How curious" (*E strano!*), she reflects, "to feel for the first time on the brink of a serious love affair." She sings at first in recitative, with orchestral commentary, more substantial than the punctuating chords of earlier recitatives; this develops into a slow aria, very melodious and wistful, "Perhaps this is the man for whom my heart has always longed" (*Ah, fors, é lui*). The key of F minor turns into brighter F major as she remembers the words he sang to her in their duet at the party, about "that love which is the pulse of the entire universe" (*Quell' amor ch'é palpito*). She rejects a heavy romance as folly for a girl of her calling (*Follie! Follie!*, another recitative section), and determines to forget the young man by revelling in a whirlpool of pleasure, *Gioir*, a brilliant cadenza, bringing the music to a new key, A flat major, for the quicker second part of the aria, commonly known as its "cabaletta". "I must always remain free" (*Sempre libera*), she sings. By a fine stroke of drama she is interrupted by the voice of her suitor, singing outside in the street about "love, the pulse of the universe", and her aria ends as a duet.

In the more conventional type of set-piece, or *scena*, the two halves of the aria are often linked by the entry of another character bearing news that stirs the principal singer to a brighter mood: Lady Macbeth's Letter Scene, for instance, where a servant announces that King Duncan will spend that night in Macbeth's castle, a prospect that excites Lady Macbeth's ambition to plans for the murder of the King. Or the whole *scena* may be addressed to the chorus, who can boost the climax of the cabaletta by supporting the singer (for example Lucy's Mad Scene in Donizetti's *Lucia di Lammermoor*). Verdi gives an effective variant in the wedding scene of *Il Trovatore*. Manrico addresses the first half, *Ah si, ben mio*, to his bride. They sing a short duet, preparing to enter the church whose organ accompanies them. But Manrico's soldiers prevent them with news that his mother has been taken prisoner and is to be burned as a witch. He determines to rescue her, and his quick cabaletta, *Di quella pira*, is supported by male chorus. When the *scena* introduces a new character (but only then), the first half is called *cavatina*.

Verdi tried constantly to surpass these old conventions so that a scene of drama might become a piece of unbroken music. Despite opposition from audiences that insisted on applauding the star singers, Verdi eventually won. If applause is permitted in the middle of a scene, its effect is marred and we miss the music that follows—we do not usually applaud a great Hamlet after one of his soliloquies. In later operas, particularly *Aïda, Otello* and *Falstaff*, musical continuity rules. The great set pieces in the third act of *Aïda* follow one another without a break, and in *Falstaff* each of the six scenes is an uninterrupted set piece, some twenty minutes long. Wagner was to go even further in this direction: the third act of *Die Meistersinger* lasts nearly two and a half hours with hardly an occasion for applause.

Verdi's Classicism

Verdi made his orchestral music infinitely more colourful and interesting than that of his predecessors; so much so that Italian critics accused him of imitating Wagner, a composer whose work he hardly knew, though both

Wagner p 229–40

Verdi, foreground, *with two companions in front of the Casa di Riposo. His comic masterpiece,* Falstaff, *was completed at the age of eighty.*

had learned their trade from Rossini and Meyerbeer. Verdi had learned not only to write more eloquently than they for orchestra, as Wagner also did, but to gear ensembles carefully, preserving an integrated structure so that at any moment we can remember what has gone before and imagine what might be to come, and feel at all times in the presence of a balanced whole. This makes for an eminently Classic quality, because Verdi, in the Romantic age, remained a watchful Classicist, his sights set on the right idea correctly presented. In the second scene of *Falstaff*, for example, the merry wives of Windsor sing an ensemble. Then their menfolk sing another. At the end of the scene, the two ensembles recur together, in different tempi, but working perfectly together. At last Verdi's rigorous schooling in counterpoint paid off with a seemingly effortless *tour de force*.

During the present century, Verdi appreciation has expanded hugely, and by the 1960s it was possible to see and hear almost all of his operas

Verdi and Wagner
Music Drama

somewhere, decently staged. As the world's larger companies added, here and there, an unfamiliar Verdi opera to repertory, the gramophone recorded it—few of his operas now remain unrecorded. His supremacy increases all the time. There isn't a Verdi opera that I am inclined to disparage.

Verdi's Followers

Verdi bestrode the operatic scene unchallenged in Italy. His last librettist, Boito, composed two operas himself; *Mefistofele*, a treatment of Goethe's *Faust* (1868), closer to Goethe than Gounod's popular piece, and a *Nero* (1919), which is still scarcely familiar. Boito also wrote the libretto for *La Gioconda* ("The Playful Woman"—it is the Italian title of the painting by Leonardo da Vinci better known as the "Mona Lisa"), set to music by Amilcare Ponchielli (1834–1886) in 1876. Crude in style beside Verdi's music of the same period, and much concerned with violence and other base emotions, it introduced the *verismo* style—the word means realism, but chiefly signifies no emotional holds barred and deals with unheroic, ignoble or merely vulgar *dramatis personae*. Verdi's dramas had certainly inspired it. The *Dance of the Hours* ballet in *La Gioconda* has remained popular; also some of the arias, chiefly the hero's *Cielo e mar* and the heroine's *Suicidio*, often extracted for separate performance.

In the foyers of Milan's La Scala, Ponchielli's bust can be found, with those of Verdi and his predecessors; also a huge one of Umberto Giordano (1867–1948), who bequeathed us the French Revolution opera *Andrea Chénier* (1896) about a historical poet sent to the guillotine out of jealousy. It is a work that blazes with revolutionary spirit and is musically very strong, with vivid, robust solos for the three principal characters, sympathetically written for voices. It stands confidently beside the work of Verdi's chief successor, Giacomo Puccini, as do the so-called "heavenly twins", Ruggiero Leoncavallo's *Pagliacci* ("The Clowns", 1892) and Pietro Mascagni's *Cavalleria Rusticana* ("Rustic Chivalry", 1890), one-act operas usually played nowadays as a popular double-bill. In them the Verdi spirit remains

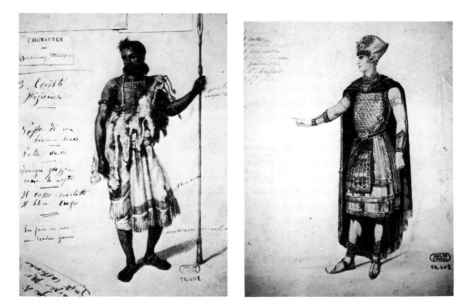

*Two costume designs from the original production of Verdi's **Aïda**.*

Gounod's *Faust* p 211–13

Long before his death in 1901, Verdi had become a national hero, as this **memorial postcard** *bears witness.*

Arrigo Boito, *Verdi's librettist for both* Otello *and* Falstaff, *was himself a skilled composer and had fought beside Garibaldi in the struggle for Italian unity.*

active, even when coarsened. The clown-manager Canio in *Pagliacci*, suspecting his wife's unfaithfulness, but obliged to go through his rigmarole for the public's admiration, has a solo *Vesti la giubba* ("On with the motley") that quickly became a favourite item. Before Verdi's death, his place at the forefront of Italian opera composers had been taken, persuasively, by Giacomo Puccini.

Giacomo Puccini (1858–1924)

An affectionate caricature of **Puccini** *in later life.*

Puccini was born in Lucca, a charming old Tuscan town where his forefathers had been city musicians, church organists, for at least one hundred and fifty years. Giacomo was raised in the family calling, and began work as an organist. A performance of Verdi's *Aïda* in neighbouring Pisa convinced him, when he was eighteen, that he must devote his musicianship to opera, and indeed he showed himself, almost at once, to be a consummate man of the theatre with a well-nigh flawless sense of just what will communicate on stage, and what might not. He studied in Milan under Ponchielli, who advised him to enter a competition for a one-act opera. *Le Villi* was unplaced, but an impromptu performance at the piano by Puccini, during a party, impressed Boito, who had it accepted for production in a Milan theatre (1884), and the publishing firm of Ricordi, which specialized in the work of Italian composers. They signed Puccini on the spot, and thereafter masterminded his immensely successful career.

Puccini's first triumph was with his third opera, *Manon Lescaut* (1893). Puccini knew Massenet's popular *Manon* on the same subject, but felt personally drawn to Prévost's novel, and contrived to narrate the story differently, though he had to employ seven authors before the libretto suited his musical intentions. *Manon Lescaut* was an international success, despite Massenet's work, and it introduced the typical Puccini heroine, a frail young delicious love-object, who is made to suffer distressfully for her charm. Puccini was particularly inspired by such fragile girls, being an enthusiast for field sports, a huntsman, as well as a womanizer. After *Manon* came *La Bohème* (1896), a French story of impoverished student life (Puccini could draw on personal experience) where the embroideress Mimi dies of consumption among her artist-friends. *La Bohème* is not the fully fledged Puccini, but as a music-drama it is almost perfect in proportions and contents. At first it was thought too frivolous and musically audacious— Puccini, all his life, made a habit of keeping up with the musical *avant-garde*. But the international public quickly appreciated its special quality and the appeal of Musetta's Waltz Song, Rodolfo's *Your tiny hand is frozen*, Mimi's *They call me Mimi*, all published separately as sheet-music and sold profusely, for performance in cultured drawing-rooms and seaside pier pavilions.

In his next opera, *Tosca* (1900), Puccini fulfilled his wish to attempt a more masculine, forceful sort of drama; in a word sadistic. Here again is the frail, brave young lady (elderly, bosomy Toscas, sometimes to be seen in performance of the opera, make nonsense of this basic premise) who has to save her lover by submitting to the lusts of the cruel police chief Scarpia (she kills him first). The drama of *Tosca* is sharp-set, and it suited Puccini's creative personality perfectly; with it, he made the *verismo* style his own. Tosca's cry of despair, "Love and music, these I have lived for" (*Vissi d'arte*), Puccinian melody at its most sumptuous, is the best known excerpt, though there are also Cavaradossi's two solos, "Strange harmony of contrasts"

Verdi and Wagner

Music Drama

Eva Turner *as Turandot in Puccini's opera, a role which she made particularly her own.*

(*Recondita armonia*) and "When the stars were brightly shining" (*E lucevan le stelle*). Puccini's natural gift for melody was excited by situations of cruelty, and there are plenty in the police-state story of *Tosca*. *Madam Butterfly* (1904) found an even more vulnerable pretty candidate for suffering in the Japanese geisha-girl who abandons her family and national traditions to marry an American sailor: he leaves her to rejoin his ship, and returns with another, American, wife, whereupon Butterfly commits hara-kiri. Her solo, "One fine day" (*Un bel dì, vedremo*), is particularly famous though *Butterfly*, as a whole, survived a disastrous first performance to become, for some time, the world's most popular opera.

These have remained Puccini's best loved operas. In the later ones he continued to enrich and develop his musical language. *The Girl of the*

Golden West (1910, New York) is about gold-mining in California; a community of rough, simple men and one woman—their spiritual guide—who falls in love with a bandit on the run and saves him from a lynching—the fragile, suffering heroine has become a tough customer. Then came "The Swallow" (*La rondine*, 1917, Monte Carlo), a light Romantic opera, and an operatic triple bill consisting of "The Cloak" (*Il tabarro*), *Sister Angelica* and *Gianni Schicchi* (New York, 1918). The last, a picaresque comedy, quickly became popular (it includes the soprano solo *O my beloved Daddy*); and the first, a horror opera about bargees on the river Seine, has slowly drawn level with it; *Angelica*, set in a nunnery and with an all-female cast, was long deprecated for its sugary religiosity. Puccini left his last opera, *Turandot*, unfinished at his death, and it was completed by his disciple, Alfano. Set in China, it contrasts Puccini's favourite fragile, suffering girl with the hard, vengeful princess Turandot, who delights in killing the men who court her, a great role for a powerful dramatic soprano. Spectacular and exotic Chinese themes and effects blended into Puccini's Italianate and particular musical language. *Turandot* effectively crowned his life's work, and seems to have been the last Italian opera to remain in the international repertory.

Richard Wagner

Verdi and Puccini never aspired further than eloquent operas of ideas, about people. Their contemporary in Germany, Wagner, had the bolder vision of a Total Work of Art (*Gesamtkunstwerk* in German), which would unite poetic drama, music, scenery and even dance in a stage spectacle which he saw as the true justification of Gluck's theories, based on those of the Florentine *Camerata*, and ultimately those of Aeschylus and his fifth century BC fellow Greeks.

Wagner thought big all his life. He wanted to revive the ideal Greek drama, an aim in which Monteverdi and Gluck had apparently failed; a drama which must be a rite participated in by all the audience. Dissatisfied by the theatres in which he worked as a young man, Wagner wrote his operatic quartet, *The Ring*, consisting of *The Rhine Gold*, *The Valkyrie*, *Siegfried* and *Twilight of the Gods*, for a theatre technically better equipped than any existing in Europe. Eventually he built it himself in Bayreuth, a small town in Bavarian Germany, and launched the still celebrated Bayreuth festivals (his temporary structure has survived and been only enlarged and improved in the light of experience: what Wagner designed is still mostly ideal, particularly the acoustics).

As a young man, Wagner was chiefly concerned to expand German opera as he had inherited it from Weber and his lesser successors. His aim was nothing less than to combine that German quality, the flavour of the countryside and the folklore, with the vividness of Rossini and the grandeur of Meyerbeer (much though he personally detested the latter), and then support it with the rich, heroic, orchestral style of Beethoven. The enormity of the notion was purest Romanticism, but Wagner was up to the challenge. His first successful opera, *Rienzi* (1842), is a German version of a Meyerbeer French *grand opéra*, skilfully copied and more melodious, dealing with revolutionary politics in medieval Rome. Wagner had declared a politically progressive hand, and thereafter became personally involved in the movements for revolution in Germany. A visit to Paris, where he found humble work as an arranger, only served to inflame his political fervour.

Gluck p 125–6
Monteverdi p 69–70

Meyerbeer p 198–200
Camerata p 26

Rossini p 196–8

***Richard Wagner**, whose life was as epic and extraordinary as anything he wrote.*

His next opera, *Der fliegende Holländer* ("The Flying Dutchman", 1843, Dresden) has nothing to do with Germany or patriotism but is simply a splendid spook-opera (on the lines of Cherubini's horror-opera) full of marvellous Weber-style music, taken a degree further by a young composer. As a work of art it far surpasses Wagner's next two operas, *Tannhäuser* (1845) and *Lohengrin* (1850), though there are fine moments in both, especially in the second act of *Lohengrin* where Wagnerian opera shows its sharply focused face in the altercations of Ortrude and Telramund, then Ortrude with the heroine Elsa. Both operas are heavily idealistic, deeply German in subject matter (though *Lohengrin* takes place in Belgium). Wagner decided that Germany must attend to Teutonic myth and legend in order to develop progressively in the art of living.

Wagner was on the brink of a new enterprise in *Lohengrin*; close to arrival at a new way of propounding opera, which he found while composing

Bayreuth Theatre

Using the fortune of his fanatical admirer and patron, King Ludwig II of Bavaria, Wagner realized his long-planned dream of a theatre devoted to the cause of ideal performances of his operas. It had to be far removed from existing cultural centres, for Wagner claimed that his works would make their maximum impact in solitude. The foundation stone was laid in Bayreuth in 1872. Much of the money required was raised by "Wagner Societies" all over the world. Four years later, the first complete "Ring" was given in the new Festspielhaus there. The most unusual feature of its fan-shaped auditorium was the curved wooden screen that effectively concealed the orchestra from both audience and singers, but threw their sound right on to the stage. (The hood curving out from the stage side being proportionately lower, the conductor sat at the top of the orchestra, commanding a view of both his players and the stage.) At Wagner's insistence, incidentally, the Bayreuth opera house was the first to darken the auditorium during performances.

Since Wagner's death (his grave lies in the garden at Bayreuth), the annual festivals have remained largely a family occasion: first masterminded by his widow Cosima, his son Siegfried, and then by his two grandsons, Wieland and Wolfgang. The latter remains in charge.

1840–1893

The tenor Fritz Soot as
Siegfried *in Wagner's
opera of the same name.
Siegfried is the part-mortal
grandson of the mighty god,
Wotan.*

In Wagner's
Götterdämmerung,
*Gunther (right, played by
Theodor Scheidel) suspects
Siegfried and Brünnhilde
(Fritz Soot & Maria Müller)
of betraying his trust.*

his next work, the enormous four-evening *Ring* (started in 1848, finished only in 1876). As a saga of man's destiny, past or future, it must be the most potent of all operas, influencing not only later composers, but everybody who is caught in its spell. Something of the glory can be heard in such familiar orchestral excerpts as *Forest Murmurs* and *The Ride of the Valkyries*, but they are only trailers for the real thing, which involves intelligible words, and a stage. Simply to hear *Die Walküre*, or any of Wagner's later operas in the concert-hall or on records is not enough: they must be experienced in the theatre, and the effect is more profound the more we see and hear them.

*In Wagner's **Siegfried**, the hero awakes the lovely Brunnhilde with a kiss. (The soprano Gertrud Bindernagel was shot by her jealous husband as she left the theatre after the performance.)*

The Ring

Wagner's source was an old folk-poem, one of a number dealing with the decline and fall of the old Norse gods. The established authority of the gods' leader, Wotan, is challenged by the material wealth of subterranean dwarfs, the Nibelungs, and by the physical strength of the race of earthly giants. To save his prestige, Wotan resorts to robbery with violence, and can no longer himself right the wrong he has done because he has compromised the morality that gave him authority. The world is saved by his human daughter, Brünnhilde, and his human grandson, Siegfried, and the cure involves the purification of earth and heaven by destructive fire and water. The symbolism suggests the confrontation of management and shop-floor in the Industrial Revolution (as Bernard Shaw explained in his book *The Perfect Wagnerite*). Today the symbols seem even more topical. Unlike

Verdi's operas, *The Ring* is not intended to be a realistic piece: there are magical transformations and magic potions—the vital stuff of old legends. It is, on the other hand, serious, and we are to perceive ourselves in it, related to the others about us. Wagner makes the characters very real; not only Siegfried, the boorish young hero, who is expected to right all wrongs and upsets everything by his naïvety and pride, but the demi-goddess Brünn-hilde and her father Wotan, who struggles all the time to resolve his guilt and be worthy of his role as governor of the world. You cannot survive if you compromise your given ethics.

The greatest Verdi operas, before *Falstaff*, end with death and general lamentation. So it is, usually, with Wagner. Rienzi, his daughter and her lover all burn to death in the Capitol in Rome, while Senta and the Flying Dutchman throw themselves into the sea so as to ascend together to heaven. Tannhäuser collapses on the corpse of Elisabeth, and Elsa expires as Lohengrin returns to Mónsalvat. In *The Ring* everybody dies except Alberich, the ambitious shop-floor steward, who will live to fight another day—such is the fascinating conclusion to *Götterdämmerung* ("The Twilight of the Gods").

In *The Ring* we are asked to consider the entire world. Wagner employs an extra voice in *The Ring*, the orchestra, which comments throughout on the action and what we are to think of it. All the time that the characters are singing, Wagner's orchestra tells us about the background of their actions and motivation, using an elaborate symphonic technique of developing and transforming themes, each with particular references of its own. As the story progresses from one opera to the next, so the web of symphonic commentary grows increasingly rich and allusive, with more and more themes (the German word is *Leitmotiv*) and topics for Wagner to draw on.

Loge (Fritz Soot), Fricka (Karin Branzell), Donner (Herbert Janssen), Freia (Maria Müller) and Froh (Jaro Dworsky) in Wagner's **Das Rheingold**.

*More scenes from early productions of **The Ring**. Below left: the two Valkyries in this 1876 production are played by Lilli Lehmann (left) and her sister Marie.*

A piano score made by Wagner of the orchestral Prelude to **Tristan und Isolde**.

The summerhouse in Munich (now demolished) where Wagner composed the final bars of **Tristan und Isolde**.

Wagner's library in the Villa Wahnfried at Bayreuth. The air of the room where he composed was specially perfumed with scent imported from France.

Because there are sections of development in this symphonic opera, there must also be recapitulations. They sometimes take place in orchestral interludes between scenes (a magnificent specimen is the prelude to the third act of *Siegfried*), sometimes in long monologues, when one character is telling another what happened in the past. These monologues are as close as Wagner comes to the old *scena* or *aria*. He had abandoned the division of an opera into separate "numbers", recitatives, duets, trios, choruses and the like. In symphonic opera the music has to flow uninterruptedly from the beginning of one act until the curtain falls at its end. In *The Ring* a chorus is only used once, in the second act of *The Twilight of the Gods*, though there is something like the effect of a chorus when the eight Valkyrie maidens foregather on a mountain top to meet their leader Brünnhilde (this is the scene known as *The Ride of the Valkyries*). It was important to Wagner that his words should all be understood, and so the characters seldom sing more than one at a time.

By alternating scenes of action, scenes of dialogue, and narrative monologues, Wagner sustains long stretches of music-drama, very diverse in mood and pace. His cast-list includes a trio of water nymphs (the Rhinemaidens) and three Norns who watch over the destiny of the world, as well as the eight Valkyries and the chorus in *Twilight*, so that some variation of vocal texture is ensured. Despite the importance of the orchestra, *The Ring* is a work with great solo singing roles: Brünnhilde, a dramatic soprano, must have power, beauty of tone, and stamina to survive the long monologue (called the Immolation Scene) which ends *The Twilight*. Wotan's is a tremendous part for a strong bass-baritone. Siegfried calls for a powerful tenor, physically agile and handsome in appearance. There are several glorious roles for deep, dark bass voices. *The Ring* is symphonic music-drama, but it is also opera, with music to be sung as beautifully as

Verdi and Wagner

Music Drama

possible, in a continuation of the *bel canto* tradition, and acted in addition by men and women who look like the characters they are portraying.

Tristan, Meistersinger and Parsifal

In the middle of *The Ring*, Wagner broke off to compose two other operas, more likely to be staged and make him some money for the building of Bayreuth, the theatre of his highly practical dreams. Both subjects were close to him. *Tristan und Isolde* (1865), taken from Arthurian legend, hymned the ideal love which cannot be consummated in human life—though in the second act love duet, as exquisitely erotic music as exists, we may ask what is consummation and what not. Richard Strauss declared that the composer of that love duet must have had the coolest head in the world to compose music so exquisitely calculated. In the orchestral prelude to the first act, which portrays the onset of that ideal love, Wagner already takes orchestral music further than it had hitherto explored in terms of tonal harmony. Isolde's long pair of monologues during the first act, sometimes called her *Narration and Curse*, and Tristan's corresponding monologues in the third act, are among the other special glories of this fervent, concentrated opera, which ends with another most ecstatic solo for Isolde, the famous *Liebestod* ("Love-death").

Wagner hoped for another popular success with his comic opera *Die Meistersinger von Nürnberg* ("The Mastersingers of Nuremberg", 1868). Like *The Ring*, it proved very difficult for singers to learn, though for us nowadays it is most singable. Walter's Prize Song, familiar to all, is spread over two scenes. Hans Sachs, a historical German composer, cobbler and philosopher, gradually becomes accepted as the hero of the whole drama, his place confirmed by his two monologues in acts two and three, as well as in duet scenes with others. It would be a beautifully devised libretto—charming, human, romantic—even if Wagner's music were not there. Wagner does use a chorus, to spectacular and sonorous purpose, most of all in the closing scene, which portrays a folk festival by the River Pegnitz, songs for the various guilds of tradesmen, a lilting waltz danced by the crowd and then Hans Sachs greeted by the townsfolk with his hymn to Luther's Reformation, *Wach auf* ("Awake"), the historical Sachs's own words set to Wagner's own music.

Once settled in his own Bayreuth festival theatre (the first festival was given there in 1876), Wagner realized how his remaining urgent project, a *Parsifal* after the old German medieval poem, would sound and he settled down to write it, finishing it in 1882, a year before his death.

Wagner had little scenic taste (unlike Verdi, whose response to stage setting was immediate and firmly discriminating), but was quick to note any deviation from his wishes as expressed in stage directions, which were always very detailed and relevant to the action. Wagner was nevertheless always thoughtful about the visual aspect of his operas. He produced them himself and enjoyed impersonation during rehearsals: his knowledge of the art of acting was praised by all who watched him at work.

Parsifal is a solemn Christian drama, at first sight not a typical Wagnerian subject: Wagner was not a model of the Christian virtues himself. And indeed *Parsifal* is fundamentally another rescue-opera (like *Fidelio*), mixed with Arthurian romance and with a sort of solemn suggestion of piety, which Wagner knew how to convey. The rejection of physical love-making in act two of *Parsifal* marks a dramatic climax greater

Engelbert Humperdinck, *composer of* Hansel & Gretel *and assistant for a time to Richard Wagner. He had a hand in the composition of the latter's* Parsifal.

Facing page: ***Richard Wagner*** *with his wife Cosima, the daughter of Liszt.*

Richard Strauss p 300–6, 319–21

than reading the text might lead one to expect. For Wagner it was clearly the turning-point of the opera. The rest traces Parsifal's training for the guardianship of the Grail, which he assumes at the very end. Wagner wanted *Parsifal* to be performed only at Bayreuth. His wish has been disregarded and it is right that people in every country should be able to experience one of opera's greatest monuments. Nevertheless I believe that Wagner's spectre looms over, and dooms, every production outside Bayreuth and protects every production within. I have never seen a bad *Parsifal* in Bayreuth, not a tolerable one anywhere else.

Wagner's Legacy
It is arguable that, after *Tristan*, *Parsifal* and *Falstaff*, the vocabulary of tonal music had little new to say and that Arnold Schoenberg's twelve-note technique was inevitable. There were, as Schoenberg himself admitted, some more good pieces to be written in C major, just as there were more good German operas after *Parsifal*. Wagner's son, Siegfried, wrote pleasant fairy-tale pieces, but the best was by the Wagner acolyte Engelbert Humperdinck (1854–1921): his *Hansel und Gretel*, nursery Wagner with folk tunes instead of motto-themes, has won audiences ever since its première (conducted by Richard Strauss) at Weimar in 1893.

Chapter 12
Nationalism
My Country

Edvard Grieg explores the native music of Norway ♦ A
Spanish tradition is founded by Felipe Pedrell and his pupils,
Albeníz, Granados and Falla ♦ Czechoslovakia's folk
tradition inspires Smetana, Dvořák and Janáček ♦ Kodály and
Bartók discover the folk music of Hungary ♦ Sibelius and
Finland ♦ Vaughan Williams, Holst and the English musical
renaissance ♦ Charles Ives "stretches the ears" of America ♦

Throughout European musical history, there has been a common language
through which composers could make contact with audiences and fellow-
musicians elsewhere. In the early eighteenth century it was the Vivaldi
language, in the late sixteenth century the Lassus variety, during the first
half of the nineteenth century, Rossini, tempered sometimes by a measure
of Beethoven. Every composer varied it a bit to suit his personal style, but it
was a *lingua franca*, analogous to Latin, which every educated person could
speak until recently.

If you were French, German or Italian, your musical language was born
within you, and others would understand it, even if they did not like it.
Musicians in other countries were less certain of international communication. They had their own heritages of folk music, sometimes quite strong, as
in Spain—though Spanish audiences in the nineteenth century were
Rossini-bewitched and wanted only Italian comic opera and its Spanish
local variety, the *zarzuela*, a mixture of songs, dances and spoken play. The
Spanish music that travelled Europe was not the *zarzuela* but the touristic
confections (excellent if unauthentic music) of the Russian Glinka, the
French Bizet and Chabrier, or the Austrian Hugo Wolf. In England,
Scandinavia, Hungary and in what we now call Czechoslovakia, the
German influence had dominated either because of political pressure or out
of local snobbery and discouragement of a local musical dialect. Promising
young musicians were sent to Leipzig for training in German compositional
technique. Eventually they began to revolt.

Edvard Grieg (1843–1907)
Grieg, a Norwegian, studied in Leipzig, then went home, foreswore German
methods and set out to base his music on the folk music of his country so

1850~1950 My Country

Norwegian folk music
*includes many vigorous
dances, perhaps none more
renowned than the nimble*
Halling.

that it would convey a Norwegian flavour. His theatre music for Ibsen's *Peer Gynt* is well known and exceptionally beautiful. *Dawn*, at the beginning of the first suite, breaks with inimitable natural fluency; the harmonic switches in *The Death of Aase*, progress in a way of their own, not Teutonic. *Solveig's Song* in the second suite touches the key of what we regard as Norwegian folk song.

Grieg was also ambitious to compose large-scale works such as Germans could, but in his own Norwegian way. In his piano concerto he sighted a target that none before him had localized. There is some Lisztian brilliance, some Schumann and Wagner and something else, very clean and undistorted, which belongs particularly to Norway, a straightforward, simple phraseology related to Norwegian folk dances. Grieg was an enthusiast in the collection of his country's folk song and in setting the two languages then current, the sophisticated *Rijksmal* and the peasant *Landsmal*. His song-cycle *Haugtussa* represents this side of his work eloquently. But other individual songs spread his popularity even more, such as *I Love You* (words by Hans Andersen), *Last Spring*, *A Swan* (words by Ibsen) and *From Monte Pincio* (a grand, rather Wagnerian song)—particularly since he travelled Europe giving song recitals with his wife, the soprano Nina Hagerup. Grieg's songs and short piano solos (such as *Wedding Day at Troldhaugen*) were performed in countless musical homes while he was still alive. His ten books of *Lyric Pieces* for piano solo contain some marvellous music, though Debussy referred to them contemptuously as "bon-bons stuffed with snow".

Above: **Edvard Grieg**, *who was instrumental in founding the Norwegian Academy of Music, was deeply concerned in the creation of a music that would sound distinctively Norwegian.*

Isaac Albeníz (1860–1909)

One country much addicted to Grieg's music was Spain. What Grieg had done for Norway, surely a native could do for Spain—that was the opinion of both Enrique Granados (1867–1916) and Manuel de Falla (1876–1946). They were much encouraged by their teacher Felipe Pedrell, the chief propagandist in Spain for a nationalistic music that could be exported, as the provincial *zarzuela* hardly could.

They were overtaken in this aim by an older composer-pianist, also a protégé of Pedrell, Isaac Albeníz. He was a wonder-boy pianist who gave his début at the age of four, composed when he was seven, was ignominiously

Left: *The opening bars of Grieg's haunting* **Solveig's Song** *from Peer Gynt.*

Far left: *Johannes Brun in the character of* The Mountain King *in* **Peer Gynt**. *At Ibsen's request, Grieg supplied the music for this bewitching drama.*

1850-1950 My Country

exploited by his parents and determined to get away from home. When he was ten he escaped to travel and give concerts, but had to return when bandits robbed him of everything. Undaunted, he ran away again two years later and stowed away on a ship going to South America, where he earned his living giving concerts. He returned to become a piano pupil of Liszt and a great virtuoso—so his charming, fantastically brilliant, almost innumerable piano pieces suggest. Albeníz gave up opus numbers somewhere in the 200s, long before his death. Pedrell persuaded him to concentrate on composition and the music of his country, not on drawing-room success in London and Paris.

During the 1890s Albeníz abandoned his career as pianist. His finest music is in the Spanish piano solo pieces which he wrote in the last three years of his life: the suite *Iberia* and its two appendices, *Azulejos* and *Navarra*. They are intensely brilliant and difficult, very evocative. Among the others are *Triana* and *El puerto*. The gramophone catalogue lists many other favourite Albeníz pieces of Spanish character, some arranged for guitar. Albeníz delighted to imitate castanets and guitar in his piano music. In *Iberia* he brought Spanish music back to Spanish authorship, the first composer since Victoria to do so in an international context.

Enrique Granados (1867–1916)

Granados was as gifted in literature and painting as in music. Best known are his *Goyescas*, a set of piano solos, completed in 1911 and based on paintings by Francesco Goya. Of these, the most famous is *La maja y el ruiseñor* ("The lover and the nightingale"), also known as a song. It conveys with wondrous voluptuousness the contrast between the woman's infatuation and the bird's uncommitted natural chirruping. The success of these lustrous piano pieces in Paris led to the commission of an operatic *Goyescas* (hence the vocal version just mentioned), which finally had its first performance in New York in 1916. Granados perished soon after. Returning

Isaac Albeníz (pictured with his daughter) was paid a lot of money by an English millionaire, Francis Money-Coutts, to write a lengthy Arthurian opera with a libretto by his benefactor.

Liszt p 185–7
Victoria p 49–50

from the *Goyescas* première in New York, his ship was torpedoed in the English Channel. He was picked up by a lifeboat, but dived back into the sea to save his wife and both were drowned.

Granados' Spanish Dances for piano and his songs in eighteenth-century Spanish style (*Tonadillas*) testify to his rousing nationalism, as do many other short pieces. Like Albeníz and Falla, he was less drawn to the landscape of Spain than to Spain's musical history and classic style.

*The paintings of **Goya** (right: The Dance of San Antonio de la Florida) were the inspiration behind Granados' marvellous series of piano pieces, Goyescas.*

Manuel de Falla (1876–1946)

Falla trained successfully as a pianist and was persuaded by his teacher, Pedrell, to help put Spain on the musical map again. It was his sojourn in Paris from 1907 until 1914 that enabled him to do so—his contact with Debussy and Ravel and with Dyagilev, Stravinsky and the Russian Ballet. He, more than either Albeníz or Granados, investigated the musical roots of his national inheritance. He was born in Cadiz and he spent years collecting and examining the traditional music of that region, Andalusia. (Strangely, Albeníz's *Iberia* also deals more with Andalusia than with his native Catalonia, much farther north.) Like all Spanish composers, including the above named, Falla wrote *zarzuelas*.

In 1904 he composed a real, serious Spanish opera, *La vida breve* ("Life is Short") and fulfilled Pedrell's wish: it was handsomely received in Paris.

Debussy p 285–9, 321   Ravel p 284

Dyagilev p 290–1   Stravinsky p 291–4, 321–4

1850-1950 *My Country*

Manuel de Falla, by Picasso. He wrote a magnificent Harpsichord Concerto for the great Wanda Landowska.

*On the death of his great colleague Albeniz, it fell to **Enrique Granados** to complete the master's last piano piece, Azulejos.*

The First World War sent him back to Spain, where he brought out the ballet *El amor brujo* ("Love the Magician"), a Spanish gypsy fantasy about spiritual possession in which occurs the popular "Ritual Fire Dance". From this time also come *Seven Popular Spanish Songs*—flamboyant original music to traditional texts. Both works appeared in 1915. A year later Falla produced a three-movement piano concerto called *Nights in the Gardens of Spain*. Brightly coloured evocative music, brilliant, truly Spanish and eminently popular, it fulfilled completely what Pedrell had longed for, and was as fine a piano concerto as any being written at the time. Falla followed it with the ballet *El sombrero de tres picos* ("The Three-cornered Hat") for Diaghilev's Russian Ballet, for which Pablo Picasso designed the settings. This is Spanish Falla at his most captivating. Splendid ballet as it is, the true Spanish Falla, not courting attention but simply putting himself on paper, is to be heard in the super-folkloric *Fantasia baetica* for solo piano (1919), written for the Polish pianist Arthur Rubinstein. Falla then turned to a sort of Spanish neoclassicism with the puppet-opera *Master Peter's Puppetshow*, based on an episode in Cervantes' *Don Quixote*, and a harpsichord concerto for Wanda Landowska, the Polish virtuoso exponent of that newly revived old keyboard instrument. Thereafter, Falla spent his energy on an oratorio called *Atlántida* (left incomplete at his death in self-imposed exile in South America); it proved unsatisfactory even in its later completed state. Falla's youth was glorious and *Nights in the Gardens of Spain* alone would justify his claim to greatness.

A later Spanish nationalist composer is Joaquín Rodrigo (born 1901), whose guitar concerto, entitled *Concierto de Aranjuez* (1939), evokes Spain with compulsive authenticity and is now one of the most popular pieces of Spanish music in existence.

The Czechoslovakia of Smetana

The title of this chapter, "My Country", comes from a collection of orchestral tone-poems celebrating the country of Bohemia; the most musical part of the Hapsburg Austro-Hungarian Empire. We last met the Bohemian composers in Mannheim, where Stamitz and other compatriots created the symphony. Their musical and literary education was almost entirely German: Czech was not a language for public usage, it was only for peasants. When peasants began to assert their rights, the Czech language revived, and with it Czech music and theatre. The Czech people complained about the Austro-Hungarian domination. Blood was spilt, but the reverses of Austria in Lombardy, thanks to Garibaldi, made Czech music possible.

Bedřich Smetana (1824–1884) returned from abroad, where he had made his name as a composer and conductor and taught himself Czech, the native language he had never learned, then began writing the music of his country. It took thirty years for the rest of the world to accept his nationalist masterpiece, *The Sold Bride* (1866—usually called, misleadingly, "The Bartered Bride"), whose countrified song, dance and comic action blaze with colour and *joie de vivre*.

Smetana's greatest opera is probably *Dalibor* (1868), a sort of *Fidelio* rescue-opera with splendid heroic music. His most patriotic achievement, the noble opera *Libuše*, is revered by Czechs and always performed on national holidays, but is probably too local in terms of reference to achieve international fame, though his six orchestral symphonic poems, *Ma Vlast* ("My Country", 1879), certainly did. They are *Vyšehrad*, the castle which dominates Prague; *Vltava*, the principal river in Bohemia; *Sarka*, an early national heroine; *From Bohemia's Woods and Fields; Tabor* and *Blanik*, places associated with the Hussite Czech Protestant movement. The contents are largely of national interest (outside Czechoslovakia, Sarka and the Hussites mean very little), but Smetana's inspired music has sustained attention to the whole cycle, unified in the *Vyšehrad* theme. Smetana borrowed this theme from his contemporary, Zdeněk Fibich (1850–1900), a likeable writer of romantic music, more German in manner. *Vltava* (sometimes identified by its German name *Moldau*) has always been the most frequently performed; a vivid documentary of the river's course from its spring, through varied countryside, dividing and meeting again before flowing past the towering castle of Vyšehrad in Prague. Smetana's two string quartets (the first subtitled "From my Life") touchingly describe the deafness from which he suffered in later years. The second of them depicts a repeated high note that whistled repeatedly in his ears before his hearing disappeared altogether. Smetana conducted the Czech National Opera in Prague between 1866 and 1874. In his orchestra sat a viola-player called Dvořák who was to rival him among the ranks of Czech composers.

*A costume design by Picasso for the Diaghilev ballet **The Three-cornered Hat**, with music by Manuel de Falla.*

Nationalism

My Country

A view across the Vltava to
St Vitus' Cathedral,
Prague.

Antonin Dvořák (1841–1904)

Dvořák had the advantage over Smetana as a Czech composer in that he came from a peasant background and his first language was Czech, in speech as well as in music. Bohemian traditional music was with him from childhood: his own compositions often include Czech dances such as the *dumka* and the *furiant*, and his melodies are close to traditional Bohemian ones but seldom need to borrow existing tunes: to Dvořák, as to Schubert, melodies sprang unbidden all the time. As soon as Dvořák's musical gifts became clear, his parents were willing for him to be a musician, not a butcher as his ancestors had been: he was sent away to learn music in Prague.

Musically he was influenced by both Wagner and Brahms: the latter persuaded his own publisher, Simrock, to take Dvořák's works and urged Dvořák to leave Prague for Vienna. Brahms was a strong influence on Dvořák's music—in the sixth and seventh symphonies, for example. We can sometimes hear Dvořák consciously putting on the style of the Austrian Empire, then reverting to his own Bohemian origins—Viennese art-music alternated with Czech folk music. Dvořák's cello concerto, one of his finest works, is an eloquent example, most of the time pure Dvořák and Bohemian rusticity, with moments of urban grandeur aimed at Vienna. His eighth symphony (in G major), written for London, chiefly suggests the simple

Wagner p 229–40   Schubert p 163–8
Brahms p 187–90

rustic delight of a countryman (in the slow movement you may hear the cooing of pigeons, whose breeding was Dvořák's chief extra-musical hobby, alongside cards and train-spotting); but the energetic finale looks towards the big, busy city.

For a long time Dvořák resisted all efforts to remove him from the Czech countryside to some cultural metropolis. The English took greatly to his choral music. Big festivals in industrial centres, such as Leeds and Birmingham, enjoyed *The Spectre's Bride*, *Stabat Mater* and *St Ludmilla* and made him welcome. Eventually he left the respectable German publishing house of Simrock for the London publisher Novello, because his

Above: ***The Bohemian countryside*** *was an inspiration to such composers as* **Smetana** *(left) and Dvořák.*

Below: ***Dvořák*** *and two costume sketches for his last opera,* **Armida***.*

Nationalism

My Country

Leos Janáček *with Zdenka Schulzova, before their marriage in 1881.*

music sold best in Britain—and has always remained very popular with audiences there.

Through friendship with Chaikovsky, Dvořák paid a visit to Russia, where his music was well liked. But his most famous voyage was to America in 1891, when he became the first principal of a new musical academy in New York. There he composed his *American* string quartet and his ninth symphony, *From the New World*, both supposedly influenced by Red Indian or African black music—though scholars differ on the subject, and Czech musicians find those American tunes perfectly Czech in flavour. The deliberately Czech Dvořák can be heard in his *Slavonic Dances* (originally for piano duet, 1887, later scored for orchestra) and *Slavonic Rhapsodies*.

Chaikovsky p 275–7

Janáček in the garden of
his house in Brno, in 1927.

Dvořák's *Gypsy Songs* include the old favourite *Songs my Mother taught me* (recorded by many a great singer), and his *Biblical Songs* are well known too. He wrote operas throughout an active life, the best of them perhaps *The Jacobin* (1889), an amusing, gentle, rather Romantic score about an alien in a village, much suspected by the inhabitants until he proves to be the rightful heir to the local squirearchy. *Rusalka* (1901), about a water-nymph, the Undine story, contains a favourite soprano solo, *O Silver Moon*. Some of Dvořák's best pieces are not so much historically important as just enjoyable: they include the *Scherzo Capriccioso* and the *Symphonic Variations*, both for orchestra, both rather Brahmsian with strong Czech overtones.

Leoš Janáček (1854–1928)

In later years Dvořák befriended a talented composer from Brno in Moravia. Janáček was deeply rooted in country life, which he could portray in music with rare vividness as in the lively Sinfonietta (1926), a festive evocation of Brno, past and present, and the piano suite *Along Overgrown Paths*—wisps of elusive harmony and melody that are too sharply focused to rank as impressionism—or in his curious song-cycle *The Diary of a Man who Disappeared*, chiefly for tenor and piano, but also including a mezzo-soprano (as the gypsy girl who entices the young man from home) and off-stage chorus; a compelling piece. He set the Catholic Mass in the old Moravian language—it is called his *Glagolitic Mass* (1926). When Janáček composed his first masterly opera, *Jenufa* (1904), he tried to get it produced outside Brno, without success, even in Prague: it was too idiosyncratic for a national, let alone international, audience; too close to nature and primitive instincts to be admired by people intent on acquiring social graces.

Eventually *Jenufa* was performed (in Prague and elsewhere) with great success, and during the 1920s Janáček enjoyed an Indian Summer of glorious creativity, with a blissful love-affair that sparked off two ecstatic string quartets (the first is called *Kreutzer Sonata*, 1923, after Tolstoy's novel, the second, *Intimate Letters*, 1928) and numerous theatre commissions which resulted in the operas *Katya Kabanova* (1922, based on Ostrovsky's play *The Storm*); *The Cunning Little Vixen* (1926), a play about animals that ought to repel an opera audience, but is so tastefully and enthusiastically done that one cannot help loving it; *The Makropoulos Case* (1926), on a play by Karel Čapek about an opera singer who lives two hundred years, another curious story set to riveting music, with perhaps the best part for a prima donna after Puccini's *Turandot*; and finally *From the House of the Dead*, an all-male opera about a prison camp in nineteenth-century Russia, as described by Dostoyevsky. Janáček's opera subjects were all unconventional, like his music, as if he dared himself each time to achieve the impossible. He found fame in the last years of his life, but only worldwide acclaim after the Second World War, when he gradually emerged as a great pioneer of modern music-theatre, indeed as another Wagner from a different part of Europe, much more concerned with the humanity of life on earth. "In every creature is a spark of God," he said.

The Music of Hungary

Across the Austro-Hungarian border from Czechoslovakia, Hungarian musicians were no less talented. Liszt, and others, hymned the excellent Hungarian gypsy orchestras, and Ferenc Erkel (1810–1893) lauded the Hungarian nation in his operas *Hunyadi Laszló* (1844) and *Bánk Bán* (1852).

A view across the Tisza, in the Tokay region of north-east **Hungary**.

which other countries have also found exhilarating in recent years. Hungarian composers of that period assumed that gypsy music was the true folk music of Hungary. They were also, perhaps through Liszt, drawn in their compositions towards Wagner to an extent where personal and national character could not emerge. The sources for a real Hungarian music were there, however, in the music of non-gypsy peasant Magyars, as Zoltán Kodály (1882–1967) realized later. In 1905 he began travelling round Hungary collecting traditional songs and dances and recording or writing them down; he was soon assisted by his friend Bela Bartók (1881–1945). They had both been trained as professional, German-orientated composers and both had enjoyed some success. Bartók's *Kossuth* Symphony (1903) is a decent piece of pseudo-Richard Strauss, with some personality of its own, a virtuoso style and a good Hungarian revolutionary streak to impress a native audience.

Kodály and Bartók netted an invaluable bag of real Hungarian traditional music, just before its memory was expunged by the arrival of radio and the cinema, which substituted international light music for the memory of each village's musical heritage. Kodály's experience led him to a jovial national opera, *Háry János*; a superb choral work, *Psalmus Hungaricus*; the virtuoso *Peacock* variations for orchestra—all close to his experience of Hungarian folk music. His method of musical education for Hungarians, based on their own musical inheritance, is still a feature of Hungarian schooling and brings remarkable results.

Bartók also taught music to a generation of Hungarians (his *Mikrokosmos*, six volumes of piano-teaching pieces, are now learned everywhere),

Zoltán Kodály *in his study in Budapest, transcribing folk music collected from far and wide throughout his native Hungary.*

Bela Bartók, around 1912, playing a large hurdy-gurdy. The furniture behind him was made for the composer by a peasant craftsman.

but his *métier* was composition. The study of folk music soon drew him away from the attractions of Liszt, Wagner and Richard Strauss. His fourteen *Bagatelles* for solo piano, opus 6 (1908), are as much an introduction to twentieth-century composition as anything in modern music; short, succinct and strictly to the point. Like Falla, Bartók had learned from Debussy and his music developed his Hungarian musical findings along French rather than German lines, as we hear in the elusive, masterly opera *Duke Bluebeard's Castle* (1918), in which Bluebeard brings his seventh bride back home. She insists on learning about his past and, in turn, he allows her to open doors to the rich outposts of his kingdom, lastly to the room where her predecessors wanly live, and where she goes at the end.

The Significance of Bartók
Bartók became one of the founding fathers of progressive twentieth-century music. His six string quartets, the most beautiful and demanding since Beethoven's, are built on what he learned from other European composers (especially Debussy, but perhaps also early Stravinsky), yet he and they would have made scarcely any mark in the history of music without his investigation of Hungarian peasant musical diction. The second of them may be the most accessible, the sixth entertaining as well as serious.

Bartók's music, whether in the virtuoso elaboration of his two sonatas for violin and piano and three piano concertos, his later very robust sonata for two pianos and percussion or even his very late, deliberately popular

Stravinsky p 291–4, 321–4   Falla p 245–7

Debussy p 285–9

concerto for orchestra (written during his final years of exile in North America), chiefly represents the emergence of Hungary as one of Europe's great musical nations, perhaps nurtured by the Hapsburgs, but only able to flourish when the Empire collapsed. One cannot easily select a single masterpiece out of so much adventurous, poetic, superbly crafted, creative work; but I do urgently recommend Bartók's second violin concerto as one glorious summit.

The greatest twentieth-century composers have all been international figures, writing music in a *lingua franca* of some sort. Stravinsky and Schoenberg internationalized their music. Bartók, their peer, remained

*Above: **Bartók** spent a long time collecting the folk music of Hungary. He also took many photographs of the peasants whose songs he recorded.*

Schoenberg p 307–9

255

Nationalism

My Country

Sibelius at the piano while
his wife, Aino, listens. For
the last thirty years of his
life, after completing the
mighty Tapiola, *he wrote
virtually no music at all.*

Hungarian and obliged the rest of the world to learn his musical language.
He died miserably in the USA before he could return to his native land.

Finland and Sibelius (1865–1957)

In Finland, German-orientated at the end of the nineteenth century like
every other European country, the talented Jean Sibelius (who spoke
Swedish, not Finnish at home) as a boy developed a fascination for the
national epic, the *Kalevala*, a book which brings together all old legends of
Scandinavia. He was, like other young musicians of his day, sent to study in
Germany and, like Grieg, he revolted, determined to write music in a way
appropriate to a Scandinavian. His sights were set higher than Grieg's.
Orchestral tone-poems on national subjects were important to him: in *En
Saga* (simply "A Story") and *Tapiola* (a portrait of windswept Finnish
forests) he achieved masterpieces in a perfectly individual music language,
clearly of its time and country. He went further in his seven symphonies, of

Grieg p 241–3

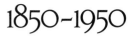

which the first two begin quite traditionally but gradually become more perverse, inclined to concentrate or omit sections which other composers would naturally repeat. The later Sibelius symphonies refine their musical language increasingly boldly, and move with a strange but convinced authority. The fourth in A minor is the most succinct and, perhaps, ideal, of the seven, though a case for supremacy could be made for several of them. Sibelius had great influence on English composers of the early twentieth century, largely in matters of technique more than expression. Since his death, his individual, commanding tone of musical voice has been increasingly appreciated all over the world.

England—Vaughan Williams and Holst

One of his great admirers was the English composer Ralph Vaughan Williams (1872–1958), who dedicated his fifth symphony "in sincere flattery" to Sibelius, though the music is not imitative at all, actually derived from an opera on Bunyan's *The Pilgrim's Progress*. After conventional musical schooling (his later teachers were Bruch and Ravel), Vaughan Williams and his friend Gustav Holst (1874–1934) determined to seek out the traditional songs of England as Bartók and Kodály were doing in Hungary, though unbeknown to them. The English composers too wanted to write music outside the prevalent German tradition. Holst succeeded quickly with his orchestral suite *The Planets* (1916), a poetic and imaginative interpretation of astrology in which his enthusiasm had been roused. He later painted a sombre, compelling portrait of Thomas Hardy's Wessex in *Egdon Heath*. Reading a book on Hindu literature, he became so interested that he learned the Sanskrit language so as to translate the poems of *Rig Veda* into English himself, and set them to music. Later he learned ancient Greek in order to make his own text for the choral and orchestral *Hymn of Jesus* (1917). English folk song remained for Holst a fascinating study, but it took a very small part in his music. With such a searching, original mind, he had no difficulty in writing his own, quite un-German sort of music.

English folk song penetrated more deeply into Vaughan Williams's musical language, and his inspiration was almost purely English—whether landscape as *In the Fen Country*, an orchestral tone-poem (1904), and three *Norfolk Rhapsodies* (1905–6); or old English music in *Fantasia on a Theme by Thomas Tallis* (1910). This was his first national and greatest international success, a meditation for solo string quartet and two string orchestras, the smaller one placed farther away from the others. His inspiration could be English painting, as in the ballet *Job* (1930) based on William Blake's illustrations to the Bible story. Equally, English literature such as Bunyan's allegory *The Pilgrim's Progress* (he set one episode in 1921, and completed a four-act opera on the subject in 1949); or English life in the past, as with *Hugh the Drover* (1914), a romantic, partly ballad-opera, about English village life in the early nineteenth century. In *Riders to the Sea* (1932) he took for once an Irish subject, J.M. Synge's play of that name, set in an Irish fishing village on the savage Atlantic coast, where the sea destroys all who earn their living upon it.

The first of Vaughan Williams's nine symphonies was inspired by the sea which surrounds Great Britain. *A Sea Symphony* (1909) is a vocal work, with soloists, chorus and orchestra; the poems are not English, but by the American Walt Whitman, a favourite also of Holst, and of another English

Tallis p 49, 55

Ravel p 284

*Like Kodály and Bartók in Hungary, **Gustav Holst** (in knee-breeches) and **Vaughan Williams** (with walking stick) were Britain's great hunters of their native folk music.*

contemporary, Frederick Delius. Vaughan Williams continued with the purely orchestral *London Symphony* (1913), which brings together familiar sights and sounds in the capital's life before the First World War, as a symphonic tone-poem. These are stirring pieces, but not the authentic Vaughan Williams, a voice first heard in his third, Pastoral Symphony (1921), which blends folk and pastoral sounds into a finespun orchestral, still symphonic, texture (it includes a wordless offstage soprano solo in the last movement, eminently neo-Romantic in effect, almost other-worldly). The fifth, *Pilgrim's Progress*, symphony revives an aspect of this serene, visionary Vaughan Williams; the fourth (1934) and sixth (1947) symphonies have a much more uncomfortable, indeed alarming effect. Number four seemed, at the time, to react violently against the rise of Fascism in Germany and Italy, number six to the horrors of the resultant war ended by atomic bombing. Vaughan Williams denied those interpretations, but the continuing prestige of the two works is surely connected with their relevance to violence in our own age. After them, his last three symphonies come as something of an anticlimax, though number seven, the *Antarctic Symphony* (1952), reworked from music composed for the film *Scott of the Antarctic* (1948), has a certain heroic character, naturally enough. It is a reminder that Vaughan Williams gave much of his energy in later years to the quite new medium of film-music, starting with war films in 1940, and ending with *The Vision of William Blake* in 1957 (a return to the world of

Early Music Renaissance

After the introduction of the piano around 1790, the harpsichord was virtually unheard for more than a hundred years. Its revival was due to the efforts of two people, Arnold Dolmetsch (1858–1940) and the Polish virtuoso Wanda Landowska (1879–1959). Dolmetsch, excited by the immense quantity of undiscovered and unperformed early music, manufactured viols, recorders, lutes and harpsichords to re-create the sounds that composers heard in their own time. Landowska, a brilliant pianist, commissioned a harpsichord from the firm of Pleyel in Paris early in the twentieth century, and set about reconstructing from available evidence how Bach, Scarlatti and Couperin would have performed their own music on the instrument.

Scholarship in this area was deficient. Landowska's harpsichord, for example, was made with an iron frame, pedals to change the stops, and a clanging sonority quite foreign to true harpsichord sound. Her performances, on the other hand, were nothing less than thrilling, as recordings still show. (She even took her harpsichord to Russia to play to Tolstoy, the instrument carried to his house through the snow, on the back of a sleigh. Another performance, illustrated here, took place in the studio of the sculptor Rodin.)

Interest in early music, especially keyboard music, had continued through the nineteenth century: Brahms, for example, owned a priceless manuscript of Scarlatti sonatas and had edited the harpsichord suites of Couperin. But the piano had remained the ne plus ultra *of instruments for performing them. It is still through Dolmetsch and Landowska (for making the harpsichord sound a familiar one all over the world) that we have learned to love this music the way it was meant to sound.*

1850–1950 My Country

Charles Ives *was a very private musician. He kept many of his compositions secret, and only rarely went to listen to music.*

Job). Vaughan Williams, like Holst, was essentially a practical composer, writing music for immediate performance by forces whose size and abilities determined what he wrote. Throughout his working life, novelty always combined with tradition.

America—Charles Ives (1874–1954)

In the USA, the most idiosyncratic of all composers, Charles Ives was writing music to make listeners "stretch their ears", so his father advised him. Ives made a prosperous living as a businessman, and until 1920 composed in his spare time music that his contemporaries detested (if they ever heard it), it being far in advance of the vanguard movements. His orchestral work *Three Places in New England* paints musical landscapes worthy of any in Europe. Ives's inspiration was not so much American folk song as hymn-tunes and community songs, popular music of the day which he would put together in different keys and rhythms. He experimented with quarter-tone scales too—ideas not then current but dreamed up by his father, who was an army bandmaster but not a composer. It was sometimes said that Charlie Ives composed his father's unwritten music. Memories of Ives's boyhood, books, games (he was a fine sportsman), girls, tunes, places all mingle in his five symphonies, his *Concord* sonata for piano, his string quartets, and many songs, with unconventional, uncanny perception. Ives was one of music's greatest visionaries and pioneers, as can best be heard in his fourth symphony or in *The Unanswered Question*. He was proud to call himself an American. He, more than later European-orientated American composers (Aaron Copland is the most celebrated example), has yet to be understood by the rest of the world; perhaps even by his compatriots.

Copland p 363

Chapter 13
The Music of Russia
The Mighty Fistful

Ballad operas and folk songs inspire a new Russian music ♦
Glinka and Dargomïzhsky set the scene ♦ The Brothers
Rubinstein provide the platform ♦ The Mighty Fistful:
Balakirev, Cui, Borodin, Musorgsky and Rimsky-Korsakov ♦
The mightiest of them all—Chaikovsky ♦ After the Fistful—
Rakhmaninov and Skryabin ♦

The nationalist musical movement was particularly influential in Russia. It
had always been a musical country, with a strong tradition of folk music,
and of church music for the Greek Orthodox Rite. But secular art music was
for the ruling classes, who expected it to come from the west; largely from
Italy, France or Germany. If a cultivated amateur did compose music, it
would ape the current Italian or French manner. Glinka, one such amateur,
brought the sound of Russia into his music. His example fired composers of
the next generation. The brothers Anton and Nicholas Rubinstein started
concert societies, where the paying public could hear new Russian music,
and conservatories in which young musicians would be professionally
trained. Already a talented group of amateur composers was gathering, all
eager to write music as loyal Russians. There were five of them, and some
people called them "The Five", though they made such an impact on the
musical world that they were also nicknamed *Moguchaya Kuchka*, the
"Mighty Clutch" or "Mighty Fistful"—there are five fingers to a fist, as in
the phrase "a bunch of fives". The greatest Russian composer, Chaikovsky,
was considered too westernized (he alone had profited from professional
academic training) to be included in the *Kuchka*. Their successors, all
professional musicians, thought in western as much as in Russian musical
ways. In the early twentieth century the Russian impresario Dyagilev
brought the music of the *Kuchka* to western Europe with his famous
Russian ballet company and allied enterprises. But anti-western *Kuchka*
philosophies of music have persisted in Soviet Russia since the Revolution.

The Oak Tree and the Acorn
Chaikovsky once likened Glinka's orchestral piece *Kamarinskaya* (1848) to
"an acorn in which you can see the whole oak tree of Russian music".
"Sapling" would have been more accurate: the acorns were in Russian

Russian folk musicians.
This group, from Georgia,
claims to be the world's
oldest orchestra: together
the age of the six musicians
adds up to 500 years.

ballad-operas of the late eighteenth century, plays with interpolated folk songs, along the lines of *The Beggar's Opera* in England. Catherine the Great (1729–1796) encouraged her Italian court composers to set opera librettos in Russian, and sent some Russian musicians to Italy for serious musical studies. The most successful was a serf (a peasant slave) called Evstigney Ipatovich Fomin (1761–1800) who was privileged to be educated in St Petersburg (serf orchestras were common), then sent to study music in Italy with Padre Martini (who also taught Mozart), and returned to compose several stage-works with Russian texts and with music of a Russian flavour (though some of it was by other composers). Fomin's opera *Coachmen at the Staging Post* (1787) imitates the balalaika in its overture, and his other works adapt national tunes to his own musical purposes. Catherine the Great herself wrote the Russian text for his French-styled opera-ballet *Boeslavich, the Hero of Novgorod* (1786).

Glinka

From the acorns to the sapling: Mikhail Ivanovich Glinka (1804–1857) wrote the first real, abiding Russian opera, *Ivan Susanin*, subtitled *A Life for the Tsar* (1836). He came from a wealthy family and divided his energies between music and womanizing, with hypochondria as a powerful side-interest. A desire to visit Italy was gratified when he complained of illness. There he became an addict of opera, in particular the works of Rossini, Bellini and Donizetti, and he determined to do for Russia what they had done for Italy. But he lacked the compositional technique to accomplish the task, so he went to Berlin for lessons. The result was *A Life for the Tsar*, which tells how in 1613 a peasant, Ivan Susanin, prevented conspirators from murdering Tsar Michael Romanov, but at the sacrifice of his own life.

The score of Glinka's opera
A Life for the Tsar. *"I*
could not be an Italian
composer . . . I had to think
and write like a Russian,"
declared Glinka.

Bellini p 203–5   Rossini p 196–8

Donizetti p 200–3

Glinka's operas (he composed another, *Ruslan and Ludmilla*, 1842) have a European sound with a Russian accent, Bellini and Russian folk song variously balanced. *Ruslan*, the more nationalist in idiom, has a fantastic rescue-story involving supernatural forces. It was derived from a poem by Alexander Pushkin (1799–1837), the great Russian nationalist poet and advanced thinker, who was one of Glinka's intimate friends until Pushkin's death following a duel. He was a major literary inspiration to Russian musicians in general, then and subsequently. Glinka later stayed in Paris, where he studied further and made friends with Berlioz. He then went to Spain, where the local music inspired him to several orchestral and solo piano works (eg the First Spanish Overture, 1845, based on the celebrated dance-tune called *Jota aragonesa*), at that time astounding for their brilliant evocation of that country's music and important for their influence on later non-Spanish composers, such as Bizet and Chabrier.

Glinka never shook off the superficiality of his upbringing. Eventually he found a lovely girl and wed her, but he never took his marriage seriously and his wife left him because of his continued womanizing. He was swayed by the western taste of the élite Russian public, remained indifferent to the revolutionary aspirations of friends such as Pushkin, and was happy to compose songs and piano pieces (he was an accomplished singer and pianist) which parallel his attractive memoirs like a musical diary of his experience. One piano piece commemorates his first journey by the newly invented railway train, others are inspired by parting from some sweetheart or group of friends, as in the series *Farewell to St Petersburg*. Glinka did invent the

Glinka, a portrait by Ilya Repin. His opera A Life for the Tsar *rapidly became a favourite of Russian audiences (including the Tsar himself).*

specifically Russian narrative style of symphonic composition, derived from whole melodies, not short thematic fragments as in Germany, and had aspirations for a new sort of Russian church music. He was studying for this last task in Berlin when he died. Glinka was friendly with Balakirev and gave him every encouragement, and his sister, Ludmilla Shestakova, became a spiritual matriarch to the *Kuchka*. He was likeable, in some ways a surprisingly admirable man. His drawing-room songs in particular repay investigation.

Dargomïzhsky

Alexander Dargomizhsky. *His opera to Pushkin's text,* The Stone Guest, *greatly influenced later Russian composers.*

Another sapling of the Russian musical forest was Alexander Dargomïzhsky (1813–1869). Born into a well-to-do musical family, he learned the piano and singing as well as the violin, but was discouraged from his keenness for composition and put into the civil service. Glinka befriended him and proved a soulmate since both lived chiefly for music and girls: Dargomïzhsky became a successful singing teacher (women pupils only, and without financial payment). He wrote numerous songs for them, and that sent him to Russian folk song and a study of intonation in Russian speech (such as Janáček was to investigate later with the Czech language), all of which found fruit in his opera *The Stone Guest* (written in the 1860s, left incomplete at his death, but completed by Cui and Rimsky-Korsakov, and first performed in 1872). *The Stone Guest* is impressive in performance on record, and clearly influenced Musorgsky and other Russian composers, though its first performance turned other composers away from it. Dargomïzhsky's more conventional opera *Rusalka* (another Pushkin derivation, 1856), also set by Dvořák, was immediately successful, and remains in Soviet repertory to this day.

The Brothers Rubinstein

In 1859 Anton Rubinstein formed the Imperial Russian Musical Society in St Petersburg as a concert-giving society which gave regular public performances of contemporary Russian music, the first of their kind in Russia. A year later his brother Nicholas inaugurated a similar society in Moscow, with equal success. In 1862 a musical conservatory was opened in St Petersburg: one of the first enrolled pupils was Chaikovsky. Both brothers were closely affiliated with western European music, academic (therefore anti-Berlioz and Wagner) and vocally opposed to the nationalist innovations of the *Kuchka*. Their conflict was publicly stated; Nicholas is famous still for his vitriolic reception of Chaikovsky's first piano concerto, perhaps that composer's most popular work. Of all Anton's many compositions only his *Melody in F* is often heard today. The brothers, despite their conservatism, did provide a platform for their younger, more Russian-minded colleagues.

Balakirev

Chief among them was Mily Balakirev (1837–1910). He was trained as a pianist and had a few theory lessons from German teachers. He made friends with Glinka, with whom he found himself in agreement about the future of Russian music. Seldom can so much have been made out of so little. Balakirev won his leading place in the *Kuchka*, which he founded, because he was the most experienced technically, the greatest enthusiast for a new Russian music, and a determined guide to his colleagues. He had

The Rubinstein brothers
*were for a long time the
keystone of music in 19th-
century Russia. This is a
caricature of Anton, the
great pianist of his era.*

no doubt about how they should write their music. Chaikovsky was told exactly what keys to use and what sort of themes and textures to compose for his *Romeo and Juliet* overture. Balakirev must also have been behind Chaikovsky's first piano concerto, since it is in B flat minor also, a remote key that Balakirev favoured (his other preferred keys were D major and B minor: yet Balakirev's finest work, his Symphony, is in C major—perhaps that is why it took more than thirty years to write). In 1905 Balakirev produced a fine, very personal piano sonata—its key was, predictably, B flat minor; his disciple Borodin's second symphony was in B minor. The mania for five flats and two sharps temporarily monopolized Russian music like a disease.

Balakirev was aware of the larger geographical Russian context, in modern times comprehended in the USSR. His tremendously brilliant piano solo piece *Islamey* borrows atmosphere and ideas from the remoter regions of the Imperial Russian Empire (1868), and his symphonic poem *Tamara* (1882) describes an eastern Russian story about a seductress who murdered all her lovers (rather like Carlo Gozzi's *Turandot*).

Balakirev led the inspiration of western musicians to oriental topics,

The Music of Russia
The Mighty Fistful

The exotic skyline of **Moscow** proclaims its reputation as "The most western outpost of the Orient".

Balakirev's *introverted personality lost him both friends and opportunities, though he eventually won the prestigious post of director to the Imperial court chapel.*

not as remote subjects but as material for the fashionable voluptuous sadism. His sonata-form movements are quite unlike the German variety; they are based on long melodies to be varied and transformed, not merely themes to be argued. This method, taken over from Glinka, is central to the Russian symphony from Balakirev, through Borodin and Chaikovsky, to Shostakovich and later Russian composers. It has been their decisive break from traditional German teaching: the Russian symphony is fundamentally a different article from the older German variety, not a whit less valid. An eventful narrative is not to be thought less estimable than an intellectual argument by anyone who admires both Homer's *Iliad* and Hobbes's *Leviathan*.

The Fistful

Balakirev recruited an élite of amateur composers. Least famous today is Cesar Cui (1835–1918), a professor of military engineering by profession, and a leading authority on fortifications, who had also studied musical theory in youth. Cui was a fairly prolific and an ambitious composer, but well aware that, with all his pro-Russian feelings, he was creatively not attuned to the Russian new music, being half-French and half-Lithuanian himself. He was a stern but enthusiastic critic, a successful writer of songs and piano solos. He also wrote some impassioned operas, such as *Angelo* (1876, based on a play by Victor Hugo).

Sonata form p 141

Borodin's music is most familiar in a work he never wrote. The musical Kismet *is based on many of his most popular melodies.*

Borodin

Alexander Borodin (1833–1887) was a chemist by trade, a musician because his gifts were fostered by his natural father, a prince who named his bastard son after one of his serfs (slavery was still rampant in Russia). Borodin's fame rests on a few works of vibrant quality: the opera *Prince Igor*, which contains the *Polovtsian Dances*; two symphonies (number two in B minor is especially captivating) and an incomplete third one; two string quartets, the second magically evocative of eastern Russia. The American musical *Kismet* raided Borodin's music to fairly sensitive purpose, though *Prince Igor*, already a document of east–west confrontation, makes the point much more cogently, and would be acknowledged, if it were regularly in repertory, as the equal of Musorgsky's *Boris Godunov*.

Musorgsky

Like all these *Kuchka* composers, Modest Musorgsky (1839–1881) came from a well-to-do family which encouraged musical talent at a strictly amateur level. His musical gifts emerged in boyhood, composition included, but he was put through the army, from which he emerged to become a civil servant. How Musorgsky and the other composers of the *Kuchka* acquired their expertise in composition without professional tuition remains a mystery. In Musorgsky's case there is perhaps less mystery, since his music, pioneering and unacademic, followed its own rules, essentially the furthest

Like other members of the mighty fistful, **Cui** *was predominantly an amateur musician. He pursued a most successful military career, reaching the rank of Lieutenant-General.*

from western practice. Balakirev gave him some lessons in basic compositional technique: in his piano suite *Pictures at an Exhibition* (1874), and his
song-set *Sunless*, Musorgsky unfolds his musical ideas bluntly but with real
sensibility. We are listening to a great musician, not one who sounds like an
amateur, though he is obviously striking out along new paths, for example
in the *Catacombs* section of *Pictures*. Musorgsky's songs are numerous and
very fine. *Tell me, little star* is pure visionary lyricism: the sets called
The Nursery, and *Songs and Dances of Death* are, respectively, charmingly
comic and compulsively macabre.

His orchestral tone-poem *A Night on Bald Mountain*, concerned with
witches and their ceremonies on St John's Eve, Midsummer's night, assails
the ear in the composer's own version—it is usually heard in the prettified
adaptation made later by his friend Rimsky-Korsakov, and that too was the
fate of his great opera *Boris Godunov*. Musorgsky wrote his own text, based
on Pushkin's interpretation of history. The real Boris Godunov (1552–1605)
was thought to have done away with the infant Tsar so as to succeed him.
The opera is like a scenic pageant of Russian history, dominated, paradoxically, by the oppressed Russian mob. Musorgsky's first composition of the
text (1869) was turned down by the St Petersburg opera; even the second
version (1874) was not fully successful, its music too harsh and unsophisticated for popular taste.

After Musorgsky's death it was thoroughly revised, even recomposed,
by Rimsky-Korsakov, and so became internationally appreciated. The
harsher, more realistic original score became available only in 1928, since

*Boris Godunov,
Musorgsky's masterpiece,
was re-orchestrated by
Rimsky-Korsakov to render
the work more palatable.*

Facing page: *A composer of
genius,* **Musorgsky**
*wrecked his life by a
remorseless addiction to
drink. This marvellous
picture by Repin portrays
the decline of a man
haunted by epilepsy and
delirium tremens.*

1840–1943 The Mighty Fistful

Moscow Conservatory

The first music schools in Moscow go back to the eighteenth century. Their purpose was largely that of training sufficient members of the serving classes in enough instrumental skill to play in bands for their masters: the wealthy employed their own musicians to instruct them up to a proper level of musical achievement. In 1772 a Czech musician, Johann Kerzelli, who had settled in Moscow with his family, opened a music school in Moscow for "the nobility, the bourgeoisie and the serfs"; and within the next decade the Kerzellis had found business sufficiently good to warrant another music college, this time exclusively for the training of serfs.

It was not until 1866 that the Conservatory was founded, however, though for some years there had been a series of music classes available through the Russian Musical Society. The Conservatory was opened by Nicholas Rubinstein, to complement the one founded in St Petersburg by his brother Anton four years previously. Chaikovsky was professor of harmony at the new Conservatory, an appointment made by the far-sighted Rubinstein that proved to be of the highest importance. From it there came composers who formed what might well be called the Moscow School: Arensky and Taneyev were both Chaikovsky pupils. Not that Chaikovsky was happy for long at the Conservatory: the pay was niggardly, and Rubinstein's drinking made life extremely difficult. Below: N. Zverev with his pupils. To his left sits Skryabin, to his right stands Rakhmaninov.

when it has been staged and recorded, but has not yet completely supplanted Rimsky's benevolent meddling. In either version the great moments come across potently: the coronation scene with its splendid processions and cries of "Glory!" contrasted with Boris's misgivings; the comedy of the country innkeeper and her wandering monk guests; the clock scene; Boris's death; and the revolution scene in Kromy Forest, which ends with a village idiot's lament for strife-torn Russia.

Musorgsky's other operas include *Khovanshchina* ("The Khovansky Affair", 1886), more Russian history from the time of Peter the Great; *The Wedding*, a short comedy after Gogol; and *The Fair at Sorochints*, which includes a well known *Gopak*. Much of this was left incomplete when Musorgsky died of alcoholic epilepsy following a long and hopeless fight against alcoholism, and was only afterwards rendered performable by Rimsky-Korsakov, Cui and others.

Nicholas Rimsky-Korsakov (1844–1908)

Rimsky-Korsakov came from a naval family and followed them into the service, though the passion of his boyhood was already opera. His voyages may have drawn him to such exotic subjects as the *Spanish Caprice* for orchestra (1877) and the quasi-symphony *Sheherazade* (1888), based on the *Arabian Nights*, though they had to be composed later, being essentially virtuoso studies in orchestral colour, a subject of which the young naval officer knew nothing. He spent his first period in the navy writing a symphony in E flat minor, under the encouragement of Balakirev, who helped him to score it for orchestra. Soon Rimsky-Korsakov was regarded among the *Kuchka* as their greatest expert in instrumentation, and he was besought by them for advice. He took his reputation seriously, read the available books and relished a new job on shore as Inspector of Naval Bands, because it required him to study in detail the method and technical possibilities of all wind and brass instruments such as came into his responsibility. He became a great expert, and passed on his knowledge to his pupils after he left naval service and became professor of composition at the Conservatory in St. Petersburg.

During one famous winter (1871–1872), Rimsky shared lodgings with Musorgsky, who was composing *Boris Godunov* in the mornings while Rimsky wrote his opera *The Maid of Pskov* in the afternoons. Balakirev had alerted Rimsky to the non-Russian classics, and in 1875 Rimsky conducted the first performance in Russia of Bach's *St Matthew Passion*. But Russian folk song had been deep in his consciousness from childhood, since his mother's family were country folk and he was weaned on the traditional music of his homeland.

As his sense of scholarship developed, he collected and arranged Russian folk songs, edited the works of Glinka for publication, and completed the unfinished works of deceased friends and predecessors. He taught music and, fortunately for us, began to write his memoirs—an excellent and informative volume. His scholarly interest in orchestral technique was heightened by his first hearing of Wagner's *Ring* brought by a first-rate German touring company to St Petersburg in 1889, and thereafter his orchestral music reflected Wagner's colouring, though not his melody or harmony—Rimsky was by now a master of the Russian style at a superior professional level. Opera was Rimsky's principal interest: he wrote a dozen or more of them, mostly on Russian subjects. *The Maid of Pskov*

1840-1943 The Mighty Fistful

Rimsky-Korsakov
*pursued a naval career until
his thirtieth year,
completing his first
symphony while still in the
service.*

went into three versions. *May Night* (1880), *Snow Maiden* (1882), *Mlada* (1892), *Christmas Eve* (1895), *Sadko* (1898), *The Tsar's Bride* (1899) and *The Tale of Tsar Saltan* (1900) show how industriously he worked. They are all occasionally to be found and are worth looking for; likewise *The Invisible City of Kitezh* (1907) and his last opera, *The Golden Cock*, the most popular of all (performed first in 1909 after the composer's death). Rimsky-Korsakov's music is of a glossier variety than the works of the other *Kuchka* composers; great on atmosphere and non-committal on character, compared with the persons of Musorgsky's operas, or of *Prince Igor*. Drama seems not to have interested Rimsky nearly as much as musical evocation. It would be ungenerous and cynical to pretend that Rimsky's best works were those written not by him, but by his pupils: Glazunov's violin concertos and symphonies, Stravinsky's *Firebird*, or Prokofiev's opera *Love for Three Oranges*: it is tempting to say so all the same, because all derive clearly from Rimsky's teaching.

Stravinsky p 291–4, 321–4   Glazunov p 339

Prokofiev p 339–40

Ballet

In common with several types of dance, the art of ballet was largely developed in France. It was originally a courtly entertainment: King Louis XIV in particular was an enthusiast, and was a skilled and frequent performer in ballets at his own court. But it was not until much later that the art became dramatic: early ballet had made much use of singing and recitation.

An important figure in the concept of narrating a story by means of dance was Jean Georges Noverre, an eighteenth-century Frenchman, ballet-master to Queen Marie Antoinette and a friend of Voltaire and Frederick the Great. He removed much of the over-stylized ritual, substituting a concentration upon personal expression and natural movement. Subsequent generations have continued to lean heavily on Noverre's principles.

For an art based upon movement and rhythm, ballet is of course closely linked with music. This, like Fokin's Les Sylphides *(to orchestrated arrangements of Chopin piano pieces), may be music that already exists; or it may be music specially composed, such as Chaikovsky's ballets for Moscow, or Stravinsky's scores for Dyagilev. The choreographer's role is harder to define. Inasmuch as he devises and rehearses the ballet, his work has been likened to that of a film director, to which must be added the deepest knowledge of music and of the dance. For the latter reason, many successful choreographers have been professional dancers themselves.*

The Music of Russia

The Mighty Fistful

Pyotr Ilyich Chaikovsky (1840–1893)

These then were the Mighty Fistful. Mightier than any of them and the friendly colleague of all (except the critic Cui, who regularly abused his new works) was Chaikovsky. He, like other Russian composers of his day, was well-born. He was put into the study of Law, then made a clerk in the Ministry of Justice. His family had moved from the country to St Petersburg when he was eight; his precocious musical gifts were admired and fostered—he learned to sing and play the piano (the vocal accomplishment of all these Russian composers seems central to their common emphasis on lyricism as the principal element in all music, hence the special characteristic of the Russian symphony).

After four years as a civil servant, Chaikovsky enrolled as a student at the new St Petersburg conservatory, whose western basis he did not resist, though Russian traditional melody had always been in the forefront of his musical experience. Chaikovsky's affinity with Russian folk music is manifest in his brilliant treatment of *The Crane* in the finale of the second symphony, of *The Birch Tree* in the finale of his fourth symphony, and in the shaping of many other principal melodies that he used symphonically. His violin concerto seems to derive, in every theme, from Russian traditional song. Equally you can hear Russian art-music (eg Glinka) in the duet that begins *Eugene Onegin*. The dance-movements, so enchanting in

*This scene of **Tsar Nicholas II attending the opera** captures the spirit of Imperial Russia in its last, extravagant hours.*

Facing page: ***Chaikovsky*** *by the Russian painter Kusnetsov. "He was", said Stravinsky, "the most Russian of all of us."*

1840–1943 The Mighty Fistful

Chaikovsky, *with his friend and pupil (also a pupil of Liszt), the brilliant young pianist and conductor Aleksandr Siloti.*

Chaikovsky's country house *at Klin, half-way between Moscow and St Petersburg. When friends came to see him, the composer enjoyed drinking with them late into the night, often over a piano duet or game of cards.*

all his music, are Russian international—the waltzes, the polonaises and mazurkas from Russian environs, the set-pieces in his ballets (*The Sleeping Beauty*, *Swan Lake*, *The Nutcracker*), the central movements of his symphonies, even the quick waltz, borrowed from a French cabaret song *Je veux danser et rire* ("I want to dance and laugh"), in the middle movement of his first piano concerto, and particularly the set dances in his operas *Onegin* and *Queen of Spades*.

Chaikovsky acquired his technique from conservatory, and it was sound. He had a natural inheritance of Russian music. It is professionalism, artistic polish, that distinguishes his music, even when second-best, compared to that of his Russian *Kuchka* colleagues. They accused him of Germanism, but all his music exhales the atmosphere of Russia, from the *Winter Dreams* first symphony to the *Pathetic* number six, the C major string serenade, full of Russian effects and rhythms (especially in its last movement), the piano trio in memory of Nicholas Rubinstein, above all in the ballets, and in the operas, which are still largely unexplored outside Russia. For piano solo, never Chaikovsky's forte, there is a weighty sonata in G major that has never found much favour in the west. But there is some miraculous keyboard writing in arrangements of fifty Russian folk songs that the composer made for piano duet.

Chaikovsky's musical purview extends beyond Russian folk song and brave amateurism, hence his rejection by the *Kuchka*, and particularly their critical mouthpiece, Cui. One example is the *Italian Caprice*, a fantasy for orchestra on impressions of a holiday, in the manner of popular Italian music: another is the *Manfred* symphony, unnumbered, dating from between symphonies four and five, based on Lord Byron's poetic drama. It was written just after his disastrous marriage to a fanatical, perhaps nymphomanic girl, whose advances reminded him of Tatyana in the opera *Onegin*. Chaikovsky determined not to make Onegin's mistake and he wed her, but found immediately that his homosexual temperament was repelled by contact with a woman, and was obliged to divorce her. Yet he needed a female confidante and fortunately found one in a wealthy, sexually wounded widow, Nadezhda von Meck, who gave him an annual subvention and exchanged intimate, intellectual letters with him, though they took care never to meet. Neither desired physical contact with the opposite sex, but both needed the spiritual and mental contact. Mme Meck helped Chaikovsky enormously, giving him the creative confidence that he lacked.

Chaikovsky composed distinguished music in all forms: for the Church, the opera and ballet, the theatre, orchestra, chamber music ensembles, music for soloists, songs and piano solos. He died, perhaps a suicide as the result of a disastrous homosexual liaison at court, and he has been revered ever since, outside and inside Russia. His home at Klin is now a Chaikovsky museum and every concert hall in the world is partly his shrine, shared, as he wished, with his favourite composers, Bach and Mozart.

After the Fistful

Soviet Russian music today owes everything to the *Kuchka*, whose immediate scions, however, looked firmly to the west for their inspiration—but variously, as individuals, not as any anti-Russian school. Rakhmaninov and Stravinsky both left Russia for the west: both remained profoundly Russian in their music, as did Nicolas Medtner, who settled in England. Prokofiev, disinclined to stay in Russia after the Revolution of 1917, travelled widely,

Cui p 266

1840-1943 The Mighty Fistful

*One revolutionary listening to the music of another: **Lenin** visits Gorky in 1920, while Dobroven plays them the music of Beethoven.*

then returned to spend his last fruitful years in the USSR. Skryabin died (of blood poisoning, from a sore on his lip) before he might have defected: his ideals were less Russian than French and oriental.

Rakhmaninov

The *Kuchka*'s successors were a motley collection. The most closely connected were Sergei Rakhmaninov (1873–1943) and Alexander Skryabin (1872–1915), both graduates of a strict military-style academy for pianists. At first Skryabin seemed unambitious, content to write charming salon pieces in the Chopin manner. Rakhmaninov essayed a major symphony, his first in D minor, which was execrated for its modernism (actually borrowed from Chaikovsky and Richard Strauss) and which he destroyed, though the orchestral parts survived, were reconstituted and the whole symphony restored to popular approval. Rakhmaninov was distraught by the failure of the symphony and lost all creative self-confidence. Mercifully he was saved by a hypnotist, who repeatedly told the unconscious patient that his new piano concerto for London would be fluently, effortlessly composed and of good quality. The treatment worked; the concerto was his second, in C

Chopin p 180–4

Richard Strauss p 300–6, 319–21

Sergei Rakhmaninov
made up his mind to leave
Russia while on a tour of
Sweden in 1917.

minor, the best loved of all his works. It was a period for him of ripe masterpieces; the second symphony, which brims with passion, allure and a light melancholy; the cello sonata; the second suite for two pianos; and many piano solos.

Rakhmaninov conducted the Bolshoi Opera for some time and wrote operas himself. Later he made a career as conductor of his own orchestral music. But his *métier* was the piano and, although he completed three symphonies (the third for America), his reputation rests on his piano music. Notable are his solo pieces (a sumptuous set of preludes, two sonatas and some elaborate, picturesque *Etudes-tableaux*) and his four piano concertos, which are the finest to come out of Russia: they are not just pianistic like Chopin's but truly symphonic, the piano solos intimately mingled with the orchestral music. Here are Chaikovsky and Liszt and something structural, perhaps Brahms, combining to make a new Russian brand of piano concerto, firmly built as well as slavonically melancholic, brilliant and dance-like. There is also a scintillating, very much loved *Rhapsody on a Theme by Paganini* (1934), in which Rakhmaninov created one of his most admired and typical melodies simply by turning Paganini's theme upside down!

Rakhmaninov composed his third, most strenuous and monumental piano concerto for his pianistic début in the United States. Eventually he settled in California and died there. The music of his American period is all of a piece, reflecting the move to America. Typical of this change are the *Symphonic Dances* for orchestra, discreetly impassioned, subtle in content, masterfully imagined for orchestra. When he died, he seemed a relic from

A revolutionary poster of
1918: "**A year of
Proletarian
Dictatorship**."

Skryabin wanted to "suffocate in ecstasy". He thought big—his piece Mysterium *was to be performed in India, to which listeners would be summoned by bells suspended from the clouds and then treated to billows of incense and coloured lights.*

Skryabin's **Prometheus** *or* The Poem of Fire *includes directions for a colour organ, which projects lights on to a large screen. Each note had a different colour—the note E was "pearly white and shimmer of moonlight".*

another age, his later music a disappointing shadow of his pre-Revolution Russian self. His position today is secure, for the late as well as the earlier music; the poker-face as well as the heart on sleeve.

Skryabin (1872–1915)

It is easier to appreciate the emergence of Rakhmaninov from his Russian inheritance (you can hear bits of Balakirev, Musorgsky and Glinka for example) than to appreciate how Alexander Skryabin fits into the story of Russian music, unless unconventionalism can be accepted as a cause. Skryabin would not accept the technique wished on his friend Rakhmaninov, who learned the Liszt method, with all its agility and power: Skryabin's piano playing came from Chopin. His first piano pieces are simply Chopin more elaborated, the melodies thrown into the sky like fireworks, as in the lustrous close of the fourth sonata. Skryabin's music was concerned with blazing, compelling, voluptuous belief. He was a minor Wagner. His symphonies, *The Divine Poem*, *The Poem of Ecstasy*, *Prometheus* and his *Last Rite* were composed to prepare humanity for a final, willing, gratified extinction. Fortunately for us, it never happened. Skryabin's music is still attractive, especially his symphonies and his last piano pieces, which included experiments in necromancy: the *Black Mass* and *White Mass* sonatas.

Rimsky-Korsakov's last pupil was Prokofiev. He and Stravinsky belong to the early twentieth century. Both, like Rakhmaninov, left Russia at the time of the Revolution in 1917. Soviet philosophy decreed that henceforward music must hymn past achievements or exhort citizens to new deeds of heroism. The ideal was promising, the reality frustrating and unfruitful for the highest traditions of Russian music.

Chopin p 180–4

Liszt p 185–7

Prokofiev p 339–40

Chapter 14
Vantage Point

The Turn of the Century

"Only connect!" ♦ The influence of eastern music ♦ The inter-relation of painting, poetry and music ♦ Claude Debussy—a musical impressionist ♦ Dyagilev's Ballets Russes ♦ *The Rite of Spring* makes artistic history ♦ The post-Wagnerians ♦ Expressionism and Symbolism ♦ Stretching the limits—Mahler and Richard Strauss ♦ Looking back ♦

By the end of the nineteenth century, European music was bursting, on all sides, out of the seams of the old musical *lingua franca*, which had been intelligible in every country. Nationalism was by no means a spent force: it even influenced composers living far away. Western music was, not for the first time, exposed to the artistic cultures of the Orient (poetry and painting as well as music). Another country, the mind, invaded music with the findings of psychologists, and there was also a growing interest in the music of the past.

In the *fin de siècle* period (roughly from 1890 to 1914), there were plenty of excellent composers working in Europe; but the story of those brilliant years is less about them than about the artistic ideas that united them in their efforts wherever they worked. So the outstanding figures of that time have to be discussed according to their various spheres of achievement, and in relation to one another. Where they lived meant less than which paths they fruitfully followed. This was a great period in which to follow E.M. Forster's doctrine of "Only connect!". The individual's achievement is not lessened by the greater importance of the common trends.

Everybody understood German music (only the Latin countries found it boring) just as everybody loved French, Italian and Spanish music (except the Germans, who found it frivolous). At least music now travelled more speedily thanks to modern methods of transport, and today's new score could, if required, be performed in another country very shortly afterwards: music could now keep up with space as well as time.

Lure of the East

Eastern cultures, particularly in India, Japan, China and neighbouring countries, had maintained since earliest times a flourishing musical culture that was individual to each country and its regions; highly developed since

1875–1920 The Turn of the Century

ancient times, it was never written down, being passed on by tradition from one generation to the next.

Explorers had returned with tales of far-off countries, and sometimes with specimens of their art, though not music. Chinese interludes were put into stage works by Lully and Purcell for exoticism's sake. There was a craze for Turkish music in the Austria of Mozart's time, excited by martial politics and French imperialism, which threw up such exotic opera subjects as Bizet's *The Pearl Fishers* (1863), set in Ceylon, Délibes' *Lakmé* (1883), about an Indian temple priestess and two soldiers from France, and Meyerbeer's last opera, *The African Girl* (1885), about Vasco da Gama's discovery of Madagascar. None of these pieces managed to imitate the true sound of eastern music, if only because it was unknown in the west.

The most important event for the bringing together of eastern and western music must have been the Universal Exhibition, which took place in Paris in 1889. It brought the Mighty Fistful composers from Russia to the attention of France and its neighbours. The work of Musorgsky was particularly influential. Verdi's *The Force of Destiny* had, dynamically and structurally, influenced Musorgsky's *Boris Godunov*, and now the methods of *Boris* affected opera elsewhere, particularly Debussy's *Pelléas et Mélisande* (1902), probably the most beautiful opera since Wagner's *Tristan und Isolde* (1864). Just as great a discovery for visitors to this Exhibition was the display of Indonesian *gamelan* music containing brazen, glittering timbres, exotic scales and lithe, sensuous, refined musical phrases that fascinated European composers, even outside France.

The lure of the east had already exerted itself on painters with the appearance of Chinese watercolours and Japanese colour prints. Poetry from Persia, India, China and Japan was translated into western-European languages. Music about the Far East or derived from the sound of its music was now a potent inspiration to western composers. Puccini's *Madama Butterfly* (1904) made a poignant human point out of the contrast between the American boat-stop philanderer and the faithful Japanese geisha-girl, who renounces all her Japanese past to become his wife and mother of his child. In Mascagni's *Iris* (1898), the pure, parentally protected Japanese heroine is abducted and taken to a brothel. Her blind father curses her and she drowns herself in a sewer. Other similar subjects include Mahler's song-symphony *Das Lied von der Erde*, its six symphonic movements set to German translations of old Chinese poems (1908); the French Albert Roussel's *Padmavati* (1914), an opera-ballet on an Indian theme, the score making use of Indian musical scales, and Stravinsky's *The Nightingale* (1909–1914) on a fairy-tale about China by Hans Andersen. All these brought a new sound and feeling to European opera, and to Mahler's vocal symphonic music a new character—part tragic, part playful—in line with his new ideals. A good example is Mahler's exquisite orchestral song *Ich atmet einen linden Duft* (1902), which is set to a German poem by Rückert, but in feeling is close to the delicacy of Chinese watercolours. The eastern vogue had already been satirized by Gilbert and Sullivan with their operetta *The Mikado* (1885), later followed, part-seriously, by Lehár's *Land of Smiles* (1929), which contains the famous air *You are my Heart's Delight*.

The sound of the gamelan orchestra found its way into Claude Debussy's piano piece *Pagodas* (1903) and oriental influence can also be traced in his String Quartet (1893). For the score of his symphonic-poem *La*

*Facing page: At the close of the 19th century, the oriental influence loomed strong in many branches of western art. This elegant portrait by **Whistler** shows many such touches: note the spray of blossom, and the Japanese fan.*

Purcell p 72

Musorgsky p 267–71

Meyerbeer p 198–200

Force of Destiny p 217–19

Lully p 71, 122–4

Bizet p 211–13

1875-1920 The Turn of the Century

The Wave. Hokusai's meticulous approach to his art set an example that was eagerly taken up by the western aesthetic movement.

*Gilbert & Sullivan's **The Mikado** was directly inspired by oriental features at the great Paris Exhibition.*

Mer (1904), he took as frontispiece the Japanese Hokusai's painting of *The Wave*—a gigantic breaker about to engulf a tiny boat. Ravel's piano piece *Little Ugly, Empress of the Pagodas* (from his *Mother Goose* suite, 1908), translates gamelan music into modern western pianistic terms (the suite was later scored for orchestra), and his *Songs of Madagascar* (1926), for voice and instrumental ensemble, reflect exotic influence quite violently as, now and then, does the song *Asie* in his orchestral song-set *Shéhérazade* (1903).

Painting and Music

The decades surrounding 1900 were as rich in new artistic developments in European painting and sculpture as they were in music. In France, which seemed to be the artistic capital of Europe, Cézanne, Gauguin, Van Gogh and the other post-Impressionists would soon give way to the Cubists—Picasso (a Spanish *émigré*), Braque and their followers. Another line branched into the New Art, so-called *art nouveau*: (in Vienna they called it *Jügendstil*, "the style of youth", and it prospered there too), Klimt being its noblest exponent.

Music has tended to lag several decades behind experiment in the other arts, so it is perhaps no surprise that during this period the main influence of painting on music was Impressionism, which had flourished in France between 1863 and about 1880, and was chiefly associated with such painters as Claude Monet, whose picture of a sunset, entitled "Impressions", gave the movement its name, though the series portraying Rouen Cathedral in

Gamelan

The Gamelan orchestra's unique sound comes from Indonesia and Siam. It has attracted many western composers, from Debussy (who heard it at the Great Exhibition in Paris in 1889 and echoed its sonorities in piano pieces) to Benjamin Britten.

The Gamelan's forces are divided between bowed instruments and percussion. The basis of the bowed sound is the rabab, which has only two strings and produces a viol-like sonority. The various percussion instruments are composed of bonangs (an agreeably onomatopoeic word), suspended gongs beaten by small hammers: wooden xylophones; and tuned hand-drums. Rattles and bass drums also have a part to play. There are also some woodwind sounds in the Gamelan that produce oboe- and flute-like noises, yet the sonority that stays with the listener is always the complex and haunting counterpoint of the little gongs that are tapped with such intricate care.

various lights perhaps best typifies the aims of Impressionism. The Irish painter and art historian William Orpen described Impressionism as "the substitution of a simultaneous vision, that sees a scene as a whole, in place of a consecutive vision that sees nature piece by piece", adding that the Impressionist artist's palette of colours, being concerned with light above all, was based on the solar spectrum, rather than on shades between black and white.

Claude Debussy (1864–1918)
The Impressionists' hazing of detail and purification of colour were musically reflected, to strong purpose, in the work of Debussy. He was, in any case, a man who numbered among his friends as many poets and painters as musicians. One was the American-born Impressionist painter

1875–1920 The Turn of the Century

Claude Debussy at the age of 24. A portrait that now hangs in the Villa Medici in Rome.

James Whistler, whose *Nocturnes*, studies of the River Thames at Chelsea by night, gave their name and something of their character to three of Debussy's evocations of Paris at night: *Clouds*, *Festivals* and *Sirens*. Two of his poet friends were Paul Verlaine, whose *Ariettes oubliées* ("Forgotten Ditties", 1888) and *Fêtes galantes* ("Pastoral Pleasures", 1891 and 1904) are among Debussy's most striking songs; and Stephane Mallarmé for whose poem "The Afternoon of a Faun" Debussy wrote his orchestral *Prélude* (1894), a new sort of romantic music; lazy, sensual and dreamlike, which some musicians, Boulez among them, claim as a major source of modern music.

Debussy's first musical success was a student cantata *The Blessed*

Boulez p 346–7

The Blessed Damozel by
Dante Gabriel Rossetti,
subject of a cantata
composed by Debussy.

Damozel (1888) to a poem by the English Pre-Raphaelite Dante Gabriel
Rossetti, the music chastely modal in vocabulary; a breakaway from the
pseudo-Gounod prettiness of his earliest compositions, and a musical
manner that was to persist, throughout his creative life, for the evocation of
classical Greek or otherwise mythical scenes. There are examples in the
three *Songs of Bilitis* (1899—its second song, *The Necklace*, a little
monument of blameless eroticism), in the solo piano preludes, *Dancers of
Delphi*, *The Girl with the Flaxen Hair*, *The Submerged Cathedral* and, as
may be expected, the piano-duet *Six antique epigrams* (intended to go with
the *Bilitis* songs).

The Impressionist Debussy is heard in the three orchestral *Images*

The Turn of the Century

*A Dyagilev production for the **Ballets Russes** of Ode (1928, to the music of one of his protégés, Nabokov), and designed by Tchelichev.*

*Mary Garden as the heroine in Debussy's **Pelléas et Mélisande**. As early as 1902 she made recordings, with the composer accompanying at the piano.*

(1909), consisting of *Gigues*, which quotes a northern English folk tune, *Weel may the Keel Row*, amid a foggy imaginary landscape; *Rounds of Springtime*, which quotes a French folk song, *We'll to the woods no more*, and *Iberia*, a three-movement suite vividly evocative of Spain, as is the piano-piece *Evening in Granada*—though it was a country that much-travelled Debussy never visited. His orchestral masterpiece is, arguably at least, the near-symphony *The Sea* (1904), completed while staying at a hotel in Eastbourne—its three movements are entitled *Upon the sea from dawn till noon*, *Waves at play* and *Dialogue of the wind and the sea*. The work has been well likened to Cézanne's sense of colour and form.

Debussy was a thorough-going Parisian of his day, fond of travel, a sharp wit (his writings on music, entitled "M. Croche, the dilettante-hater", are good reading). His wit is musically evident in the piano-pieces *Homage to Samuel Pickwick*, *The Golliwog's Cakewalk* (jazz and Wagner's *Tristan* combined), *Dr Gradus ad Parnassum* (a take-off of piano exercises), and indeed *Fireworks*, a French equivalent of Guy Fawkes Night. He had an eventful, tempestuous love-life, with two wives and numerous mistresses. He was acquainted with virtually every leading composer of his day, from Liszt to Stravinsky, and quarrelled with just about all of them; yet his music influenced every progressive composer of the twentieth century from Bartók and Ravel to Boulez and Stockhausen, excepting Richard Strauss, who found Debussy's music wholly unsympathetic. Debussy was trained for a career as piano virtuoso, and his piano music is as important and copious as that of Chopin or Bartók. That he remained a decent pianist, though he seldom played in public, is attested by the story that, when Stravinsky completed *The Rite of Spring*, he tried it out in piano-duet form

NIJINSKY
dans "La Péri"

Aquarelle de Léon BAKST.

*The cover for the programme of the 1911 season of the **Ballets Russes** shows Bakst's costume design for Nijinsky in* La Péri.

with Debussy, who sight-read the lower parts almost flawlessly, though it was in a quite new musical style, and spoke admiringly of it. There is, incidentally, a most graceful and attractive piano duet by Debussy himself: *Petite Suite*, which is often heard in an orchestrated version.

Debussy was such a versatile composer that several of his works have been claimed as his "greatest" this or that. Strictly speaking, a composer can only have one "masterpiece", and Debussy's is surely his opera *Pelléas and Mélisande* (1902), which furnishes Maurice Maeterlinck's play with a tactful, dreamlike, yet logically constructed musical setting, infinitely more subtle and momentous than its text. Set in a mythical country called "Allemonde" (which sounds like the French name for Germany), it is about a prince who finds a beautiful foreign princess lost in a forest, takes her home as his bride, but loses her to his younger half-brother Pelléas. The lovers are caught, Pelléas is slain, and Mélisande dies in childbirth. *Pelléas and Mélisande* gathers together all aspects of Debussy's music, some plainsong and modes, some Wagner (*Parsifal*) and Musorgsky (*Boris Godunov*), some *art nouveau*, the French tradition from Léonin and Dufay to Massenet which was Debussy's inheritance, as well as his own original vision, which fuses all those ingredients into one integral musical style. *Pelléas* is exquisitely composed for singing voices and for a large orchestra, discreetly used. The linking of the several scenes, in each act until the last, by orchestral interludes, perhaps derives from Wagner's transformation scenes, but in any case, it was taken over by later composers, notably Berg in *Wozzeck* and *Lulu*, by Britten in *Peter Grimes* and *The Turn of the Screw* and even by Richard Strauss, in his comic opera *Intermezzo*. Debussy was ready to learn from Wagner, but not at the expense of his Frenchness as an artist. He inscribed his last works, three sonatas for violin, cello and a trio of instruments, as the work of Claude Debussy, "French musician". His most "advanced" composition, the ballet *Jeux* (1912), is completely French in atmosphere, a game of tennis regarded as a symbol of love games. It was composed for Sergei Dyagilev's Russian Ballet, which had made Paris its centre and was already regarded as a major force on the progressive artistic scene of the time.

Dyagilev's Russian Ballet

Sergei Pavlovich Dyagilev (1872–1929) capitalized on his talents as a cultivated enthusiast for the arts with a flair for business, by studying law, editing an arts magazine, then organizing a series of Russian concerts in Paris which included performances of *Boris Godunov* with the great Shalyapin in the name part (1908). A year later he formed a company of Russian ballet dancers for a season in Paris. St Petersburg had the finest ballet dancers in the world at the Maryinsky Theatre in Theatre Street (the company now called the Kirov Ballet), but they were, Dyagilev recognized, wasted on bad old productions of the classics, and feeble new concoctions. Dyagilev aspired to Wagner's concept of a "total work of art", though he was ready to keep poetry and singing in reserve, so as to promote dance, music, scenery, drama, costumes and acting, all in perfect and artistically adventurous collaboration. Two of his first new ventures delighted Paris: *Les Sylphides*, a short sequence of dances for wood nymphs at night, set to music by Chopin, and a danced version of Rimsky-Korsakov's four-movement oriental symphonic poem *Shéhérazade*. They are still repertory works for ballet companies the world over.

Designs by Goncharova *for Dyagilev's production of* The Wedding, *performed by the Ballets Russes.*

Boris Godunov p 269–71   *Parsifal* p 238–9

Britten p 333   Berg p 308, 335–6

Jean Cocteau (left*) with the impresario Sergei Dyagilev. Cocteau formulated many of the principles for the group known as* Les Six.

Igor Stravinsky (1882–1971)

For his first new ballet with new music, Dyagilev chose the old Russian fairy-tale of *The Firebird*. When his chosen composer, Lyadov, showed no interest in producing the music, Dyagilev turned instead to Rimsky-Korsakov's brilliant young pupil, Stravinsky, who quickly produced a very Russian, gorgeously coloured score which delighted one and all, and instantly made an international star-composer of Stravinsky. *Firebird* was decidedly "Mighty Fistful" stuff, and Stravinsky was anxious to dispense with the mantle of Rimsky, which he did in the next Dyagilev ballet, *Petrushka* (1911); the melodic lines are harder, the colours brighter and sharper, the harmonies much more challenging and the tone of voice more earthy, as befits the scene of a popular Carnival fair (peasants and showmen, not fairy-tale princes and princesses). *Petrushka* is about puppets who live lives of their own, and the Pierrot, here Petrushka ("little Peter"), survives murder to cackle and mock at the audience.

It was with his third ballet, *The Rite of Spring* (1913), that Stravinsky turned the western musical world topsy-turvy. Its subject was the primitive Russian peasants' appeasement of the new year deity that presides over earthly fertility, and therefore over man's survival. The savage theme

Vantage Point
The Turn of the Century

Igor Stravinsky *in 1915.*
A portrait by Jacques Emile
Blanche.

prescribed savage music. Stravinsky's score for *The Rite of Spring* evokes the first spring thaw for primitive man, with reiterated rhythms, harsh, massive blocks of harmony and dour, menacing scraps of basic melodic material. The indignant furore created by the fashionable Parisian audience at the first performance made artistic history ("just what I wanted", commented Dyagilev) and, specifically, musical history. Nothing so patently revolutionary and so durably compelling had been heard since Wagner's *Tristan und Isolde*. *The Rite* is music's reply to the painters' *fauvisme* and *bruitism*, and Stravinsky's triumphant riposte to the music of the new mechanical age, and to the dominance of German music in particular.

As a ballet *The Rite* did not keep its place intact in the repertory: later generations have preferred to match Stravinsky's music with new choreography and scenic design. The orchestral score, on the other hand, soon found a leading place in the syllabus of the virtuoso symphony orchestra and the star orchestral conductor. It begat imitations, some of them presentable, such as Prokofiev's *Ala and Lolly* (an unsuccessful ballet but a popular orchestral work known as *Scythian Suite*), Varèse's orchestral *Arcana* and perhaps also *Mars* in Gustav Holst's suite *The Planets*. It had great formative influence on the Bavarian composer Carl Orff, though his most popular work, the choral *Carmina Burana* (1936), derives more closely from Stravinsky's subsequent choral ballet *The Wedding*, a Russian peasant rite set in an age closer to modern times (1923). For other composers, Stravinsky's *Rite of Spring* has remained a musical landmark. He could have capitalized on that particular style of music in a series of

*Stravinsky's **The Rite of Spring**, in which a young girl dances herself to death in a pagan ritual.*

1875-1920 The Turn of the Century

similar works, but his creative vision regarded *The Rite* as a transition to other musical concerns.

The Heirs of Wagner

The influence of Wagner on European music was widely resented: some instances have already been recorded in the last two chapters. In France the retreat from Wagner was led, purposefully and not without admiration, by Debussy. Paris was in the throes of a Wagner cult, and "Tristanizing" was a favourite pastime in all the arts and among cultured society, notwithstanding France's ignominious defeat in the Franco-Prussian war. One branch of French music, which centred on the figure of the Belgian-born César Franck, was called *Schola Cantorum* by its founder, Vincent D'Indy. Its adherents adapted Wagnerian techniques to non-operatic music, as in the songs of Henri Duparc, the symphonies of D'Indy and of Ernest Chausson, Chabrier's opera *Gwendoline*, as well as the piano sonata and the symphonic tone-poem *The Sorcerer's Apprentice* by Paul Dukas—to name but a few of the best known products of that school.

The Post-Wagnerians

The Wagnerian influence did not have to be monumental in design or resource: among his disciples were Engelbert Humperdinck, whose fairy-story opera *Hansel and Gretel* (1893) uses nursery-rhymes instead of *Leitmotive*, and Wagner's son Siegfried, whose operas also deal in German folk themes—*Der Bärenhäuter* is the least obscure. In Austria the enthusiastic Wagnerite Hugo Wolf (1860–1903) concentrated his creative energy on songs with piano accompaniment, remarkable for fine poetic taste and scrupulous word-setting matched to music sometimes grandiloquent (*i.e. Prometheus*), but often sharply focused and curtly epigrammatic in design, as witness the Tuscan peasant poetry, set in German translation as the *Italienisches Liederbuch* ("Italian Songbook"). Wolf, as a typical romantic, carried on a muscial love-affair with Spain in his *Spanish Songbook* and operas *Der Corregidor* and *Manuel Venegas* (the latter unfinished).

Hugo Wolf *worked for a time as a music critic in Vienna, where he made himself very unpopular for his refusal to accept the music of Brahms.*

Wolf's songs, composed in short bursts of extraordinary creative concentration, made little impression on his contemporaries; he died insane in a mental hospital, impoverished and unappreciated. Today he is admired and loved the world over as a song composer comparable with Dowland and Schubert, Schumann, Loewe, Brahms, Strauss, Mahler and Fauré, who was a great French song-composer in his own right, or more recently Poulenc and Britten. As royal lines go, this one is illustrious.

Elgar and Delius

Some chauvinistic German, at the end of the nineteenth century, damned England as "the land without music", doubtless wholly ignorant of musical history before the time of Schütz, the first respectable German composer. In previous centuries England's music had been as influential in Europe as Germany's was not. By 1900 England was more than ripe for some musical nationalism; the work of Vaughan Williams and Holst has already been discussed in that direction. Before them, not as folk song composers in particular, came two British composers, acclaimed first in Germany, later appreciated world-wide. They were Edward Elgar (1857–1934) and Frederick Delius (1862–1934). Both grew up in the English provinces outside

Vaughan Williams p 257–60   Humperdinck p 240

Holst p 257

Elgar, *photographed in his music-room at Severn House in Hampstead, London.*

Delius spent his last years crippled and helpless at his house near Fontainebleau in France.

London amid grand, hilly English countryside; Elgar in Worcestershire, Delius in Yorkshire. Elgar's *Introduction and Allegro* for string orchestra and string quartet quotes a Welsh folk song (so he declared) and he composed *Pomp and Circumstance* marches for national occasions. Delius used the Norfolk folk song *Brigg Fair* for a rhapsodic variation-work, but their work is otherwise entirely personal; music about themselves. Elgar's finest works, two symphonies, concertos for violin and for cello, the orchestral *Enigma Variations*, musical portraits of friends, all derive from Schumann and Mendelssohn and Wagner, as his cantata *The Dream of Gerontius* derives from *Parsifal*. The English, supposedly, were cold fish, but Elgar's musical temperament was, audibly in his music, as hot-blooded as any Latin. He had a special love for Italy, which is musically evoked in his second symphony, inspired by Venice, as is much of his violin concerto; and

his orchestral overture *In the South* represents a holiday diary from the town of Alassio.

Frederick Delius left his native Yorkshire town as soon as possible and travelled in America, Norway, Germany and France, where he finally settled in a village south of Paris. His music was mostly concerned with post-Impressionist nature, as in *Summer Night on the River* or *A Song of the High Hills*, which evokes Norway (he was a disciple of Grieg). From his American years come his *Appalachia* variations and the cantata *Sea Drift*, to a text by Walt Whitman. During his last years he was blind and paralyzed, but was able to dictate new music to an amanuensis, young Eric Fenby, who has written vividly about the experience. Both composers were contented foreign disciples of Wagner.

The Wagnerian musical legacy continued to show profits in the masterly, influential compositions of Mahler and Richard Strauss, also their joint younger protégé, the Viennese Arnold Schoenberg (1874–1951). All of them changed musical direction during their careers. It was said of Schoenberg that he began as an imitator of Wagner and ended as an imitator of Brahms (the two anti-poles of later nineteenth-century German musical taste). Similarly it could be said that Mahler began as a Wagner disciple and ended as a follower of Debussy and forerunner of Alban Berg. Strauss, a staunch Bavarian unlike those two Austrians, began as disciple of Mendelssohn, Schumann and Brahms, then was converted to become a spiritual descendant of the Viennese Classics, especially of Mozart. Those are glib generalizations, but perhaps more illustrative than such sweeping conclusions usually are. It remains to add that Arnold Schoenberg was, together with Debussy, the greatest musical innovator of the twentieth century.

Psychoanalysis and Music
What changed the course of music for Mahler, Strauss, Schoenberg and other early twentieth-century composers was the study of psychoanalysis,

*Van Gogh's **The Potato Eaters** exemplifies the identification with the lot of the common man in the nineteenth century.*

*Gustave Charpentier drew upon his own experiences of life in Montmartre for his opera **Louise**.*

1875–1920 The Turn of the Century

associated primarily with the work of Sigmund Freud and Carl Jung, who developed it along scientific lines from the findings of earlier philosophers (and perceptive physicians). Psychoanalysis, explicitly or implicitly, put into more generally perceptible focus the egoism of the Romantic sensibility, explaining not only the nature and cause of abnormal actions and thoughts, but the eccentricity of otherwise conventional people.

The artistic interpretation of such studies in abnormal psychology was stylized as Expressionism, and grew directly out of such late-Romantic stimuli as Symbolism (in which the prime topic, too sacred or too terrible to be named directly, is suggested by poetic analogy) and Realism, which found poetic material not in grandly heroic subject-matter and noble ideals, but in dramas or situations drawn from down-to-earth everyday life. Realism was a style in painting familiar in the nineteenth century from the work of Courbet, Millet, Daumier, Goya and the young Van Gogh, all of whom took working-class life as their subjects, sometimes contrasting them uncomfortably with the effete existence of their social so-styled "superiors", and with devastating effect.

In poetry, Realism could draw on the plebeian vernacular for its language (as in Rudyard Kipling's anti-heroic poems of army life). In the theatrical arts, and the climate of Romanticism, such frankness was considered unsuitable for aristocratic or respectable bourgeois audiences (Bizet's *Carmen* with its cigarette-makers, smugglers and uninhibited gypsy heroine was hardly allowed on stage, for fear of shocking a family audience). "Realistic" opera got off the ground in Italy with the *verismo* works of Puccini and others.

Realism was not confined to Italy. Eugen d'Albert, a Glasgow-born adoptive German composer and a great virtuoso pianist, composed a telling veristic opera, *Tiefland* (1903), about peasant life in the Pyrenees, its music along post-Wagnerian lines. Gustave Charpentier's *Louise* (1900) promises everything for French *verismo*: conflict in a Paris working-class family when the daughter falls in love with a poet, a scene in a factory, popular revelry in Montparnasse, and appallingly reactionary parents for the ordinary and adorable heroine. The central act, with its carnival and nightmare, turns fantastic and unreal, highly imaginative but not quite compelling. It flaws, but does not mar, the vitality and allure of the realistic subject and its adorable music, summed up in Louise's solo *Depuis le jour* at the beginning of the third act; a confession of love that strikes a chord in all who have ever been in love.

In the *verismo* context must be mentioned Schoenberg's *Verklärte Nacht* (1899), already unusual as a descriptive narrative instrumental composition, not for symphony orchestra but for string sextet. It is relevant here for its frank, unconventional context. It is about a young woman walking at night with her lover and admitting that she is pregnant by another man—a casual but welcome seducer—her present lover accepts the situation as part of his love for her. The music is passionate, heavily post-Wagnerian, and delicate, ethereal in texture. Schoenberg's early post-Wagnerian music also included a sumptuous tone-poem about *Pelléas and Mélisande* (1903), again indicative of the retreat from Wagnerian density; and the monumental saga of the *Gurrelieder* (1911), a gargantuan feast of heroic emotionalism, yet including moments of the tenderest lyricism (the *Song of the Wood Dove*), and of novel invention (the monologue, half-sung, half-spoken by Klaus the Jester) that heralds the supreme creator of later years.

Carmen p 211, 213
Puccini p 226–9

Gustav Mahler, an etching made in 1902 by Emil Orlik.

Gustav Mahler (1860–1911)

Schoenberg's *Gurrelieder* closely mirrors Mahler's *Das klagende Lied* (1880), an epic cantata on the folk tale of the singing bone. Neither is typical of the composers' later, most characteristic, music. Mahler subsequently divided his energies (necessarily restricted to summer vacations, since he was a busy conductor of opera during the other months) between songs, often with orchestral accompaniment, and symphonies. These (there are ten of them) were spiritually and Romantically autobiographical, eternally searching after truths about the nature of human existence and the possibility of an after-life, fears of annihilation, or nightmares of the soul, alternating with visions of celestial bliss. His songs include a number of German or Austrian folk poems from the collection *Des Knaben Wunderhorn* ("The Boy's Miraculous Horn") made by Arnim and Brentano (1808), a major document of German romantic nationalism and as such a psychological prop to Mahler, a Jewish peasant from remote Bohemia, who felt himself a stranger in sophisticated, anti-Semitic Vienna. Mahler included some *Wunderhorn* songs, as well as quotations from his own settings of them, in some of his symphonies. He had to balance the grand visions in his music with trivial or naïve references, perhaps to a village band or a military signal; memories of childhood, so he admitted to Freud during a professional consultation. This manifestation of "the short and simple annals of the poor" was for him a psychological necessity. His huge symphonic frescoes (the first and fourth symphonies are the least expansive) were slow to win popularity, and had no obvious successors (unless in some by Shostakovich, a self-confessed Mahler devotee), though his boldly progressive treatment of tonality and harmony certainly had great impact on Schoenberg and his followers Berg and Webern, also Britten and later composers.

Stretching the Limits

Mahler took tonal music to limits where it is sometimes impossible to state what key a symphony by him is "in". The fourth symphony, for example, begins in G major via B minor and ends in E major. Later symphonic composers, often independently, gave numbers or names, rather than keys, to their works, an indication (as in Mahler) that the music travels from one point to another without having to use a return ticket, so to speak. The long-established hierarchy of major–minor tonality was on the point of exhaustion. Something like a warning signal to this effect occurs at the climax of the first movement in Mahler's tenth symphony, a gigantic screaming discord that sounds as if it must contain all twelve notes of the chromatic scale, though a careful count reveals only nine of them. Mahler never quite abandoned tonality: his last work, the tenth symphony (left incomplete at his death, but completed for practical performance by Deryck Cooke in the 1960s), begins and ends unequivocally in F sharp major—admittedly an advanced and significance-loaded key, seldom used by the classical masters of tonality.

Richard Strauss (1864–1949)

By then, Richard Strauss had already, in his opera *Elektra* (1909), taken tonality and chromatic dissonance to his own proposed limits, from which he felt able only to retreat in subsequent works. *Elektra* is a study in extreme psychological abnormality, a document of musical Expressionism if ever there was one. It was preceded by another lurid one-act opera, *Salome* (1906), almost as hysterical in tone, but more sensuously coloured—*Elektra* has a texture like monolithic granite. By 1900 Strauss had won fame, sometimes notoriety, with a series of orchestral symphonic poems, immensely brilliant in execution, most of them portraying literary characters in some psychological and realistic detail, and in defiantly progressive post-Wagnerian musical language. Thus *Don Juan* (1888) uses an enlarged sonata-form to describe the name part as adventurer and as insatiable lover (a graphic theme for massed horns), in pursuit of aristocratic, perhaps Junoesque, Donna Anna and the gentler Elvira. Strauss insisted that one could hear the colour of her hair—but only because in German productions of Mozart's opera just then it was traditional for the character of Elvira to always wear the red wig of a prostitute.

Till Eulenspiegel (1895) is a busy comedy of a legendary practical joker,

Facing page: *Richard Strauss's opera* **Salome** *was based upon the play (written in French) by Oscar Wilde.*

SALOME.
Drama nach Oscar Wilde's gleichnamiger Dichtung.
Musik
von
Richard Strauss.
Op. 54.
Klavier-Auszug mit Text Pr. netto M 16.
Klavier-Auszug mit französisch-italienischem Text „ netto „ 16.
Soloscene der Salome für Gesang und Klavier „ netto „ 5.
Soloscene der Salome für Gesang und Klavier mit französisch-italienischem Text „ netto „ 5.
Für Klavier
Klavier-Auszug mit überlegtem Text „ netto „ 16.
Klavier-Auszug mit überlegtem französisch-italienischem Text „ netto „ 16.
Salomes Tanz zu zwei Händen „ netto „ 3.
Salomes Tanz zu vier Händen „ netto „ 5.
Eigentum des Verlegers für alle Länder
Berlin W.
Adolph Fürstner.
Per l'Italia: G. Ricordi e C., Milano.
Représentants exclusifs pour la France et la Belgique:
Société Musicale G Astruc et Cie, Paris.
Aufführungsrecht vorbehalten.
V. N. A. 5507. 5508. 5511. F.

Richard Strauss
*maintained that, when
conducting, the right-hand
thumb need never leave the
waistcoat pocket. Klob's
etching shows him ignoring
his own dictum.*

Elektra produced strong reactions among the public, as this cartoon of Strauss playing selections upon the cornet shows.

his exploits recounted in vivid detail: hubbub in a market, a group of scholars arguing heatedly, a love affair, eventually a gruesome execution by hanging—within the form of a double rondo whose first theme represents the past, its second theme (a swaggering horn solo, elusively notated off the beat) representing Till Owlglass himself.

Don Quixote (1897) plots the adventures of Cervantes' distraught knight-errant in the form of variations, the hero characterized by solo cello so that the work resembles a concerto. The windmills, the sheep, the sacred procession, the midnight vigil, the ducking in a weir, and Quixote's death scene, his last words unfinished—all carried Strauss's fame as a musical mimic to new extremes; yet *Quixote* abounds in touching human observation and lyric poetry.

For his last three symphonic poems Strauss resorted to autobiography, romanticized in *Ein Heldenleben* (1898), which shows Strauss and his wife battling triumphantly against hostile music-critics, then comically realistic

*The Almanac of the Expressionist **Blaue Reiter** movement (published in 1912) aimed at a synthesis of all the arts, to be created out of music, the visual arts and literature.*

and self-deflatory in the *Domestic Symphony* (1903), which describes a day in the life of father, mother and noisy baby. Strauss was particularly vilified for composing music about himself, as if Berlioz had not already done the same, not to mention Chaikovsky. Today these contrasting self-portraits seem endearing rather than repugnant.

After the ultra-violent *Elektra*, Strauss returned to a more euphonious diatonic musical idiom in *Der Rosenkavalier* (1911), still the opera for which he is best known; a non-Expressionist romantic comedy about high society in mid-eighteenth-century Vienna. His pioneering days were over and he was content to exercise his creative genius and unequalled technical expertise on pleasing conservative listeners. As such, his later works are

Berlioz p 205–11
Chaikovsky p 275–7

Recording

A frequent complaint of musicians and music-lovers is the impossibility of hearing how music sounded at the time of its first performance: the gramophone, though rectifying this omission for most musical events of the twentieth century, has, if anything, sharpened the sense of loss for the musical performances of earlier generations. But we are not totally without evidence of how Handel, Haydn or Mozart intended their music to sound: there are "recordings" of performances that may well have been made under their supervision. All three composers wrote music for mechanical instruments, Handel for a mechanical organ attached to a set of bells, and Mozart and Haydn for small mechanical clocks. These played tunes at regular intervals throughout the day; careful restoration makes it possible for us to hear what they heard, to listen to the tempo, for example, that Haydn intended for the little minuets that these costly timepieces can still reproduce.

But when recording arrived, late in the nineteenth century, it was long viewed with suspicion; many great artists avoided making recordings at all, which has been a great loss to us. But it was a loss to them as well, for the rewards were enormous. Caruso was among the first to recognize the great potential of the medium: he cut his first record in 1902, and was eventually to make himself more than a million dollars from record sales. The great soprano Emma Calvé was another who made a pretty penny through the gramophone (though her tendency to dance around while singing into the recording horn was hard for the engineers to cope with). Yet even she at first had been more than wary of the implications of the recording studio: "Never in my life will I enter such a place. It is a tavern, not a manufactory. I shall be robbed there," she declared.

Those who have listened to such early recordings must be aware of the difficulties involved when attempting to capture the sound of an orchestra on wax: the accompanying instruments behind the two singers just mentioned, for example, sound tinny and far away. For a time this was remedied by specially designed musical instruments fitted with horns instead of their usual sound boxes, that directed the notes produced towards the large recording horn; but it was not until the advent of electrical recording complete with microphones in the 1920s that matters showed a marked improvement.

Since then, the technique has been tremendously refined, though not fundamentally altered. Tape and long-playing records have brought improvements and benefits familiar to us all. Tape has also brought the dubious benefit of permitting an artist to isolate and re-record sections of his performance that displease him, as many times as he wishes: such an availability has complex implications as far as a true recorded performance is concerned. Beyond this, the universal accessibility that we now have to great music has become cheapened by overexposure as background music everywhere. These not inconsiderable disadvantages have been outweighed by the obvious benefits, at least for the world at large, to a point where the effects of recording upon the music industry can be justifiably compared with the effect of the printing press upon the written word.

Arnold Schoenberg *was a close friend of the painter Kandinsky, whose painting "The Blue Rider" gave the* Blaue Reiter *movement its name.*

not of historical interest, except that in harking back to the Hellenic world which he so loved, in *The Egyptian Helen* (1928) and *The Love of Danae* (1944), to the Vienna of the waltzing Strausses (no relations) in *Arabella* (1933) and to the Paris of Gluck's time in *Capriccio* (1942), he was following trends of his contemporaries, moving away from Wagner and Expressionism, towards neoclassicism and neo-Hellenism. Late in his long life Strauss returned to orchestral music, composing an oboe concerto and a study for twenty-three solo strings entitled *Metamorphoses* of high, purely Classical quality. His farewell to music in *Four Last Songs* (1948) for soprano and orchestra remind us that he was the last of the great *lieder*-composers; a royal line, now apparently extinct.

Expressionism
Much of this was far away in 1900, the year on which this chapter is based. What I have already described as Expressionism was a style of painting

Gluck p 125–6
Wagner p 229–40

*Schoenberg's **Pierrot Lunaire** (this production starred Mary Thomas as the crazed clown) is a setting of poems by the Belgian Albert Giraud.*

associated with the work of Franz Marc, Emil Nolde and Vasily Kandinsky of the *Blaue Reiter* movement (to which Schoenberg, as a Sunday painter, was also affiliated) from about 1909 (the year of *Elektra*) onwards. Its essence was to be abstract, subjective and intolerant of all discipline.

The dividing line between post-Impressionism, Symbolism and Expressionism was slender: Van Gogh in the late 1880s and Edvard Munch in the 1890s had effectively visualized Expressionism as we now recognize the style. It is the nightmare world of the mind that we can recognize in the first two movements of Mahler's sixth symphony, or the scherzo of his ninth and in *Salome* and *Elektra*. In such works as Schoenberg's monodrama *Waiting* (1909), we witness the interior agony of a woman waiting at night in a forest for the lover who, she is convinced, will not arrive; is he dead, has she murdered him, or is he altogether imaginary? Schoenberg's singer, at her wit's end, has her vocal powers stretched to breaking point throughout, though the large orchestra is deployed with finesse and self-control, at odds with the notion of Expressionism as anarchical. It is atonal music—the boundaries of tonality crossed into a sound-world where the only control is anarchy, the reality behind unreality. Schoenberg wrote proudly of his song-cycle *The Book of the Hanging Gardens* (1910), that he had "broken through every restriction of a bygone aesthetic". He claimed to have "emancipated the dissonance"; that is to say, no chord was any longer to be regarded as less agreeable, or more disagreeable, than any other chord, less or more apt to conclude a piece of music by virtue of its lack of emotional ambiguity. Debussy had already claimed much the same with his "non-functional harmony"—outlandish chords (he used to play them on the piano to fellow students at the Paris Conservatoire, calling them "a banquet for the ears") that could be resolved in any direction.

Both composers, nevertheless, out of artistic necessity, followed each harmony with another, more pleasing or more confusing, according to the

1875~1920 The Turn of the Century

natural (if no longer academic) principle of tension and relaxation. If you listen to an unfamiliar piece of non-tonal music, you cannot tell what will follow, but your ear and the composer's sense of fitness will ensure that you sense changing sound in terms of tension heightened or relieved. The same holds true of Schoenberg's other non-tonal music, notably the song-cycle *The Book of the Hanging Garden* to poems by the Austrian symbolist Stefan George; the first Chamber Symphony (1906—still supposedly tonal, in E major, though only just); the *Five Orchestral Pieces* (1909) in which emotional sensibility completely replaces intellectual argument, and the song-cycle *Pierrot Lunaire* for voice and a mixed piano quintet ensemble (1912). This last became a key-work of its period, partly because the vocal part is hardly ever pitched precisely, but designed in a sing-song style where each note is roughly touched, then quitted in a downward slide, as in speech, before the next note is attacked. The *Sprechgesang*, or "speech-song", was much used by Schoenberg and his pupil Berg later, as well as by composers of our own day.

Pierrot Lunaire is fanciful, capricious and absurd, as befits a *commedia dell' arte* circus turn, but also an excursion into the soul of the Pierrot inside each of us, therefore not really frivolous. If the Symbolist, rather Surrealist texts are understood (German translations of a French original), and if the instrumental accompaniment is played with knowledge and flair, the piece has the vitality of an Italian *opera buffa*, a counterblast to the common supposition that Schoenberg's music was always humourless and auto-cratic.

Tilly Wedekind as her husband's heroine, **Lulu**. *It was from two of Wedekind's plays that Berg derived the libretto for* Lulu.

The New Language of Schoenberg, Webern and Berg

From these non-tonal compositions Schoenberg, having fortified his position with a masterly treatise on traditional tonal harmony, was to launch a new formulation of non-tonal language, based on all twelve semitones—a substitute for the exhausted diatonic method. His pupils Berg and Webern accompanied him (some scholars opine that they taught him as much as he taught them). For all his pioneering zeal, Schoenberg was temperamentally a classic stylist, in the mould of Brahms or J.S. Bach. Webern was the radical, his musical thought naturally most akin to the concise style most appropriate to non-tonal music—when you cannot take any movement for granted from one note to another, how can you absorb a new composition lasting more than a few minutes? Schoenberg's structural and rhetorical achievement in *Erwartung*, which lasts some twenty minutes, is the more to be admired in this light.

Webern had his own row to hoe. Berg's aims were communicative, human and more in line with tradition. He accompanied Schoenberg all the way into dodecaphony, or serial music as we now call it, but in his works the old tonal music never disappeared. Tonal and non-tonal music are mixed in his opera *Wozzeck* (1925), a supreme document of Expressionism, interna-tionally accepted and loved for its compassionate qualities long before the other products of the Second Viennese School, though almost preceded in popular favour by his violin concerto (1936), which courts attention by quoting Bach and Austrian folk song, as well as the open strings of the violin, all in a twelve-note composition. His last opera, *Lulu*, another exemplary Expressionist drama of woman as destroyer, then victim, of man, was left unfinished at his premature death, but has been completed and performed in the late 1970s.

Schoenberg's greatest achievements after his formulation of twelve-note composition, were the unfinished opera *Moses and Aaron*, a string trio of blinding virtuosity and uncompromising severity, concertos for violin and piano which renew the grandeur of their Romantic models (Schumann and Brahms, no less), and the later of his five admirable string quartets. His own personality, didactic and uncompromising, makes it hard for audiences, even now, to fall in love with his music, but there is, when one has crossed the threshold of the language, sweetness in it, and joy, and Viennese relaxation. When you break through the cocoon of the chrysalis, a butterfly, not an ogre, emerges.

Looking Back

The introduction to this book refers to the long accepted doctrine that music had improved from generation to generation and century to century—so that Brahms, for a late Victorian, was accepted as artistically and technically superior to the composers who lived before him. By now it will have become clear that the doctrine was no longer wholly accepted.

Scholars and enthusiasts had revived the glories of plainsong, of Palestrina's age, of J.S. Bach and Handel, with editions and performances and teaching. The nineteenth century saw the launch of new, scholarly, complete editions of the music of Europe's outstanding composers from earlier centuries; such active composers as Brahms were not too proud to lend a hand. Few thought to delve beyond the printed notes: executant musicians were content to play what they read, and in opera houses singers were actively discouraged, by conductors as scrupulous and renowned as

Above: *In his Violin Concerto* **Alban Berg** *imbued the twelve-note system with a passionate Romanticism.*

Above left: **Anton Webern's** *music is extremely concise. His published output consists of little more than four hours' music.*

Above: **Max Reger** wrote much of his orchestral music while director of the renowned Meiningen Orchestra.

Above right: **Busoni** spent the first part of his life as a virtuoso pianist. "Bach is the foundation of piano playing: Liszt is the summit," he declared.

Mahler, from embellishing the written notes in the style expected by earlier composers. Brahms and d'Indy, for example, were avid collectors and editors of pre-classical music: Brahms's edition of the keyboard suites of Couperin is still in use today.

Back to Ancient Greece

When the excesses of musical Romanticism could go no further and C major began to sound like an extinct remnant of those earlier days, musicians and their audiences, not to mention their interpreters, turned their thoughts to a new music. A music which would ignore the Romantic era and build on the pre-classics—Bach, Handel, even Palestrina and plainsong—as a purer, more vital inspiration, perhaps capable of breathing new life into the idea of tonal music. There was even an attempt to construct a system of modal harmony, even though the old modes essentially contained their own implied harmony and required no further implementation.

Around 1900, glutted with the legacy of Wagner and polychromaticism ("the cult of the dominant umpteenth" as one composer fancifully described it), composers almost everywhere in Europe turned their creative minds to inspiration from the past (this was the time when Arnold Dolmetsch pioneered the return to old instruments; the viols, the recorder, harpsichord and clavichord). For some it was a romanticized classical Greek or Arcadian source, a simpler, pastoral world with pure ideals, unpolluted emotions, few but essential and eloquent notes, the lyre and flute dominant (as in

Plainsong p 23–5

Debussy's late sonata for flute, viola and harp), the emotions chaste, hieratic and noble.

The cult of classical Greece resulted in Debussy's infinitely pure and infinitely erotic *Chansons de Bilitis* (1897), among the most captivating of all his songs. The same inspiration was behind Ravel's ballet score *Daphnis et Chloé* (1912), a vast but economically inhibited musical canvas, every note and timbre eventful—the opening *Daybreak* of the last scene among the most ravishing musical evocations of nature ever put to music—the very spirit of benign Nature (Stravinsky's *Rite of Spring* had already proposed a less idyllic interpretation). Richard Strauss's closely felt sympathy with Arcadian Greece, already mentioned, involved more adipose tissue in, for example, the pastoral *Daphne* (1938), rather a teutonic view of primitive Hellas. Greece for Strauss meant the toughness of *Elektra*, as he showed again in *The Egyptian Helen* (1929), which almost revives that granite, discordant insistence.

Among French composers of about 1900 Fauré's songs will be found often, whatever their poetry, to espouse the cool, clean, sparing textures that French composers associated with Hellenic culture. Erik Satie (1866–1925) gave the most complete demonstration of new keyboard harmony in a Hellenic manner of any composer. His last work, a static drama called *Socrate* (1919), has the quality of a rite with its austere lines, timbres and manner of singing. Much of Satie's music seems needlessly cynical; tolerable jokes overelaborated for the sake of protest. *Socrate* is serious, and uplifted in tone of voice and accompaniment; truly French-Greek of its period, a noble example to Satie's successors, more of whom later.

Back to the Eighteenth Century

The branch of neoclassicism in music which took as its slogan "Back to Bach" is usually associated with Europe in the interwar years (1919–1939), but the movement had put down viable roots before 1900, some might say in the finale of Brahms's fourth symphony (1886) or as early as the first movement of Saint-Säens' fourth piano concerto (1844).

Max Reger (1873–1916) picked up the gauntlet. He was a brilliant, natural contrapuntist and devotee of convoluted chromatic harmony (as a young man he declared that he could distinguish no difference between harmony and counterpoint). Bach was his idol and he composed profusely for the organ and in most other forms except opera. Although an admirer of Wagner, Reger believed firmly in the virtues of abstract music, and was not drawn at all to Expressionism. His rather Brahmsian piano concerto (1910), clarinet quintet (1915) and sets of variations, for orchestra on a theme by Mozart (1914), for piano on themes by Bach (1904) and Telemann (1914), show an individual cast of mind with a positive solution to the creative problems of his age.

He may be viewed as a spiritual link between Brahms and Paul Hindemith (1895–1963), whose music began with Expressionist post-Wagnerian fantasy (*Mörder, Hoffnung der Frauen*, 1919) and underwent many varied influences, always anti-Romantic, in pursuit of the fashionable 1920's *Neue Sachlichkeit*, or "New Objectivity", or Sound For Its Own Sake, settling into linear counterpoint in the J.S. Bach tradition, spare and muscular, not atonal but newly regulated by an idiosyncratic harmonic system based on natural overtones; more of Hindemith later.

Ferruccio Busoni (1866–1924), half-Italian, half-German by ancestry,

Hindemith p 333–4

among the greatest virtuoso pianists of his age, was also a composer and musical philosopher of advanced views soundly based on the music of the past. His *Fantasia contrappuntistica* for piano, or two pianos (1910–1922), shows Busoni's Bach-orientated personal style at its most impressive and, with his *Duettino concertante* for two pianos on the last movement of Mozart's F major piano concerto, K 459, reminds us of Busoni's attempt to pioneer a movement based on the aesthetics and practice of J.S. Bach and Mozart. Busoni's musical affiliations were numerous. His monumental piano concerto (1904) with choral finale has Lisztian affiliations, and closely reconciles the composer's Latin and teutonic ancestral allegiances. Two operas, *Turandot* (1917) and *Arlecchino* (1916), return to the Italian *commedia dell' arte* with so much creative fervour and excellent invention that they must win over all who hear them—but neither has yet become a repertory work. More often staged is the posthumously completed *Doktor Faust*, a new, partly symbolic treatment of the old legend, greatly impressive in performance, in essence not modern at all for our time; highly clever, juggling with essentially Romantic notions. Busoni could not bring his creative self into the post-war world, any more than Elgar.

Elements of the "Back to the Eighteenth Century" movement may be found in the texture or style of Ravel's Piano Trio (1915) and piano suite *Le tombeau de Couperin* (1917); in the dance movements of Schoenberg's Piano Suite, opus twenty-five (his first twelve-note work, 1925), and in Berg's *Wozzeck*, each of its fifteen scenes adopting a traditional musical form, as do those of *Lulu*, more elaborately. Not in Berg's operas, but often elsewhere, the neoclassic attraction resulted in a suggestion of self-conscious mimicry, or even parody. Perfect examples are Richard Strauss's incidental music to Molière's *Le Bourgeois gentilhomme* (1912) originally devised as the curtain-raiser to the opera *Ariadne auf Naxos*, though eventually the two works were separated. Strauss's "historicizing" was doubtless superior in its day, but now it sounds heavy-handed and the quite unacademic opera proves the more effective, especially when given a new behind-the-scenes prologue, with an extra starring role for the boy-genius who is supposed to have composed the opera. Here the neoclassic trend is dropped often, as in the composer's Hymn to music, and the duet with the pretty comedienne Zerbinetta. There is more of the Rococo spirit, naturally poured out, in such moments of *Der Rosenkavalier* as the breakfast scene and the Marschallin's first monologue, though the post-Romantic Strauss wells up in the closing scene of the opera, with its glorious trio for female voices. The neoclassic Strauss was to come forward later. The epitome of pre-First World War music then seemed to be the waltz music of *Der Rosenkavalier*, sumptuous, spectacular, luscious.

These were the most significant of the many trends binding together the profuse innovatory activity around the turn from the nineteenth to the twentieth century. Many of the composers discussed have either been mentioned earlier, or are due to recur later. The turn of a century is seldom a catalyst that produces instant change—it is rather a moment to take stock.

Mozart's piano concertos p 155–6

Chapter 15
Serialism and the Jazz Age
War and Peace

Music and the machine age ◆ The player-piano and the gramophone ◆ Music goes to the movies ◆ The effects of war ◆ The eclecticism of Igor Stravinsky ◆ Satie and *Les Six* ◆ The Armistice spirit ◆ Jazz ◆ Paul Hindemith and Kurt Weill ◆ The second Viennese school ◆ Audiences for the New Music ◆ Music in Russia ◆ America: source and centre ◆

Wartime has always been bad for music and the other arts, because it discourages fine feelings and noble sentiments, and exhorts civilized human beings to become predatory, homicidal beasts again. They are told by their leaders to sacrifice their individualities and better selves, their lives included, for the triumph of their country over another country, which really means for the greater power and glory of their leaders.

During the period covered by the previous chapter, artists, including musicians, were doing their damnedest to turn civilized thought away from the bombastic dreams of Romantic egotism towards a truthfully, more refined, more self-aware attitude to life. Being individualists, the artists went to work in many diverse ways, and couldn't convince their fellow humans to discredit the power politicians. So in 1914 another war began involving almost every country in the world, the most destructive ever known, not only in killing and ruining towns or cities, but in provoking international hatred. When it ended, with the Armistice of 1918, the rejoicing and spiritual relief found musical expression in uninhibited, irresponsible merriment and carousal. The Machine Age was making the world smaller. Europe discovered a new American music, the jazz of black slaves from Africa who had invented it to ease their miserable way of life. Although slavery had been abolished in America, its black inhabitants were still second-class citizens, and had plenty of despair to voice.

There was a new wave of musical nationalism, too, in countries that were made independent by the peace treaties of 1919 and were quick to assert that independence. A few composers wrote serious new music, designed to make their listeners think, but the general irresponsibility and prevailing concern to be entertained, even to forget that the world had changed since 1914, allowed power politicians to continue their fatal excesses until 1939, when a second world war began, and music was once

1880–1960 *War and Peace*

An image of war: *Eric Gill's* Westward Ho! *(1921)*.

more, even more disastrously, subjugated to patriotism, the "war effort", and savage mindlessness.

Nearly forty years after the ending of that second murderous orgy (in a sense it was a Crusade against Hitler) with the explosion of two atom bombs on Japan, it seems as if those two world wars were really one bout of carnage, with a half-time interval in which the opposing sides, far from determining to mend their ways, simply made ready to intensify their beastliness to one another.

The Music of Machines

The nineteenth century prided itself on being the age of the Industrial Revolution and increased mass-production through new mechanical inventions. To the musician a machine means regular rhythm. Beethoven celebrated Mälzel's metronome in a vocal canon (*Ta ta ta ta*, 1812), to be sung while the machine ticked out the beats at the desired speed: he re-worked the music as the second movement of his Eighth Symphony (1812). Wagner put the spinning-wheel into his opera *The Flying Dutchman* (1843), where the whirring of the regular foot-treadle accompanies a chorus of girls at their work. The later sewing-machine (patented in 1851 by Isaac Singer) was likewise notated in the orchestral score of Charpentier's opera *Louise* (1900) for a scene in a dressmaker's shop. Berlioz and Glinka both celebrated the invention of the railway train, the former in a cantata, *Chant des chemins de fer* ("Song of the Railways", 1846), the latter in *Farewell to St Petersburg* (1840).

For musicians of their age as well as ours, the essence of rhythm in music is that it should not be constrained to regularity but, once set up, can be varied ever so slightly all the time in the interest of musical expressive-ness. You can appreciate this by setting a metronome or a stop-watch to a gramophone record, and then listening to the subsequent bending of the beat by the interpretation. Better still, if you yourself are a performing musician, try to play a piece while exactly following the tick of a metronome, if you can manage it: the result is quite unmusical. Wagner did manage it for a few moments in the Nibelung factory music of his opera *The Rhine Gold*, with eighteen anvils exactly synchronized.

After the railway train came the motor car, the aeroplane, the telephone, the cinema, the player-piano and the phonograph. They made for quick, close connection between countries and even continents; all affected music beneficially to some extent, and were in time duly hymned in music. The Swiss composer Arthur Honegger was to portray the physical activity, as well as the soul (he said) of the express train in his orchestral tone-poem *Pacific 231* (1923). Benjamin Britten made a less high-powered portrait of a rural engine in his early, poetical and economical film-score *Night Mail* (1936). The arrival of the aeroplane in 1903 was much later turned to musical account by George Antheil in his *Airplane Sonata* for solo piano (1922). It was a conscious protest against Straussian monumentalism and Debussy's Impressionism, avowedly realistic in the "motoric" style which young Sergei Prokofiev had been pursuing in pre-Revolution Russia, from his first piano concerto (1911) onwards. Antheil subsequently composed a *Ballet mécanique* (1924), first scored for sixteen player-pianos, later recast (1926) for eight pianos, one pianola, four xylophones, two electric bells, two aircraft-propellers, a tam-tam (a large, rimless gong), four bass drums and an electric siren.

Music could not draw much inspiration from the telephone beyond mimicry of its ring, as in Strauss's opera *Intermezzo* (1924) and Berg's *Lulu* (1936, a more interesting sound), though Gian-Carlo Menotti was much later to write a whole opera, *The Telephone* (1947), about a girl so besotted with the instrument that her lover has to leave her apartment and propose marriage from a neighbouring telephone-box.

The motor car did badly out of music, considering its regular use for travel throughout the twentieth century: only Prokofiev's "motor" style suggests the internal combustion engine—and you may nowadays as usefully listen to Stravinsky's *Rite of Spring*, with all its repetitive ostinatos suggesting sacrificial processions, in terms of a car-industry evidently bent on ritual suicide. The *Springtime Rounds* and *Procession of Old Men* may suggest the old De Dion Bouton, but Stravinsky never said so.

The Rhine Gold p 229
Stravinsky p 291–4, 321–4

1880–1960 *War and Peace*

*The perfect parody of the machine age: **Chaplin's Modern Times** (1936).*

One Russian composer did deliberately make music out of industrial machinery: Alexander Mossolov, with his *Steel Foundry* (1927) for orchestra, a work widely performed at the time, and recorded because of its topicality, but in no way musically distinctive. Outside Soviet Russia factories do not inspire much music.

The Player-piano

To a generation of composers fed up with the caprices of Romantic pianists, the player-piano, or pianola, offered the ideal possibility of a completely accurate, inflexible reproduction of their anti-romantic music. Hence the attraction of it for Antheil and for Stravinsky, who engraved his own performances of his piano works on pianola-rolls and scored one version of his cantata *The Wedding* for player-piano accompaniment—significantly he settled, in the end, for four live pianists and percussion with singing voices. Even Stravinsky needed a little metrical flexibility for his music.

The player-piano is now chiefly valuable for posterity as a memento of early twentieth-century composers and pianists (Godowsky, Mahler, Grieg and Saint-Saëns among them) who did not later record for the gramophone. It did have one advantage over the gramophone record: the person playing the piano-roll has to take a physical part in the reproduction of the music, by pedalling with the feet, as on a harmonium and adding "expression" by means of some hand controls, and so can imaginatively become its executant, with all the attendant illusions of grandeur. One is not so personally involved when playing a gramophone record!

Electronics

Electronic instruments have more of a history than is generally supposed: the first experiments extend back into the nineteenth century. It was as the result of an accident that the first instrument, the Singing Arc, was evolved. When the new carbon-arc street lamps were found to emit a persistent whistle, the English scientist William Duddell, who was investigating this problem, constructed a keyboard on the same principle, for demonstration purposes, in 1897.

The most wonderful electronic instrument was evolved some five or six years later, in the United States. Thaddeus Cahill's Telharmonium was a masterpiece of engineering: it cost several fortunes to build, and weighed more than two hundred tons. It was designed to relay "high-class" music over the New York telephone system to hotels, restaurants and private houses—loudspeakers had not yet been invented. The instrument's limitations, however, were glaring, and its gigantic size was soon rendered obsolete. One of the twelve rotors of this mighty behemoth is illustrated here.

There is an important distinction to be made among those instruments which amplify and reproduce external musical sounds, such as the electric guitar or electric organ, and those which create the sounds themselves—pure electronic instruments such as the synthesizer. An early pure electronic instrument that enjoyed a vogue for some years was the Theremin. In this, the frequency of an oscillating current was raised or lowered according to the proximity of the performer's hand to an aerial, resulting in a wailing glissando *much favoured by composers of early sci-fi film music.*

Studios for the study of electronic music were set up after the war in America, France, Italy and, most importantly, in Germany, where young musicians such as Karlheinz Stockhausen began in the 1950s to codify and study the possibilities that were offered. The process of electronic composition has become marvellously sophisticated since then, reaching its ultimate (at the time of writing) in the synthesizer which, theoretically, can analyse and reconstitute any conceivable sound or combination of sounds, and create a foreseeably unlimited range of new sounds besides. The ondes martenot, *much used by Honegger and other inter-war composers, notably Messiaen, produces a variable electronic sound via a keyboard of six octaves. Its distinctive sonority, featured prominently in Messiaen's* Turangalîla Symphony, *is created in a complex fashion, involving an acoustic lyre-shaped soundbox fitted with sympathetic strings. The great pianist Alfred Cortot was sufficiently impressed by the instrument to write the introduction to Martenot's manual on how to play it.*

1880-1960 War and Peace

*By the 1920s, **the gramophone** had become the indispensable accompaniment to social activities of every kind, as this illustration from a contemporary advertisement shows.*

***Joseph Joachim** became the first Director of the prestigious Berlin Hochschule für Musik, and an early recording star.*

The Phonograph

The gramophone record had been invented in 1877 by Thomas Edison and had the superior advantage that it could reproduce voices, instruments and even an orchestra. One prototype claims to reproduce the voice of Jenny Lind (1820–1887), the "Swedish Nightingale" and most beloved soprano of her day. Another, of an extract from *Tristan and Isolde*, is said to have been conducted in Bayreuth by Wagner himself. Brahms recorded one of his Hungarian Dances, announcing his name first. The great Hungarian violinist Joseph Joachim, Debussy, the young Caruso and the elderly, still great soprano Lilli Lehmann (who sang Mozart, Bellini and Wagner with equal mastery, as no soprano now can), all recorded for the gramophone. There are even some tantalizing records of opera performed live at the Metropolitan in New York in 1901, with Jean de Reszke, the greatest operatic tenor of his time, who never recorded commercially for the gramophone.

If only the phonograph had been invented as early as the camera, we could now hear Chopin, Liszt and Paganini, Malibran and the legendary *bel canto* singers of her generation, especially those supposedly unsurpassed tenors, Mario and Rubini. When gramophone recording did take music seriously, it moved fast. The first composition to use it was Resphighi's orchestral symphonic poem *The Pines of Rome* (1924), which includes the singing of a nightingale recorded for interpolation at a particular spot in the music. The gramophone's importance, not only as a record of musical performance but as an ingredient in composition, affirmatively arrived with the invention of tape-recording, commercially feasible from the 1930s onward. From 1949 it became the standard method of recording for the gramophone and shortly afterwards was marketed for domestic use, after which composers began to use it as an ingredient of new music.

Jenny Lind p 201

Film Music

Of all these new technologies, the cinema was going to profit most from music's cooperation. Silent movies needed musical accompaniment, and it had to match the cinematic drama exactly, a new technique for composers. Richard Strauss adapted his *Rosenkavalier*, with some additions from existing occasional pieces, for a silent film version (1926); and in 1930 Schoenberg composed his orchestral *Music for a Film Scene*, presumably silent, its contents only vaguely specified and therefore unidentifiable by students of the cinema. It must have inspired his pupil Alban Berg to include a silent film sequence in his second opera *Lulu* (1936), with detailed orchestral accompaniment, which shows how the heroine is tried and imprisoned for murder, and how she escapes from prison with the heroic assistance of her lesbian admirer, Countess Geschwitz. By that date, paradoxically, the cinema had begun to talk (and to be filmed, primitively, in colour).

It was only then that serious composers were persuaded to work for the cinema. Some significant film-scores of the 1930s, good music professionally matched to the stop-watch needs of kinetic drama, were composed in England by Arthur Bliss (the proto-science fiction H.G. Wells film *Things to Come*, 1933), in Russia by Shostakovich (*New Babylon*, 1929, was his first of many cinematic scores) and in France by Georges Auric (born 1899). Auric wrote the music for Jean Cocteau's famous films *A Poet's Blood* (1930), *The Eternal Return* (1943), *Beauty and the Beast* (1946), *The Eagle Has Two Heads* (1947) and *Orpheus* (1949), and for many movies by other directors. In Hollywood Aaron Copland (born 1900) contributed distinctive scores for *Of Mice and Men* (1939), *The Red Pony* (1948) and *Something Wild* (1961).

Old-fashioned composers were sometimes unwilling to have their inspiration controlled by the second-hand of a stop-watch, but some lived to make film-music not only honourable, but exemplary for the whole world. Notably the elderly Vaughan Williams in a number of feature films, culminating in *Scott of the Antarctic* (1948); the no longer young John Ireland in *The Overlanders*, a film about Australian rural life (1947); and particularly William Walton in music for three Shakespeare films directed by Laurence Olivier (*Henry V*, 1944, *Hamlet*, 1948 and *Richard III*, 1956). In Hollywood some admirable film-music was written by specialist composers of distinction, whose work was virtually unknown in the concert-hall— the best known being Erich Wolfgang Korngold, whose opera *The Dead City* (1920) is still performed.

Between the wars, film music was an important art-form, well known to the public at large—an example is Walton's *Spitfire Prelude and Fugue* from the feature film *The First of the Few* (1942). Likewise Richard Addinsell's *Warsaw Concerto*, a Rakhmaninov pastiche commissioned for a wartime film, *Dangerous Moonlight* (1941), because Rakhmaninov's own second piano concerto was not available, though it was later used as incidental music for another film (*Brief Encounter*, 1946).

*The glorious soprano voice of **Lilli Lehmann**, who sang as a Rhinemaiden in the first performance of* The Ring *cycle, can still be heard on early recordings.*

The Great War

In the horrors of the 1914–1918 war, the stultification of twentieth-century music, highly promising at a European, even intercontinental level, seemed of small importance. The Great War drove Richard Strauss, Germany's leading composer, into voluntary retirement at his country home in Bavaria, where he devoted himself to a sublime, metaphysical opera—his

1880-1960 War and Peace

Film Music

The first film music was played live, from the pit, by a pianist or small instrumental group; or later by the mighty Wurlitzer, embellished with extra effects that could add wolf-whistles, train whistles, hoofbeats or waves on the seashore. Innumerable miniature tone-poems were supplied for the use of accompanists to silent epics, bearing titles such as "Blank amazement", "Battle commences" or "Homeward through the Snow".

But since the arrival of talking pictures and the possibility of an integrated sound-track of music, the procedure of composing for the films has become incalculably more sophisticated. The film score is generally written when shooting and editing are complete: this can involve the composer in working to an uncomfortably tight deadline. After getting to know the film thoroughly, he agrees with the director which parts of it are going to need music and which will be dramatically stronger unsupported by a score, and sets to work accordingly. Timing has to be done to fractions of a second to synchronize the music with the action. At the recording session, the conductor (often the composer himself) watches the film on a screen erected behind the orchestra to cope with the process of synchronization: cuts and fades can be added later. Shown here are a scene from Irving Berlin's classic, Annie Get Your Gun, and a photograph taken during the recording of William Walton's music for the Olivier film of Hamlet.

greatest—*The Woman without a Shadow* (1919). It is about humankind's quest for the validity of child-bearing—the procreation of our species which makes life worthwhile for those of us not intent on power and the destruction of others. We do not deserve children, the opera says, unless they will survive to make this world better. Strauss was no narrow chauvinist, and as an international composer he preferred to remain neutral. Debussy in France, dying of cancer, became embittered, subscribed his last pieces, three new classic instrumental sonatas, as the works of a "French musician", and added a sad, sour, self-pitying song, the *Carol of Homeless Children*. He had no optimism left to buoy his musicianship above the catastrophe.

Composers lost contact with their colleagues overseas, or across boundaries: some were obliged to enlist, some were killed in action or permanently brain-damaged, like the gifted English song-writer Ivor Gurney. Alban Berg was conscripted, and acquired from war the compassion and loathing to write his first, terrifyingly great opera, *Wozzeck* (refused production until 1925), about a soldier tormented and mocked by his superiors until he loses his reason, cutting the throat of his mistress, and drowning himself.

Stravinsky had left Russia and found exile in neutral Switzerland. There he turned wartime deprivation to artistic virtue in his little drama *The Soldier's Tale* (1918). It uses three speaking actors, one non-speaking dancer and a tiny instrumental chamber ensemble, whose musical textures of taut phrases much repeated clearly derive from *The Rite of Spring*, but even more look forward to the Parisian career of Stravinsky between the two world wars. Dyagilev was, for the moment, unable to commission ballets from him: Stravinsky had to satisfy his hunger for the musical stage with this shoestring entertainment to be toured round villages. *The Soldier's Tale* has outlived its original wartime circumstances and is constantly produced today the world over.

*Stanley Kubrick's film **2001** featured music by such disparate composers as Johann Strauss and Ligeti, with marvellous electronic effects.*

Stravinsky at 88. *One of his last works, the* Requiem Canticles, *was performed at his own funeral in Venice.*

Stravinsky as Frenchman

Some surmised that Stravinsky had, in some Symbolist fashion, forecast the First World War with the barbarous sacrificial ceremony of *The Rite of Spring*. Similarly it might be suggested that he made music's tombstone for the wasteful deaths of that war when it ended in 1918, with his *Symphonies of Wind Instruments* (1920). This short, one-movement dirge, austerely Classical in tone of voice, completely abstract in content, unlike his previous works, was in fact written in memory of Debussy. At first hearing it may sound quite un-Russian. Stravinsky had by then made his home in Paris and become a French citizen. After completing *The Wedding*, an evocation of old Russian peasant customs, staged by Dyagilev (Paris 1923), Stravinsky chiefly pursued the neoclassical manner of *Symphonies*, as in the ballet *Apollo Musagetes* ("Apollo, Leader of the Muses", 1928) and in a fine Violin Concerto (1931). For public appearances as a pianist, he composed a Piano Sonata (1924), in which the debt to J.S. Bach is clear, a Piano Concerto (1924) with wind accompaniment, and a Capriccio for piano and orchestra (1929). For Dyagilev's Russian Ballet company he had compiled *Pulcinella* (1920) by stringing together a quantity of melodies supposedly by Pergolesi, harmonizing and scoring them in his own modern

Dyagilev p 290–1

manner: he later referred to the composition of *Pulcinella* as "a cheerful rape", and he followed it with another, when he re-worked some lesser-known melodies by Chaikovsky as the ballet *The Fairy's Kiss* (1928).

Stravinsky's soul, he said, was still Russian, as could be heard in the short opera *Mavra* (1922), based on a story by Pushkin in which the new cook turns out to be the lover of the daughter of the house, who disguises him as an old woman. The sound of Russian church music mingles with neo-Baroque counterpoint in the choral *Symphony of Psalms* (1930), "dedicated to the Glory of God and the Boston Symphony Orchestra", so the title page naïvely declares. This is surely the greatest work of Stravinsky during his French years, together with the Latin opera-oratorio *Oedipus Rex* (1927), set to a Latin text and deliberately statuesque in effect, its music a whole anthology of neoclassic styles from Bach and Handel to Gluck. A narrator stands to one side of the stage and explains, in the language of the audience (French originally, and the narrator was Jean Cocteau, who had written the text which was then translated into Latin), what is going on. The effect of *Oedipus Rex*, essentially artificial, can be powerfully moving. Stravinsky's wife died in Paris and he removed to Los Angeles, re-married and began a third life as an American citizen, composing two more purely orchestral symphonies, one in C major (1940), the other "in Three Movements" (1945), both neoclassical and dynamic—rather monumental, as one might expect from the music of an elderly master.

Dyagilev had died in 1929, but Stravinsky returned to the ballet in collaboration with George Balanchine, a Russian emigré disciple of

Stravinsky's ballet The Wedding *scored for four pianos and percussion.*

*A pencil sketch of **Dyagilev**, hastily executed by the designer Alexandre Benois on the back of a programme for the première of* The Wedding.

1880–1960 War and Peace

Ravel's *meticulous approach to composition led Stravinsky to refer to him as "The Swiss Clockmaker".*

Dyagilev, a choreographer of genius and an expert musician himself, who worked for a long time at the New York City Ballet. This last, eventful phase of Stravinsky's working life belongs to the next chapter.

Armistice Music

The USA had made a belated but significant appearance in the First World War. Recruiting propaganda was led by the world's leading operatic tenor, Enrico Caruso, singing in English the recorded hit-song *Over There* by the young and brilliant George M. Cohan. (In Britain the parallel song was *Keep the Home Fires Burning*, a more demure appeal to patriotism by the

even younger and apparently more brilliant Ivor Novello.) More or less simultaneously with the Armistice, records of black American ragtime, or jazz, began to arrive in Europe. Stravinsky in Paris responded to this new, vital influence with his *Ragtime* for eleven instruments (1920) and *Piano Rag-music* (1919), though he took this flirtation less seriously than other young European composers of the time, more like a lepidopterist catching his specimen and pinning it to a mounting-board, colourful but inanimate. Paris was still the capital city of new music and the home of the hectically jocular, uproariously satirical, cabaret-style music associated with the Armistice in Europe.

*When **Satie** was criticized for the formlessness of his music, he responded by composing* Three pear-shaped pieces.

Les Six

Armistice music was especially associated with six young French composers, disciples of the composer Erik Satie and the writer Jean Cocteau, who were nicknamed *Les Six*. I have already mentioned Satie's *Socrates* in Chapter 14, and his cynicism. He was a curious mixture: much taken with religious mysticism, ashamed of his technical limitations as a composer, though he made a virtue of them in his piano pieces (1898), later orchestrated by his friend Debussy, called *Three Gymnopédies* (the title taken from a festival in ancient Sparta at which boys and men danced naked) in which cool melody is matched to plain chords, with now and then a surprising harmonic switch. He loved to give his pieces eccentric titles, such as *Three Pear-shaped Pieces* (an anthology of music he wrote during years of work in Parisian music-hall, the so-called *café-concert* which had inspired Chabrier and was again, through Satie, to fire the imagination of *Les Six*). And he often wrote comic performance instructions to his players, not to be passed on to the audience. One piano piece, *Vexations* (1893)

consists of a few, simple bars of music, to be repeated 840 times.

Satie was concerned to draw music away from pretentiousness. In 1920 he collaborated with his disciple Milhaud in composing "Furniture Music" (*musique d'ameublement*) to be performed during intervals at concerts, and regarded as what we call background music or Muzak—how ashamed Satie would be to learn what a horror his musical furniture has propagated.

Debussy and Ravel were friends and disciples of Satie's music, his ideals and personality. Both championed his work, but it was Cocteau who used most influence to bring Satie to public notice. He collaborated with Satie in the Dyagilev ballet *Parade* (1917) whose first performance in Paris caused a public outrage. The score is famous for the inclusion of a typewriter, siren, revolver, roulette wheel and other extra-musical effects. His oriental-styled *Gnossiennes* for piano were first fruits of the 1889 Paris Exhibition. He was quick to espouse the Dada movement, of which he was a progenitor in his ballet *Relâche* ("No Performance"), a zany affair with a René Clair film as intermezzo, familiar to cinema enthusiasts.

Debussy, Ravel, *Les Six*, later Varèse and John Cage, all hailed Satie's originality, hatred of pretentiousness, cult of pure simplicity, and studied eccentricity—if he was a *poseur*, he was completely sincere, influential, and the creator of some lovely music.

In exactly the same way as the nineteenth-century Mighty Fistful in Russia, the French *Six* were of unequal importance. Germaine Tailleferre (born 1892) is nowadays remembered as a female composer when there were still few women creating music. Louis Durey wrote well about music, but his compositions are seldom played. Georges Auric (born 1899) wrote ballets, songs, piano music and orchestral music, but made a speciality of

Georges Auric composed *some delightful film scores, such as* Moulin Rouge *and* The Lavender Hill Mob.

Facing page: *Arthur Honegger* (seated) *photographed with his friend Jean Cocteau.*

Milhaud p 331

1880–1960 War and Peace

Les Six *(minus the composer Durey, and with some friends): Germaine Tailleferre, flanked by Milhaud and Honegger, poses with Auric and Poulenc. Also in the picture are Cocteau (back right), and the pianists Meyer and Wiener.*

film-music, as mentioned earlier, and he was an early French convert to Schoenberg's serialism.

Arthur Honegger (1892–1955), Swiss-born, composed five symphonies, at least four of them worth getting to know (number two, composed in Paris during the Second World War, is a modern *Eroica* for string orchestra with trumpet solo at the end). His big choral works, *King David* (composed in 1921 for the folk theatre at Mézières, near Lausanne), *Joan of Arc at the Stake* (1938) and *The Dance of Death* (1938), brought the visual quality of cinematic drama to the visionary field of sacred oratorio, encouraging stage production which they hardly need (they make a strong effect on records). To his famous locomotive tone poem *Pacific 231* written in 1924, he later added an enjoyable, sympathetic orchestral evocation of his favourite sport, *Rugby* (1928). He wrote a ballet, *Semiramis* (1934), which made use of an electric "Musical Waves" machine, invented by the musician Maurice Martenot, which was capable of producing vibrato and glissando effects from a keyboard. Honnegger was the least obviously frivolous of the *Six*— his output was very large and varied.

Francis Poulenc (1899–1963) at first appeared the typical Parisian Armistice composer; he emerged precociously with a jazz-derived *African Rhapsody* (1918), then settled down to lightly frivolous pieces derived from Satie, Chabrier and French cabaret, as in his *Mouvements perpetuels* for piano solo (1918, "Perpetual Motion" of a relaxed nature), or his Dyagilev ballet *Les biches* ("The House Party", intended to shock prudish audiences, Paris 1923). Poulenc had a particular affinity for Symbolist or Surrealist French poetry. His songs, prolific and as fine as any ever composed by a Frenchman, include masterly settings of Éluard, Apollinaire, Aragon,

*Set to a libretto by Apollinaire, Poulenc's surreal opera **Les Mamelles de Tirésias**; the heroine lets fly two balloons (representing her breasts) from inside her blouse and grows a beard, to liberate herself.*

Francis Poulenc, *leaving Milan's Hotel Continental. Though he enjoyed the reputation of being one of France's more frivolous composers, Poulenc was also a profoundly religious man.*

indeed all the leading modernist French poets of his day, exquisitely designed for singing voice and piano—he had a long-lived concert partnership with the superb singer Pierre Bernac.

Poulenc's art was wide in range, embracing the hilarious (and ultimately serious) Surrealist comic opera *Les Mamelles de Tirésias* ("Tiresias's Breasts", 1944), considered shocking at the time, now acclaimed international repertory material, and the fervent Roman Catholic tragedy of nuns guillotined during the French Revolution, *Dialogues of the Carmelites* (1957), as well as an almost Berliozian *Gloria* (1959) for chorus and orchestra. Poulenc could be flippant and deadly serious almost in the same breath. His sonata for violin and piano (1943) is almost café music, really a statement of profound tragedy. His cantata for unaccompanied chorus, *La Figure humaine* ("The Human Face", 1943), hymns the invincible human spirit, at a time of deepest despair, with an eloquence still shattering in emotional effect, as does the short, equally classical and non-committal song *C* (1943), about the crossing of the French bridge at the village of Cé while the Nazi invaders were occupying France.

Poulenc was never one of music's pioneers but already, not quite twenty years after his death (when most popular composers are still being rejected by immediate posterity), he remains one of the most profound and lovable of all French musicians.

The most prolific of *Les Six* was Darius Milhaud (1892–1974), often frivolous or satirical, as in his three mini-operas (*opéra-minutes*) on classical myths, absurdly treated, or his song-settings of a flower catalogue and a brochure on farm machinery. Of all the *Six*, Milhaud was the most fruitfully influenced by American jazz, heard to good advantage in his ballet *The Ox on the Roof* (1919), named after a café in Paris. In later years his music became gently serious in tone. His many string quartets include two which may also be played simultaneously as a string octet, a feat worthy of his Lowland ancestors. Like many other good European composers, Milhaud, a Jew from the delectable and historic town of Aix-en-Provence, forsook France before 1939 for California, where he taught a lucky generation of American music students, and was still enthusiastically attentive to the newest developments in music.

The Armistice Spirit in France
Those were *Les Six*. Stravinsky was not numbered among them, but belonged to their company, more or less aloof, through Dyagilev and his new muse, the poet Jean Cocteau. Like Satie, Stravinsky exerted a pervasive influence. Ravel blossomed anew in this Armistice scene, with his Violin Sonata (1920), whose middle movement is a jazz-derived blues, and his two concertos for piano, one for both hands (1931) is typically hectic and jollificatory in its outer movements, elegiac in the central slow movement, and contains the most beautiful tune he ever wrote. A concerto for left-handed pianist (completed in 1931 too) was commissioned by Paul Wittgenstein, an Austrian pianist who had lost his right arm in the First World War and, being rich, commissioned similar works from Richard Strauss, Prokofiev and Britten: all are of fine quality and Wittgenstein found them all disagreeably modern. Other pianists, fortunately, disagreed, and Ravel's left-hand piano concerto, a sombre yet scintillating one-movement piece, typifies the elegiac music of his last years, not Armistice at all, but jeremiad, like Vaughan Williams's fourth symphony.

Popular Idiom for England
The defiant Armistice spirit spread outwards from Paris. In England across the Channel it inspired William Walton (born 1902) to his satirical entertainment *Façade* (1922), in which nonsense poems by his friend Edith Sitwell, words arranged for their verbal musical colour, were declaimed against jolly, popular-orientated music for a small instrumental band—waltz, foxtrot, tango, tarantella, even the current popular song *I do like to be beside the seaside*. The flavour was distinctly unusual, the virtuosity irresistible, the effect deplorable to older folk. *Façade* was a hit, and has remained so ever since. Walton's natural appreciation of all popular idioms, including jazz, sustained his inspiration for a while, until he fell into a melancholy, neo-Romantic strain of erotic yearning and unfulfilment. This

Edith Sitwell,
*photographed by Cecil
Beaton. Her absurd verses
to her friend William
Walton's* Façade *remain
fresh and funny after more
than sixty years of
repetition.*

was poignantly voiced in concertos for viola, violin and cello, and in a first symphony (1935) which has remained the outstanding British musical document of the inter-war years, unsurpassed by later works, though his jubilantly secular oratorio *Belshazzar's Feast* (1931) lit a fireworks display beneath the seat of British complacency that remains as explosive as ever. Britain was not much addicted to Armistice jollification in music, though young Benjamin Britten (1913–1976) let off a noisy banger with his festival cantata *Our Hunting Fathers* (1936), which launched him on a happily brilliant and unpredictable career.

Functional Art for Germany

In Germany, defeated after the Great War, impoverished and struggling, young Paul Hindemith gladly espoused jazz in his first *Chamber Music* and *Piano Suite* (both 1922), and went on to shock, surprise or delight his audiences with operas on inflammatory and satirical subjects, before settling down to write sturdy music for practical purposes. He found his place as the musical spokesman of the functional art advocated by Walter Gropius's *Bauhaus* movement, art that was useful and pleasant to perform or listen to. He prided himself on being able to play every instrument in the orchestra and he wrote at least one sonata for every standard orchestral instrument. He was a modern Telemann, the complete general practitioner in music. Performing musicians should be grateful to him: all his music is demanding to play and interesting for intelligent audiences. Dissatisfied by Schoenberg's twelve-note technique, Hindemith formulated another one of his own, based on the natural series of harmonic overtones. For him it made

*Paul **Hindemith** (centre), flanked by Kurt Weill (extreme left) and Bertolt Brecht, seen extracting spectacles from his pocket.*

good music, not for his disciples. In his best work, the Concert Music for Strings and Brass (1931, the so-called *Boston Symphony*) and the opera *Mathis the Painter* (staged in Zurich in 1938, having been banned by the Nazis, causing his eventual retirement to America), he proved himself a major influence on the music of his period.

Kurt Weill

A more piquant voice in German music of the inter-war years was that of Kurt Weill (1900–1950), a Busoni pupil who rose to international fame through his collaboration with the poet Bertolt Brecht in *The Threepenny Opera* (1928), a revised and updated version of John Gay's *The Beggar's Opera*, now set in London during the early 1900s. Weill retained one of the original ballad-tunes (the first sung number in both versions) but, for the rest, composed his own tunes in the style of Berlin cabaret, tough, bitter and jazzy. Almost everybody knows the *Ballad of Mack the Knife*, which has become a pop-song standard and is typical of the score (though Weill's original scoring is tastier than any of the later "cover versions").

Brecht and Weill collaborated further in *The Rise and Fall of Mahagonny Town* (1930), about gold-miners in Alaska, again deeply cynical and satirical: the *Alabama Song* and *Benares Song* are the choicest pieces here. And there was *Happy End* (1929) about gangsters and the Salvation Army, with the heroine's haunting *Surabaya Johnny* song about the bad-hat lover she cannot give up. When Hitler came to power in 1933, Brecht and Weill parted company, and both left Germany in haste; they collaborated briefly in Paris on an opera-ballet *The Seven Deadly Sins* (1933). Brecht returned to a glorious career in the straight theatre, collaborating chiefly with the composer Hanns Eisler when his plays needed music. Weill gravitated to New York, and some less memorable Broadway musicals. Like other eminent refugees from Europe, he found asylum in America, but little stimulation and less appreciation.

Vienna Between the Wars

After the end of the First World War, Austria ceased to be the headquarters of the Holy Roman Empire and became a republic. Vienna was still an attraction to musical people, with its State Opera and illustrious singers, its Vienna Philharmonic Orchestra, and Vienna Boys Choir. It was still, in a sense, the headquarters of modern music as the home of Arnold Schoenberg and his pupils, chiefly Alban Berg and Anton Webern, who were composing the most far-reaching and serious new music of any in Europe (with the important exception of Bartók in Hungary).

Schoenberg and his School

It was in the early 1920s that Schoenberg formulated his "technique of composing music with twelve notes related only to one another", later called "twelve-note" or "dodecaphonic" or "serial" music. Schoenberg's creative mentality, despite his searching after a new organization for non-tonal music, was based on the musical forms of the Viennese classics up to Brahms—the freer, newer forms of his idol Mahler already contained the seeds of disorganization which he needed to tidy up. In Schoenberg's third and fourth string quartets, and his Variations for Orchestra (1928), and the later, superb concertos for violin and for piano with orchestra, he matched Classical forms with his new concepts of melody and harmony to masterly

Serialism

By the beginning of the twentieth century, the resources of tonal music, in major or minor keys, had been so stretched by chromatic elaboration and key-switching that the very principle of tonality seemed exhausted. Already in Wagner's operas there are long passages of music to which one cannot confidently ascribe a key. The young Schoenberg, in such works as Five Orchestral Pieces *and* Pierrot Lunaire, *completely abandoned the key-system, and this music is described as "atonal" (meaning keyless, though he preferred to call it "pantonal"—in all keys at once).*

Schoenberg (right) found this state of musical anarchy impossible to continue, so from 1920 onwards he elaborated an alternative discipline for musical composition. He called it "Composition with twelve notes related only to one another". Other composers, such as Berg and Webern in Austria, Lutyens and Searle in England, Auric in France, Dallapiccola in Italy and Krenek in America, took up the method: it became familiarly known as "12-note" or "dodecaphonic" music, more recently "serialism", since the technique has extended further. After 1945, young composers in Europe and America quickly took up and developed Schoenberg's method to serialize note-lengths and dynamics (levels of volume) as well as the pitch of the notes. Such music, quite obviously, is demanding to play and to hear—and, as one critic put it, exceedingly hard to whistle. Today's music is often serial, but much less strictly so.

Perhaps the most familiar and approachable piece of serial music is Berg's Violin Concerto. He dedicated it "to the memory of an angel", who was the dead young daughter of Alma Mahler. The work is sumptuous and deeply moving.

purpose. Yet he realized that new ideas needed new forms and structures of their own, as he showed with the superb string trio (1946) of his years in America (it is not an easy work for a listener to become familiar with, but supremely worth the trouble). And long before then he was experimenting with forms, in the operas *The Lucky Hand* (1913) and *From Today until Tomorrow* (1929) for example.

Berg had completed his opera *Wozzeck* before Schoenberg's twelve-note technique was worked out: its music is freely non-tonal, controlled elaborately by strict old musical structures, such as variation, fugue or passacaglia. Berg's creative nature was more Romantic, his twelve-note music

*The New Zealand soprano Kiri Te Kanawa in a Royal Opera House production of Richard Strauss's **Arabella**.*

more immediately attractive in sound than Schoenberg's, as can be heard in his Violin Concerto (1935), which can quote from Austrian folk song and from J.S. Bach without their seeming incongruous. His second opera, *Lulu*, does use twelve-note technique throughout, and with great variety of mood and character. His most masterly, elaborate twelve-note composition is surely the Concerto for Piano, Violin and Thirteen Wind Instruments (1925), into whose themes he wove the musical notes in the names of Schoenberg, Webern and Berg.

Webern was, even before twelve-note music, the miniaturist, or epigrammatist, of the so-called "Second Viennese School", sparing of notes and placing each one with infinite care. None of his thirty opus-numbered works lasts more than a few minutes (he had composed his share of extended, rich-textured music as a young student), and often his themes are only three or four notes long (a twelve-note series is most conveniently divided by three or four, as simple arithmetic reminds us). His Symphony (1924) and Concerto (1934) are both chamber works and both compact in duration, but very intense in character and as action-packed (if you concentrate thoroughly) as a Romantic forty-five-minute work. After 1945,

Berg p 308

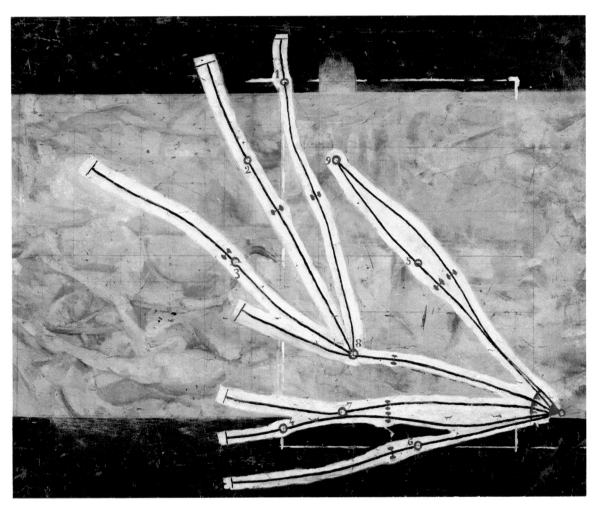

the young *avant-garde* were to find most inspiration in Webern's methods and ideals of composition.

For Vienna in the 1920s and 1930s, Schoenberg's music, and that of his pupils, was of little interest. The Viennese even remembered Mahler chiefly as a great conductor, and seldom demanded to hear his symphonies. The great new voice in music, for the Viennese, was the prodigiously gifted Erich Wolfgang Korngold (1897–1957), whose luscious, fantastical dream-opera *Die tote Stadt* ("The Dead Town", 1920) made music-drama in a tone of voice that conveniently forgot times had changed and Franz-Josef was no longer on the Austrian throne. Korngold had other successes (it helped that his father was the most influential music critic in Vienna), among them an earlier opera *Violanta* (1916). When Hitler annexed Austria, Korngold removed to Hollywood and became an immensely successful composer of film-music—unlike Bartók, Schoenberg, Stravinsky and others. He was a survivor, and one can only congratulate him since his music was always of expert quality.

A superior talent, it must be suggested, was that of Franz Lehár (1870–1948), who kept the Johann Strauss operetta tradition alive in Vienna, at

Nonsense had reached the arts in the late nineteenth century, in the writing of Charles Cros and the music of Satie, for example. **Network of Stoppages** *by Marcel Duchamp (1914) typifies the absurd fun of the period.*

first with *The Merry Widow* (1905), followed regularly with such Romantic melodious, never sub-standard delights as *The Count of Luxemburg* (1909), *Paganini* (1925), *Land of Smiles* (1929) and finally—a full-blown opera for the State Opera House—*Giuditta* (1934). Those are only the most beloved in a distinguished succession of works, which includes the sumptuous waltz *Gold and Silver*.

Richard Strauss, who was artistic director of the Vienna Opera briefly after 1919, envied Lehár's success intensely, longing to write operettas himself. He did not have the light touch however, and his nearest approaches, in *Intermezzo* (1924) and *Arabella* (1933), were only internationally popular long after his death. He did lighten his style during these years: *The Egyptian Helen* (1928) is still a heavy, Freudian piece, quite spectacular; *The Love of Danae* (1944), an uneasy blend of operetta and Wagnerian myth; and *Capriccio* (1942), a charming operatic conversation-piece. The finest of Strauss's later operas is *Friedenstag* ("Peace Day", 1938), not at all popular in Hitler's Germany, nor elsewhere, since it preaches international brotherhood and the futility of war.

Finding an Audience

Music, from the very first, had always been a method of communication with other people who might not speak the same verbal language, but would understand messages sung or played. Courts and Church establishments gradually provided musicians with audiences and incentives to compose new music. Until the nineteenth century, all the music regularly performed was newly composed. As the courts and Church establishments became less important to music than public concerts, subscribers to those concerts began to demand what they already knew, rather than the unknown. Most music played today is old music.

In Vienna Schoenberg had to form his Society for Private Performances in order to get an audience, however small, for the newest compositions of himself and his colleagues. They were noisy affairs: at one, Mahler was a spectator and berated his neighbour for hissing a new piece by Schoenberg. "Don't worry, Mr Mahler," replied the remonstrater, "I hiss your symphonies too." In France, Germany and Italy, new works still always find an audience, delighted to attend so as to boo and whistle and even hurl stink-bombs. In America, Britain and some other places, audiences demonstrate either by walking out, or by never walking into the hall. So there arose the idea of special jamborees, called festivals, at which interested parties would gather to hear new compositions by leaders of the vanguard. Strauss and Mahler took part, in the early years of this century, at a Lower Rhine Festival in Alsace. In 1922 a gathering of composers in Salzburg led to the institution of the International Society for Contemporary Music, whose annual festivals still present the cream of new music from all countries, each time in a different location. Other festivals of new music grew up elsewhere, always exciting and sociable, and always including some dud premières, which have the useful purpose of spotlighting the masterpieces. Two years before the ISCM's beginning in Salzburg, another gathering there of Richard Strauss, Hugo von Hofmannsthal and the great theatre producer Max Reinhardt resulted in the founding of the Salzburg Festival, for superb performances of great music and theatre by internationally outstanding performers. The standard was only made possible because international travel had become easier—though it was not until after 1945

R. Strauss p 300–6, 319–21

that travel of this kind became available to other than rich people, and international festivals, whether specialist or of general appeal, grew to their present quantity.

Above: **Dmitri Shostakovich**, *at ease with a copy of* Pravda.

Soviet Russia

By 1917, when the Bolshevik Revolution overthrew the government, assassinated the effete royal family and established Soviet rule, the *Kuchka* were dead, likewise Skryabin. Rakhmaninov and Stravinsky had moved to Europe, as had Prokofiev. Glazunov (1865–1936), a lesser academic, was left. The new Soviet regime was, in principle, enthusiastic for artistic experiment at the moment, and welcomed its first venturesome composer, Dmitri Shostakovich (1906–1975), at first an Armistice figure, with his defiantly jocular and satirical early symphonies and first piano concerto (1933). A subordinate melancholy, evident in Shostakovich's precocious first symphony (1926), was encouraged by a short-lived, intense cult of Mahler's music in Leningrad during the mid-1920s. For Shostakovich it was crucial, expressing the ambivalent attitudes which always dominated his music.

Above left: *An album snapshot of* **Sergei Prokofiev** *with his wife, taken in 1946.*

Shostakovich's pioneering socialist music, exactly what Communism needed, was not officially appreciated when Stalin became Russia's leader. Music was expected to appeal to the least tutored audience: authority ignored the appeal of genius (though every audience can appreciate it), and denigrated enterprise, in the shape of Shostakovich's opera *Lady Macbeth of Mtsensk* (1934). Stalinism went on to disparage the best work of Shostakovich and Prokofiev (who had returned home in 1934). Shostakovich stayed in Russia and composed fifteen symphonies, traditional in language, striking and even controversial in content. Prokofiev toured America and Europe, playing his piano concertos with fervent virtuosity. He also

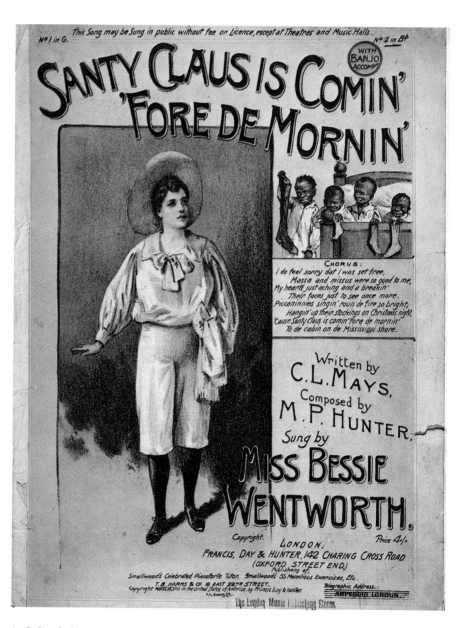

Black music *first reached Europe in a rather unreal and bowdlerized form, as witness this tasteless "piccaninny" song of the period.*

indulged his generation's interest in fantastic psychological incident, memorably in his opera *The Love for Three Oranges* (1919), heroic, hilarious and Surrealist, but also in the witchcraft theme of *The Fiery Angel* (1926). After these captivating pieces, Prokofiev returned to Russia and thereafter composed blameless lyrical music until his death, though his ballet *Romeo and Juliet* (1935) is as inventive and dramatic as any in the repertory and his *Cinderella* (1944) is a masterpiece of comic charm and romance.

America: Source and Centre

One of George Gershwin's most attractive orchestral works is the symphonic poem *An American in Paris* (1928). The capital of France (arguably

the capital of modern music and of art in general in the early twentieth century) had also become Mecca for aspiring American musicians. They no longer went to Leipzig or Berlin to learn composition, but to Paris, where Nadia Boulanger, a devoted Stravinsky acolyte and strict musical disciplinarian, taught gifted young musicians mastery of their profession. Among her pupils were the Americans Aaron Copland, Virgil Thomson and Elliott Carter, each of whom found an American identity as well as a professional expertise quite uncommon in the 1920s. America had brought jazz to France around 1918: it was right that France should repay America with sophisticated, masterful musical technique.

America became a new centre for exciting musical activity. It was the land of opportunity for European artists, rich and enterprising, at least in theory (the reality became less welcoming). By 1939, when the Second World War began, Rakhmaninov and Stravinsky from Russia, Bartók from Hungary, Hindemith and Weill from Germany, Schoenberg and Korngold from Austria and Britten from England were all in residence there.

America had become, by 1939, a lively musical country, chiefly at a popular level. It was the home of black ragtime, the exhilarating music of Scott Joplin, the gospel songs which had inspired Dvořák during his stay in the 1890s, the introvert blues and the extravert jazz which white musicians copied, but only black musicians naturally commanded. Take for example Louis Armstrong and King Oliver on the trumpet, Duke Ellington on the piano. Other fine jazz musicians were white skinned, but learned to play good jazz too, such as the trumpeter Bix Beiderbecke and the clarinettist Benny Goodman. At a grander level there was the big showband of Paul Whiteman, who launched Bing Crosby as a singer and Gershwin as a composer.

Americans had still not properly assimilated black people into their

*An early (and rare) picture of an original **jazz band**: Lil Hardin (Mrs Louis Armstrong), flanked by King Oliver, and with the immortal Johnny Dodds on clarinet.*

***Aaron Copland** was a pupil of Nadia Boulanger: from his earliest days as a composer, he determined to bring America's native music into his formalized and classical structures.*

society, but their music demanded it. The white Americans, Charles Griffes, Howard Hanson, Roy Harris and Samuel Barber, were writing decent American music, but they were surpassed all the time by their more inspired and inventive black jazz colleagues. Jazz music was essentially improvised, different in each performance, and so nobody could discuss a jazz piece in finite terms, even when a record was marketed. I can only say that there were choruses for full orchestra interleaved with virtuoso breaks, much as in a Vivaldi *concerto grosso*, and that the jazz improvisation was at least as brilliant as anything done in the Baroque period, and as firmly controlled. Creative improvisation was audibly still a lively art.

At a less uninhibited or improvised level American music brought forth, as before, the brilliant, spectacular, delightfully tuneful musical shows associated with the Broadway stage and the Hollywood musical films of Irving Berlin, Jerome Kern, Cole Porter and George Gershwin, lavish in melody and richly scored.

Gershwin (1898–1937) went further with his piano concerto (1925), *Rhapsody in Blue* (1924), *An American in Paris* and chiefly his opera *Porgy and Bess* (1935), a black jazzy music drama by a white American composer, still the only valid American opera, black or white.

1939–1945

When the Second World War began in 1939, America was host to some of the world's greatest composers. Rakhmaninov, before his death in 1943, produced a brilliant third symphony (1936) for the Philadelphia Orchestra, a set of symphonic dances (1940), almost a symphony and particularly rich in sardonic and sour-sweet ideas, and the *Paganini Rhapsody* (1934) for piano and orchestra, the summary of his life's venture into the relationship between piano virtuosity and colourful orchestral music.

He and Korngold were the successes. Bartók, a greater composer, could not make the compromise: even his brilliant *Concerto for Orchestra* (1943) commissioned for Koussevitsky's Boston Symphony Orchestra, took time to be admired, as did his third piano concerto (1945), a legacy for his pianist-wife. Schoenberg and Stravinsky in Hollywood and Weill in New York were massively ignored. Modern music was not wanted, either in America or Europe. It did not mix easily with jazz or popular idioms, though to survive, it had to push ahead of its audiences. When the Second World War ended in 1945, Bartók and Webern both died in neglect. The popular audiences for new music seemed farther away than ever.

Korngold p 337

Rakhmaninov p 278–80

Bartók p 253–6

Chapter 16
Freedom and Beyond
Today and Tomorrow

The post-war school in Darmstadt ♦ *Musique concrète* ♦
Stockhausen ♦ The indeterminate music of John Cage ♦
Happenings ♦ Music theatre ♦ The last years of Shostakovich
and Stravinsky ♦ The Polish school ♦ Music in time ♦

With the defeat of the Nazis and the end of the Second World War in 1945, Germany and other Nazi-occupied countries were free at last to discover what had been happening in music and the other arts elsewhere. Fascist politics had kept its subjects in complete ignorance of such developments. The new exposure to Schoenberg and his Viennese school, to Stravinsky, Bartók, Hindemith and other composers of the recent past who had taken refuge in the USA, hastened the establishment of a new vanguard in Europe—assisted in its resources by rapid advances in technology, some of which also affected Popular music.

The Antithesis
At first the new vanguard, which had Darmstadt in Germany as its focal point, seemed united in pursuit of an extended, stricter application of Schoenberg's twelve-note compositional techniques (they taught only how to compose music, not what sort of music). Soon another branch of the vanguard, visitors to Darmstadt from the USA, championed greater freedom of expression and design, a looser rather than tauter sort of music, often inspired by eastern thought.

These two extremes, the completely organized, even pre-ordained, composition, and the completely informal, almost extempore sort of music, have continued to interact throughout Europe and the Americas, Australasia and the Far East too: Asia, while lending its own musical ways to western composers, showed a taste as well as an aptitude for western music, past and present. At the time of writing, in 1982, western music is as fruitfully cultivated in the East as the political regime prevalent in each country allows.

Communism, as represented by Russia and China, disapproves of musical adventure as much as Hitler and Mussolini did. After 1945, composers in Soviet-dominated countries were encouraged to write only the most simple and immediately accessible music on topics acceptable to Soviet

*Three young musicians at
Darmstadt in the 1950s:
Boulez (seated) with
Maderna (centre) and
Stockhausen.*

ideology. A "cultural thaw" has been permitted in some of Russia's
dependent countries, giving the semblance of a liberal musical climate.
Nevertheless, Communist thought dogmatically prefers the crowd to the
individual, and therefore discourages the original, exploratory genius, who
throughout the history of music has kept tradition alive; whether conservative, like Palestrina and Bach and Mozart, or revolutionary, like Beethoven,
Wagner or Boulez.

Against this background of three conflicting musical tendencies, this
chapter pinpoints some major post-war composers and their works, and
attempts to find, if possible, a compass-bearing towards the future.

Catching up with the Past
In the aftermath of the Second World War, Germany, Italy, France, all
Europe indeed, was hard up and ill-equipped to resume peacetime civilized
activity. Musicians and ordinary musical folk were ignorant of such
twentieth-century masterpieces as Stravinsky's *Rite of Spring*, Schoenberg's *Pierrot Lunaire* and Bartók's string quartets. Records were hard to
come by and, like printed music, had to be imported; concert performances
could only take place when the unfamiliar music had been obtained, learned
and rehearsed. The victorious occupation armies made sure that the arts

Olivier Messiaen, in addition to his work as a composer, was organist at the church of the Trinité in Paris for more than forty years.

were fostered, in particular modern non-Nazi works, including music. Radio broadcasts helped to re-educate the repressed generation.

For musicians, two new events were particularly valuable: the *Musica Viva* series of concerts devoted to progressive twentieth-century music, initiated in Munich just after the war by the composer Karl-Amadeus Hartmann (1905–1963, a lively middle-of-the-road symphonist) and much copied elsewhere; and the International Summer School, initiated at Darmstadt in West Germany in 1946, likewise copied elsewhere.

The Darmstadt School

The Darmstadt Summer School was intentionally educational, with lectures by scholars and teachers on the great composers of the twentieth century, and concerts including their works, alongside some by students attending the course. Some of the latter were Henze, Stockhausen, Zimmermann and Kagel from Germany; Nono, Berio, Bussotti and Maderna from Italy; Boulez from France; all now recognized as the leaders of their musical generation. All had studied Schoenberg's twelve-note technique as music students elsewhere, and were using it brilliantly to write music far different from Schoenberg's. All had yet to make their reputations.

Schoenberg was still living, teaching and composing in Los Angeles,

Twelve-note music p 334–6

Schoenberg p 307–9

Freedom and Beyond
Today and Tomorrow

Pierre Boulez was a pupil in Paris of Olivier Messiaen.

respected but not much loved, and hardly performed. At Darmstadt and in Munich at least, his works were played, appreciated, and exerted influence, though Boulez was already suggesting that Schoenberg's application of his twelve-note method to Classical and Romantic musical forms (Haydn and Brahms re-composed atonally) was a misdirection to his successors, who must find their own forms from each newly invented set of musical material: the note-series, the voices or instruments involved, the character of the work in mind. Boulez was equally scathing about Stravinsky, another Los Angeles resident, who had "composed nothing but pastiche since *The Rite of Spring*" (an exaggeration for those who know *The Wedding* and the *Symphonies of Wind Instruments*, to name but two). Boulez and his Darmstadt friends learned plenty from Stravinsky, reject him though they might. Their major inspiration from the recent past was Webern, who, like Bartók, had died hardly appreciated in 1945. Webern's music was valued by the Darmstadt school for its concentrated epigrammatic style, where each note does as much work as a hundred in a Romantic composition; where the musical textures are so refined, and the nuances so widely ranging, from loud to soft, harsh to delicate, smooth to jagged. Webern's Symphony and Concerto were particularly admired, and studied and discussed as the stepping-stones for developments to be made.

Total Serialization

These Darmstadt students spent as much fruitful time arguing about New Music as writing it, and the lecturers also took part. One of them was Boulez's teacher, Olivier Messiaen (born 1908). During the 1949 Summer School Messiaen composed his piano piece *Mode de valeurs et d'intensités* ("Mode of Durations and Nuances"). It did not use twelve-note technique, which Messiaen never cared for; but it did, as Boulez and his friends had

Webern p 336–7

Pierre Henry,
*photographed in 1955
during an electronic
performance at the Ballets
de l'Etoile.*

proposed, systematize every note-value (half-notes, quarter-notes etc), every method of touch (staccato, legato, etc) and dynamic (forte, piano, etc) according to a preconceived, logically organized plan. The chosen notes were selected too, not on Schoenberg's lines, but according to modes, not so much like Gregorian plainsong, rather resembling the systems of Oriental music, especially the Indian *ragas*. Boulez's *Structures* for two pianos, his second piano sonata, and the song-cycle with chamber accompaniment, *Le Marteau sans maître* ("The Hammer without a Master"), splendidly exemplify the "total serialization" which overtook the Darmstadt school, and its disciples elsewhere, for a while.

Stockhausen's *Kreuzspiel* and *Zeitmasze*, Berio's *Circles* (with a novel special attraction involving movement by the performers on stage, bringing a sort of theatre into the concert-hall), and Nono's cantata *Il canto sospeso*, are all further evidence of this search for a creative, expressive alliance between mathematics and music, such as the ancient Greeks had appreciated. There was still a historical continuity, as there always has been: nothing is new under the sun. Some good music was produced by the doctrine of total serialization: all the pieces just mentioned are worth hearing nowadays, and give pleasure once you have learned the language, not necessarily by studying the grammar and syntax, but by living with it and becoming accustomed to the sound of it.

Music from Machines
The danger of total serialization was that, once the parameters had been decided, the composition could write itself: a machine could have invented it; a living, sentient human musician was no longer needed as creator. Just then the machines became available.

In Paris in 1948, two composers, Pierre Henry (born 1927) and Pierre

Schaeffer (born 1910), recorded commonplace sounds—dustbins, heart-beats, train noises, for example—on to discs, and composed music from them by slowing them down or speeding them up, raising or lowering the pitch, turning the volume control up or down, and altering the characteristic of the original sound-source. They called their invention "concrete music", to signify that its origins were real, not abstract. Henry's *Symphonie pour un homme seul* ("Symphony for Solo Male") and Schaeffer's *Train Music* sound crude today, though certainly still imaginative.

When tape-recorders and musical synthesizers became readily available after 1950, the musical manipulation of sound-sources could be much more sophisticated. Studios of electronic music were set up all over the world, from Japan to the USA, though the best known was one in Cologne, Germany, where Karlheinz Stockhausen (born 1926) lived and worked. There a composer could apply electronic control (the work of a record producer and engineer in a modern recording studio) to live sounds, or tones generated electronically, and build up the textures, musical events and the structures he desired. The almost immediate result was Stockhausen's *Gesang der Jünglinge* ("Song of the Boys in the Fiery Furnace"), elaborated on tape from a boy singing a fragment of that biblical text in German translation and turning it into a moving musical experience which calls upon all the traditional resources of familiar music. Stockhausen moved from this "concrete music" to true electronic music, in which the given sound materials, based on a series even if not actually twelve-note, are electronically generated and manipulated to yield the musical textures and sequence of events desired by the composer. Most enterprising composers of the 1950s and later have experimented with electronic music; the more imaginative have preferred to manipulate some form of human musical performance, to de-mechanize the "concrete music", and make it their own, controlled, non-mechanical work. Stockhausen has led the way in this field.

Tape-recorders and synthesizers can manipulate given music—live, recorded, or broadcast—yielding new, personally transformed music to which a composer might honourably put his signature. An example is Stockhausen's *Hymnen*, a long electronic work based on the national anthems of the world, so manipulated as to make a personal, international statement about the composer's anti-nationalistic ideals. Being based on existing material, we may call it a "collage" rather than original, wholly invented music. Music based on quotations was to become a popular feature with the vanguard of this period. Stockhausen soon formed his own musical techniques and in the realization of his creative instructions to them, which have taken very varied forms, from fully notated music to sign-language and purely verbal directions. Modern music is often said to repel the ordinary music-loving public. Yet Stockhausen, whatever he may turn his mind to, can always entice a large audience to his concerts, where he sits at a console in the middle of the auditorium, manipulating the dials which control and transform live musical performance into a new electronic sound-product. The audience can see, as well as hear, a new piece of music being created on the spot by its composer. It is a one-off musical occasion, as it was when Bach or Mozart extemporized in public.

Recorded Improvisation

There is a difference nowadays. Bach's extemporizations, or Mozart's improvised cadenzas in a concerto, would be different when elaborated for

Stockhausen has composed much music that combines live performers with pre-recorded sounds.

A much acclaimed piece of **music theatre** *in recent years was Mike Westbrook's jazz cabaret* Mama Chicago.

writing down. With the invention of tape-recording, extemporized music could be recorded live, perpetuated, for better or worse, and so made available to anybody in the world. The art of extemporization gradually became less admired during the nineteenth century in Classical music circles, as though good music had to be written down. This sentiment has never died out: few concert soloists now improvise in public, except organists. Jazz, on the other hand, is essentially an art of improvisation, only rehearable if it is recorded. The gramophone made it possible, in short stretches at first, usually two and a half minutes. When the long-playing record appeared, not only the repertory of Classical music was benefited. Long jazz improvisations could also be recorded, and less sophisticated pop music could break out of the "single" format into extended rock compositions, lasting up to half an hour or more. These "albums" might include some short pieces for the hit parade of best-selling "single" records, or could use a whole side for a long piece of music, worked out on tape—many jazz or rock musicians saw no virtue in learning musical notation. Examples are The Who's *Tommy*, Led Zeppelin's *Physical Graffiti*, the second side of The Beatles' *Abbey Road*, or Pink Floyd's *Dark Side of the Moon* and *Wish You Were Here*, all compositions which move quite close to the ideals of modern Classical music in length, style and tonal quality—and have won a much larger public.

The Pre-Classical Revival

In a democratic age, Classical music was still branded with its old function of music for the élite, in church or at court. The new admirers of sophisticated rock music were now, nevertheless, more easily inclined to explore records of Baroque music, Bach, Handel, Vivaldi, then the earlier Monteverdi, and even medieval music, and after that to go and hear such music in concert. The growing popularity of pre-Classical music (*i.e.* music before Haydn and the other Viennese Classical composers) ran concurrently with a performers' movement towards "authentic" performance on old instruments, or good copies, and old methods of playing them. Small choirs and chamber ensembles of a size prescribed by the composers, rather than the blowzy, Romantic, inflated performances inherited from the nineteenth century, helped to make this music more acceptable to an audience that did not care for the sound of a Romantic symphony orchestra, or for opera singers trained for Puccini and Wagner, with the grand style and generous vocal vibrato that Rossini and Verdi would have despised as wobbly. Some addicts of rock were drawn to Beethoven and Mozart, and to later Romantic music in general. Thanks to records and tapes and radio music stations, you and I are privileged nowadays to become familiar with all the music mentioned in this book. We can identify it, more or less exactly, when we hear it, and relate each composer to the others in terms of sound and style, and the climate of history, which gives every piece of music its identity.

The Vanguard and the Public

The Darmstadt school of composers, with their total serialism, were writing music for one another, but it was unattractive to the outside world, sometimes unintelligible. Boulez (born 1926) may rest assured that *Pli selon pli* (1963) will eventually become as popular as any of Mahler's or Chaikovsky's symphonies are today. But Mahler's motto, "My time will come", is poor comfort to any living composer, and total serialism soon faded

*As well as working as a composer, **Xenakis** is also an engineer and architect. He designed the Philips Pavilion for the 1958 Brussels World Fair.*

in favour of a vanguard music that might communicate instantly with a non-professional audience. New technology, tape-recorders, tone-generators, synthesizers, might render New Music more alluring, like a ladies' cosmetic apparatus; but the real need was for the notes themselves to communicate. There are still some Puritan composers who refuse to compromise and insist on hoeing their own row, honourably, for those who eventually may appreciate what they have done.

One is Yannis Xenakis (born 1922), a Greek pupil of Messiaen, who composes such strict music that, having himself worked out his materials (themes, etc), he feeds them through a computer and calls the results "stochastic music", giving his pieces the initials ST followed by a number indicating how many performers are required—thus ST4 requires a string quartet. The results are heroic and adventurous, but appallingly difficult for live musicians to perform, and decidedly impersonal in effect.

A few new instruments have emerged: the electric guitar has not completely replaced the clean, honest sound of the acoustic guitar; the electric piano has some valuable and some coarse sounds to add to the tonal spectrum; throat microphones can alter the character of the singing voice. "New" instruments in modern music have, rather, been imported from exotic countries—from China, Japan, South America and Africa, for example.

The cult of instrumental virtuosity is as old as time, and the art of executant supremacy is still rampant. Modern composers owe much to such

Freedom and Beyond

Today and Tomorrow

The oboist and composer **Heinz Holliger**.

executants as the flautist Severino Gazzelloni and oboist Heinz Holliger—himself a resourceful composer of advanced persuasion like the trombonist Vinko Globokar. They, and others, have developed a new technique of blowing double-stops and chords on instruments expected to play only one note at a time; their virtuosity, and that of others less famous, has been responsible for new developments in music. No less important was the development of recorded sound, from LP to stereophonic, then multi-channel sound, giving an illusion of music wrapped round the listener on all sides—this was Leopold Stokowski's intention for the Walt Disney cartoon film *Fantasia* (1938). Stereophonic and wrap-round sound have influenced both popular and new classical music, the latter quite dramatically in the Scottish Thea Musgrave's Horn Concerto, where the soloist and orchestra are finally surrounded by a multitude of other horn-players, stationed all round the auditorium—a renovation of Gabrieli's music for St Mark's, Venice, in the early seventeenth century.

The high-minded Darmstadt call for total control of all the elements in musical composition failed, because the resultant music was too unattractive to the ordinary musical public, though it may have brought their idol Webern's music back into general appreciation for its clean, economical, sensitive and genuinely lovable qualities. Fortunately Darmstadt was visited in 1959 by the champion of informal unsystematized music.

John Cage is a native of California, a state whose clement climate is conducive to relaxation and harmony, a creative atmosphere similar to

Facing page: *One of* **Thea Musgrave's** *greatest successes has been her opera* Mary Queen of Scots *(1977)*.

G. Gabrieli p 50, 62, 80, 208

John Cage, looking over the shoulder of his friend and colleague, the avant-garde *pianist **David Tudor**.*

Vienna rather than Berlin. Since he has brought international vanguard music back from the total serialization of the Darmstadt movement into a variety of more liberal, unrestricted styles, he must be accounted a major composer of our time. However, his music is infrequently performed, in Europe at least, and nothing that he has composed has been as important as his beneficial influence upon others.

John Cage (born 1912)

His education involved literature, art and architecture as well as music, and travel throughout western Europe. He has always been involved in the dance, chiefly with the outstanding Merce Cunningham company, as music director. His musical studies were with Henry Cowell (1897–1965), the American composer, a leader of the interwar American vanguard, who invented the now common idea of playing the piano not on its keyboard but inside its mechanism, on the string, midway between a harp and, beaten with hammers, the Hungarian cimbalom. Cowell also invented "note

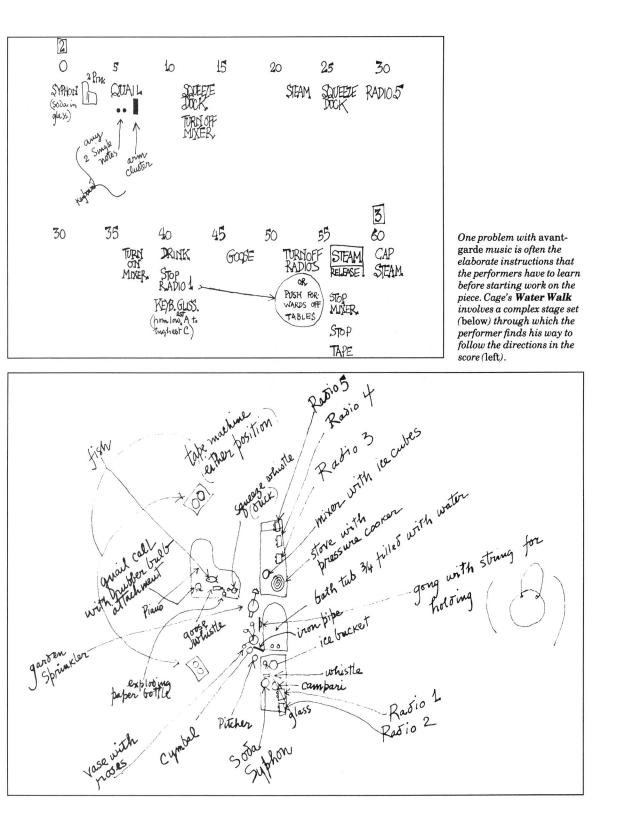

One problem with avant-garde music is often the elaborate instructions that the performers have to learn before starting work on the piece. Cage's **Water Walk** involves a complex stage set (below) through which the performer finds his way to follow the directions in the score (left).

clusters", all adjacent notes depressed together, perhaps by the whole forearm. Cage, logically, went one further and invented the "prepared piano", an instrument whose strings were interspersed with elastic bands, drawing pins, erasers, bolts, screws and bits of plastic, so as to turn it into a real percussion instrument (conventional musicians still regard the piano as a percussive instrument to be transformed into a singing voice). His most notorious piano piece is *4'33" for Henry Flint*, in which the pianist sits at his keyboard for the time specified, without touching the instrument—a Wagnerian presumption, insisting that the silence is the composer's private property, which it certainly is not.

Cage worked in a radio station, and was composing a sort of electronic music in 1942, long before Pierre Henry's *musique concrète*. His studies of eastern thought led him to Zen Buddhism, to *I Ching*, the Chinese theory of chance (you throw a dice to decide which idea, and even which note, comes next), to new graphic methods of notating music (an exhibition of this won an art award), to the Bali gamelan orchestra, as well as music from external sources distorted, random music (given notes to be played in any order for as long as prescribed), and mixtures of radio sound. He even used balancing equipment to render incomprehensible his own lecture, declaring the result to be a new work of art. Most of these devices were later attempted by European composers.

Cage's own music, so international in purview, so multifarious, so rich in new ideas, carefully attuned to a western notion of eastern thought, is unique, often most attractive. Its effect on other American composers was in effect, exhilarating: he liberated the music of the United States, which had become stuck in traditions inherited from refugees (such as Schoenberg, Hindemith and Stravinsky), or from teaching in Paris—all good American composers had to serve their term with the incomparable teacher Nadia Boulanger, who sent her pupils home with an impeccable ear, Stravinsky to the core. Of Cage's compositions, *Sonatas and Interludes* for prepared piano is probably most easily available on record, *Fontana Mix*, an early electronic composition, decidedly influential, *Concert for Piano and Orchestra* (1958)

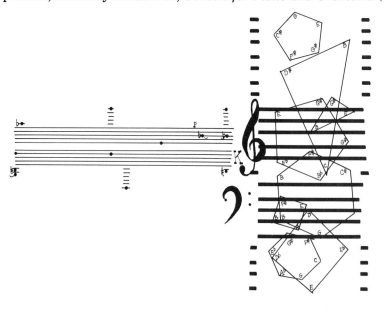

A page from **John Cage's** *massive Piano Concerto, which has an ornately graphic score.*

Gamelan p 285

Henry p 347–8
Boulanger p 341, 358

A page from the performing score of Kagel's **Ludwig van**, *which consists of objects wrapped up in pages of Beethoven chamber music and photographed.*

perhaps the most enjoyable. His adventurous and widely ranging interests may have changed the face of music more than any of his compositions. He proposed, instead of Darmstadt's total serialization, a composer's total freedom, which involved freedom for the executant and for the listener. Music everywhere responded to the unassuming yet eloquent charm of John Cage, though his totally liberated music is, by his own admission, often boring to hear.

Anarchy and Fun

Music was much too solemn, too strait-jacketed, Cage suggested. A composer's imagination needed a freedom far from the automatism of total serialization, and the listener needed it too. We all need to be entertained sometimes by music, something that doctrinaire Darmstadt had almost forgotten. Cage proposed a sort of music—Random Music—merely notes on which the performers should improvise until recalled by the conductor to the next section. The tyranny of the nineteenth-century composer was to be abolished; the age of ornamentation, written down music demanding embellishment, had returned.

In Europe, the idea was more cautiously taken. Stockhausen's *Piano Piece XI*, consists of nineteen short sections, very dynamic, to be played in any order until one section has been heard three times. His percussion piece

Freedom and Beyond
Today and Tomorrow

*Many of America's leading composers were pupils in Paris of **Nadia Boulanger**, among them Aaron Copland, Walter Piston and Virgil Thomson.*

Zyklus is similarly designed, its score so printed and bound that changes can be made in part, as well as wholesale. His *Solo*, for any melody instrument, is improvised above a shortwave radio broadcast indistinctly tuned. Boulez, in his Third Piano Sonata (still incomplete), arrived at interchangeable structure, but from the influence of the French poet Mallarmé's *A Dice-Throw*. Hans Werner Henze sometimes includes "boxes" of notes to be played at random until the next call to action, as if they were entr'actes. Lutoslawski has, as cautiously, allowed a small degree of freedom within controlled music. Even the conservative Benjamin Britten, in his late works, planned a degree of flexible ensemble and repetition, ended with his "Curlew" sign (∿).

Butterfly Music
New forms of graphic notation, developed chiefly by composers of more enterprise than importance, introduced a sort of indeterminacy by showing only roughly which note was to be performed: the method is not unlike that of Schoenberg's "speech-song" in *Pierrot Lunaire* where the pitched note, as written, is only to be approximated. A more extreme form of indeterminacy, stemming from Cage, is textual music, which for a time attracted Stockhausen, and is chiefly associated with Cage's pupil, La Monte Young (born 1936). The performer has to realize the music, not from reading notes, but

Blind Man's Buff *by Peter Maxwell Davies: the première at London's Roundhouse.*

Two generations of English composers: **Sir William Walton** *(left) with* **Peter Maxwell Davies**.

words which say what is to be done. An example is Young's "Turn a butterfly (or any number of butterflies) loose in the performance area ... the doors and windows may be opened, and the composition finishes when the butterfly flies away". Stockhausen, more musically responsible, told performers, for instance, to "play a vibration in the rhythm of your thinking". He called it "intuitive music" and climaxed it in *Sternklang* ("Starsound", 1971) for five ensembles, playing intuitively within mutual earshot in a Berlin public park. Such vague musical instructions easily led to performances which no responsible composer would wish to put his name to, and random text-music soon went into abeyance.

Musical Games
Young's Butterfly piece was more a game than a piece of music, and modern musical experiments have included many such games, more or less serious, partly in the name of music-theatre. The postwar vanguard hated opera, but could not do without dramatic music. Several composers turned a straightforward or instrumental piece into a sort of spectacle: Kagel's *Match* is a competition for two solo cellos, with a drummer as voluble referee; Boulez's *Domaines* is a clarinet concerto in which the soloist moves from one group of players to another, each time making music with them (the choice of partners is made at random, in the second half more closely prescribed, as in the Spanish dice game of *dados*). Xenakis' *Duel* is for two conductors and ensembles, contesting against one another. Peter Maxwell Davies and his "Fires of London" group have produced many concert spectacles, such as *Songs for a Mad King*, in which the lunatic George III tries to instruct his private aviary (solo instrumentalists in cages) how to warble his favourite songs by Handel. Or *Vesalii Icones*, which partners the instrumental group with a naked black dancer who mimes the sacred stations of the Cross in terms of an old book on human anatomy—I don't understand the connection either, but it regularly knocks me out in performance (the record is no substitute, though helpful homework).

Opera Survives
Opera, much inveighed against, has continued. Almost the first musical event after the end of the Second World War was the première in London of Britten's *Peter Grimes* (1945), the first British opera to achieve success overseas and at home: it was no vanguard effort, traditionally based on Puccini and Berg, and a little of much else, but masterfully put together, personal and durable. Britten went on to compose many other operas, more progressive in manner, some closely influenced by Oriental theatre (*Curlew River* for example). Henze made a great career in opera, from *Boulevard Solitude* to *The Bassarids* (1966), much more advanced in language (he was younger than Britten) but essentially in the old style; *The Bassarids* is the greatest of all modern operas. Subsequently he espoused Communism, and found his subject-matter in social conflict, grandly in the spectacular war-opera *We Come to the River* (1976), perhaps more potently in the concentrated semi-theatrical piece *El Cimarron* (1971), about a South American slave on the run.

Music-theatre
Some composers were ashamed of opera as an élite art-form: and so music-theatre was invented. Opera had never been élitist in Italy or Germany, nor

indeed in France, where the opera was a meeting place, like a market, at which marriages were often arranged between two families. The success of *Grimes* turned Britain into a keenly operatic country, with companies regularly proliferating, and new operas constantly reaching the stage. Michael Tippett (born 1905) has contributed copiously, with challenging subject-matter and action (he writes his own librettos): I find *The Knot Garden* (1970) his most venturesome achievement, though his first opera, *The Midsummer Marriage* (1956), deeply involved in legend and psychology, is the most effective in theatrical magic. Foreign composers, Henze apart, have avoided opera, except György Ligeti (born 1923) whose *Le grand macabre* (1978) is at once original, thought-provoking, and often very comical. Its vinegary character is shared by an earlier English opera, Harrison Birtwistle's *Punch and Judy* (1968), a new, very violent treatment of the old street-show. Among other postwar operas of importance are Stravinsky's *The Rake's Progress* (1951), which puts the manners of the eighteenth-century *opera buffa* to the composer's own personal uses, an extreme example of the "pastiche" Stravinsky to which Boulez so objected; and Schoenberg's *Moses and Aaron*, left unfinished at his death in 1951, a grand biblical spectacular, involving some splendid choruses and an extended ballet for the *Dance round the Golden Calf*—the part of Moses is spoken throughout, to show that he lacks the eloquence of his brother Aaron, a tenor singer.

This postwar period has also seen the rise of the American musical comedy, with such triumphs as Irving Berlin's *Annie Get Your Gun* (1946), Leonard Bernstein's *West Side Story* (1957), Frederick Loewe's *My Fair Lady* (1956), Cole Porter's *Kiss Me Kate* (1948), Richard Rodgers' *The Sound of Music* (1959). Galt MacDermot's *Hair* (1967), the English Andrew Lloyd Webber's *Jesus Christ Superstar* (1970) and Richard O'Brien's provocative *Rocky Horror Show* are examples of the newer rock musical.

Some Leading Composers

In the above survey of experiments and trends during the last four decades, some important composers have either gone unmentioned or been given less attention than they deserved.

In Russia Dmitri Shostakovich (1906–1975), who had suffered public

Above: *Britten's opera* **Peter Grimes** *(1945) brought the composer international fame. It tells a powerful story of life and death set in a remote fishing village on the Suffolk coast.*

Above left: **Benjamin Britten** (left) *photographed in Moscow in 1963 meeting* **Dmitri Shostakovich**. *In the centre is the English tenor* **Peter Pears**.

Hans Werner Henze. As early as 1953 he made the decision to abandon his native Germany, and has since lived in Italy.

*Henze's opera **The Bassarids** (1966), based on the* Bacchae *of Euripides, has an Intermezzo set in the eighteenth century that deals with the judgment of Calliope.*

rebuke for his incisive, cheerful, but too venturesome music, settled down to extend the quantity of his symphonies to fifteen and string quartets to thirteen; he added two concertos each for violin and cello, and a second piano concerto, moderately easy, for his son, Maxim (who eventually became a conductor and, after his father's death, defected with his family to the West). Of the symphonies, number ten (1953) is surely the finest, a true Russian epic; number thirteen, nicknamed *Babi-Yar*, caused a stir by voicing protest against Soviet anti-Jewish policies, number fourteen is for two singers and smallish orchestra, dwells on death, and was dedicated to his friend Benjamin Britten; and number fifteen ended the series enigmatically, quoting cheerfully from Rossini's *William Tell* and mournfully from Wagner's *Twilight of the Gods*. Shostakovich's later string quartets, the private counterparts of his more public symphonies in terms of rhetoric, emphasize even more the loneliness and pessimism to which he latterly became a victim. He remained in Russia until his death, the only outstanding Soviet composer after Prokofiev. No Russian composer of their stature has come forward to succeed them in the noble lineage of Glinka.

Within the Soviet Russian empire, Hungary produced György Ligeti, a real original, whose talent only became known after 1956 when he defected to Germany, where he worked with Stockhausen in Cologne before settling in Vienna. Ligeti's music quickly excited attention when it was borrowed to accompany Stanley Kubrick's film *2001, A Space Odyssey*, for whose astronautical adventures Ligeti's dense yet delicate impressionist textures, neither tuneful nor harmonious, but most attractive to the ear, were very

Györgÿ Ligeti's scores are well known for the complex intricacy of their part-writing.

apt. *Atmospheres, Melodies, Lontano* and *Ramifications*, all for orchestra, are among the most engaging of them. After 1970 Ligeti moved, as it were, his musical camera more closely into focus on the world about him. *San Francisco Polyphony* (1972) exemplifies his return to audible melody and sinewy counterpoint, *Clocks and Clouds* a new interest in pulse, and the opera *Le grand Macabre* his spicy, ribald wit.

The "cultural thaw" in Poland revealed a new clutch of expert, interesting composers, led by Witold Lutoslawski (born 1913) and Krzysztof Penderecki (born 1933), the latter addicted to a variant of Ligeti's dense pointillist textures, impressive enough in the choral work *Utrenja*, the *St Luke Passion*, and the opera *The Devils of Loudun*, but more communicative and diverse in such recent works as the Violin Concerto (1976) and the opera *Paradise Lost* (1978). Lutoslawski's elegant, precisely delineated music, discriminatingly alive to vanguard tendencies elsewhere, has readily won an international audience. His concertos for cello, and for oboe and harp, show the refined yet bold quality of his mind.

In America Stravinsky enjoyed an Indian summer after joining the serialist vanguard in his late works, the splendid ballet *Agon* (only partly twelve-note), the choral *Threni* (strongly Russian in character), and the scintillating Movements for piano and orchestra. Aaron Copland (born 1900) seemed at one time to typify the music of the American countryside, clean, tuneful, relaxed and beautiful: during the 1950s he too embraced Schoenberg's serialism: his *Connotations* (1962) is a forthcoming, likable orchestral piece in this vein. The outstanding American composer today is surely Elliot Carter, born 1908, who essays formidable mathematical feats that never sound unbeguiling, for example in his Double Concerto for harpsichord and piano (1961), or his monumental Piano Concerto (1965), which showed that the age of virtuosity was far from exhausted. In Paris, Messiaen's harmony class brought generations of young musicians to the musical vanguard. Messiaen has derived inspiration from his studies in bird-song (*The Bird Catalogue*) and from the mysterious East in, chiefly, the huge symphony *Turangalîla* (1948), increasingly vital to his listeners, if they can bear the sweetness.

Conclusion

The state of Classical music in the 1980s, so much experiment in so many directions, has led at least one writer on music to maintain that the continuing history of music stopped around 1960 and cannot be traced further. He meant that there is no longer a *lingua franca* spoken, or rather written, by all composers. There has been a sort of self-imposed musical Iron Curtain during these last two decades. Yet I have no doubt that, when the dust settles, music will be found alive and well, and still moving forward along lines accessible to every interested listener, however untrained in the language of music. There will always be honourable conservative composers, and always a vanguard as outrageous as possible, I hope. Perhaps this vanguard will be more readily communicative with the worldwide musical public than in the past, thanks to radio, the record-player, and other modern diffusers of music. Music, like all the arts, and like us, cannot stop the clock. It must move forward, to reflect the changes and chances of this fleeting world in remorseless time. But our receptivity has to move forward as well. We have to keep "stretching our ears", as Ives's father said, all the time.

Plus ça change . . . scores from the Middle Ages and from our own time (Stockhausen's Refrain *for 3 players).*

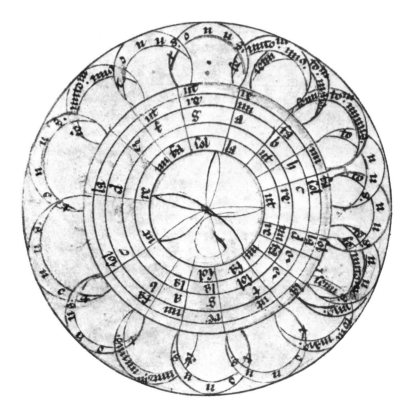

Messian p 346–7

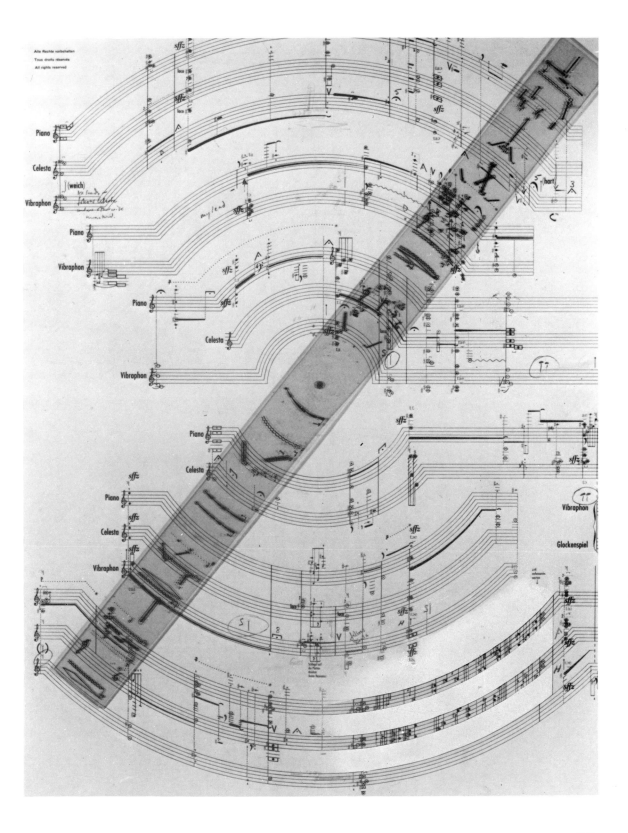

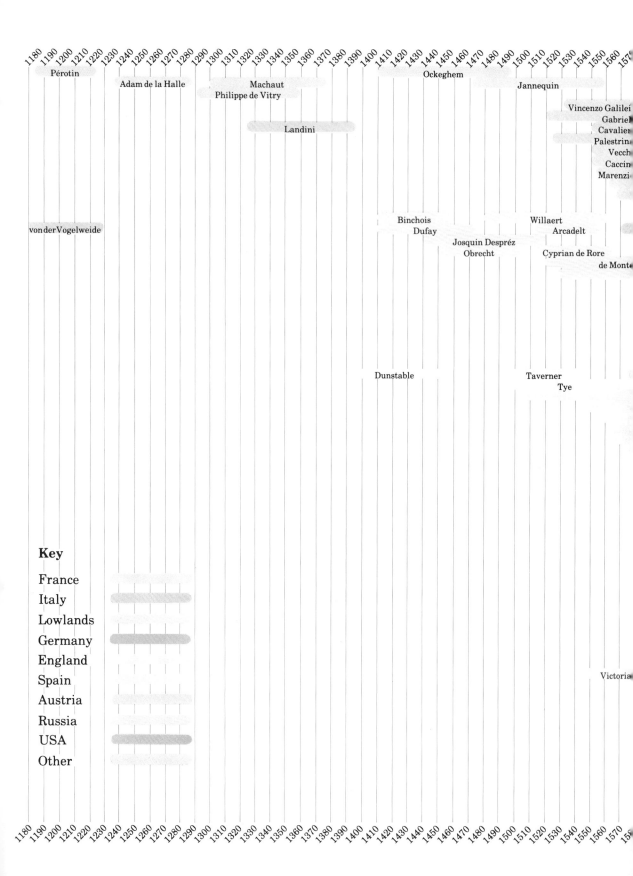

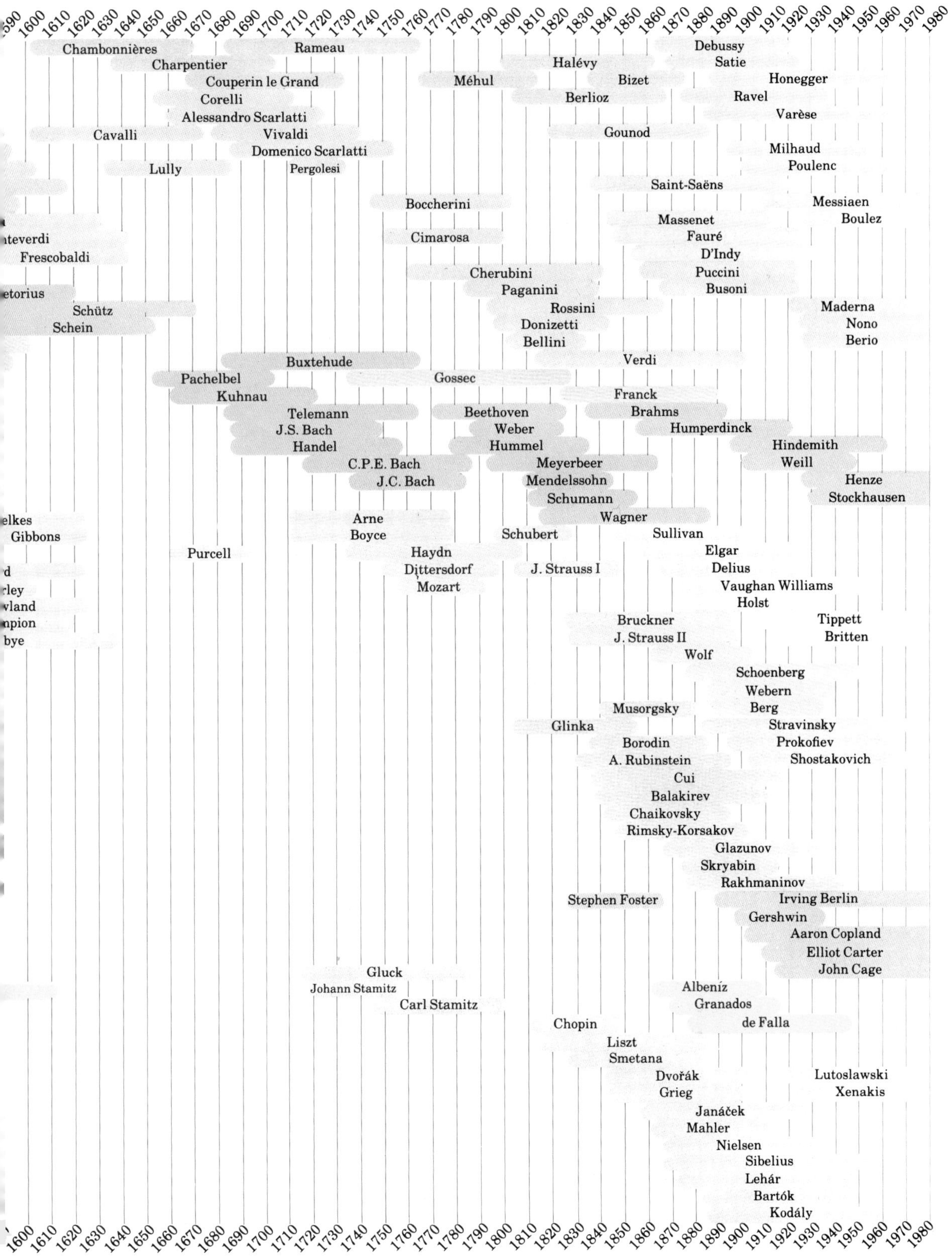

Chambonnières
Charpentier
Couperin le Grand
Corelli
Alessandro Scarlatti
Cavalli
Vivaldi
Domenico Scarlatti
Lully
Pergolesi
Rameau

Debussy
Satie
Halévy
Honegger
Méhul
Bizet
Ravel
Berlioz
Varèse
Gounod
Milhaud
Poulenc

teverdi
Frescobaldi
etorius
Schütz
Schein

Saint-Saëns
Messiaen
Boccherini
Massenet
Boulez
Cimarosa
Fauré
D'Indy
Cherubini
Puccini
Paganini
Busoni
Rossini
Maderna
Donizetti
Nono
Bellini
Berio

Buxtehude
Verdi
Pachelbel
Gossec
Kuhnau
Franck
Telemann
Beethoven
Brahms
J.S. Bach
Weber
Humperdinck
Handel
Hummel
Hindemith
C.P.E. Bach
Meyerbeer
Weill
J.C. Bach
Mendelssohn
Henze
Schumann
Stockhausen

elkes
Gibbons
Arne
Boyce
Wagner
rd
Purcell
Schubert
Sullivan
rley
Haydn
Elgar
vland
Dittersdorf
J. Strauss I
Delius
mpion
Mozart
Vaughan Williams
bye
Holst

Bruckner
Tippett
J. Strauss II
Britten
Wolf

Schoenberg
Webern
Musorgsky
Berg
Glinka
Stravinsky
Borodin
Prokofiev
A. Rubinstein
Shostakovich
Cui
Balakirev
Chaikovsky
Rimsky-Korsakov

Glazunov
Skryabin
Rakhmaninov
Stephen Foster
Irving Berlin
Gershwin
Aaron Copland
Elliot Carter
John Cage

Gluck
Albeníz
Johann Stamitz
Granados
Carl Stamitz
de Falla
Chopin
Liszt
Smetana
Dvořák
Lutoslawski
Grieg
Xenakis
Janáček
Mahler
Nielsen
Sibelius
Lehár
Bartók
Kodály

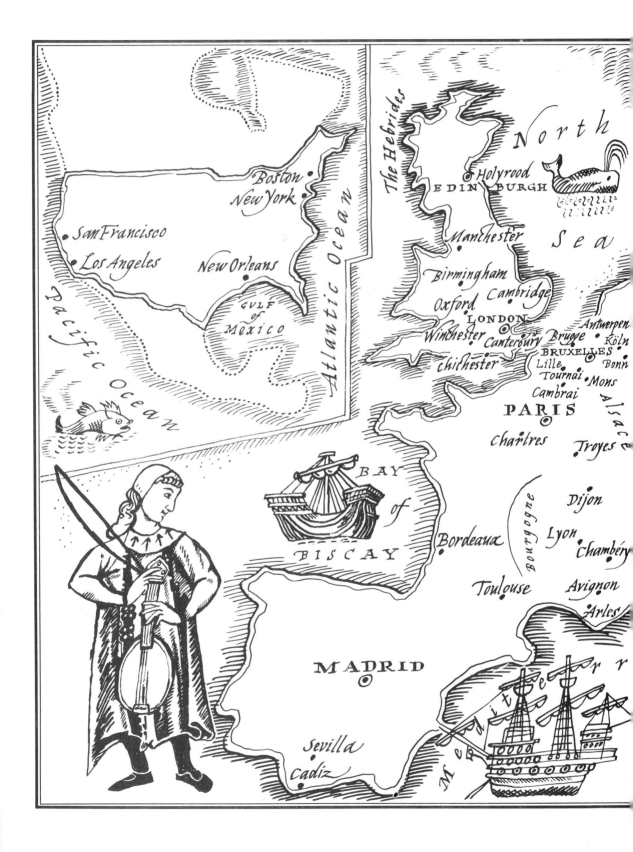

OSLO

Tapiola
HELSINKI

St Petersburg

STOCKHOLM

Baltic sea

MOSKVA

Kirov

Elsinore
KÖBENHAVN

Lübeck
Hamburg
Elberfeld

Hannover *Potsdam* BERLIN
Wittenberg
Köthen

WARSZAWA

Halle
Eisenach *Weimar* *Leipzig* *Dresden* *Wroclaw*
Frankfurt *Arnstadt*

Darmstadt *Bayreuth* PRAHA *Kraków*

Mannheim *Nürnberg*

Brno
Stuttgart *Schönbrunn*
Zürich *München* *Linz* WIEN BUDAPEST

Salzburg *Eisenstadt*

Bergamo
Milano *Brescia*
Cremona *Padova* *Venezia*

Torino *Busseto* *Mantova*
Ferrara
Modena *Bologna*
Lucca *Firenze* *Pesaro*
Pisa

Arezzo
Perugia

Adriatic sea

a n e a n
sea

ROMA
Napoli

sea *Palermo*

Music Library

Below is a list of recordings, arranged by chapter to supplement the four-record set of albums designed to accompany this volume. Artists are recommended in only a few instances, for there is such a wealth of excellence available in recorded performances today that it would be unnecessary to list here.

Also included is a list of more specialized reading, with more detailed information that lies beyond the scope of this general work. The dates and facts of *Music in Time* are those of the great musical encyclopedia *The New Grove*, as is the transliteration of Russian names, incidentally.

Chapter 1 *Records*

Evening Ragas (Indian)

Chapter 1 *Books*

Karl Geiringer Instruments in the History of Western Music
ALLEN & UNWIN, 1978
Denis Stevens, ed. A History of Song
HUTCHINSON

Chapter 2 *Records*

Easter Sunday Vespers *Monks of Mount Athos*
Divine Orthodox Liturgy
Adam de la Halle:
  Le jeu de Robin et Marion
The following recordings by The Early Music Consort/David Munrow:
Gothic Era
Machaut & his Contemporaries
The Court of Burgundy
Music of the Crusades
14th Century Florence

Chapter 3 *Records*

Dufay (including *Se la face est pale*)
Art of the Netherlands (Josquin, Obrecht, Isaac, etc) *Early Music Consort*
Ockeghem   *Prague Madrigal Singers*
Josquin:
  Absalon, fili mei *Wells Cathedral Choir*
Tallis:
  Lamentations
  Spem in alium *Clerkes of Oxenford*
Palestrina:
  Hodie Christus Natus est, etc *Kings College Chapel Choir*
Jannequin:
  Cries of Paris *Consort of Music*
  La guerre *King's singers*
Lassus:
  Recital of Motets *Collegium Vocale c. Herrewegh*
  Madrigals etc *Paris Polyphonic Ensemble*
Victoria:
  Requiem etc *St John's College Choir recital*

Chapter 4 *Records*

Florentine Music
Musica Reservata
Vecchi:
  L'anfiparnaso *Deller Consort*
Gesualdo: Tenebrae etc
Byrd: Masses etc (3 records)
Tomkins: Madrigals
Gibbons: The Silver Swan etc
Morley: O Mistress Mine etc
Weelkes, Wilbye etc *King's Singers*
Dowland:
  Lachrimae
  Consort Pieces
  Songs *Consort of Music*
Fitzwilliam Virginal Book
Marini:
  Recital *Consort of Music*
Monteverdi:
  Orfeo
  Incoronazione di Poppaea
  Vespers 1610 *Early Music Consort*
Lully:
  Armide
  Isis *Paillard Orchestra*
Purcell:
  Chacony in G minor
  Trumpet Tune & Air
  Come ye sons of Art
  Funeral Music of Queen Mary
  Monteverdi Choir/Gardner
  Verse Anthems *Deller Consort*
  Dido & Aeneas
  King Arthur

Chapter 4 *Books*

E.H. Fellowes Byrd
Joseph Kerman The Elizabethan Madrigal
Alfred Einstein The Italian Madrigal
David Brown Weelkes
          Wilbye
Denis Arnold Monteverdi
Jane Glover Cavalli
F.B. Zimmerman Purcell

Chapter 5 *Records*

Praetorius: *Early Music Consort*
Schütz:
  Musikalische Exequien

St Matthew Passion
J.S. Bach:
  6 Brandenburg Concertos
  4 Orchestral Overtures
  St Matthew Passion
  Mass in B minor
  Harpsichord concertos
  Concerto for 2 violins
  Christmas Oratorio
  Magnificat
  The Well-tempered Clavier
  Motet: Jesu meine Freude
  Cantata 140 Wachet auf
        106 Gottes Zeit
        82 Ich habe genug
        80 Ein feste Burg
        65 Sie werden alle
Buxtehude:
  In dulci jubilo
Couperin:
  Harpsichord suites
  Leçons de Tenèbres
  Les goûts réunis, suites
Kuhnau:
  Biblical Sonatas
Corelli:
  La folie d'Espagne
  Concerti grossi op 6
Vivaldi:
  The Four Seasons
  Various Concertos *English Concert* or *Academy of Ancient Music*
Telemann:
  Darmstadt Overtures

Chapter 5 *Books*

P.M. Young The Bachs
C. Girdlestone Rameau
W. Mellers Couperin
E.J. Dent Alesssandro Scarlatti
R. Kirkpatrick Domenico Scarlatti
M. Talbot Vivaldi

Chapter 6 *Records*

Handel:
  Water Music
  Concerti Grossi op 6
  Messiah
  Belshazzar
  Zadok the Priest
  Ariodante
  Acis & Galatea
  Cantata, Lucrezia
A. Scarlatti:
  Il giardino d'amor
  Arie amorose *Janet Baker*
D. Scarlatti:
  Harpsichord sonatas
Hasse:
  La clemenza di Tito, Arias
Pergolesi:
  Stabat Mater
  La serva padrona

Music Library

Berlioz:
Symphonie fantastique
Les Troyens
Nuits d'été, voice and orchestra
Grande messe des morts
Alkan:
Piano music *Lewenthal* or *R. Smith*
Gounod:
Faust
Roméo et Juliette
Melodies
Bizet:
Symphony in C major
Carmen
St Saëns:
Symphony 3 in C minor
Piano concerto 2 in G minor
Carnival of the Animals
Samson et Dalila
Massenet:
Manon
Werther

Chapter 10 *Books*
H. Weinberg Rossini
Berlioz Memoirs
W. Dean Bizet
J. Harding Gounod
      Massenet
      St Saëns & his circle

Chapter 11 *Records*
Verdi:
Nabucco
Macbeth
La Traviata
Don Carlos
Aida
Otello
Falstaff
Missa da Requiem
Ponchielli:
La Gioconda
Leoncavallo:
Pagliacci
Mascagni:
Cavalleria Rusticana
Wagner:
Der fliegende Holländer
Der Ring des Nibelungen
Tristan und Isolde
Die Meistersinger
Parsifal
Siegfried Idyll
Humperdinck:
Hänsel und Gretel

Chapter 11 *Books*
W. Weaver Verdi, Documentary study
J. Budden Verdi's Operas (3 vols)
C. Westernhagen Wagner
G.B. Shaw The Perfect Wagnerite
M. Carner Puccini

Chapter 12 *Records*
Grieg:
Peer Gynt
Piano Concerto
Songs
Lyric Pieces, solo piano
Albeníz:
Iberia
Granados:
Goyescas, piano
Falla:
El sombrero de tres picos
Nights in the gardens of Spain
7 Spanish popular songs
Rodrigo:
Concierto de Aranjuez
Smetana:
The Bartered Bride
Dalibor
Ma Vlast
Dvořák:
Symphonies 8–9
Cello Concerto in B minor
Piano Quintet
Slavonic Dances
Gypsy Songs
The Jacobin
Janáček:
Sinfonietta
Glagolitic Mass
Jenufa
String Quartet 2 (Intimate Letters)
Bartók:
Concerto for Orchestra
Violin Concerto 2
Music for Strings, Percussion
    and Celesta
String Quartet 6
14 Bagatelles, piano
Bluebeard's Castle
Sibelius:
Symphony 5
En Saga, orchestra
Vaughan Williams:
Symphony 6
The Lark Ascending
Fantasia on a theme by Thomas Tallis
Serenade to Music
On Wenlock Edge
Ives:
Symphony 4
Three places in New England
The Unanswered Question
Songs

Chapter 12 *Books*
J. Horton Grieg
B. Large Smetana
J. Clapham Dvořák
J. Vogel Janáček
H. Stevens Bartók
R. Layton Sibelius
M. Kennedy R. Vaughan Williams

I. Holst Gustav Holst
H. Cowell Charles Ives & his Music

Chapter 13 *Records*
Glinka:
Kamarinskaya
Songs
A Life for the Tsar
Balakirev:
Symphony in C major
Islamey, piano solo
Borodin:
Symphony 2 in B minor
String Quartet 2 in D
Prince Igor
Musorgsky:
Night on the Bare Mountain
Pictures at an Exhibition, piano solo
Boris Godunov
The Nursery, songs
Rimsky Korsakov:
Sheherazade, for orchestra
Capriccio Espagnol
Chaikovsky:
Symphonies 2, 6
Piano Concerto 1
Violin Concerto
Romeo & Juliet, orchestra
Piano Trio
Swan Lake, ballet music
Serenade for strings
Eugene Onegin
Songs
Rakhmaninov:
Symphony 2
Piano Concerto 2
Symphonic Dances
Skryabin:
Prometheus, Poem of Fire
Piano Sonatas 4, 9

Chapter 13 *Books*
R. A. Leonard History of Russian Music
D. Brown Glinka
M. D. Calvacoressi Musorgsky
N. Rimsky-Korsakov My Musical Life
J. Warrack Tchaikovsky
G. Norris Rakhmaninov
H. Macdonald Skryabin

Chapter 14 *Records*
Debussy:
Prélude à l'aprés-midi d'un faune
La Mer
Préludes, piano
Pelléas et Mélisande
Chansons de Bilitis
Stravinsky:
The Firebird
Petrushka
The Rite of Spring
Franck:
Symphonic Variations

(Piano & Orchestra)
Symphony in D minor
Chausson:
Poème, violin & orchestra
Wolf:
Italienisches Liederbuch
Dukas:
L'apprenti sorcier
Elgar:
Enigma Variations
Symphony 2
Violin Concerto
Serenade for strings
The Dream of Gerontius
Delius:
On hearing the first Cuckoo in Spring
Brigg Fair
Sea Drift
A Mass of Life
Schoenberg:
Verklärte Nacht
Five Orchestral Pieces
Pierrot Lunaire
Violin Concerto
A Survivor from Warsaw
Mahler:
Symphony 4
Das Lied von der Erde
Rückert songs
R. Strauss:
Don Juan
Oboe Concerto
Metamorphosen, strings
Der Rosenkavalier
Four Last Songs
Berg:
Wozzeck
Violin Concerto
Ravel:
Daphnis et Chloé
Piano Trio
Gaspard de la nuit, piano
Sheherazade, songs
Fauré:
Requiem
Songs
Satie:
Piano recital/Ciccolini
Reger:
Piano Concerto
Busoni:
Arlecchino
Piano Concerto

Chapter 14 *Books*
E. Lockspeiser Debussy
C. Debussy M. Croche, dilettantehater
M. Kennedy Mahler
R. Nichols Ravel
E.W. White Stravinsky
F. Walker Hugo Wolf
M. Kennedy Elgar
T. Beecham Delius

C. Rosen Schoenberg
M. Kennedy Richard Strauss
R. Orledge Fauré
E.J. Dent Busoni

Chapter 15 *Records*
Honegger:
Pacific 231
Le Roi David
Respighi:
I pini di Roma
Prokofiev:
Piano Concerto 1
Scythian Suite
Violin Concerto 1
Romeo and Juliet, ballet
Stravinsky:
Symphonies of Wind Instruments
Apollo
Oedipus Rex
Poulenc:
Mouvements perpetuels, piano
Les biches, ballet
Song recitals: F. Palmer *or* H. Cuénod
Hindemith:
Concert Music for Strings and Brass
Horn Concerto
Symphony, Mathis der Maler
Das Marienleben, songs
Gershwin:
Rhapsody in Blue
Piano Concerto
An American in Paris
Porgy and Bess
Webern:
Six Pieces for orchestra
Concerto

Chapter 15 *Books*
P. Griffiths A Concise History of Modern Music
I. Nestyev Prokofiev
H. Moldenhauer Webern
M. Carner Berg

Chapter 16 *Records*
Messiaen:
Turangalîla, symphony
20 regards sur l'enfant Jésus, piano
Oiseaux exotiques, piano & orchestra
Boulez:
Pli selon pli, orchestra
Le marteau sans maître, songs
Berio:
Cries of London
Circles
Sinfonia
Stockhausen:
Gruppen
Gesang der Jünglinge
Telemusik
Nono:
Il canto sospeso

The Who:
Tommy
Led Zeppelin:
Physical Graffiti
The Beatles:
Sergent Pepper
Abbey Road
Pink Floyd:
Dark Side of the Moon
Xenakis:
Antikthon etc *National Philharmonic Orchestra c. Howarth*
Musgrave:
Horn Concerto
Cage:
Sonatas and Interludes
Kagel:
Match
Maxwell-Davies:
Songs for a Mad King
Symphony 1
Britten:
Serenade
War Requiem
Turn of the Screw
Cello Symphony
Henze:
Symphony 6
Voices
Tippett:
Symphony 3
A Child of Our Time
The Midsummer Marriage
Ligeti:
Aventures
Melodien
Requiem
Birtwistle:
Punch & Judy
Lutoslawski:
Concerto for Oboe and Harp
Penderecki:
St Luke Passion
Violin Concerto
Stravinsky:
Agon
Movements
Copland:
Billy the Kid
Connotations
Shostakovich:
Symphonies 1, 4, 10, 14
Cello Concerto 1
String Quartet 8
The Nose
Carter:
Double Concerto
Piano Concerto

Chapter 16 *Books*
P. Griffiths Modern Music
M. Kennedy Britten
P. Griffiths A Guide to Electronic Music

Index

Compiled by Frederick Smyth member of the Society of Indexers

Page numbers in bold (**75**) indicate the principal references. Those in italic figures (*75*) direct the reader to illustrations or their captions. 'q.' stands for 'quoted'.

The titles of all stage works, films and oratorios are alphabetically indexed. Under composers' names are listed only those of their works of which mention is made *other than* in the relevant principal sections (bold-figure references) of the text.

Titled musical works, wherever listed (always in *italic type*), are operas unless otherwise described or unless the title itself clearly indicates to the contrary.

Literary works and musical collections, also listed in *italic type*, are distinguished by their publication dates.

Index

Index

Index

Index